The Green Pages

The Complete Indoor Plant Catalog

Edited by Maggie Oster
Designed by Marsha E. Gold

A Tree Communications Edition
Published by Ballantine Books, Inc., New York

Contents

Copyright © 1977 by Tree Communications, Inc. All rights reserved. No part of this work may be reproduced or transmitted in any form by any means, electronic or mechanical, including photocopying and recording, or by any information storage or retrieval system, without permission in writing from the publisher. Published in the United States by Ballantine Books, a division of Random House, Inc., New York, and simultaneously in Canada by Ballantine Books of Canada, Ltd., Toronto, Canada.

Library of Congress Catalog Card Number: 76-30469

ISBN 0-345-25898-3

Manufactured in the United States of America
First edition: April, 1977

Page 151, "Everyday Stress," reprinted from *Plants as Therapy* by Elvin McDonald. Copyright 1976 by Praeger Publishers, Inc., New York. Excerpted and reprinted by permission.

Page 174, "Pinching, Pruning and Shaping," reprinted from *Garden in Your House*. Revised and enlarged edition copyright © 1958, 1971 by Ernesta Drinker Ballard. By permission of Harper and Row Publishers.

Page 181, "Clothing The New Baby: Containers," reprinted from *Practicing Plant Parenthood*. Copyright © 1975 Maggie Baylis, with permission of the publisher, 101 Productions.

Pages 190-191, "Problem/Cause/Cure Chart," reprinted from *First Aid for House Plants*. Copyright 1976 by Shirley Ross. Used with permission of McGraw-Hill Book Company.

Introduction

Do you know which is the best book on cacti, or bromeliads, or begonias? Where the nearest horticultural library or public garden is? How to re-pot an orchid, start a seed, grow tomatoes in your window, or propagate a fern? How to begin a career in horticulture? Where to buy a window greenhouse? Who manufactures a clear, lucite watering can in the shape of a swan?

The Green Pages puts the answers to these questions and much, much more—right at your fingertips. Here is an A to Z guide through the maze of information that has unfolded as people have become more involved with plants. For example, well-known garden experts have furnished concise introductions for most of the sections; the best books on each subject have been evaluated; step-by-step how-to drawings lead you from beginning to end. We've also included plant societies, magazines, and gardens to visit—all to lead you to sources for even more information about growing plants. Most important of all, you now have access to hundreds of sources for plants and gardening supplies and equipment.

Descriptions

For each product you will find a description, often a picture, and information about their products.

Under each company listing that offers plants or seeds, we have included the cost, if any, of the catalog or plant list, whether they are open to visitors, and what types of plants are available. We have tried to list companies under the category—or categories—that most represents their listings. Companies offering a very wide range of plants to grow indoors are listed in *Houseplants*. Those offering both indoor and outdoor plants, plus supplies and equipment, are in *General Sources*.

Many people are afraid to order plants through the mail, but when reputable nurseries are involved, there is really little to fear. And the advantages in buying plants by mail order make it worth the effort. You'll have access to thousands of plants that otherwise could never be yours. Often, the companies have seasonal sales or offer special collections that give you discounts. Many companies are also willing to help you with plant problems. And for many people, it's just plain fun to get things through the mail.

Make ordering easier

When ordering either plants or products through the mail, keep these points in mind:
- Many of the companies listed are small, family operations; they may not be able to handle a large volume of mail quickly, so be patient.
- When sending for catalogs, brochures, and plant lists, be sure to include the amount of money specified, if there is a charge.

- Take advantage of the chance to compare company prices, return or refund policies, and guarantees.
- When ready to place an order, be sure to read the instructions carefully; things to look for include minimum order, taxes, postage, substitutions, and so forth. Use the order blank provided, typing or printing the order; keep a copy for yourself.
- Keep in mind that most companies prefer not to ship from November to April in order to avoid cold damage to plants. Seeds can usually be shipped year round, except for those tropicals which have a short life.
- Companies usually ship small plants in 2-, 2½-, or 3-inch pots; some companies offer cuttings or seeds. Know what you're ordering.
- Even if a company doesn't require a minimum order, several plants should be ordered at once as the packing, handling, and shipping costs do not justify sending one plant.
- Whenever writing a company, for whatever reason, always include a stamped, self-addressed envelope.

The Green Pages was written for the rookie and the veteran alike. No matter how much (or how little) you know, as you browse through it you'll find tidbits, or perhaps whole chunks, of information that will make indoor gardening easier, richer, and, of course, more fun.

Maggie Oster

Created and produced by Tree Communications, Inc., 250 Park Avenue South, New York, New York 10003.

Photographer: Stephen Mays
Production manager: Lucille O'Brien
Contributing editors: Nancy Bruning, Linda Hetzer, Jill Munves.
Design staff: Yaron Fidler, Christopher Jones, Anthony McCall, Alan Okada

Assisting in the production of this book: Delores Barry, Anisa Beazer, Debi Bracken, Sally Clark, Mary Clarke, Kattie M. Cumbo-Baker, George Drapeau, Wayne Ferrante, Andrew Feigenbaum, Frankie Freilich, Rodney Friedman, Phillip Gim, Marina Givotovsky, Eva Gold, Ronald Gross, Elizabeth Henley, Tina Isaris, Judith Jessurum-Lobo, Susan Keller, Silvia Kelley, Helen Kessler, Norman Lee, Patricia Lee, Paul Levin, Robert Levine, Lori Matus, Lynn Matus, Bruce Michel, Ruth Michel, Tom Morgan, Patricia Murray, Nancy Naglin, Patrick O'Connell, Jane Opper, George and Lucille Oster, Carolyn Parqueth, Douglas Porcaro, David A. Pottinger, Iris Rautenberg, Judith Ress, Marcia Sanders, Mary Ellen Slate, Gordon Stein, Kenneth Weinberg, Alicia Zanelli.

Special thanks to Brooklyn Botanic Garden, Logee's Greenhouses, Planting Field Arboretum, and Anna Thornhill for allowing us to photograph their plants.

Note: We have tried to include companies that are known for service and quality. Mistakes can happen and circumstances can change; we apologize for any problems or inconveniences as you use this catalog.

African violets

Just about everyone who grows plants has had, at one time or another, at least one African violet. It's a plant that readily adapts to the home environment, and provides flowers year round. Not a violet, but native to Africa, African violets are members of the best all-around, flowering houseplant family (see *Gesneriads*).

All colors and forms

Intensive hybridization efforts have produced a wide assortment of plants from which to choose. Leaves may be plain, quilted, fluted, rippled, serrated, or variegated. Flower colors range from intense purple to shades of violet, magenta, rose, pink, and white. Often contrasting colors edge, splash, spot, or center the flower. Beside the familiar plain single blossom, there are also single-fringed, single-starred, semidouble, and fringed or crested double flowers. In addition, trailing and miniature varieties are also available in a variety of leaf forms and flower colors.

Easy to care for

Growing African violets successfully is really rather easy. They prefer room temperatures in the low seventies and bright, but not direct, sunlight, or you can grow your plants under fluorescent lamps. If using natural light, rotate the plants regularly to maintain the uniform, even growth. One-sided light is the cause of lopsided plants. Insufficient light is usually the cause for cessation of flowering, giving rise to the fallacy that African violets have a dormant period. Violets do especially well with morning sun.

For potting, use one of the soilless mixes or prepackaged African violet soil (additional coarse sand or perlite is often needed to improve drainage of these) or a soil mix of equal parts

sterilized loam, leafmold or peat moss, and sand, perlite, or vermiculite. Water from the the top with lukewarm water when the soil surface is dry to the touch. Water is most likely to injure leaves when it is cold. If using special self-watering planters, water according to directions.

Fertilize biweekly with a water-soluble fertilizer at half strength, or use a special African violet brand following directions. African violets are usually propagated by leaf cuttings, although divisions and seed are sometimes used. Adequate humidity is also important to African violet health and flowering. The most prevalent pests are mealy bugs, cyclamen mites, nematodes, thrips, springtails; mildew, as well as crown, stem, and root rot, are other hazards.

Ruth Katzenberger

Ruth Katzenberger, who has developed a hybrid gesneriad, Sinningia 'Dollbaby,' is a director of the American Gloxinia and Gesneriad Society.

Assured success

Trying to choose from among the myriad of African violet varieties available is not nearly so awesome a task as it may seem. Two series of African violet varieties (Rhapsodie and Ballet) have been hybridized and selected for their continuous, long-lasting bloom, strong, vigorous growth, and resistance to disease. In other words, plants anyone can grow. Each series contains varieties in a range of colors and with both single and double flowers. The variety Lisa, of the Ballet series, is noted especially for its ease of culture and quantity of flowers.

Side shoots

Side shoots (or suckers) are a pair of tiny leaves that form on the main stem of African violets. They should be carefully pinched or cut off or they will drain the plant's energy and cause it to stop flowering.

Long necks

Occasionally an African violet will shed its lower leaves, causing a long neck to form. To remedy this unattractive situation, cut off the top and reroot it in moist propagating medium.

Societies

African Violet Society of America
Box 1326
Knoxville, Tennessee 37901
Members receive *The African Violet Maga-zine* 5 times a year. Dues are $6.00 per year.

Saintpaulia International
Alma Wright
Box 10604
Knoxville, Tennessee 37919
Dues are $5.25 a year and members receive a bimonthly publication, *The Gesneriad-Saint-paulia News.*

Books

Helen Van Pelt Wilson's African Violet Book, by Helen Van Pelt Wilson, Hawthorn Books, 260 Madison Ave., New York, New York 10016, 1970, hardbound, 240 pages, $7.95. A very complete and thorough book which covers all aspects of growing African violets. Included are sections on soils, fertil-izers, pots, lighting, propagating, pest and dis-ease control, hybridizing, exhibiting, and judg-ing plus information about varieties, species, miniatures, and other gesneriads. The author has written the book from both personal experi-ence and thorough research; her advice is not only helpful but also fun to read.

Violet coloured African

Plant sources

ABC Nursery and Greenhouse, Route 1, Box 313, Lecoma, Missouri 65540. (314) 435-6389. Catalog. Open daily at 8:00 a.m. (closed Saturday). Wide selection of African violet leaf cuttings (standard, variegated foliage, and trailers); also many houseplants and herbs.

Antonelli Brothers, 2545 Capitola Road, Santa Cruz, California 95062. (408) 475-5222. Open daily. Illustrated catalog. An assortment of African violets is offered in addition to other houseplants and supplies.

Buell's Greenhouses, Box 218, Weeks Road, Eastford, Connecticut 06242. (203) 974-0623. Descriptive plant list 25 cents plus bus-iness-size, stamped, self-addressed envelope. Open Monday through Saturday 8:00 a.m. to 5:00 p.m. Over 500 standard, miniature, and trailing African violets are offered by this ges-neriad specialist. Growing instructions are sent with all plants. Supplies and books available.

Castle Violets, 614 Castle Road, Colorado Springs, Colorado 80904. Send stamped, self-addressed envelope for plant list. Violets raised with love by a retired school librarian. Leaf cut-tings. Memo comes with extensive leaf-culture notes and general culture information.

Dode's Gardens, 1490 Saturn Street, Merritt Island, Florida 32952. Plant list and catalog. Visitors welcome Sunday and other days by appointment. Varied selection of African violet leaf cuttings. Good, illustrated information sheet on how to root leaf cuttings plus numerous supplies from African violet starter kits (great for beginners or as gifts), gravel, and fertilizers to planters.

Fischer Greenhouses, Department 4, Lin-wood, New Jersey 08221. Color catalog 25 cents. Open daily 9:00 a.m. to 5:00 p.m. Visitors welcome. Large selection of African violet and hybrids with color illustrations, plus some bromeliads and orchids.

Harborcrest Nurseries, 4634 West Saanich Road, Victoria, British Columbia, V8Z 3G8, Canada. Descriptive list 25 cents. Extensive selection of standard and miniature African vio-lets offered as leaf cuttings or plants. Also avail-able are other gesneriads and houseplants.

Heavenly Violets, Mrs. Mary V. Boose, 9 Turney Place, Trumbull, Connecticut 06611. (203) 268-7368. Plant list 25 cents. Open by appointment only. Offering African violet leaves and episcias.

The House of Violets, Charlyne and Ralph Reed, 936 Garland Street Southwest, Camden, Arkansas 71701. (501) 836-3016. For plant list send stamped, self-addressed envelope. Open Monday through Saturday 9:00 a.m. to 5:00 p.m. Growers of African violets exclusively. Supplies and equipment, including self-water-ing planters, also available.

Klinkel's African Violets, 1553 Harding Street, Enumclaw, Washington 98022. (206) 825-4442. Plant list 25 cents. Call before visit-ing. Large selection of African violets including some miniatures, semi-miniatures, small grow-ers, and variegated plants. Leaf cuttings only; sent with propagation instructions.

Mrs. Velma Knowlton, 715 W. Housatonic Street, Pittsfield, Massachusetts 01201. (413) 442-3251. Plant list. Open daily 9:00 a.m. to 9:00 p.m. Large range of African violet leaf cut-tings available, including new and old varieties.

Lyndon Lyon, 14 Mutchler Street, Dolgeville, New York 13329. Plant list. Open daily 8:00 a.m. to 6:00 p.m. Visitors welcome. Specialist in breeding and growing African violets and other gesneriads plus miniature roses adapted for fluorescent light gardening. Notes on lighting, watering, feeding, temperature, propagation, and insect pests. Publishers of *The African Violet Magazine* which appears in January, March, June, September, and November.

Mimi's African Violets, 1100 Stevens Ave-nue, Box 2967, Deland, Florida 32720. (904) 734-1675. Open Monday through Friday 8:30 a.m. to 9:30 p.m. Although this African violet nursery is geared to volume growers, they do ship African violet starter plants (minimum of 12) in 2½-inch pots (their choice). Also, a large hanging pot kit is available.

The Plant Room, 6373 Trafalgar Road, Horn-by, Ontario, L0P 1E0, Canada. (416) 878-4984. Descriptive plant list $1.00. Open daily 10:00 a.m. to 4:00 p.m. (closed Wednesday). Visitors welcome. An assortment of standard and miniature African violets available as leaf cuttings. Also many other gesneriads and houseplants offered.

San Francisco Plant Company, Box 575, Colma Station, Daly City, California 94014. Nursery address is 2000 Cabrillo Highway Pacifica, California 94044. (415) 992-9998. For plant list, send stamped, self-addressed envel-ope plus 25 cents. African violets and other ges-neriads. Nursery is moving in the near future; it will expand offerings as well as open the green-houses to visitors.

Tinari Greenhouses, 2325 Valley Road, Box 190, Huntingdon Valley, Pennsylvania 19006. (215) 947-0144. Color-illustrated catalog 25 cents. Greenhouse in Bethayres, Pennsylvania. Visitors welcome. Open Monday through Saturday 8:00 a.m. to 5:00 p.m.; Sunday 1:00 p.m. to 5:00 p.m. except from June through September. Specialist in African violets including variegated foliage varieties, minia-tures, and semi-miniatures. All listed by hybrid name with flower descriptions. African violet equipment from lights, stands, carts to fertil-izers, ceramic jars, and books.

Volkmann Brothers Greenhouses, 2714 Minert Street, Dallas, Texas 75219. (214) 526-3484. Catalog. Open Monday through Friday 8:00 a.m. to 4:30; Saturday 8:00 a.m. to noon. Specialized growers of African violets. New and tested varieties including miniatures. Complete African violet supplies available from reservoir wick pots, plant stands, and lights to fertilizers and potting soils.

Wood's African Violets, Proton Station, Ontario, N0C 1L0, Canada. Open 10:00 a.m. to 7:00 p.m. A wide selection of African violets available in rooted clumps or fresh leaf cuttings. African violet supplies. Own originations; also variegated, mixtures, species, plus episcias.

Wilson Brothers Floral Company, Roach-dale, Indiana 46172. (317) 596-3455. Color-illustrated catalog. Greenhouse is on US 231, 5 miles west of Roachdale; open daily 8:30 a.m. to 5:00 p.m. Visitors welcome. Selection of African violet plants, including Ballet and Rhapsodie varieties. Also, some miniature and trailing varieties and African violet seed mix-ture. Pots, African violet spray, and soil are available, plus geraniums and houseplants.

Ailments

Plant diseases fall into two broad categories: *nonparasitic* and *parasitic*. Nonparasitic diseases are also called cultural diseases because they are caused by improper culture or environmental deficiencies—too much or too little light, water, or humidity; temperatures that are too high or too low; too much or too little fertilizer; drafts; stagnant or polluted air; a soil pH balance that is too acidic or too alkaline; physical injury. These are the factors to consider first when a plant looks sickly without showing symptoms of insect infestation. Fortunately, cultural diseases are not contagious and can be checked in the early stages by correcting the cultural problem (see *Problems*).

Parasitic diseases, on the other hand, are highly contagious. In indoor gardens they are most often caused by bacteria or fungi passed from plant to plant by hands, tools, water, soil, airborne dust, or insects. Both enter plants through wounds or natural openings, but fungi can also penetrate unbroken plant epidermis. These microorganisms normally perform an invaluable service in nature by breaking down organic matter so that soil nutrients can be utilized by plants. Improper culture, however, stimulates growth of bacteria and fungi which attack healthy plant tissue.

The chart in this section describes the symptoms, cultural causes, and treatment of some of the most common parasitic houseplant afflictions. You will notice that some of the diseases listed are aggravated by the very thing that we always think our plants can't get enough of: humidity. In the name of humidity we are advised to mist our plants continually, position them close together, or close them up in plastic bags. Indeed, under certain circumstances with certain plants this is good advice. But the precautions about these practices should also be considered.

Misting should never be done after dark, when the leaves feel chilly to the touch, or during hot, humid weather. Plants grouped together to help raise humidity should never touch, and there should always be plenty of space between them for good air circulation. A plastic tent is a good way to help raise humidity for a traumatized plant—one that has been repotted, root pruned, or divided. The high humidity of a plastic tent also helps support cuttings and seedlings while they are working to develop root systems. But the bag should always be poked with holes to admit fresh air and should always be propped up to prevent it from resting on the foliage, trapping excess moisture (the ideal growing medium for bacteria and fungi) in between.

Sanitation indoors is important to plant health. The use of only sterile potting materials cannot be overemphasized; also, diseased plant parts should be cut out and burned. This and any other kind of surgery, be it pinching out tip growth, root pruning, or taking cuttings, should be performed with clean-scrubbed hands and sterile tools. Cutting edges of razor blades, knives, or scissors can be sterilized by swabbing the blade with alcohol or by running it through a flame. After surgery, dust wounds with fungicide to be on the safe side. Dead or dying leaves, including those that have fallen into the pot, should be picked out and burned since they can harbor fungus spores. And always wash your hands after handling a diseased plant before handling a healthy one.

Gayle Fankhauser

Gayle Fankhauser is managing editor of gardening books for Publications International, the publisher of Consumer Guide Magazine, and is presently completing a book about vegetables.

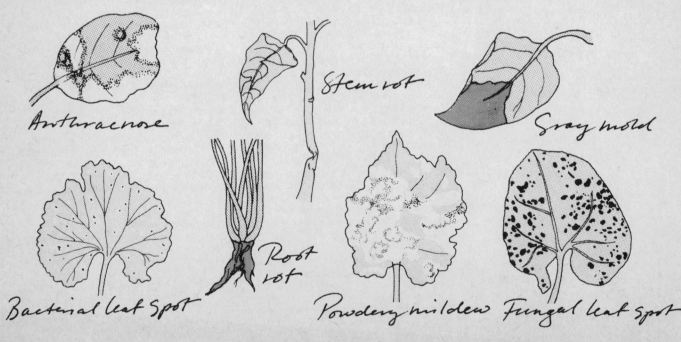

Anthracnose

Stem rot

Gray mold

Bacterial leaf spot

Root rot

Powdery mildew

Fungal leaf spot

Ailment control chart

Disease symptoms	Causes	Treatment
Anthracnose Fungal disease causing dry, depressed leaf spots, usually with tan-to-black centers and darker margins. Leaf tips may turn brown, dry, and shriveled with dark bands running across dead area.	Overwatering, too high humidity with poor ventilation, sudden chilling.	Remove infected plant parts. Cease misting; grow on the dry side. Apply foliar fungicide such as Bordeaux mixture, ferbam, maneb, or zineb. Benomyl's systemic action protects against further attack.
Damping-off Soil-borne fungi attacking seedlings, cuttings. Wilting is followed by stem collapse.	Unsterile potting medium, overwatering, temperature and humidity too high.	Drench soil with benomyl or captan. In the future use only sterile, soilless mix for cuttings and seedlings. Dust cuttings with fungicide, or rooting hormone containing fungicide, before potting.
Leaf spot May be bacterial or fungal in origin. *Fungal:* dark, dry spots with definite outline and tiny pimplelike dots. Also may have dark margins. Can take shape of ring (ringspot) with smaller rings inside. *Bacterial:* smooth, damp-looking irregular spots, sometimes surrounded by yellowish halo. Can be depressed or blistered. (Anthracnose is a kind of leaf spot disease usually classified by itself.)	Physical injury resulting in wound through which organism enters. Overwatering, high humidity, low light, sudden chilling, poor ventilation.	Remove and destroy diseased plant parts. Dust wounds with benomyl, captan, or zineb. Follow up with captan or zineb in spray, or with benomyl applied to soil for systemic protection. Reduce watering, cease misting.
Mold—black, sooty Foliage fungi which grow on honeydew secreted by aphids, mealybugs, scales, whiteflies. Not parasitic to plant but does block out light and interfere with photosynthesis.	Insect infestation. Aggravated by high humidity and poor ventilation.	Wipe mold from foliage with warm, soapy water or summer oil solution. Treat insect infestation.
Mold—white or gray Soil fungi which create a white-to-gray fuzzy substance on topsoil. By itself does little damage but does slow down soil drying time and portends root rot and other disease.	Overwatering, too much organic fertilizer.	Scrape away mold, aerate soil. Drench soil with fungicide. Reduce watering.
Powdery mildew Fungi feeding on plant, creating white-to-gray powdery coating on foliage. Results in stunted growth, curled leaves, deformed buds.	Too-high humidity combined with poor air circulation. Brought on by cool nights followed by warm days.	Remove badly damaged leaves. Dust foliage with sulfur or Karathane. Or apply benomyl as drench or spray. Correct culture.
Rot—crown and stem Fungal attack resulting in dark, mushy stems, crowns.	Overwatering, excessive humidity, poor ventilation. Extremely high or low temperatures.	Cut out and destroy infected areas; dust wounds with captan, ferbam, zineb. Repot in fresh soil in clay pot. Or take cuttings from healthy growth and destroy parent plant.
Rot—root Fungal attack which reduces ability of roots to absorb water. New growth dies back. Plant wilts, appearing to need water when the opposite is true. Roots look discolored, shriveled, pulpy.	Overwatering. Unsterile soil.	Cut out infected roots; dust wounds with fungicide. Repot in clay pot (smaller than previous pot if much of root ball has been cut away) in sterile medium. Drench soil with fungicide first two or three waterings thereafter.

Books

The Indoor Gardener's First Aid Book, by Jack Kramer, Simon and Schuster, 630 Fifth Ave., New York, New York 10020, 1975, hardbound, 128 pages, $6.95. Descriptions of the diseases— how to detect and treat them— are too brief to be very helpful, but this is a good beginner's book on the subject.

Plant Disease Handbook, by Cynthia Wescott, Van Nostrand Reinhold Co., 450 W. 33 St., New York, New York 10001, 1971, hardbound, 825 pages, $13.50. This is a serious reference work. The excellent opening chapters and the introductory discussions of each disease are highly informative and comprehensible to the laymen.

The Plant Doctor, by Richard Nicholls, Running Press, 38 S. 19 St., Philadelphia, Pennsylvania 19103, 1975, paperback, 108 pages, $3.95. This book gives good overall coverage of houseplant hygiene as it relates to plant pests and diseases. Cultural diseases are discussed along with basic care techniques, but parasitic diseases are in a chapter by themselves. The diagnostic chart is cross-referenced with full explanations in the text.

First Aid for House Plants, by Shirley Ross, McGraw-Hill Book Co., 1221 Avenue of the Americas, New York, New York 10020, 1976, paperback, 216 pages, $5.95. This book contains individual discussions of 100 common houseplants, their care requirements, and the pests and diseases they are most likely to develop. There is an excellent handling of parasitic and nonparasitic diseases in chart form but no background explanation of them.

Houseplant Rx, by Doc and Katy Abraham, Countryside Books, A.B. Morse Co., Barrington, Illinois, 1976, paperback, 48 pages, $1.50. This book contains a good diagnostic chart for handling parasitic and cultural diseases but is rather weak on the background information that would help the reader make good use of the chart. The book includes color photographs of diseased plants.

How to Control Plant Diseases in Home and Garden, by Malcolm C. Shurtleff, Iowa State University Press, Ames, Iowa 50010, hardbound, 520 pages, $4.95. A valuable reference book for gardeners with a serious interest in plant diseases, this book explains the basics of this complex subject, answering the hows and whys in an organized and well-written way.

Rx for Ailing House Plants, by Charles M. Evans and Roberta Lee Pliner, Random House, 201 E. 50 St., New York, New York 10022, 1974, paperback, 106 pages, $3.95. This well-organized book includes cultural and parasitic diseases as well as insect pests. The diagnostic chart is helpful as are the individual discussions of diseases. Background information explaining bacteria, fungi, and viruses as they attack plants is missing.

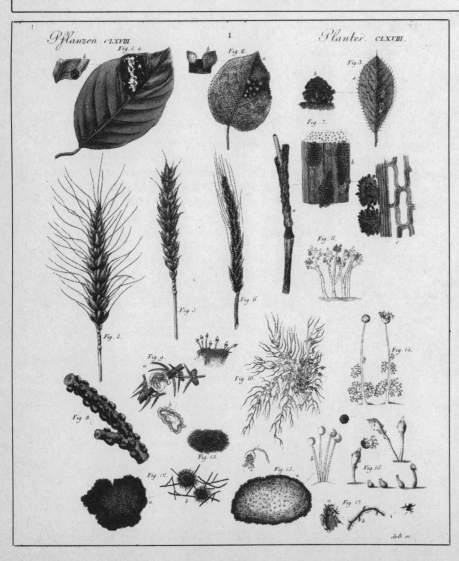

Supplies & equipment

Mite-e-funge controls fungus and mites on a wide variety of plants. Squeeze-duster applicator eliminates leaf burn and allows easy application. Does not harm beneficial insects. Contains 98 percent sulfur.
For brochure and mail-order information, write:
**Organic Control
Box 25382
Los Angeles, CA 90025**

Fungicides to apply as sprays or dusts are available from B.G. Pratt; included are wettable sulfur, Bordeaux mixture, and benomyl.
For buying information write:
**B.G. Pratt Division
Gabriel Chemicals, Ltd.
204 21st Avenue
Paterson, NJ 07509**

Fungicides designed for the indoor plant grower are available in consumer-size containers from Bonide. Specific and general-purpose formulations for spraying and soil treatment are offered. They are sold in the East and Midwest in garden centers and hardware stores.
For buying information write:
**Bonide Chemical Company
2 Wurz Avenue
Yorkville, NY 13495**

Ortho fungicides include a wide range of specific and multi-purpose products for indoor plant protection. These are distributed nationally and can be found in many retail outlets.
For additional information write:
**Chevron Chemical Company
575 Market Street
San Francisco, CA 94119**

Aquatic plants

Imagine an oasis of liquid, shimmering silence as part of your home. Though impressive, you don't need a huge sunken pool, replete with expensive exotic fish and giant waterlilies, to capture the essence of an underwater-world. All you need is a simple fishpond or tank from the five and dime. Simply add a few easy-to-care-for plants, one or two goldfish, and perhaps some dramatic lighting, and you've created a perpetual living picture enchanting enough to compete with any other form of entertainment. If you already have a fish tank, adding live plants to it imparts a more natural, complete appearance. And your fish will love having real plants to nibble and hide in. On the practical side, an aquarium will increase the humidity in the home to the benefit of all the inhabitants, including other houseplants.

Aquatic plants

A wide variety of plants can be grown in aquariums. There is even a miniature water lily available from Three Springs Fisheries that will grow indoors in a sunny window or under a plant light. Most aquatic plants absorb nutrients from all over their surfaces, not just their roots; some have no roots at all. When selecting plants, have some that are rooted, such as sagittaria, vallisneria, and cryptocoryne; some bunch plants, such as

cabomba (fanwort), myriophyllum (milfoil), and anacharis (elodea); and one or two floating plants, such as duckweed or nitella. It is also important to choose plants that have the same light requirements; light duration is more important than intensity. Tropical and subtropical plants do well with twelve hours of light; those from the temperate zone require up to fourteen hours for healthy foliage and up to 16 hours to produce flowers.

Fish: Balance is the basis

The secret to a successful plant and fish aquarium is balance. Fish and plants should come from the same climate and so have similar needs. Although fish and plants in an aquatic community interact and support each others' life systems, they are still in an artificially created environment. All their needs will not be satisfied automatically. Make sure you know your fish's requirements. Proper feeding keeps them healthy and beautiful, and maintains a clean tank. As a rule, feed fish only once a day; give them only as much as they can consume in five minutes. One day a week, force them to scavenge for food remnants by withholding food. Feed even less frequently in winter.

You may wish to add scavengers, such as snails, newts, or turtles. They consume the refuse in the water, keeping the tank clean.

Waterscaping

When designing your "waterscape," you need to keep two things in mind: try to arrive at a pleasing effect aesthetically, while satisfying the needs of the plants and fish.

Begin by choosing the proper container. For plants alone, any glass container will do, even a large bottle like the ones used for terrariums. (If you use such a bottle, which has a narrow neck, you will need terrarium-planting implements, such as a funnel, dowel, and pruning tool.) For fish, of course, use fish bowls or a fish tank, in any size.

Pour in about a 2-inch layer of clean, aquarium gravel or very coarse sand. Create hills and valleys in the planting medium to resemble a natural terrain. If you add small and large stones, old branches, shells, and other found objects, they must be clean, disinfected, and without crevices that harbor bacteria and bits of organic matter which will pollute the water. Pour in about 6 inches of rain water or tap water.

Next, add the plants. For each plant, create a cavity in the planting medium with a stick and insert the roots, making sure they hang straight down. Then fill in the cavity with the medium, covering and anchoring the roots.

When arranging the plants, consider the view from all sides. Do not

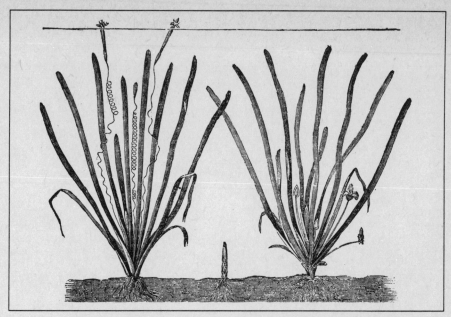

use so many plants that light is not adequate. Having too many plants will also obliterate the fish; keep the front and most of the center of the aquarium sparsely planted so fish can be seen. The best arrangement is one in which tall plants are grouped in the back, with shorter plants around them.

When you have finished planting, add water almost to the top and put on a glass cover. When using tap water, let the aquarium sit for a week so the chlorine has a chance to escape. Then add the fish. The temperature should be maintained at about 70 degrees F.

Maintenance

For a plants-only water garden, simply maintain the water level by adding rain water, or tap water which has been left standing for several days. Trim off any dead, decaying leaves or roots.

If your water garden includes fish, change the water two or three times a year, transferring the fish to a container filled with the same water in which they have been living.

Cloudy water is a common occurrence, especially in newly established aquariums. It is caused by the growth of algae and usually subsides in five to ten days. Fresh water is full of the embryos of algae and protozoa, plus the minerals they need to reproduce. Once they have consumed all the nutrients, they die. Do not add more water if the water turns cloudy. This merely introduces more embryos and minerals. If cloudy water persists, use a substance specially formulated to treat the condition, and switch to rain water or install a filtering system.

Nancy Bruning

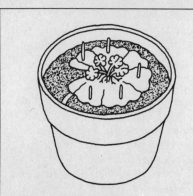

The viviparous water lily
The miniature water lily, Margaret Mary, grows in indoor aquariums. These tiny wonders are viviparous, which means they reproduce by sprouting miniature plants from the center of their leaves. To root the young plant, cut off the leaf and pin it to the surface of the soil in a flowerpot. Plunge the pot, up to its rim, into a container of water. The new plant will soon take root and be suitable for planting in another water garden.

Plants for an indoor water garden

Acorus gramineus (Japanese rush)
Acorus gramineus variegatus (variegated Japanese rush)
Anacharis densa and *canadensis* (elodea)
Aponegeton fenestralis (lace plant)
Azolla caroliniana (floating moss)
Bacopa caroliniana and monniera
Cabomba caroliniana (fanwort)
Ceratopteris thalictroides (water fern)
Ceterophyllum demersum (hornwort)
Cryptocoryne cordata (water trumpet)
Echinodorus tenellus (sword plant)
Eichhornia crassipes (water hyacinth)
Eleocharis acicularis (hair grass)
Hydrocleys commersonii (water poppy)
Hygrophila polysperma (water star)
Lagarosiphon muscoides (false elodea)
Lemna gibba, minor, and *triocula* (duckweed)
Ludwigia mulertii (swamp spoon)
Lysimachia nummularia (moneywort)
Myriophyllum prosperinacoides (milfoil)
Nitella flexis
Nomaphila stricta (giant Indian water star)
Nymphoides aquatica (banana plant)
Synnema triflorum (water wisteria)
Sagittaria graminea (arrowhead)
Vallisneria spiralis (eel grass)

Goldfish by the inch

Three Springs Fisheries, one of the suppliers listed in this section, has this suggestion for determining how many goldfish you should buy for your aquarium: Measure the water surface of the fish tank in square inches. Then (not counting the tail) buy one inch of goldfish per 20 square inches. For example, a 10-by-20-inch fish tank has a 200-square-inch water surface, and would accommodate ten 1-inch goldfish.

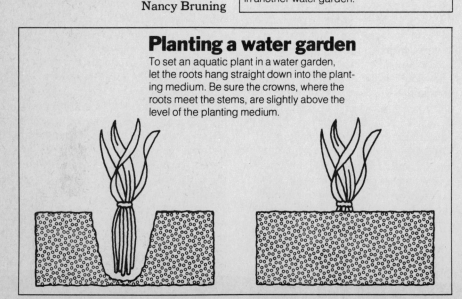

Planting a water garden

To set an aquatic plant in a water garden, let the roots hang straight down into the planting medium. Be sure the crowns, where the roots meet the stems, are slightly above the level of the planting medium.

Books

Aquarium Plants and Decoration, by R.F. O'Connell, Charles Scribner's Sons, 597 Fifth Ave., New York, New York 10017, 1973, paperback, 94 pages, $3.95. Describes a variety of aquatic plants, giving details of their origin and growth habits. Also gives advice on designing a tropical aquarium. Illustrated with line drawings and color photos. Written by an aquarist with many years of experience, in an informative and easily readable style.

Aquarium Fishes and Plants, by K. Rataj and R. Zukal, Hamlyn House, Feltham, Middlesex, England, 1971, hardbound, 134 pages. A book that will be difficult to locate, but worth the effort. Includes information on designing the aquarium and offers guidance on heating and lighting the tank and nourishing the plants and fish. The main body of the text is devoted to pairing up species of fish and plants in accordance with the geographical region from which they originate and describing how to care for them.

A Guide To Water Gardening, by Phillipp Swindells, Charles Scribner's Sons, 597 Fifth Ave., New York, New York 10017, hardbound, 224 pages, $7.95. One chapter on water gardening indoors.

Plant sources

Paradise Gardens, 14 May Street, Whitman, Massachusetts 02382. (617) 447-4711. Illustrated catalog $1.00. Open Monday through Saturday 8:00 a.m. to 6:00 p.m. These specialists in water gardening offer many aquatic plants (cattail, flowering rush, water hyacinth, floating fern, water sprite) and some varieties of hardy and tropical water lilies. Extensive materials for pools are offered, including liners, pumps, filters, fountains, and deodorants. Some directions for plant culture included in catalog.

Slocum Water Gardens, 1101 Cypress Gardens Road, Winter Haven, Florida 33880. (813) 292-7151. Color-illustrated catalog $1.00. Open Monday through Saturday. Visitors welcome. Water liles, goldfish, scavengers, and oxygenating plants.

Three Springs Fisheries, Lilypons, Maryland 21717. (301) 874-5133. Color-illustrated catalog $1.00. Open Monday through Saturday 9:00 a.m. to 3:30 p.m.; Sunday 12:30 p.m. to 3:30 p.m. March 15 through September 15. Remainder of year open Monday through Saturday 9:00 a.m. to 3:30 p.m.; closed holidays. Although this nursery for aquatic plants is geared primarily towards outdoor ponds, streams, and pools, it does include some miniature water lilies, such as Margaret Mary, suitable for indoor aquariums. Wide selection of lilies, including many tropical varieties. Also lotus, water iris, and aquatic plants. Tips on culture and numerous water accessories are offered, including large choice of goldfish.

William Tricker, Allendale Avenue, Saddle River, New Jersey 07458. (201) 327-0721. Catalog 25 cents. Open Monday through Saturday 8:00 a.m. to 5:00 p.m. Aquatic plants, particularly water lilies. Fiberglass pools, goldfish, and water garden accessories.

Van Ness Water Gardens, 2460 North Euclid Avenue, Upland, California 91786. (714) 982-2425. Illustrated color catalog 50 cents. Open Tuesday through Saturday 8:00 a.m. to 5:00 p.m. Large selection of water lilies, plus many aquatic plants, fish, equipment, and related books. Very informative and helpful catalog with detailed explanations for water gardeners.

Supplies & equipment

Pools for use in garden planning have been developed by Russel Rielle of Hermitage Gardens. Most are free-form in design; they range in surface size from 41½ by 45½ inches to 77 by 108 inches. Made of molded plastic, they can be used alone or in combinations with wooden bridges and rock waterfalls. Connectors, lights, pumps, and filters are supplied. Sold by garden centers, landscapers, and by mail.

For catalog ($1.00) and mail-order information, write:
Russell A. Rielle
Box 361
Route 5 West of Canastota, NY 13032

Fountains in over 700 combinations are offered by Roman Fountains. Suitable for both indoor and outdoor installation, they range in size from small indoor fountains to large installations and waterfall units. Available at garden centers, nurseries, and florist shops.

For catalog and mail-order information, write:
Roman Fountains
Box 10190
Albuquerque, NM 87114

Baskets

One of the easiest ways to decorate with plants, and even make many look more spectacular, is to put them in an interesting container.

With the current interest in natural fibers, fabrics, and colors, some of the most unusual, interesting, and often reasonably priced choices today are baskets. From the dime store version, to the elaborate lacquered foreign imports, there are enough different weaves, shapes and sizes to offer endless decorating possibilities.

Create dramatic displays

Try one basket, or a cluster of individual plants each in its own basket of the same size, or varying sizes. For an even more dramatic display, take two or three smaller plants and arrange them in one large basket. To keep the individual pots from showing, put some sphagnum moss around the tops of the pots. Several small ferns, for example, will give the appearance of one large plant when arranged this way.

Baskets can also serve as a practical problem solver for covering up unattractive pots.

And don't forget some of the colored baskets, which can be particularly attractive when color is a theme at a dinner party. And there's no reason not to consider using your plants, especially favorites in bloom, as a centerpiece on your kitchen or dining room table. Remember that for the price of cut flowers today, you can still have the green plant when you'd be throwing out the dead flowers.

Do's and don'ts

There are some do's and don'ts about using baskets. Do remember to put a dish or lining of foil in the bottom of the basket so water won't leak. This saves the basket from getting wet, too, and avoids the chore of trying to get rid of unsightly water marks on tables. If the plant is a little too low for the basket, you can prop up the pot with pebbles or an overturned saucer.

Some hangups

There are just as many ways to hang baskets with plants, which is an interesting way to show off the plant as well as the container and perhaps even one of the variety of macramé or shell ropes. There also are some basket-like containers such as wicker bird cages which are excellent for vines and trailing plants. Again, remember with the hanging baskets to put a dish in the bottom.

You can change the baskets around, spray them with different color paints, and add decorations like ribbons and bows for a special touch.

And don't forget to consider the large baskets for your bigger plants which sit on the floor. Since there is a more limited variety of very large pots, baskets are a good way to hide unsightly ones. And perhaps nicest of all, when you're tired of the basket, or a tragedy befalls the plant, you can always fill them with fruit, some of your homemade bread, or toss magazines in the large ones.

Penny Girard

Penny Girard is a news reporter for Fairchild Publications in Washington, D.C. She has written articles on plants for Washingtonian Magazine *and* Plants Alive *and also teaches courses on plants and gardening at the Open University in Washington.*

Natural fibers: a glossary of terms

Aloe: A fiber which comes from the East Indian variety of the sisal plant, more off-white in color than other varieties of sisal.

Bacbac: The bark of the abaca hemp plant, which is actually a banana. Peeled in strips and fashioned, when damp, into baskets. The texture is hairy and rough.

Bamboo: To distinguish it from rattan, which is a vine, bamboo is a species of woody grass. It is brittle and hollow. It cannot be steam bent and is difficult to work with.

Banana: The bark of the banana plant peeled in strips and used in basketry.

Coco: Also known as Coir (pronounced coy-yer), it comes from the tough fibrous husk of one of 36 species of the coco palm. The very best quality coco comes from special unripened fruit. Natives of India's southern Malabar coast remove the husks and soak them for several months in brackish pools. The fiber is separated from the pulp by pounding. Hand spinning the yarn has been a cottage industry for years. The color is tobacco brown, although you can get a lighter coloring by soaking the fiber in sea water for more than a year—other colors are dyed. Coco has a rough finish and is especially resistant to dirt and heat. Mid-rib of the palm leaf is used in the manufacture of basketware.

Fern: Flowerless, forest plant with leaflike fronds which are cut and split. Very pliant, and suitable for weaving into baskets.

Lake Grass: From northern and central provinces of China, a marshy reed which is harvested and handcrafted in trivets and matting.

Latanier: Palm leaf from the coconut tree, yellow/white in color. Commercial production comes from Haiti, hence the French name.

Maize: It is made from the outer husk of corn. First, workers strip the husk; while it is damp, it is worked into braids; then patterns and the ends tied off underneath. It dries almost white, and the rugs are smooth-textured and flat. Chinese maize rugs are made in agricultural communes in the Shantung and Tientsin areas.

Palm: A tree with fan-shaped leaves. Can also be a shrub or a vine found in tropical and sub-tropical areas. The mid-rib portion of the leaf is suitable for baskets.

Ramie: A strong, lustrous bast fiber from a nettle family plant.

Rattan: From the stem of a thorny climbing jungle palm. Not to be confused with the bamboo because distinctive joints or nodes every few feet make the two look alike. Rattan, however, is solid and bamboo is hollow. Bamboo cannot be readily bent or machined, and is not strong like rattan. The vines (the big ones are 7 to 10 years old and up to 600 feet in length) are cut off 3 feet above the ground, dried, and the outer bark removed. Rattan will last indefinitely. It has greater tensile strength than steel. It is very strong and very lightweight. Rattan is almost white in its natural state, though it is generally stained to give it color. The "tortoise shell" finish used both on rattan and bamboo is made by scorching with a flame which darkens the surface.

Reed: A general term for any hollow stalk, mostly varieties of native grasses or canes, indigenous to a particular geographic area: Totora, Duda, Tule, Nito, Casso, Kayabang, Canastro, Tiboli, and Tiruray (the latter two names actually refer to the primitive tribes who fashion the baskets, which bear their names, from local jungle flora).

Rice Straw: A by-product of the tremendous rice production in China, rice straw is used in both doormats and rugs, utilizing the shaft of the grain. Its color is a warm beige/tan.

Rush: Akin to seagrass, it is less waxy and softer. It has a sweet odor like new-mown hay. Colors vary—Haitian rush, the least expensive, is a yellowish tan/green; Chinese rush comes in shades of brown.

Seagrass: Grown in marshy areas, it is harvested and woven into braids while moist, then sun dried. Indigenous to many tropical areas, the most important production comes from Taiwan and has been used in rug production for years. The rugs characteristically feature open-work and filigree type patterns in a crisp, flat weave.

Sisal: A long, strong fiber obtained from the lower, mature leaves of the agave, a giant yuccalike plant grown on plantations. It originated in Mexico's Yucatan peninsula, but today the best sisal comes from East Africa. It is also grown in India, Taiwan, Haiti, and Brazil. Sisal varies in color from country to country, but the natural, undyed fiber is cream colored and it may be bleached to a pure white. As it has great tensile strength, sisal is used to make marine ropes.

Wheat Straw: The fibers come from the stem of the common wheat plant. A shiny golden yellow color, the Chinese use it in rugs, handbags, baskets, and home accessories.

Wicker: There is no such thing as a wicker material. Wicker is merely a style of furniture, mostly rattan, or accessories. Wicker has, to a large degree, become the generic name for rattan.

Willow: Comes from a family of trees and shrubs. It is characteristically a red/brown woody material that does not bend smoothly. Often when plaited or woven, it will flatten out and create a corner. It is formed when wet, and some people advise that it should be moistened occasionally to prevent brittleness. It does not have the stability of rattan and it's available also in the peeled state from China in a cream color, and in an orange/tan color from Eastern Europe where the willow is peeled by a steaming process.

Reprinted by permission from a leaflet compiled by Import Specialists, 82 Wall St., New York, New York 10005.

How to waterproof a pot-covering basket

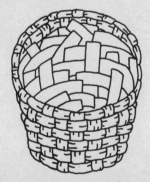

1. Cover the interior of the basket with strips of paper such as newsprint. Be sure there are no spaces between the strips. Overlap or use more than one thickness to ensure complete coverage.

2. Fold or cut the top edges of the paper strips so that they end at least an inch below the basket rim.

3. Waterproof by painting a resin sealer over the paper; be careful not to miss a spot.

4. If the paper shows between the plant's pot and the basket, fill in the empty space with sphagnum moss or bark.

Supplies & equipment

Wicker plant accessories are available from Fran's Basket House. Among the many items offered are plant stands with metal liners, sea grass planters in open or closed weave, hanging rattan planters, and window-sill rattan planters.

For the catalog and mail-order information, write:

**Fran's Basket House
Route 10
Succasunna, NJ 07876**

Woven planters and baskets. A wide range of imported decorator accessories for use with potted plants are available to indoor gardeners. Included are baskets, cylinders, pot pads, and planters made of woven bamboo, latanier, palm midrib, bacbac, coco midrib, nito vine, bacul and many other materials—from Mexico, Ecuador, Haiti, and the Philipines, to name but a few. Available at garden centers, resort gift shops, and department, hardware, and decorator stores. No mail order.

**Import Specialists
82 Wall Street
New York, NY 10005.**

Begonias

Begonias are a stimulating group of plants which offer such an abundant variety that they can be intriguing to the beginner as well as the very experienced plant grower. The eight major groupings of begonias—cane-like ("angel wings"), shrublike, thick stemmed, semperflorens ("wax begonias"), rhizomatous, rex, tuberous, and trailing-scandent—display an unequalled diversity of growth habits, colors and color patterns, leaf sizes and shapes, inflorescences, and blooming times.

Adaptable

Versatility and general ease of culture make begonias, in most cases, suitable for various growing environments, including window gardening, fluorescent light gardening, and greenhouse growing, plus outdoor gardening, when temperatures permit. There are also many miniature rhizomatous and rex begonias that are particularly suited to terrarium growing.

Basic culture

The basic culture of begonias is relatively uncomplicated. All begonias need plenty of light and/or sunlight in various amounts. Usually canelike, bare-leaved shrublike, most trailing-scandent, and semperflorens types require the most sunlight; rhizomatous, hairy-leaved shrublike, trailing-scandent, and tuberous types do well with filtered sunlight or bright light most of the day. The grower must consider the intensity of the sun in his geographic location, and adjust amounts of sunlight accordingly. Rex begonias do not tolerate bright sunlight and are especially suited to fluorescent light gardening.

Although most begonias are not too demanding as far as temperature is concerned, they will grow ideally

when the temperature range is between 58 and 72 degrees F. The relative humidity should be between 40 and 60 percent for best results with all types of begonias except rex begonias. They prefer a slightly higher relative humidity. Careful watering is essential; it must be done thoroughly only when the soil surface is slightly dry to the touch. The potting soil must be light, porous, and coarse to ensure proper drainage for good root development. Begonias should be repotted only when the root system fills the pot, and then moved only to the next size pot, preferably a clay pot because of its porosity. Because begonias are shallow-rooted plants, it is preferable to use squatty-type pots for most begonias. The exceptions are the taller-growing types, which can use a deeper pot when they are fully mature.

For beautiful begonias that are vigorous, healthy, and disease-resistant, regular feeding with a complete well-balanced fertilizer is of utmost importance. Begonias have relatively few diseases and attract few insects. Since prevention is far easier than cure, regular spraying should be done with broad spectrum insecticides and fungicides. A begonia is beautiful and a pleasure to grow only when it is vigorous, healthy, insect-free, and well-groomed.

The relative simplicity of culture and the unparalleled diversity accounts for the growing popularity of begonias today.

Mildred L. and Edward J. Thompson

Mildred and Edward Thompson are plumbers by trade. In 1961, they decided to start growing begonias as a hobby; they now have three greenhouses and grow about 850 different species and cultivars of begonias.

Leaf-vein cuttings for begonias

1. This method works for large-veined begonias. Start with a sturdy, adult leaf. Make tiny slashes across the most prominent veins with a sharp knife. Place the leaf, underside down, on moist propagating medium such as sand, burying the stem.

2. Keep the cuts in close contact with the damp medium by pinning them down with toothpicks, U-shaped wire loops, or small pebbles. Maintain humidity by covering the container with a glass lid or by placing it in a plastic bag.

3. Each slash should send out roots; eventually, small plants will form. When plants are large enough to handle, pot them separately.

Begonia x crestabruchii (lettuce-leaf begonia)

Begonia masoniana (iron cross begonia)

Rex begonia

Plant sources

ABC Nursery and Greenhouse, Route 1, Box 313, Lecoma, Missouri 65540. (314) 435-6389. Plant list. Open Monday through Friday from 8:00 a.m. Visitors welcome. An assortment of begonias in addition to other houseplants.

Maxine V. Beam, Route 1, Box 93, Roanoke, Texas 76262. (817) 431-1403. Send stamp for plant list. Visitors welcome by appointment. An assortment of all types of begonias available as cuttings; also some African violets and assorted gesneriads.

Begonia Paradise Nursery, Route 1, Box 94, Bear Creek, North Carolina. Plant list 25 cents. Open Saturday and Sunday 9:00 a.m. to 4:00 p.m. Visitors welcome. Extensive list of rhizomatous, rex, and various types of fibrous-rooted begonias.

Edelweiss Gardens, 54 Robbinsville-Allentown Road, Box 66R, Robbinsville, New Jersey 08691. (609) 259-2831. Plant list 35 cents. Open until 4:00 p.m. every day. Angel wing, cane, fibrous-rooted, rex, rhizomatous, semperflorens, and other begonias; also many other houseplants.

Green of the Earth, 1295 Lownes Place, Pomona, California 91766. (714) 623-7809. Plant list 50 cents. An assortment of different kinds of begonias in addition to many other houseplants.

Hewston Green, Box 3115, Seattle, Washington 98114. Plant list 50 cents. An assortment of all types of begonias in addition to many other kinds of houseplants.

Kartuz Greenhouses, 92 Chestnut Street, Wilmington, Massachusetts 01887. (617) 658-9017. Color-illustrated catalog $1.00. Open Tuesday through Saturday 9:00 a.m. to 5:00 p.m. Visitors welcome. Cane, shrub, rhizomatous, rex, semperflorens, calla, tuberous, semi-tuberous, hiemalis, and trailing begonias; also other houseplants.

Lauray of Salisbury, Under Mountain Road, Salisbury, Connecticut 06068. (203) 435-2263. Catalog 50 cents. Open daily 10:00 a.m. to 5:00 p.m. Visitors welcome. Angel wing, small-leaved, rhizomatous, and assorted other begonias as well as many other houseplants.

Logee's Greenhouses, 55 North Street, Danielson, Connecticut 06239. (203) 774-8038. Illustrated catalog $2.00. Open daily 9:00 a.m. to 4:00 p.m. Visitors welcome. Very large selection of rex, angel wing, cane, felted-leaved, hairy-leaved, hanging, fibrous-rooted, rhizomatous, procumbent, semi-tuberous, semperflorens, and calla begonias; also, many other houseplants.

Merry Gardens, Camden, Maine 04843. Pictorial handbook $1.00; plant list 50 cents. Open Monday through Saturday 9:00 a.m. to 4:30 p.m. Visitors welcome. Fibrous-rooted, rhizomatous, angel wing, small-leaved, hairy-leaved, semperflorens, and trailing begonias; many other houseplants are also offered.

The Plant Room, 6373 Trafalgar Road, Hornby, Ontario, LOP 1EO, Canada. (416) 878-4984. Plant list $1.00. Open daily 10:00 a.m. to 4:00 p.m. (closed Wednesday). Visitors welcome. An assortment of begonias plus many other houseplants.

Rainbow Begonia Gardens, Box 991, Westminster, California 92683. (714) 897-4463. Plant list. Extensive selection of begonias available as leaf or stem cuttings. List gives brief description of flower and leaf.

Wilson Brothers Floral Company, Roachdale, Indiana 46172. (317) 596-3455. Color-illustrated catalog. Greenhouse is on US 231, 5 miles west of Roachdale. Open daily 8:30 a.m. to 5:00 p.m. Visitors welcome. Rex, angel wing, calla, semperflorens, and other kinds of begonias; also, geraniums and other houseplants.

Begonia limmingheiana (shrimp begonia)

Begonia semperflorens albo-foliis (calla-lily begonia)

Begonia x erythrophylla (beefsteak begonia)

Canelike begonia

Societies

American Begonia Society, Jacqueline Garinger, 8302 Kittyhawk Avenue, Los Angeles, California 90045. Founded in 1932 as the California Begonia Society, this organization took its present name in 1934. The purposes of the Society are to stimulate and promote interest in begonias and other shade-loving plants; to encourage introduction and development of new types of begonias; to standardize nomenclature of begonias; and to gather and publish information in regard to propagation and culture of begonias and companion plants.

Annual membership dues are $5.00. All members receive a subscription to *The Begonian* and a culture bulletin on begonias. Members also have access to the 50 libraries the Society maintains across the United States, 80 round-robin letters on begonia growing, a correspondence course in judging begonia shows, and a seed bank.

A national show is held at the end of August or beginning of September in Orange County, California. There is also a regional convention in the East in the fall.

Books

Begonia Guide, by Mildred L. Thompson and Edward J. Thompson, 310-A Hill St., Southampton, New York 11968, 1976, 975 pages, Volume I: $19.75, Volume II: $18.75, Volume III will be distributed in winter 1977 with the price to be set then. A three-volume work in loose-leaf format suitable for both the beginning grower and the experienced collector, this set contains the history of the *Begoniaceae*, culture in various parts of the country and around the world, horticultural classification, parentages of hybrids, propagation, bloom information, glossary, an extensive bibliography, black and white photographs, and drawings. To order write the Thompsons at the above address.

Begonias Chevalier, translated by Alva Graham, California, 1975, 165 pages, $10.00. A translation from the French of an important work on begonias done in the 1930s by Charles Chevalier, this book gives cultural and historical information on species and cultivars of begonias. It is profusely illustrated with both color and black and white photographs. To order, write the American Begonia Society Librarian, Mrs. Lydia Austin, 15329 Eastwood Ave., Lawndale, California 90260.

Wedge-shaped begonia leaf cuttings

Use this method for large-leaved begonias with prominent veins, such as the rex and other rhizomatous, thick-rooted varieties.

1. Cut a healthy, mature leaf into triangles using a sharp knife. Make sure each piece has a major vein and a piece of stem. Trimming off the top quarter of the triangles will reduce wilting.

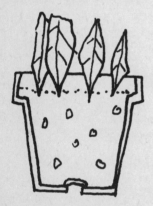

2. Poke a hole in moist rooting medium such as vermiculite and insert the triangle, pointed end down. Keep the medium moist and cover with a glass lid or enclose in a plastic bag to maintain humidity.

3. Pot each section separately when it has rooted, or wait until plantlets form.

Begonias to try

Canelike
Barbara Ann
Corallina de Lucerna
Corinthian
Dorothy Barton
Esther Albertine
Flo'Belle Moseley
Frances Lyons
Hannah Serr
Irene Nuss
Kentwood
Laura Engelbert
Lenore Olivier
Lil O'Neill
Martha Floro
Matild
Nancy Gail
Nora Hanson
Orange Rubra
Orpha C. Fox
Question Mark
Robinson's Peach
Rubric
Sophie Cecile
Wayne Newton

Shrublike
acuminata
acutifolia
Alleryi
Argenteo-guttata
Bayern
Catalina
China Boy
Concord
Corbeille de Feu
cubensis hort.
Dancing Girl
Dearest Mae
Decker's Select
fruticosa
Gwenn Lowell
Lory Hansen
Magdalene Madsen
Medora
metallica
Mrs. Fred T. Scripps
Multiflora Rosea
Nelly Bly

Perfectiflora
Preussen
Richmondensis
Rutherfordiana
Sachen
scharffiana
scharffii
Selover
Thrustonii
Waltanna

Thick stemmed
friburgensis
Marie B. Reed
parilis
ulmifolia

Semperflorens
Bois de Vaux
Carmen
Comet
cucullata
Derby
Flamingo
Gee-Gee
Gin
Indian Maid
Kallaking
leptotricha
Linda
Othello
Pink Pearl
Pink Profusion
Rosabella
Scarletta
schmidtiana
Tausendschoen
Whiskey
White Pearl

Rhizomatous
Aladdin
Angie
Arcola
Aries
Baby Perfectifolia
Beatrice Haddrell
Black Falcon
Bow-Arriola
Bow-Chancee

Bow-Imp
Bow-Joe
Bow-Nigra
bowerae
bowerae var.
  nigramarga
Brocade
Chantilly Lace
Charro
China Doll
Christine
Chumash
Cleopatra
Ed Bates
Edith M.
El MacWhorter
Elaine Wilkerson
Ella Frost
Elsie Picot
English Lace
Fischer's ricinifolia
Frances Fickewirth
Freddie
Geminii
Goldie Frost
Heather Ann
Kifujin
King Leo
Leopon
Libby Lee
Little Darling
Little Joe
Mercury
Midget
Needham
Neptune
Nod
Oceanside
Olive Milliman
Patricia Ogdon
Penny O'Day
Ricinifolia
Robert Shatzer
Rosetta White
Sir Percy
Skeezar
Smidgens
Squiggles

Stallion
Stash
Texastar
Universe
Vermash
Verbob
Whiskers
Winkum
Zee Bowman
Zugario

Rex
Beau Rouge
Christine Blais
Ed Thompson
Ember
Fairy
Granny
Helen Teupel
Julie Blais
Marion Louise
Peter Pan
Peace
Robin
Shirtsleeves
Shorty
Silver Sweet
Tweed

Tuberous and semituberous
Aphrodite series
dregei
evansiana
Helene Harmes
Maxwelton
Rambouillet
Schwabenland series
suffruticosa
Weltonensis

Trailing-scandent
Bob-o-link
convolvulacea
Delores
Ellen Dee
Florence Carrell
glabra
Marjorie Daw
procumbens

Begonia rex 'Merry Christmas'

Begonia x 'Corallina de Lucerna'

Bonsai

Wisteria

same guidelines are in effect. The plant should have:
- —small leaves or needles
- —short internodes (distance between leaves)
- —attractive bark
- —sturdy main stem
- —branching pattern that will produce good formations

Styles of bonsai
There are five basic styles which can be adapted in numerous ways. They are formal upright, informal upright, slanting, cascade, and semicascade. These styles are based on the overall shape of the tree and the direction or angle the trunk slants away from the main axis. Other styles include miniature bonsai called mame (under six inches), rock, twin, group plantings, literati, driftwood, multiple trunk, sinuous, windswept, and broom style.

Pots
In choosing a pot for a bonsai planting, the goal is always compatability with the plant, the style, and with nature. Small, shallow pots and traylike containers are specifically made for bonsai. They may be round, oval, hexagonal, square or rectangular. The colors are always muted: brown, gray, black, green, tan, or off-white.

Training, pruning, and wiring
To train the tree or shrub to grow in a specific shape, the foliage and roots are cut back and the branches are wrapped with wire. The equipment needed for this artful persuasion is relatively simple: pruning shears, sharpened dowel or chopstick, palette knife, short-bladed scissors, long tweezers, scoop, wire cutters, and copper wire (the lower the number, the heavier the wire).

Maintenance
Growing bonsai is quite a commitment in terms of time and patience. They must be watered every day, judicious pruning and pinching is a constant process during the growing periods, and some must be repotted as often as every six months. But to the bonsai grower, the investment is a wise one because of the satisfaction derived from having captured the spirit of nature in a tiny tree.

Nancy Bruning

First developed by the Chinese and later elaborated on by the Japanese, bonsai (pronounced bone-sigh) is an intriguing combination of art and horticulture. Miniaturized trees and shrubs, grown in special small containers, attempt to recreate a bit of nature, including all the characteristics of a mature specimen.

Traditional bonsai
The Japanese took centuries to evolve a system of rules and guidelines governing bonsai shape and design. In traditional bonsai, only hardy conifers and deciduous trees are used. Unfortunately, these plants must be grown and enjoyed outdoors, since they will survive the indoor life for only a very short period.

American bonsai
Americans have developed a much freer concept of bonsai. They have dispensed with many of the restrictions but have retained the artistic principles. In addition to hardy outdoor plants, more people are working with tropical and subtropical plants which can be grown and enjoyed indoors year round. Many of these plants will be familiar to you, since they (or their relatives) are often grown as ordinary houseplants.

When choosing plants suitable for bonsai, whether hardy or tropical, the

Tropical and subtropical plants suitable for indoor bonsai

Acacia baileyana (golden mimosa)
Bougainvillea species (paper flower)
Breynia nivosa var. *roseo-picta* (Jacob's coat)
Bucida buceras (black olive)
Buxus microphylla japonica (boxwood)
Calliandra haematocephala (powder puff plant)
Callistemon lanceolatus (bottle brush)
Camellia sasanqua
Carissa grandiflora (natal plum)
Citrus (calamondin orange, Meyer lemon, grapefruit)
Clerodedrum thomsonae (glorybower)
Coccoloba uvifera (sea grape)
Corokia cotoneaster (zigzag bush)
Cuphea hyssopifolia (elfin herb)
Eugenia myrtifolia (brush cherry)
Eugenia uniflora (Surinam cherry)
Ficus aurea (strangler fig)
Ficus benjamina (weeping fig)
Ficus diversifolia (mistletoe fig)
Ficus pumila (creeping fig)
Ficus retusa nitida (Indian laurel)
Gardenia jasminoides radicans (miniature gardenia)
Hibiscus rosa-sinensis (variegated hibiscus)
Homalocladium platycladum (tapeworm plant)
Ilex vomitoria (yaupon holly)
Ixora species (flame-of-the-woods)
Jacaranda acutifolia (mimosa-leaved ebony)
Lagerstroemia indica (crape myrtle)
Lantana species (shrub verbena)
Laurus nobilis (bay laurel)
Leptospermum scoparium (tea tree)
Malpighia coccigera (Singapore holly)
Murraya exotica (orange jessamine)
Myrsine africana (African boxwood)
Nicodemia diversifolia (indoor oak)
Pittosporum tobira (mock orange)
Pittosporum tobira 'Variegatum' (variegated mock orange)
Podocarpus macrophyllus 'Maki' (southern yew)
Polyscias species (Ming aralia)
Psidium cattleianum (strawberry guava)
Punica granatum nana (dwarf pomegranate)
Raphiolepis indica (Indian hawthorne)
Rosmarinus officinalis (rosemary)
Serissa foetida variegata (yellow-edged serissa)
Trachelospermum jasminoides (confederate jasmine)
Ulmus parvifolia (Chinese elm)

Societies

American Bonsai Society, 222 Rosemont Avenue, Erie, Pennsylvania 16505. The American Bonsai Society is a nonprofit educational organization that specializes in disseminating information on bonsai techniques. It is geared to all people interested in cultivating these miniature trees. Members are brought into contact with enthusiasts and bonsai clubs in their locale. All members receive the quarterly *Bonsai Journal* as well as *ABStracts*, a members' newsletter. In addition, members have access to the Society's library, a question-and-answer service, special tours, slide programs, and correspondence lists. Annual membership dues, which vary depending on the type of membership, start at $10.00 ($6.00 for students).

Bonsai Clubs International, Raymond B. Boardman, President, 19446 Edinborough Road, Detroit, Michigan 48219, or P.O. Box 2098, Sunnyvale, California 94087. Formed in 1968, this Society is a nonprofit, educational organization of over 150 bonsai clubs and more than 3,000 individual members throughout the world. Their purpose is to promote and advance the knowledge, interest, and appreciation of the art of bonsai. Membership is open to anyone interested and dues for individual members are $7.50 per year. Members receive a subscription to *Bonsai Magazine*, a 32-page publication published ten times a year. The magazine contains educational articles on the art of bonsai, Japanese gardens, saikei and suiseki, bonsai club information, shows, conventions, tools, book, sources of trees, pots, and related subjects. Other publications are available, including "How to Start A Bonsai Club" and "Bonsai Sources;" also available is a book purchase service, book-lending library, seed service, and color slide and tape programs. National conventions are held annually throughout the United States. Some sections of the country hold regional shows. Tours are usually available in conjunction with the national convention, as are occasional tours to Japan and the Orient.

Plant sources

John Brudy's Rare Plant House, Box 1348, Cocoa Beach, Florida 32931. (305) 783-4225. Catalog $1.00 (refundable with order). Mail order only. Seeds of hardy and tender plants suitable for training as bonsai.

Chung's Mountain Studio, Box 47-K, Route 1, Gold Beach, Oregon 97444. Visitors by appointment only. Young Douglas fir trees to be used for bonsai work. Also young coast pines.

Fuku-Bonsai, Box 178, Homestead Road, Kurtistown, Hawaii 96760. Brochure; send a stamped, self-addressed envelope. Specialist in Hawaiian lava rock plantings and bonsai for indoors; items available include prepared bonsai stock, lava-planted bonsai, potted bonsai, and other items related to lava planting and bonsai. The plantings are very unique.

Hortica Gardens, Box 308, Placerville, California 95667. (916) 622-7089. Catalog 25 cents (deductible with order). Nursery open by appointment; located at 6309 Green Valley Road. This nursery offers an unusual selection of hardy plants suitable for bonsai training. Excellent source for the beginner or experienced bonsai gardener. Special bonsai tools and fertilizers are offered, plus a recommended book.

King's Chrysanthemums, 3723 East Castro Valley Boulevard, Castro Valley, California 94546. (415) 582-7172. Catalog $1.00 (refundable with order). Flowering display open Saturday and Sunday in October and November. In addition to the excellent selection of greenhouse mums offered, King's also has special miniature mum varieties suitable for training as bonsai.

Mellinger's, 2310 West South Range, North Lima, Ohio 44452. Catalog. Selected and started hardy and tropical bonsai plants; also bonsai tools and pots.

Western Arboretum, Box 2827, Pasadena, California 91105. Illustrated catalog $1.00. Offers a wide selection of all the materials the bonsai gardener needs: trees and shrubs, books, kits, tools, planting mixes, wire, fertilizer, and containers, plus stands for displaying bonsai. Their catalog includes many valuable tips for the beginner.

Many of the tropical and semitropical plants suitable for bonsai are available from companies listed in *Houseplants*.

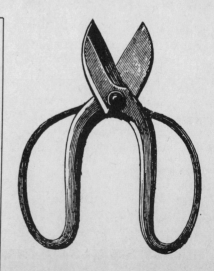

A rare and priceless collection of fifty bonsai plants was presented to the American people by the Nippon Bonsai Association of Japan in Tokyo on March 20, 1976, to commemorate America's Bicentennial. The United States National Arboretum in Washington, D.C., which is administered by USDA's Agricultural Research Service, is displaying the plants in a natural Japanese garden setting. The viewing pavilion is designed to permit visitors to see the plants to their best advantage. In addition, there are facilities for lectures and classes for the growing number of bonsai enthusiasts. American bonsai experts have volunteered to do the yearly conditioning that is necessary to give these plants their unique forms. Arboretum horticulturists will take care of the daily needs of the plants.

Basic styles of bonsai

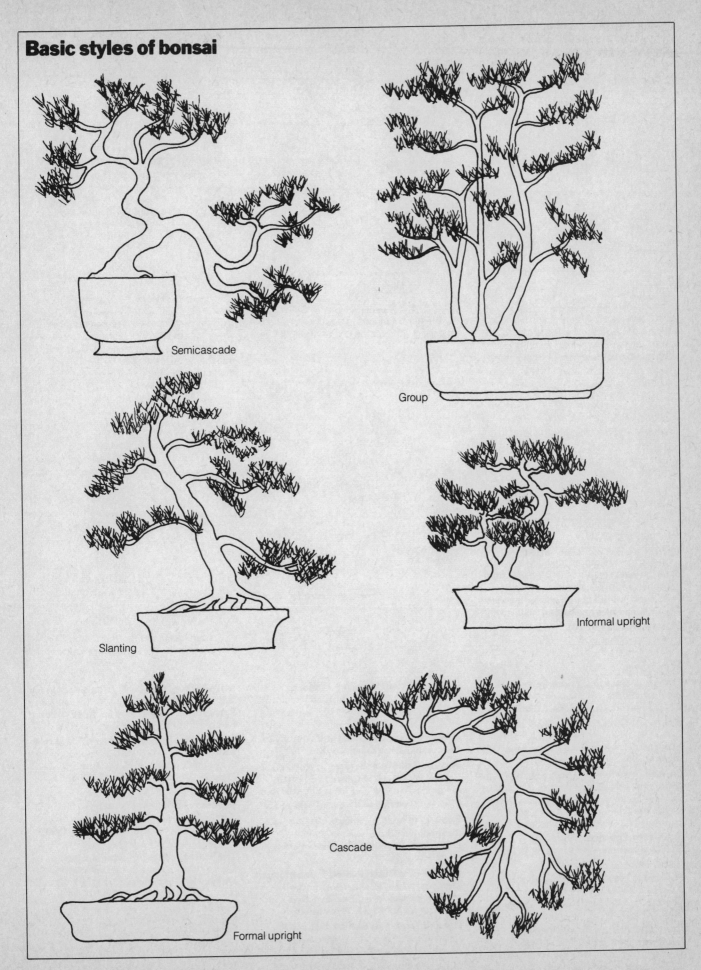

Semicascade

Group

Slanting

Informal upright

Formal upright

Cascade

Basic steps in bonsai

1. In bonsai, special pruning and wiring techniques are used to train a tree to a particular shape. The first step is to choose a style that is compatible with the natural shape of the tree. Prune lower branches at the front and any dead or diseased wood.

2. The next branches to be cut off are those that grow opposite the ones that will remain.

3. Then branches, which create a "cartwheel" effect by growing at the same level, are thinned out as well as those that grow from one side to the other by curving around the front or the back.

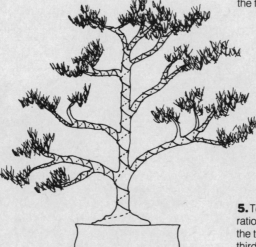

4. Wiring is the most difficult part and subtle part of the training process. The wire is anchored in the soil or the container's drainage holes and around the base of the tree. From the trunk, the wire winds its way up the main branch, then on to the smaller branches, and all the way up to the smallest twigs. The windings are always kept at a 45-degree angle to the branch and ¼ inch apart. Once the wiring is completed, the branches are gently and gradually bent by hand to grow in the desired direction. The wiring is removed after twelve to eighteen months to avoid damaging the bark.

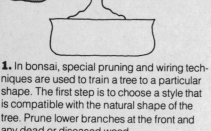

5. To maintain a balanced root-to-foliage ratio, the roots of the bonsai are pruned when the top is heavily pruned. Usually one-to-two-thirds of the root ball is removed.

Books

The Art of Dwarfing Trees, by Ann Pipe, Hawthorn Books, 260 Madison Ave., New York, New York 10016, 1964, $7.95.

The Art of Training Plants, by Ernesta Ballard, Barnes and Noble, 10 E. 53rd St., New York, New York 10022, paperback, 122 pages, $1.95.

Bonsai: Creation and Design Using Propagation Techniques, by William N. Valvanis, Symmes Systems, Box 8101, Atlanta, Georgia 30306, 1975, paperback, 40 pages, $3.95, Vol. One, Encyclopedia of Classical Bonsai Art.

Bonsai for Americans, by George F. Hull, Doubleday and Co., 245 Park Ave., New York, New York 10017, 1964, $7.95.

Bonsai for Pleasure, by Keija Murata and Takama Takeuchi, Japan Publications, 1255 Howard St., San Francisco, California 94103, 1969.

Bonsai: Miniature Potted Trees, by Norio Kobayashi, Japan Publications, 1255 Howard St., San Francisco, California 94103, 1969.

Bonsai: Miniature Potted Trees, by Kyuzo Murata, Japan Publications, 1255 Howard St., San Francisco, California 94103, 1964, paperback, $5.50.

Bonsai Miniatures Quick and Easy, by Zeko Nakamura, Shufunotomo Co., Ltd., 1973.

Bonsai, Saikei and Bonkei, by Robert L. Behme, William H. Morrow and Co., 105 Madison Ave., New York, New York 10016, 1969, hardbound, $12.95, paperback, $6.45.

Bonsai: Special Techniques, Handbook of the Brooklyn Botanic Garden, 1000 Washington Ave., Brooklyn, New York 11225, order No. 51, $1.50 postpaid.

Bonsai — The Dwarf Potted Trees of Japan, Handbook of the Brooklyn Botanic Garden, 1000 Washington Ave., Brooklyn, New York 11225, order No. 13, $1.50 postpaid.

Bonsai: Trees and Shrubs, by Lynn R. Perry, Ronald Press Co., 79 Madison Ave., New York, New York 10016, 1964, $8.50.

Introductory Bonsai: The Care and Use of Bonsai Tools, by Masakuni Kawasumi, Japan Publications, 1255 Howard St., San Francisco, California 94103, 1972, $6.95.

The Japanese Art of Miniature Trees and Landscapes, by Yuji Yoshimura and Giovanna Halford, Charles E. Tuttle Co., 28 E. Main St., Rutland, Vermont 05701, 1957, paperback, $10.95.

Japanese Miniature Trees, by Kan Yashiroda, Charles T. Branford Co., 28 Union St., Newton Center, Massachusetts 02159, $6.75.

The Master's Book of Bonsai, by the Directors of the Japan Bonsai Association, Kondansha International, 10 East 53rd St., New York, New York 10022, 1961, $8.95.

Practical Bonsai for Beginners, by Kenji Murata, Japan Publications, 1255 Howard St., San Francisco, California 94103, 1964, paperback, $5.95.

Botanical names

In the fourth century B.C., Theophrastus, a Greek philosopher, pupil of Plato and Aristotle, recorded about 500 plant names. Four centuries later, Dioskorides, a Greek physician, recorded about 600. Pliny the elder, in the first century A.D. described some thousand plants in his *Natural History*. The great Swedish botanist Linnaeus in his *Species Planatarum*, first published in 1753, recorded 5,900 species in 1,098 genera. Today the estimated total of known and described species is about 200,000, with more to come.

From the earliest times, species within genera were recognized, and in those times naming was by a simple word. As more plants were recognized confusion arose in the naming of them, and soon an unwieldy description, running to twelve words, was resorted to. It was Linnaeus who founded the binomial system of plant names, a generic name with a specific epithet. This, with modifications, is with us today, making possible a high degree of unequivocacy and order in the systematic arrangement of the kingdom of plants.

Today the naming of plants follows the strict rules of the International Code of Botanical Nomenclature. The main objects of the code are: (1) to enable nomenclature of the past to be put in order; (2) to provide guidance for the present and future in clarifying and regulating nomenclature; and to stabilize spelling of names and epithets, and assign gender in case of doubt.

Protest is often heard that 'botanical names are difficult to understand', and 'Why don't you use the English name?' It has to be admitted that with some 200,000 known species, many with one or more English names, and many sharing the same name, no one would know what plant another was discussing. Gardeners are free to use what English names are familiar to them, and to do so is pleasurable, but in these pages it will soon be found that the majority of garden plants are in fact known by their botanical names to each and all of us.

An international code enables plants to be identified in every country in the world, regardless of tongue. It also enables the customer to order with certainty from his nurseryman.

Reprinted from *A Manual of Plant Names*, by C. Chicheley Plowden, Philosophical Library, Inc., 15 East 40th Street, New York, New York, 1969, hardbound, 260 pages, $10.00.

Classification and the subsequent naming of a plant begins with placing it in its proper plant family or order. This is a grouping of related genera, of which there are only a few dozen of consequence to most general gardeners and, in any case, their interest is more botanical than horticultural. Plant family names are easily recognized by their ending which is nearly always -aceae, which means "of the family of" (as in *Rosaceae*, of the rose family). One of the rare exceptions is *Compositae*, of the daisy family.

Although necessary for classification, the name of the family is not part of the plant's name. This regularly consists of the genus name which is followed by the species name, or specific, which gives the sub-division within the genus, sometimes followed by one, and, occasionally, by more specific words when closer definition becomes essential. The plant name thus stated – genus name followed by one or more specifics – is complete and precise in itself and enough to identify it exactly among several hundred thousand other known plants in the botanical world.

Nearly all genus names have been given an ending to make them look like Latin. While a few are genuine Latin, the majority consists of Greek words either singly or in combination. Of the remainder there are Latinized names commemorating people, vernacular names, geographic names, and so on. A few have no detectable parentage but it is hard to believe that they are meaningless.

Species names are often genuine Latin, generally in the form of an adjective, of which a few have been given special botanical meanings. They often give some clue regarding the plant – its color, size, shape, habit of species growth, or native habitat. Otherwise, like genus names, species names may commemorate people or be geographic or vernacular names and so on.

Reprinted from *A Gardener's Book of Plant Names*, by A.W. Smith, Harper and Row Publishers, 10 E. 53rd St., New York, New York, 10022, 1963, hardbound, 428 pages, $5.95.

Books

Flowers and Plants: An International Lexicon with Biographical Notes, by Robert Shosteck, Quadrangle/The New York Times Book Co., 10 E. 53 St., New York, New York 10022, 1974, hardbound, 330 pages, $9.95. Explanations of the botanical and common names for many houseplants are given.

A Gardeners Book of Plant Names, by A.W. Smith, Harper and Row Publishers, 10 E. 53 St., New York, New York 10022, 1963, hardbound, 428 pages, $5.95. This book is a dictionary of derivations, meanings, and uses of over 4,000 botanical terms. Included are the generic and specific names of each plant listed in alphabetical order, as well as an index of cross-reference of 1,800 common plant names and their corresponding botanical names.

A Gardener's Guide to Plant Names, by B.J. Healey, Charles Scribner's Sons, 597 Fifth Ave., New York, New York 10017, 1972, paperback, 284 pages, $3.95. Common names, Latin names, and plant histories are discussed.

How Plants Get Their Names, by Liberty Hyde Bailey, Gale Research Co., Book Tower, Detroit, Michigan 48226, hardbound, 209 pages, $8.00. A reprint from a 1933 edition written by the foremost American horticulturist, this book serves as a guide for learning, pronouncing, and applying the names of plants.

A Manual of Plant Names, by C. Chicheley Plowden, Philosophical Library Inc., 15 E. 40 St., New York, New York 10016, 1969, hardbound, 260 pages, $10.00. A scrupulously detailed encyclopedia, this book contains discussions of the generic names of plants, specific epithets, common names, plant families, a glossary of botanical terms, all listed in alphabetical order.

Pronouncing Dictionary of Plant Names. Revised edition. Florists' Publishing Co., 310 S. Michigan Ave., Chicago, Illinois 60604, 1974, 40 cents plus 15 cents postage and handling. Contains 3,000 plant names and botanical terms with pronunciations and definitions.

Bromeliads

Bromeliads—members of the pineapple family—often produce stunning, long-lasting inflorescences and are not difficult to maintain as houseplants. Many are striking foliage subjects with a great variety of banding, spotting, and coloring. Variegation consists of longitudinal striping of a brilliant white, yellow, pink, red, or purple, such as exists in no other plant family. Many new forms of variegation are appearing as a result of plant sporting.

Long-lasting flowers

With many bromeliads, rich reds and purples appear in the center of the plant at flowering time. Bracts, which are modified leaves, are part of the flower cluster, usually being bright red. The tubular flowers themselves are of all colors, with yellow perhaps predominating. Fruits, such as the colorful berries of aechmeas, will add adornment for two or three months after the flowers are gone.

Whenever a bromeliad flowers, the inflorescence comes up in the center. As the flower cluster fades, that plant dies—even though it may not be apparent for a long time—but new plants (called offsets) will arise and grow to flowering state. These can be left on, forming a clump with time, or cut off below the soil and potted separately when at least four to six leaves have developed.

Unique scales

All bromeliads are native to the Americas and are warm climate plants. They are mostly epiphytic, with some growing in soil, some on rocks. Some genera have their rosettes so formed as to make them nonleaking cups. The water that accumulates in the center remains, unless evaporated or knocked out. Examples of such kinds are the aechmeas, billbergias, and neoregelias. The water in the cups not only helps supply the plant with moisture and humidity, but also permits dissolved food and water to be absorbed by the plant by means of so-called scales on the inner surface. Scales, with adjoining special cells, are organs of absorption that do the same work as roots in supplying the plant with dissolved minerals and compounds, as well as water. Bromeliads, like all other flowering plants have

stomata, which are involved in the exchange of gasses, but only bromeliads have the complicated scale apparatus. These scales are found in all bromeliads on both the upper and lower surfaces of the leaves. In some plants, like *Aechmea fasciata* and *Aechmea chantinii*, the scales form the pronounced white crossbars. Scales are microscopic and one needs a hand lens to see them well.

Caring for your bromeliad

Bromeliads are very adaptable as to soil mixes, and as long as a mix drains quickly, should thrive. Plants do well if grown in only leaf mold or any or-

chid mix. The advantage of the following mix is that it especially holds a newly potted offset in a stable position until a good root system is formed. To pot, first put 1¼ inch or so of heavy material, such as rocks or large gravel, in the bottom of the pot, since bromeliads are easily overturned. Then add moistened soil mix around the plant.

Here are the proportions of a recommended bromeliad mix:

Orchid bark:	2 parts
Milled spaghnum:	1 part
Humus or leaf mold:	½ part
Steer manure:	¼ part
Large size perlite:	¼ part

If one is using the above formula, the soil should need watering only once a week. The "cups of bromeliads should always contain water." Use a water soluble fertilizer at one-quarter

strength once a month. Provide humidity by one of the means discussed in *Humidity*.

Insects are not often a problem with bromeliads. Scale should be washed off with mild soap or detergent, then the plant should be rinsed. Follow with a systemic insecticide. Examine all new plants for scale.

Bromeliads thrive and have beautiful color when grown properly under full-spectrum lights. They can be grown entirely under lights or fluorescents can be used in addition to natural light. If a window is small, do not place plants further back than several feet. Bromeliads are benefited by being placed outdoors in mild, temperate weather.

Starting from seed

Some people like to grow bromeliads from seeds because it is an inexpensive (but very slow) way of accumulating plants; others just like to dabble in seeds and watch seedlings grow. Use a sterilized mix for planting seeds. Fill container with a mixture of peat moss, coarse perlite, and leaf mold or humus. Press down lightly, water, and sprinkle seed on top; then put into a plastic bag and tie it up. Place in a warm shaded location. Gradually over a few days give them brighter light. After seedlings are about one-half-inch high, fertilize every two or three days at one-quarter strength as they are being watered. With the genera guzmania, tillandsia, and vriesea—these have feathered seeds—growth is exceptionally slow, taking a year to become well established.

George Kalmbacher

George Kalmbacher, for twenty years taxonomist and curator of the herbarium at the Brooklyn Botanical Garden, is presently taxonomist emeritus there.

Mr. Kalmbacher has studied plant life on every continent, has written widely on his travels and the plant life he's studied, and gives lectures which are illustrated by selections from the 22,000 slides he has amassed.

He has had the honor of having three plants named for him: Sinningia cardinalis 'George Kalmbacher,' Caralluma kalmbacheri, and Tillandsia kalmbacheri.

Plant sources

Alberts and Merkel Brothers, 2210 South Federal Highway, Boynton Beach, Florida 33435. (305) 732-2071. Plant list 75 cents. Open Monday through Saturday 8:00 a.m. to 4:30 p.m. Visitors welcome. Aechmea, billbergia, cryptanthus, guzmania, neoregelia, tillandsia, and vriesa available. Also many other tropical houseplants are offered, plus books and supplies.

Arant's Exotic Greenhouses, Route 3, Box 972, Bessemer, Alabama 35020. (205) 428-1827. Catalog $1.50 (refundable with purchase). Open Tuesday through Saturday 9:00 a.m. to 5:00 p.m. (please call before visiting). Aechmea, billbergia, cryptanthus, guzmania, neoregelia, nidularium, tillandsia, vriesia, and others. Also, ferns, orchids, cacti and succulents, and houseplants.

Ashwood Specialty Plants, 4629 Centinela Avenue, Los Angeles, California 90066. (213) 397-1945 or 822-8900. Catalog 25 cents. Aechmea, billbergia, cryptanthus, guzmania, neoregelia, nidularium, tillandsia, and vriesia are available, plus collections. Care instructions included with order.

Blossom World Bromeliads, Route 2, Box 479-B, Pine Way, Sanford, Florida 32771. (305) 841-4012. For plant list send a self-addressed, stamped envelope. Open by appointment only. Very extensive listing of bromeliads, including a wide assortment of aechmea, billbergia, cryptanthus, guzmania, neoregelia, and vriesea.

Cornelison Bromeliad Nursery, 225 San Bernadino Street, North Fort Myers, Florida 33903. (813) 995-4206. Plant list. Open Monday through Saturday. Visitors welcome. Assorted selection of over 85 bromeliads; seedlings as well as mature-size bromeliads with useful hints on growing seedlings, potting mixtures, and watering.

Down To Earth, 1611 Jackson Street, Hollywood, Florida 33020. (305) 922-4819. Catalog. Native and imported tillandsias; mounted and unmounted plants.

Hewston Green, Box 3115, Seattle, Washington 98114. Plant list 50 cents. Selection of cryptanthus and a few other bromeliads, plus many other houseplants.

Jerry Horne, 10195 Southwest 70th Street, Miami, Florida 33173. (305) 270-1235. Catalog. Open to visitors by appointment. Aechmea, cryptanthus, guzmania, neoregelia, tillandsia, vriesia, and other bromeliads, plus an assortment of rare and unusual houseplants.

Marz Bromeliads, 10782 Citrus Drive, Moorpark, California 93021. (805) 529-1897. Plant list 35 cents. Specialized bromeliad nursery with large, varied selection. Also succulent bonsai and hoyas.

The Plantarium, 1710 East Speedway, Tucson, Arizona 85719. (602) 795-1070. Plant list. Limited selection of tillandsias grouped as "small, medium, and large" varieties. Also some jatrophas, dioscoreas, and cycads, plus *Caryota mitis* (fishtail palm).

Seaborn Del Dios Nursery, Route 3, Box 455, Escondido, California 92025. (714) 745-6945. Plant list $1.00 (deductible with order). Open daily 9:00 a.m. to 5:00 p.m. Extensive collection of bromeliads, including over 180 aechmeas, 100 neoregelias, 110 tillandsias, plus billbergia, cryptanthus, dyckia, nidularium, vriesea, and others. Owner Bill Seaborn has written his own book on bromeliads containing information on culture, propagation by seeds and offsets, light requirements, soil mixes, watering, and temperature. Nursery also carries palms and cycads.

Alvim Seidel, Orquideario Catarinense, P.O. Box 1, Rua (Street) Robert Seidel, 1981, 89280, Corupa, Santa Catarina, Brazil. Catalog. One of the most complete bromeliad collections in the world, Seidel's offers hundreds of varieties representing over 30 genera. Orchid plants and houseplant seeds are also available.

Velco's Bromeliad Nursery, 2905 Washington Boulevard, Marina Del Rey, California 90291. (213) 821-2493. Plant list. Open daily 9:00 a.m. to 5:00 p.m. Visitors welcome. Fifty different kinds of tillandsias with descriptions.

Walther's Exotic House Plants, RFD 3, Box 30-T, Catskill, New York 12414. (518) 943-3730. Business located on 9-W Highway in Catskill. Plant list 25 cents; plant-sculpture catalog and list $1.00 (refundable with order). Open daily 10:00 a.m. to 5:30 p.m. Visitors welcome. Specializing in bromeliads, including large selection of aechmea, billbergia, cryptanthus, and tillandsia. Also plants mounted on cork bark and sculptured plant arrangements. Indoor plants and equipment available at business address.

Wonderly's Exotica, 531 Knotts, Bakersfield, California 93305. (805) 325-5308. Plant list. Open Wednesday through Monday 10:00 a.m. to 5:00 p.m. Selection of aechmea, guzmania, neoregelia, nidularium, tillandsia, and others.

Books

Bromeliads, by Bill Seaborn, Future Crafts Today, Gick Publishing, Laguna Hills, California 92653, 1976, paperback, 41 pages, $2.50. Information on propagation by seeds and by asexual reproduction via offsets; light requirements, watering, soil mixes, and temperature. The book contains 237 color photographs of bromeliads, some taken in Mexico in their natural habitat.

Bromeliads, by Victoria Padilla, Crown Publishers, One Park Avenue, New York, New York 10016, 1973, hardbound, 134 pages, $12.50. Nontechnical descriptions of the 500 bromeliad species most commonly found in cultivation. Includes 150 color and black-and-white illustrations.

Bromeliads Are My Hobby, by Kathy Dorr, Marka Publishing Co., Box 997, Bellflower, California 90706, paperback, $3.00. Written for the novice, this book answers the basic questions beginners most often ask about growing bromeliads. Illustrated with drawings.

Neoregelia

Bromeliads to try

Aechmea
fasciata
chantinii
Bert
bracteata
Burgundy
caudata variegata
Foster's Favorite
pineliana
recurvata var. *ortgiesii*
benrathii
weilbachii

Billbergia
amoena
Catherine Wilson
chlorostica
Fantasia
leptopoda
Muriel Waterman
pyramidalis
venezuelana
zebrina

Cryptanthus
bivattatus
bromelioides
fosterianus
Osyanus
zonatus

Guzmania
lingulata (various forms)
lindenii

musaica
monostachia
sanguinea
bittata
zahnii

Neoregelia
carolinae tricolor
ampullacea
marmorata
spectabilis
innocentii lineatum

Tillandsia
bergeri
brachycaulos
butzii
cyanea
fasciculata
flexuosa
ionantha
plumosa
tricolor
usneoides

Vriesea
carinata
fosteriana
glutinosa
guttata
Mariae
psittacina
splendens

To see large collections of bromeliads, visit these gardens:
Longwood Gardens, Kennett Square, Pennsylvania.
Brooklyn Botanic Garden, Brooklyn, New York.
Fairchild Tropical Gardens, South Miami, Florida.
Huntington Gardens, San Marina, California.
Matthaei Botanical Gardens, Ann Arbor, Michigan.

Making bromeliads bloom

To coax an otherwise reluctant bromeliad to flower, encase the plant, along with a ripe apple, in a plastic bag. Leave the plant and the apple in the bag for four days, during which the apple will release ethylene gas. The gas acts as a trigger, and the bromeliad should flower within several months. If the technique does not work the first time, wait another two months, and try again.

Bromeliad tree

Begin by acquiring an interestingly shaped piece of wood – a tree stump, a piece of driftwood, or a large dead branch that has a number of smaller branches. If you find your tree in nature, make sure it is disease- and pest-free. For stability, sink the base into a container you have filled with concrete or plaster of Paris. When dry, disguise the top with pebbles, gravel, sphagnum moss, or bark chips.

1. Remove the bromeliads you plan to use from their pots. Wrap the roots in moist sphagnum moss, securing the moss with plastic-coated wire (preferably green or brown) or strips cut from nylon stockings.

2. Plan the location of your plants. Try to place them in natural positions such as forks or curves in the branches. If necessary, create or deepen the pockets by carving or chiseling. You can also drill holes through the wood and pass the fastening wire through them. Attach the moss-wrapped root balls of the plants to the tree, using plastic-coated wire or stocking strips.

To water the plants, spray with a mister and fill the bromeliad's "cup." Use a water-soluble fertilizer in the water occasionally to give the plants the nutrients they need. Avoid water damage to floors or table tops by putting the tree in a waterproof tray.

Vriesia

Societies
The Bromeliad Society

P.O. Box 3279
Santa Monica, California 90403

The organization, in 1950, of the Bromeliad Society, greatly increased the popularity of this interesting plant family. Native to the American tropics, bromeliads include many exotic plants; among the best known are the pineapple and Spanish moss. The Society, a nonprofit organization, was formed to promote interest in and disseminate knowledge about these and other more unusual bromeliads.

The activities of the Bromeliad Society include: fostering affiliated societies; awarding medals for notable work done in creating new hybrids; sponsoring bromeliad plantings in botanical gardens and public parks; encouraging exhibits that feature bromeliads; and the distribution of seeds through the Society Seed Fund. In addition, the Society encourages correspondence among growers of all countries; has a service that answers queries about bromeliads; and awards research grants to further knowledge of bromeliads.

People interested in learning more about bromeliads and in participating in the activities of the Society are invited to become members. The fee is $10.00 per year. All members receive a subscription to the Society's bimonthly publication, *The Journal,* and a current membership roster.

berry
flower
bract
leaf
offset
roots
Parts of a bromeliad

Aechmea

Bulbs

Forcing bulbs

Anyone can interrupt a bleak winter with a welcome burst of color and fragrance simply by providing hardy bulbs with the correct conditions.

Buying and storing bulbs

Begin planning in the early fall, and buy your bulbs as soon as they are available (usually the beginning of September). Store them in a cool, well-ventilated place until you are ready to pot them. For a succession of blooms, plant several batches, each a week or two apart. Bulbs are planted for indoor forcing between September and December and bloom between December and March.

Almost any type of bulb can be used for indoor forcing: tulip, hyacinth, crocus, daffodil, narcissus, iris, and muscari are some of the most popular. The bulbs you buy should be firm, plump, and free of scars and blemishes. Bargain bulbs seldom do well indoors.

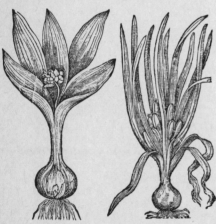

Containers

Plant bulbs in ordinary clay or plastic pots, wooden boxes, or decorative ceramic, metal, or glass pots or bowls. The depth of the container should be twice that of the bulbs so the roots have plenty of room to develop. It is safer to plant most bulbs in pots with drainage holes. For containers with no drainage holes, add a few pieces of charcoal or broken brick at the bottom to keep the water from turning sour, and regulate the watering very carefully.

Unglazed clay pots should be soaked in water overnight before planting to prevent them from absorbing water from the potting medium.

You might enjoy using the tall, clear-glass vases sold for growing pre-cooled hyacinths. These are filled with water to within ⅛ inch of the bottom of the bulb. As the roots grow, they are clearly visible through the glass — an added fascination.

Potting medium

Since bulbs have enough stored food to nourish the plant, the potting medium serves only to support and an-

chor also the bulbs and their root systems, and to keep water available. It must drain quickly, yet retain moisture. One solution is to use equal parts of packaged potting soil and coarse sand or vermiculite. Or you might prefer to use a special bulb fiber made for this purpose. Some bulbs, especially the tender ones, can be planted in pebbles, gravel, or even marbles. Never reuse soil in which bulbs have grown before. Pebbles, gravel, and marbles can be washed and reused.

Storing hardy bulbs

After planting, store hardy bulbs in any cool, dark place, such as a cellar, outdoor shed, garage, closet, refrigerator, or outdoor pit. This is the all-important stage during which the roots form and small shoots begin to emerge from the bulb. During this time the bulbs must be watered with great care and kept in complete darkness. After about twelve weeks, they will be ready to be moved to a warmer, brighter environment in your home.

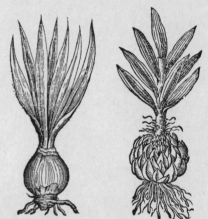

Acclimation and flowering

To allow rooted, sprouted bulbs to adjust to warmth and light, place them first in a well-ventilated, semi-dark, cool area (50 to 60 degrees F.) for about one week. Then, when leaves and buds appear, move them to a warmer (72 degrees F.), brighter spot. Water regularly until the flowers fade.

Most bulbs should be discarded after blooming, since they usually cannot be successfully forced indoors a second time. If you're of the "never say die" school of thought, try planting them outside; don't trim off the foliage — it's storing food and developing next year's flowers.

Tender bulbs

Tender bulbs include both those of tropical origin and those that can be grown outdoors in winter in the warmer parts of Florida and California. These bloom at various times throughout the year.

Some of the best ones to try include:

Amaryllis: Giant bulbs produce huge, handsome flowers and are available in a range of colors. Grown in enriched potting soil, they will blossom year after year with only a modest amount of care.

Tazetta Narcissus: Includes the ones called paper whites, Soleil d'Or, and Chinese sacred lily. These are usually grown in bowls of pebbles and water; they exhaust themselves and should not be saved after they have bloomed.

French-Roman and Fairy Hyacinth: These are also grown in pebbles and water. They are dainty, with smaller, more widely spaced bells than the regular Dutch type, but have the same delicious scent. Each rooted bulb will produce as many as six lovely sprays of flowers. Colors available are pink, blue, and white.

Agapanthus: Also called African lily or lily-of-the-Nile. Large clusters of blue or white flowers appear in the summer above the massive, glossy-green leaves. The variety 'Peter Pan' is smaller than most, with white flowers.

Caladium: It's the foliage that's important with caladiums. Shades of pink, white, green, and red form endless patterns on the leaves. These can be started any time of the year to add color to the indoor garden.

Calla lily: The classic flower of the calla is available in white, yellow, or pink, with plain or speckled leaves. These are potted in the fall and will blossom in the spring.

Sprekelia: Also called Jacobean lily or Aztec lily; scarlet, 6-inch butterfly blooms on 18-inch stems appear in late February or March when potted in October. Grow the same way as amaryllis.

Gloriosa lily: This bulb produces a climbing vine with yellow and scarlet, lily-like blooms during the summer. The plant rests during the winter months.

Tulbaghia: Commonly called pink agapanthus, its pale green leaves always look good, and if grown in the sun, it blooms off and on all year round, bearing pale lavender flowers of exquisite fragrance.

Veltheimia: When grown in a sunny window, these bulbous plants from South Africa produce large, shiny green leaves in a graceful rosette. Flower buds appear in early fall and develop slowly; finally, in mid-winter, pink flowers emerge and last for several weeks. A two- or three-week dry summer rest is needed for continued flower production.

Nancy Bruning

Amaryllis hybrid

Forcing hardy bulbs

1. Pour a layer of pebbles, or clay shards, into the container to ensure adequate drainage. Add enough potting mix so the tips of the bulbs will just reach the top edge of the pot. Do not pack the soil down tightly (packed soil prevents the roots from penetrating easily and the bulbs get pushed upwards as the roots form). Gently place the bulbs on the soil.

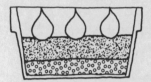

2. Place the bulbs close together to take full advantage of each pot, but without letting them touch each other or the side of the pot.

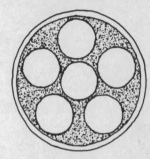

3. Add soil around the bulbs until the level reaches about ½ inch below the edge of the pot (bulb tips should remain exposed). Water the potting mixture thoroughly.

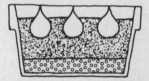

4. Store the bulbs in a cool, dark place for about twelve weeks. During this root-forming period, the temperature should be maintained at about 40 degrees F., and the potting mix must remain moist or the roots will die. Apartment-dwellers can put the bulbs in a covered box and place it on an exterior windowsill, in a cool closet, or even the refrigerator. Others can store them in a cool cellar, a garage, an outdoor shed, or in a trench or pit dug into the ground. The trench should be deep enough to cover the pots, plus about 12 inches. Spread a 3-inch layer of pebbles on the floor of the pit and set the pots on it. Cover the pots with 3 inches of sand, followed by 6 inches of soil. Water the pit regularly until freezing weather arrives. Then cover the pit with a 3-inch mulch of hay, straw, evergreen boughs, leaves, or newspaper.

When is a bulb not a bulb?

Some plants are commonly called bulbs for convenience. Although there are resemblances, corms, tubers, rhizomes, and tuberous roots are botanically different from bulbs.

Tubers

These underground stems are similar to rhizomes, but are generally much shorter and fatter. Tubers store food, and have "eyes" or buds like potatoes (which are tubers), surrounded by minute scalelike leaves. Each eye acts as a type of growth bud, and is capable of producing a new plant.

Tuberous roots

Like stem tubers, tuberous roots are thickened to store food. But they have no "eyes" or growth buds, and, when cut into pieces, cannot be used for propagation unless a part of the stem (where growth buds occur) is included.

Bulbs

This specialized form of an underground plant part contains the rudiments of the flower bud and foliage leaves, encased in layers of thick, fleshy leaves called scales. Food is stored in these special scale leaves. Scale leaves are joined at the basal plate, which is where roots develop. Bulbs reproduce by developing buds which turn into bulblets, and eventually full-sized bulbs.

Corms

Unlike bulbs, corms have no fleshy layers. On the contrary, there is one hard, solid piece of storage tissue encased in a papery tunic. The leaves and flower develop from a bud at the top. Each year, corms develop new cormels (tiny corms) at the base. As they mature, the original corm shrivels up and dies.

Rhizomes

A rhizome is a thick, food-storing stem that grows close to the soil surface, or even slightly above it. It usually grows horizontally and produces new plants by sending out more underground stems. When cut away from the parent plant, the new stems form individual plants.

Forcing lilies

Mid-Century hybrid lilies offer a new way of enjoying flowers indoors during the winter. Precooled bulbs are usually mailed in late fall or early winter and can be forced upon arrival, or stored at 34 to 40 degrees F. Once planted, they take only sixty to eighty days to bloom. Pot in a loose, porous soil, covering the bulb with two inches of soil and water thoroughly. Maintain temperatures of 55 degrees F. at night and 65 degrees F. during the day. Once growth has started, fertilize every two weeks until buds show color. Let the top of the soil dry slightly between thorough waterings. The larger the bulb, the more flowers that are produced; choose a 5- to 6-inch bulb for a single pot, or plant three smaller bulbs in a 5- or 6- inch pot.

Some of the most popular Mid-Century hybrids for forcing include:

Cinnabar	Rainbow hybrids
Enchantment	Tabasco
Joan Evans	Corsage
Pepper	Paprika

The potting dates and approximate flowering dates for Mid-Century varieties:

November 24	February 14
January 1	March 16
February 1	April 14
March 1	May 10
April 1	May 30

Books

Bulbs – A Complete Handbook, by Roy Genders, The Bobbs-Merrill Co., 4300 62nd St., Indianapolis, Indiana 46206, 1973, hardbound, 622 pages, $19.95.

Bulbs for the Home Gardener, by Bebe Miles, Grosset and Dunlap, 51 Madison Ave., New York, New York 10010, 1976, hardbound, 208 pages, $22.95.

Bulb Magic in Your Window, by Ruth Marie Peters, William Morrow and Co., 105 Madison Ave., New York, New York 10016, 1975, paperback, 212 pages, $2.45. This book explains how to grow 100 bulbs year round at home. Each type of bulb is listed alphabetically—from achimenes to zephyranthes—with complete instructions on bulb care. Sixty photographs are included.

The Complete Book of Garden Bulbs, by Marc Reynolds and William L. Meachem, Funk and Wagnalls Publishing Co., 666 Fifth Ave., New York, New York 10019, 1971, hardbound, 375 pages, $10.00.

Dwarf Bulbs, by Brian Matthew, Arco Publishing Co., 219 Park Ave., New York, New York, 10003, 1973, hardbound, 240 pages, $12.95.

Growing tazetta narcissus

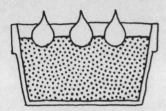

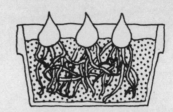

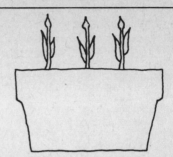

1. Use a waterproof container, such as a clear glass bowl, without a drainage hole. Fill the bowl to within 2 inches of the top with clear glass marbles, sand, gravel, pebbles, pearl chips, or charcoal. Insert the bulbs, one inch apart, so the bottom quarter is buried in the medium. Add water to just below the bottom of the bulbs.

2. Put the container in a cool (50 degrees F.), dark location until 3-to 4-inch shoots form. This will take several weeks. During this time, maintain the water level; never allow the bulbs to touch the water surface or the roots to dry out.

3. When the shoots are tall enough, move the container to a well-lighted, warmer (60 degrees F.) location for a few days. Follow with exposure to direct sunlight until the flowers open. Then move once more to bright, indirect light.

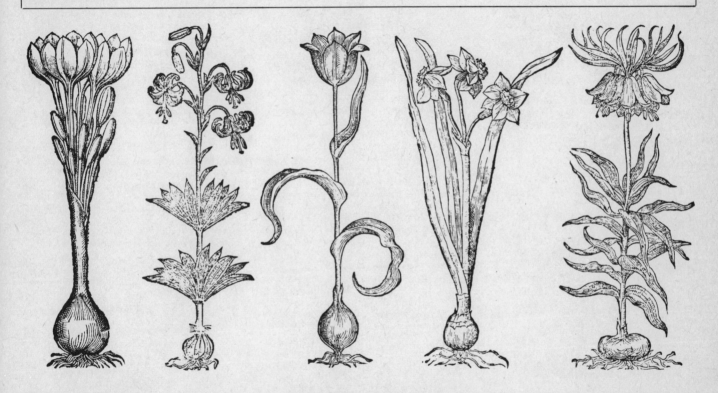

Growing amaryllis

1. Grow one bulb per pot, with 1 inch of space between the bulb and the pot. Place a clay shard over the drainage hole. Then fill the pot with potting mixture, leaving a 1-inch space at the top for watering. Bury the bottom half of the bulb in the soil.

2. Press the soil down firmly and water thoroughly. Place in a cool, dark location and don't water again until the bulb has sprouted.

3. When sprouts appear, move the plant to direct sunlight, and water it regularly.

4. When the flowers open, move to indirect sunlight. Continue to water regularly. Once a month, add water-soluble fertilizer to the water.
    When flowers and foliage fade, trim the stem (but not the leaves) to 2 inches. Set the pot in bright sunlight so the bulb can form and store food for next winter's bloom.

Sources

Amaryllis, Inc., Box 318, Baton Rouge, Louisiana 70808. (504) 924-5560. Free price list; color-illustrated catalog $1.00. Visits by appointment; flowers in bloom in April and May at 1452 Glenmore Avenue. Specialists in amaryllis bulbs of the Ludwig and Paradise varieties. Shipped in small, medium, medium-large, large, extra-large, and exhibition sizes. Also, some Hadeco African amaryllis varieties and seedlings are available.

C.A. Cruickshank, 1015 Mount Pleasant Road, Toronto, Ontario, M4P 2M1, Canada. (416) 488-8292. Color-illustrated catalogs, spring and fall, plus special bulletins. Open Monday through Saturday 9:00 a.m. to 5:00 p.m. (closed on Saturday in June, July, August, and September). For over fifty years this Canadian concern has specialized in Van Tubergen bulbs imported from Holland. Many rare and unusual varieties of tulips, narcissus, hyacinths, amaryllis, fritillaria, oxalis, and many others. Special indoor growing instructions and an assortment of indoor growing equipment.

The Daffodil Mart, Box 112, North, Virginia 23128. (804) 725-2427. Price list and brochure. The Heaths, continuing a family tradition three generations long, specialize exclusively in growing daffodils. All are planted in Virginia soil. Over 150 varieties: old standards, miniatures, hybrids, trumpet cups, triandrus, cyclamineus, tazetta, poeticus; if it's a daffodil, they have it!

De Jager Bulbs, 188 Asbury Street, South Hamilton, Massachusetts 01982. (617) 468-1622. Color-illustrated catalog $1.00. De Jager offers a selection of hardy and tender bulbs from around the world. Included are specially prepared hyacinths for indoor growing, plus various common and unusual tender bulbs ideal for indoors.

French's Bulb Importer, Box 87, Center Rutland, Vermont 05736. Catalog. Very thoughtful selection of hardy spring bulbs, plus many unusual and hard-to-find tender bulbs. Also precooled tulips, iris, and narcissus, and flower seeds for home or greenhouse. Growing instructions included.

Gladside Gardens, 61 Main Street, Northfield, Massachusetts 01360. (413) 498-2657. Price list with descriptions. Visitors welcome spring, summer, and fall. This small, friendly operation is primarily devoted to summer-blooming bulbs, including some 40 different cannas, 100 dahlias, many gladiolus. Some of the tender bulbs offered do well indoors. Also limited cacti and succulents.

International Growers Exchange, Box 397, Farmington, Michigan 48024. (313) 474-1827. Catalog $3.00. An extensive selection of rare and unusual bulbs for both indoors and out.

R.W. Longabaugh, 2144 Northeast Lakeview Drive, Sebring, Florida 33870. (813) 385-8524. Plant list 25 cents. Specialists in fancy- and lance-leaf caladium bulbs. Numerous varieties available, plus mixtures of field-grown specimens.

Grant E. Mitsch, Daffodil Haven, Box 960, Canby, Oregon 97013. (503) 266-9161. Color-illustrated catalog (contribution of $1.00 would be appreciated). Nursery is at 22695 South Haines Road, Canby. Visitors are welcome throughout flowering season in March and April (closed Sunday). Specializing in daffodils, many of their own hybrids. New and scarce cultivars.

Charles H. Mueller, River Road, New Hope, Pennsylvania 18938. (215) 862-2033. Brochure and price list with descriptions. Open daily April 1 through May 28, 10:00 a.m. to 6:00 p.m., and September 15 through December 31, 9:00 a.m. to 5:00 p.m.; January through April, open Monday through Friday 9:00 a.m. to 5:00 p.m. Visitors welcome. Over 1200 varieties of spring-flowering bulbs for fall plantings. Specializing in tulips and narcissus and their hybrids, with many new varieties. Several narcissus, amaryllis, anemones, and hyacinths for indoor growing. Also many other bulbs and wildflowers.

Oregon Bulb Farms, Box 529, Gresham, Oregon 97030. (503) 663-3133. Color-illustrated brochure. Selected lilies primarily for outdoor growing, beautifully photographed for eight-page brochure. All perennials, mostly hardy hybrids. Some are good for indoor forcing.

Picken's Caladiums, Route 3, Box 1655, Bartow, Florida 33830. (813) 533-4838. Price list and color-illustrated brochure. Open daily 8:00 a.m. to 6:00 p.m. Visitors welcome. Many varieties of fancy-leaf caladiums in mammoth, jumbo, and large-size bulbs. The most decorative 28 plants are beautifully photographed in color for the brochure.

Louis Smirnow, 85 Linden Lane, Brookville, New York 11545. (516) 626-0956. Brochure for amaryllis; catalog for peonies. Open to visitors. Varied selection of amaryllis bulbs for indoor growing. Major emphasis on outdoor peonies.

Van Bourgondien Brothers, Box A, 245 Farmingdale Road, Route 109, Babylon, New York 11702. (516) 669-3500. Color-illustrated catalogs, spring and fall. Dutch and domestic-grown bulbs and plants. Many different varieties as well as houseplants, perennial flowers, fruits, hedges, and ground covers. Established gardeners for over 125 years, this firm still operates a nursery in Hillegom, Holland.

Mary Mattison Van Schaik, Imported Dutch Bulbs, Cavendish, Vermont 05142. (802) 546-4868. Catalog 25 cents, spring and fall. Visits by appointment. After living 18 years in Holland, Mary Van Schaik has set up a nursery of exclusive Dutch imports. She brings back many new varieties every few years. Late April through May, the garden features daffodil and tulip displays.

Van Sciver's Dutch Gardens, Box 12, Tannersville, Pennsylvania 18372. (717) 629-0573. Brochures. Open daily noon to 9:00 p.m.; closed Thursday. Visitors welcome. Primarily outdoor bulbs and tuberous begonias, but some varieties of single- and double-blossomed tulips, hyacinths, and daffodils that can be forced indoors. Also gift packages of indoor crocuses and hyacinths. Cultural instructions included.

John H. Van Zonneveld Company, Box 454, Cassel Road, R.D. 1, Collegeville, Pennsylvania 19426. Color-illustrated catalog. Imported Holland bulbs. Tulips, hyacinths, narcissus, crocus, and others. Also Oregon-grown, hardy Jagra lilies. Many of these lilies can be grown indoors as well as outdoors, given the proper care. The catalog, however, is geared toward outdoor gardens. Main bulb farm still in Holland. Catalog includes directions for growing the bulbs and approximate flowering times.

Cactus and succulents

Cactus

The cacti comprise one family of succulent plants. They are native to the Americas, discovered with the New World, and their discovery created quite a sensation in the botanical and horticultural fields. At first they were considered an exotic new sort of thistle, and only the nobility and very wealthy could afford to collect these plants. Today, cacti are still being discovered, by explorers in the field and by gardeners and plant collectors, and today cacti are well within the financial reach of most enthusiasts.

In the culture of cacti, intelligence, attentive observation, and general gardening sense are probably of more value than most traditional cactus cultural advice. Cacti need food and water, light and air to grow, as do all plants, but they need these elements in slightly different proportions from many other types of plants. As they should not be kept constantly wet, they need a well-draining potting mix which dries out fairly rapidly. It should be loose and rather porous but also fairly rich. We use a mixture of sharp sand, pumice, and leaf mold, but there are almost as many mixes as there are succulent growers, and most are satisfied with their results. A mixture of equal parts of sharp sand, leaf mold, and top soil is fairly standard. Of course, a drainage hole in the container is an absolute must.

Watering is a problem to the beginning collector, but it needn't be. When the plant is actively growing, it needs more water, but in the resting season (generally fall and winter) the growth slows down or stops and the plants should be watered less frequently. When we do water, we water thoroughly. A little water only wets the top of the soil, encouraging only shallow, surface roots, and does not properly flush out accumulated fertilizer salts in the soil. Water generously but not too often, allowing the soil to start to dry out between waterings.

Most older books on cactus culture advise you not to feed cacti. To get good, healthy growth, feeding is advisable, but regular, light feedings of any well-rounded fertilizer are better than occasional large doses. Naturally, to encourage proper growth with

Powder puff cactus

feeding, the plant must have adequate light and air. Contrary to their reputation, however, few cacti can withstand constant, hot, direct sunlight and look their best. Even in the desert, where many types grow, there are shrubs and rocks for protection, particularly of the younger plants. Also, even cacti which can tolerate fairly hot, direct sunlight must be accustomed to it; sudden changes can scorch the toughest plant. The best suggestion is to be daring and experiment a bit, watch how your plants respond to your care, and vary it when the results don't seem satisfactory.

There is enormous variety of form and shade in the cactus family, and not only are they sculpturally interesting, their flowers are truly spectacular, large and colorful. A beginner's collection should include at least a few species of mammillaria, the fish-hook or pin-cushion cactus with bright rings of small flowers, of notocactus, gym-

nocalycium, and rebutia, small South American cacti which are quite easy to grow and flower under most conditions. There are, however, literally thousands of species in the family from which to choose. The image of the vicious cholla or prickly pear, with ferocious spines which go into flesh much easier than they can be removed, are only a small part of the picture.

Charles Glass and Robert Foster

Charles Glass and Robert Foster met as collectors while each was following his hobby of growing cacti and succulents. Charles Glass had taken over Cactus and Succulent Journal *and, some years later, they began to work on the magazine together.*

Succulents

Only recently have gardeners begun to discover the unique beauty, exotic aesthetic appeal, and seemingly infinite variety of succulent plants. In the past, succulents have been the misunderstood and neglected stepchildren of the plant world.

The very term succulent is even confusing to many plant lovers. Succulent is not a botanical category but a descriptive adjective meaning juicy, referring to the capacity of the plants to store water within their tissues to help them through times of drought. Succulents exist in many families of plants, including the daisy, lily, spurge, cucumber, fig, and cashew families, and most members of the stone-crop (*Crassulaceae*), cactus (*Cactaceae*), and ice plant family (*Aizoaceae*) are very succulent, to name but a few.

There are many misconceptions concerning succulent plants: that they can grow virtually without water, that they should be grown in pure sand, that they all need full, bright sun, and so forth. One must be reminded that succulents are *plants* and have the basic needs of plants: water, light, food, air. It is true that they can survive with considerable neglect, but they respond spectacularly to reasonable care. Good drainage is important, but virtually any loose, well draining, relatively rich soil mixture will do. When the soil begins to dry out, succulents like a generous watering, and they want reasonably bright light and fresh air. In general, we find that most gardeners who grow some succulents have as good or better success than do many succulent specialists.

Succulents are easily propagated, which is part of the initial appeal, by division, by even tiny cuttings, and often plants will grow from just a leaf. Depending upon their size, cuttings should be allowed to dry out (not in direct sunlight) for a few days to a few weeks, and then stood or placed on (not deeply buried in) slightly damp potting mix, and new roots should soon appear.

Many succulents have long enjoyed popularity, such as the colorful echeverias with attractive rosettes of succulent leaves; sedums and sempervivums with their bright, yellow flowers; kalanchoes, some with fuzzy, felted leaves, others with dense sprays of brilliant flowers; and some euphorbias, such as the attractive crown of thorns which bears its bright red flowers on spiny stems throughout most of the year. A wealth of others are little known, or only recently becoming familiar and gaining in popularity, such as the pachypodiums, spiny, exotic members of the oleander family; succulent pelargoniums; the bizarre members of the *Didiereaceae* from Madagascar. The stapeliads of the milkwood family, with lovely star-shaped, carrion flowers of nearly every imaginable shade and texture, offer hundreds of varieties to the collector, as do the succulent euphorbias with endless variety of form from tiny, round, nearly subterranean stems to leafy shrubs to great trees. Members of the ice plant family from southern Africa, such as tiny lithops, conophytums, and pleiospilos (little mimicry plants that resemble small rocks or pebbles consisting of just a few pairs of highly succulent leaves) have a nearly universal charm. In milder climates, aloes, agaves, and the larger euphorbias are excellent and surprisingly versatile in landscaping. Whatever your tastes in plants, succulents have a great deal to offer you.

Charles Glass and Robert Foster

Opuntia Salmiana Parm.

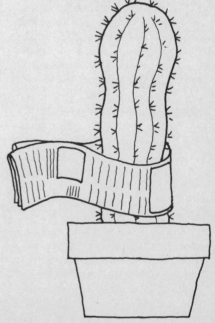

Repotting a cactus

Cacti and succulents grow so slowly they need to be moved to a larger pot only every two years, if that often. When repotting, choose a pot that seems a bit small, rather than a larger one, and a shallow, dish-shaped one, rather than a tall, deep one. As with all plants, repotting a catus is best done in the spring.

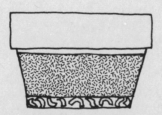

1. Place a layer of drainage material (such as clay shards from broken pots or coarse gravel) in the pot. Then add a layer of cactus potting mixture (2 parts peat moss, 1 part perlite, 1 part sharp sand).

2. Using a thick, wide strip of folded newspaper to protect your hands, remove the cactus from its old pot and transfer it to the new one. Add more potting mix up to the plant's original soil line—no higher. Smooth and tamp down the soil with a stick or spoon to remove air pockets; add more soil if necessary.

Collection of cacti

Silver sedum

Societies

Cactus and Succulent Society of America

Box 167
Reseda, CA 91335

Founded with the intention of increasing plant lovers' knowledge and awareness of cacti and succulents, the Society provides this in the activities of local chapters throughout the country. In addition, there is a biennial convention and plant show. Desert trips and visits to collections are also offered. Members receive the bimonthly *Cactus and Succulent Journal*, a well-written and illustrated publication which includes both cultural and botanical information. Dues are $12.50 per year.

International Cactus and Succulent Society

Box 691
Breckenridge, Texas 76024

The Society is a world-wide group of people who are interested in the study, propagation, and enjoyment of cacti and succulents.

The Society offers correspondence and fellowship with other cacti and succulent lovers throughout the world, plus an opportunity to have questions concerning these plants answered by professionals. A plant and seed exchange is maintained among members.

Membership is open to anyone who is interested; the fee is $7.50 per year. Membership includes a quarterly newsletter filled with information about cacti and succulents and activities of the Society.

Books

The Book of Cacti and Other Succulents, by Claude Chidamian, Doubleday and Co., 245 Park Ave., New York, New York 10017, 1958, 243 pages, $9.25. This is one of the best books for the beginning collector, illustrated with many drawings and photographs.

The Cactaceae, by Nathaniel L. Britton and J.N. Rose, Dover Publications, 180 Varick St., New York, New York 10014, 1963 reprint, 4 volumes bound in 2, 1053 pages, $35.00 for the set. The classic work on the cactus family, containing 1250 illustrations, is the most valuable of all cactus books.

Cacti, by John Borg, Blandford Press, 167 High Holborn, London, WC1V 6PH, England, 1976 reprint, 512 pages, $9.25. First printed in 1937, this book is a valuable work for the amateur, with clear, nontechnical descriptions of a large number of species.

Cacti and Succulents for the Amateur, by Charles Glass and Robert Foster, Abbey Garden Press, Box 3010, 1593 Las Canoas Rd., Santa Barbara, California 93105, 1976, 72 pages, $4.95. The most up-to-date and complete book available, it contains many new and previously unillustrated species of cacti. There are sections on care, potting, and pests.

Echeverias, by Walther (California Academy of Sciences), available from Abbey Garden Press, Box 3010, 1593 Las Canoas Rd., Santa Barbara, California 93105, 1972, 426 pages, $16.50. This is a complete monograph of their group of plants. It contains 226 photographs and 12 color plates.

Epiphyllum Handbook, by Haselton (Epiphyllum Society), available from Abbey Garden Press, Box 3010, 1593 Las Canoas Rd., Santa Barbara, California 93105, 1951, 221 pages, $6.50. The only book in print on the orchid cacti with photographs of plants and flowers and a how-to section on growing and flowering.

Growing the Mesembs, by Ed Storms, 4223 Pershing, Fort Worth, Texas 76107, 1976, paperback, 26 pages, $3.50. This book contains habitat and growing information for many genera of the living stone, or lithop, family.

Illustrated Reference on Cacti and Other Succulents, by Brian Lamb and Edgar Lamb, Blandford Press, 167 High Holborn, London, WC1V 6PH, England, 1212 pages, 4 volume set, $11.50 per volume. These are useful for plant identification with over 1300 illustrations. Each volume deals with different species and is complete in itself.

Lexicon of Succulent Plants, by Jacobsen, Blandford Press, 167 High Holborn, London WC1V 6PH, England, 1974, 664 pages, $28.50. This is the most complete listing of succulent plants with hundreds of plants both illustrated and described.

Mexican giant cactus

Black tree aeonium

Cinnamon cactus

Plant sources

Abbey Garden, 176 Toro Canyon Road, Carpinteria, California 93013. (805) 684-5112. Illustrated catalog $1.00. Retail store at 114 Toro Canyon Road, (805) 684-1179, open Friday, Saturday, and Sunday 10:00 a.m. to 4:00 p.m. Many rare and unusual succulents and cacti from a collection of euphorbias, haworthias, mesembryanthemums, asclepiads, and many others. Numerous cacti, particularly mammillaria. Catalog opens with a long essay on cacti and succulent culture, including potting medium and watering. Book list of cactus grower's guides and some plant supplies.

Arant's Exotic Greenhouses, Route 3, Box 972, Bessemer, Alabama 35020. (205) 428-1827. Catalog $1.50 (refundable with order). Open Tuesday through Saturday 9:00 a.m. to 5:00 p.m.; Monday by appointment. Call before visiting. Easter cactus, epiphyllum, rhipsalis, zygocactus, and an assortment of succulents.

Ashwood Specialty Plants, 4629 Centinela Avenue, Los Angeles, California 90066. (213) 822-8900. Catalog 25 cents. Unusual succulents, epiphyllums, and rhipsalis.

Barnett Cactus Garden, 1104 Meadowview Drive, Bossier City, Louisiana 71010. (318) 746-7172. Plant list; descriptions. Visitors welcome Saturday and Sunday. Wide selection of cacti and succulents, especially echinocactus, echinocereus, mammillaria, and opuntia. Many plants collected from Mexico.

Cactus by Mueller, 10411 Rosedale Highway, Bakersfield, California 93308. (805) 589-2674. Plant list 25 cents. Selection of cacti and succulents plus related supplies for home and greenhouse.

California EPI Center, Box 2474, Van Nuys, California 91404. Catalog 50 cents. Specialist in epiphytic cacti (over 200); mostly epiphyllum hybrids plus rhipsalis, Easter and Christmas cacti, selenicereus, hylocereus, and assorted succulents. Rooted cuttings shipped from April through November outside of California; all year round in California and warm regions.

Desert Dan's Nursery and Seed Company, West Summer Avenue, Minolta, New Jersey 08341. (609) 697-2366. Catalog with descriptions. Open by appointment. A wide selection of succulents and cacti, including cereus, mammillaria, opuntia, agave, aloe, crassula, and kalanchoe. Succulent and cactus seed mixtures available, also some books.

Desert Nursery, 21595 Box Springs Road, Riverside, California 92507. (714) 684-9995. Presently retail, mail order in future. Open 8:30 a.m. to 5:00 p.m. Visitors welcome. Extensive selection of cacti and succulents including rare euphorbias and stapeliads plus numerous species of agave, crassula, ferocactus, kalanchoe, mammillaria, and opuntia. Large cacti, yuccas, ocotillos, trees for outdoor landscaping, and many plants suitable for indoor gardening. The store has gardening tools, fertilizers, and other specialty items.

Desert Plant Company, Box 880, Marfa, Texas 79843. (915) 729-4943. Illustrated catalog $1.00. Selection of cacti of the American Southwest. Growing and planting instructions included.

Fernwood Plants, Box 268, Topanga, California 90290. (213) 455-1176. Catalog 50 cents. Open to visitors seven days a week, at 1311 Fernwood Pacific Drive in Topango. Large collection of crassula, echeveria, kalanchoe, sedum, and senecio. Many unusual mesembryanthemums and epiphytic cacti in addition to standard cacti and succulent offerings.

Grotes' Cactus Gardens, 13555 South Leland Road, Oregon City, Oregon 97045. (503) 632-4220. Open Saturday and Sunday 8:00 a.m. to 5:00 p.m., week nights by appointments. Plant list; descriptions. Large selection of cacti and succulents including many unusual types. Prices are according to size.

Ben M. Haines, 1902 Lane, Topeka, Kansas 66604. (913) 234-3543. Plant list; descriptions. Specializes in cold-climate cacti and succulents (plants which can stand −20 to 40 degrees F.) Handbook has culture information and photographs of the numerous types of cacti and related genera available ($3.25). Some seed packets also available.

Harborcrest Nurseries, 4634 West Saanich Road, Victoria, British Columbia V8Z 3G8 Canada. Plant list 25 cents. Assorted cacti and succulents with descriptions.

Henrietta's Nursery, 1345 North Brawley, Fresno, California 93711. (209) 237-7166. Not open to visitors. Illustrated catalog 35 cents.

This family-owned and operated nursery specializes in cacti and other succulents. The extensive, illustrated catalog contains a brief description of each plant along with friendly chatter on favorite types and unusual specimens. Large variety of echinocereus, gymnocalycium, mammillaria, notocactus, opuntia, rhipsalis, and trichocereus. Mixed seed packages available. Almost as wide a selection of succulents, including echinopsis hybrids. Some culture notes scattered through the catalog. Cactus and succulent books available.

Hewston Green, Box 3115, Seattle, Washington 98114. Plant list 50 cents. Assorted cacti and succulents with descriptions.

Jack's Cactus Garden, 1707 West Robindale Street, West Covina, California 91790. Plant list 25 cents. Small selection of cacti and succulents. Owners recommend a 64-page booklet *Cacti and Succulents and How to Grow Them* by Scott Haselton. Electronic moisture meter without batteries available.

K and L Cactus Nursery, 12712 Stockton Boulevard, Galt, California 95632. (209) 745-2563. Illustrated catalog 50 cents. Open Tuesday through Sunday. Visitors welcome. A family-run business, this cactus nursery has a large collection of succulents, many imported Mexican cactus species, and rare *Epithelantha micromeris, Mamillopsis senilis,* and *Neogomesis agavoides.* Also special grafted cactus from Japan, cactus and succulent seed packets (all mixtures), and books.

Kartuz Greenhouses, 92 Chestnut Street, Wilmington, Massachusetts 01887. Catalog $1.00. Open Tuesday through Saturday 9:00 a.m. to 5:00 p.m. Visitors welcome. Asclepiads, succulents, and zygocactus.

Kirkpatrick's, 27785 De Anza Street, Barstow, California 92311. (714) 252-3254. For plant list send self-addressed, stamped envelope. Open by appointment. Specializing in rare and unusual cacti and succulents, Kirkpatrick's lists a wide variety of plants and seeds. Brian and Edgar Lamb book series on cacti and succulents is available, plus their monthly notes with color photographs.

Lauray of Salisbury, Under Mountain Road, Salisbury, Connecticut 06068. (203) 435-2263. Catalog 50 cents. Open daily 9:00 a.m. to 5:00 p.m. Writing or telephoning ahead is recommended. Varied stock of cacti and succulents.

Loehman's Cactus Patch, 8014 Howe Street, Box 871, Paramount, California 90723. (714) 633-1704; 633-7187. Catalog 30 cents. Open to visitors Saturday and Sunday 11:00 a.m. to 5:00 p.m.; otherwise by appointment. Many varieties of cacti shipped bare rooted. For a small operation, Loehman's offers an extensive list.

Logee's Greenhouses, 55 North Street, Danielson, Connecticut 06239. (203) 774-8038. Catalog $2.00. Open daily 9:00 a.m. to 4:00 p.m. Visitors welcome. Assorted cacti and succulents.

Marz Bromeliads, 10782 Citrus Drive, Moorpark, California 93021. (805) 529-1897. List 35 cents. Succulent caudates and hoyas.

New Mexico Cactus Research, Box 787, Belen, New Mexico 87002. (505) 864-4027. Plant list 50 cents. Extensive selection of cacti and succulent seeds collected from the United States, Mexico, Central and South America, and South Africa. Almost 300 different species are offered, plus some seed mixtures and books.

Scotts Valley Cactus, 5311 Scotts Valley Drive, Scotts Valley, California 95066. (408) 438-0114. Catalog 25 cents. Open Monday through Saturday 9:00 a.m. to 5:00 p.m. Over 90 percent of these cacti and succulents are raised in the Scotts Valley nursery. A small, varied collection is offered which covers major genuses and species. Small, medium, and large specimens are offered where possible, plus planter kits and gardening supplies. The nursery also stocks general plants, bushes, shrubs, bedding plants, seeds, fertilizers, and soil mixture components.

Singers' Growing Things, 6385 Enfield Avenue, Reseda, California 91335. (213) 343-8304. Illustrated catalog 50 cents (deductible from first order); two newsletters are sent out each year listing new stock. This nursery specializes in succulent plants (including cacti) and cycads. The items offered are generally rare with unusual and interesting forms. Besides the individually listed plants, excellent collections are available. For the lover of the strange and exotic, this nursery's offerings are ideal.

Ed Storms, 4223 Pershing Street, Fort Worth, Texas 76107. Catalog. Just about the most complete selection of lithops available; also, many other mesembryanthemums are listed. Growing instructions included in catalog. Plus, owner Ed Storms has written a manual, *Growing The Mesembs,* based on firsthand observations in South Africa.

Sunnybrook Farms Nursery, 9448 Mayfield Road, Chesterland, Ohio 44026. (216) 729-7232 or 729-9838. Catalog 50 cents. Open Tuesday through Saturday 8:30 a.m. to 5:00 p.m. and Sunday 1:00 p.m. to 5:00 p.m. Visitors welcome. Cacti and succulents available as well as geraniums, houseplants, and herbs.

Walther's Exotic House Plants, R.D. 3, Box 30-T, Catskill, New York 12414. (518) 943-3730. Brochure with illustration and list with descriptions; $1.00 for brochure and list (refundable with order) or 25 cents for list only. Store on 9-W Highway, Catskill; open daily 10:00 a.m. to 5:30 p.m. Assorted cacti and succulents.

Dick and Ruth Wright, Route 3, Box 21, Fallbrook, California 92028. (714) 728-2383. Price list. Open to visitors, Wednesday through Sunday, 9:00 a.m. to sundown. Specializing in echeverias and other succulents, including crassula, euphorbia, kalanchoe, senecio, and sedum.

Pumice planter

Re-create a scene from nature by using a large pumice rock as a planter. You can limit yourself to one plant, or grow several, as long as they have similar growth requirements. Since pumice is light and porous, there is no danger of overwatering. Cacti and succulents are the best candidates for a pumice planter, along with bromeliads and peperomias. To obtain pumice, or Featherock, see "Stone" or "Mason Contractor's Supplies" in the yellow pages.

1. Soak the pumice rock in water to make it easier to carve. With a hammer and chisel, create a space for the planting. You can tap the chisel with the hammer to loosen large chunks first.

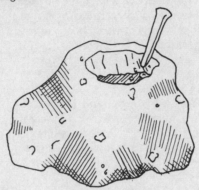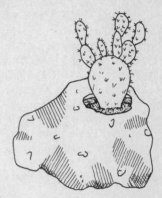

2. Then refine and smooth the cavity by carving it with the chisel. Make sure the cavity is slightly larger than the plant's pot.

3. Fill the cavity with a sterile growing medium suitable for the plant you intend to use. Insert the plant and water it well. Keep the planter in a waterproof tray, lined with pebbles if you wish, to catch the excess water.

Grafting a cactus

Attaching one type of cactus to another is a method you can use to create new, unique plants of your very own. Most often, either a globe-type cactus or a trailing type is grafted onto a taller species. The best time to graft is in the spring.

1. Using a sharp knife that has been sterilized in alcohol, slice off the top of the taller cactus (the stock).

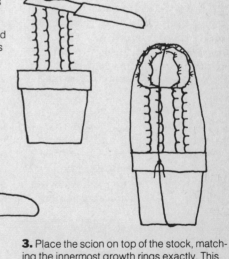

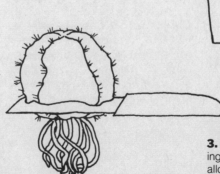

2. Remove the cactus to be grafted on top (the scion) from its pot and slice off the roots, again using a sterilized knife.

3. Place the scion on top of the stock, matching the innermost growth rings exactly. This allows nutrients and water to flow from the stock to the scion, which keeps the plant alive. Press down gently to force out any air bubbles that could cause drying or bacterial decay. Secure the graft with string or rubber bands, and place the new plant in a warm, shady location. When the graft takes (a few weeks) remove the string or rubber bands, and place the cactus in a sunnier location.

Carnivorous plants

Plants that consume insects (and sometimes small animals) are somewhat of a turnabout for growers. In order to adapt to usually very wet, poorly drained, acid, and mineral-poor natural habitats, these plants have greatly modified leaves that trap and digest insects, then absorb needed nutrients, particularly nitrogen. The leaf modifications are quite varied, and include the snap-trap of the famous but mysterious Venus flytrap which closes on its prey in a fraction of a second; the pitfall traps of the tubular, cornucopialike pitcher plants where an insect lured to the precipice of the pitcher cavity falls in and is digested; the sticky or flypaper traps of sundews and butterworts whose surface glands secrete a sweet, mucilaginous material to which the wandering insect adheres while other glands secrete digestive fluid; and the tiny, almost microscopic water traps of the bladderworts which trap very small aquatic animals and have an amazingly complex trap for their size.

Most of the carnivorous plants are very striking and colorful in appearance. They are rewarding horticultural subjects that require some extra effort, but the effort is well worth the often beautiful result. However, many of our carnivorous plants are becoming quite rare in nature and the grower should acquire his material from commercial sources, not from picking plants in the wild.

Basic growing requirements for practically all species include a salt and nutrient poor material such as live sphagnum moss or a 50-50 mix of washed pure white silica sand and Canadian peat (black peats are too rich). A plastic pot with drainhole and frequent watering with soft water are preferred over undrained pots since

the latter will eventually accumulate toxic salts due to surface evaporation. Keep the moss or soil moist at all times. High humidity is a requirement that will be difficult to meet in the average home, but no problem in the greenhouse or terrarium under fluorescent lights (caution: do not expose a closed terrarium to sunlight) where many of the smaller, compact species may be grown.

The two most frequent growing mistakes I encounter are not allowing for dormancy requirements of temperate species and overfeeding with meats or fertilizers. Most of these plants are dormant in the winter at which time they should be in a cool location, given less light, and the soil kept just barely damp. Resumption of growth indicates the end of dormancy. If forcing is attempted during the winter months, the plants will surely rot. Never feed your plants animal or fertilizer matter — it is too easy to overdo it. Carnivorous plants do not require much animal nourishment and tiny insects always present in homes, greenhouses, or even terraria will be adequate. If you like, during warm weather in more humid regions, you may place your plants outdoors to trap their prey.

Donald Schnell

Donald Schnell has been working with carnivorous plants for almost twenty years and also grows native orchids. He maintains several greenhouses of his own and also grows plants under lights.

Books

The Carnivorous Plants, by Francis E. Lloyd, Dover Publications, 180 Varick St., New York, New York 10014, 1976, 352 pages, $4.50. This classic study in anatomy and physiology, first published in 1942, has black and white photographs, drawings, and an index. Although much of the physiological matter is dated, it is still an important reference from the historical, anatomical, and bibliographical point of view.

Carnivorous Plants, by Randall Schwartz, Avon Books, 959 Eighth Ave., New York, New York 10019, 1975, paperback, 128 pages, $1.25. The book has a sampling of species from each genus mentioned. There is some information on foreign genera and growing, black and white photographs, and an index.

Carnivorous Plants, by John F. Waters, Franklin-Watts, 845 Third Ave., New York, New York 10022, 1974, 60 pages, $3.90. This is a good book for ten to fourteen-year-olds with drawings, black and white photographs, and an index.

Carnivorous Plants of the United States and Canada, by Donald Schnell, John F. Blair, Publisher, 1406 Plaza Dr. S.W., Winston-Salem, North Carolina 27103, 1976, 125 pages, $19.95. The most complete book of its type. Covers all the carnivorous plants of the continent with detailed growing instructions, 117 color photographs, glossary, index.

Cultivating Carnivorous Plants, by Allen A. Swenson, Doubleday and Co., 245 Park Ave., New York, New York 10017, 1977, hardbound, 160 pages, $7.95. An excellent book by the owner of Armstrong Associates.

Insect-Eating Plants, by Lynn and Gray Poole, Thomas Y. Crowell, 666 Fifth Ave., New York, New York 10019, 1963, 87 pages, $4.50. This book for young readers has drawings and an index, plus information on plant habits and growing instructions.

The World of Carnivorous Plants, by J. and P. Pietropaolo, Peter Pauls Nurseries, Darcey Rd., Canandaigua, New York 14424, 1974, 128 pages, $6.30. This book has black and white photographs and an index; written by people with many years of experience growing carnivorous plants.

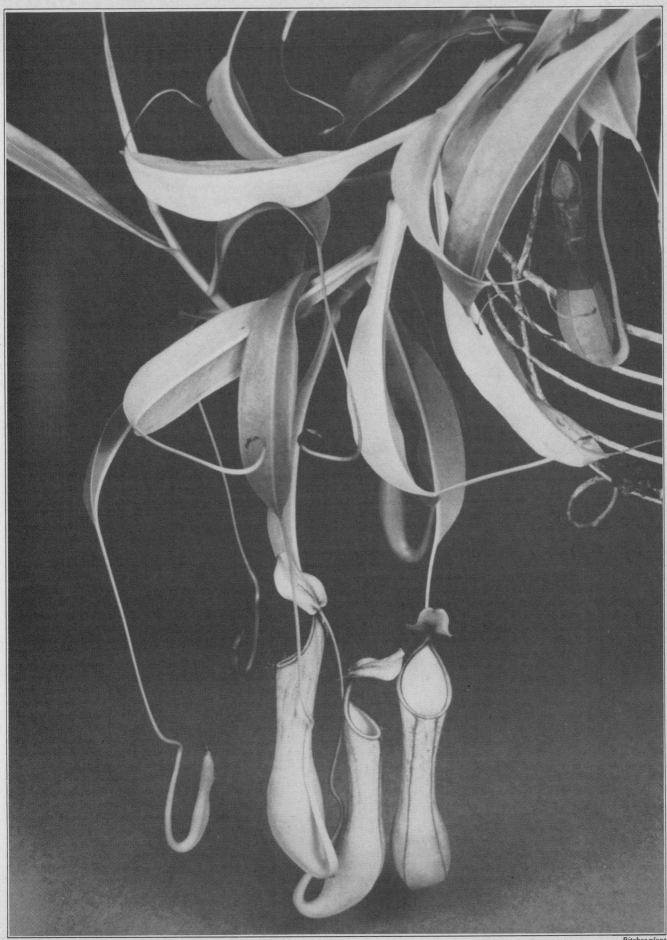

Pitcher plant

Plant collections to visit

University of California Botanic Garden
Strawberry Canyon
Berkeley, California 94720
Representatives of all genera except genlisea; many genera represented extensively.

Sea World
1720 South Shores Road
Mission Bay
San Diego, California 92109
Darlingtonia, sarracenia, nepenthes, drosera, dionaea, pinguicula; also graphic display.

Humboldt State University Greenhouse
Arcata, California 95521
Small but fairly good collection.

California State University Greenhouses
Fullerton, California 92634
Large numbers of sarracenia, drosera, and nepenthes. Open Monday through Friday 9:00 a.m. to 5:00 p.m. by appointment.

Denver Botanical Garden
903 York Street
Denver, Colorado 80206
Nepenthes, cephalotus, drosera.

Brookside Gardens
1500 Glennallan Drive
Wheaton, Maryland 20906
(In Wheaton Regional Park)
Drosera, dionaea, sarracenia, cephalotus, pinguicula, nepenthes.

University of Michigan Matthaei Botanical Gardens
1800 Dixboro Road
Ann Arbor, Michigan 48105
Sarracenia, darlingtonia, cephalotus, dionaea, utricularia, drosera, pinguicula; (open to Carnivorous Plant Newsletter subscribers).

Missouri Botanical Garden
2315 Tower Grove Avenue
St. Louis, Missouri 63110
Nepenthes, drosera, dionaea, few sarracenia.

Brooklyn Botanic Garden
1000 Washington Avenue
Brooklyn, New York 11225
Good, developing collection; well grown.

North Carolina Botanical Garden
University of North Carolina
Chapel Hill, North Carolina 27514
All United States genera with most species. Greenhouse and outdoor habitat plantings.

University of North Carolina Asheville Botanical Garden
Asheville, North Carolina 28804
Sarracenias, drosera, dionaea, scattered in habitat planting.

Longwood Gardens
Kennett Square, Pennsylvania 19348
Long known for its outstanding nepenthes collection in public and "prop" houses.

Information used by permission from the *Carnivorous Plant Newsletter*. Volume V, No. 2, June, 1976.

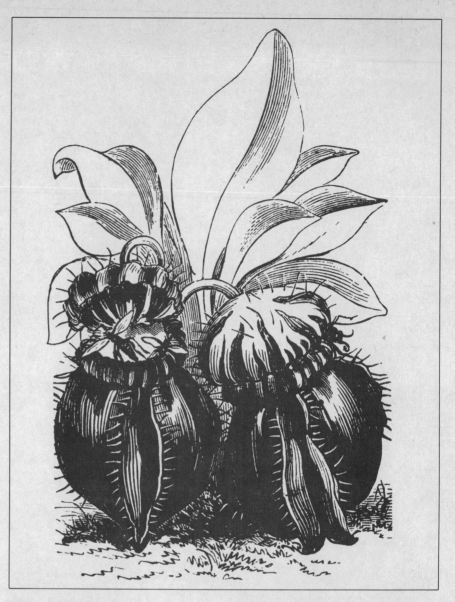

Plant sources

Armstrong Associates, Box 94, Kennebunk, Maine 04043. (207) 674-1480. Color-illustrated catalog. Venus flytrap bulbs and a selection of various pitcher plants plus butterworts, sundews, and cobra lily plant. The catalog contains general descriptive and culture information as well as gardening supplies including terrariums and tools. Allan S. Swenson, company president, is author of a new book, *Cultivating Carnivorous Plants*, published by Doubleday.

Black Copper Kits, 266 Kipp Street, Hackensack, New Jersey 07601. Catalog. Selection of Venus flytrap and pitcher plants sold as rhizomes or plants. Several kits, mini-greenhouses, and terrarium combinations available. Also helpful information sheets on terrarium culture and carnivorous plants in general.

Peter Pauls Nurseries, Route 2, Canandaigua, New York 14424. (716) 394-7397. For catalog, send a stamped, self-addressed envelope. Open only by appointment. For over twenty years, the Pietropaolos, authors of *The World of Carnivorous Plants*, have propagated and sold carnivorous plants, including many rare varieties and some seeds, plus several terrarium kits with Venus flytraps or pitcher plants. Recent additions are woodland plant terrarium kits including partridge berries, periwinkle, and trailing arbutus. General culture information is given and supplies are carried.

Sun Dew Environments, Box 111, Denver, New York 12421. Color-illustrated catalog 50 cents. Specializing in sundews and related genera (bladderworts, rainbow plant). Highly informative catalog with references is valuable for any grower of carnivorous plants. Includes article on carnivorous plants in general, with specific discussion of various sundews and their culture requirements.

Children's gardening

Thousands of years ago when men and women first learned to cultivate plants, they took a giant step forward, an achievement almost greater than going to the moon. For the first time they had a little power over their environment.

In these days when 70 percent of America lives in urban areas, both adults and children have gotten a long way from the world of growing things. Food comes prepackaged, flowers come ready cut, in bunches of six. So for a child, growing plants indoors can be more than a pleasant hobby. It is a way to get in touch with the basic patterns of nature. There are lessons of ecology to be learned from repotting a plant that can be applied to large trees and natural growth.

But in addition, what is important to each of us is the vital nonverbal communication that takes place in the sharing of gardening activity when, for example, one gives a cutting from a favorite plant to a friend. There is also a unique pleasure when the first green sprouts appear at the top of a dull-looking narcissus bulb and later when the fragrant flower appears. We are sure that this magic will occur, but there is a sense of fulfillment, a sense of renewal each time. And it is very important for children to be in touch with that kind of feeling, in the noisy, tense modern world in which we live.

Aside from providing somewhere for the beginning gardener to work (somewhere, incidentally, with a washable floor, for soil has a way of getting spread around) there isn't much advice I can give you.

From my own experience of working with youngsters, I find that they need comparatively little supervision, perhaps some help in arranging for the few tools and items necessary.

Reprinted from *Kids Gardening, A First Indoor Gardening Book For Children* by Aileen Paul, Doubleday and Co., 245 Fifth Ave., New York, New York 10017, 1972.

It's a state of mind

Seen from the child's point of view, there really are no disasters or failures in gardening: *whatever* happens will be interesting to him. The plant that dies can be dug up for a postmortem. Can he see that the soil is too wet, that the plant's stem has become heavy and waterlogged? The poor thing drowned. Or what about the plant that has become tall and spindly, its leaves yellow and sickly? It has been yearning for light, and without it, its root system has become thin and sparse.

You and your children will find enormous rewards in just a pot or two of a growing anything. Literally, anything. And from strictly gardening ventures your interests will branch out – as has this book – to embrace a love of nature, the study of birds, the preparation of good food, and an appreciation of herbs. All this becomes part of the package as you grow with your gardening.

And consider what all this will give your children: a rapport with nature in all its diversity; a never-ending sense of wonder at the precision and beauty of it all; and a lifelong interest in growing things. Not bad dividends gained from an open heart.

Reprinted from *Growing Up Green,* by Alice Skelsey and Gloria Huckaby, Workman Publishing Co., 231 E. 51st St., New York, New York 10022, 1973.

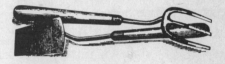

Books

Fun With Growing Things, by Joan Eckstein and Joyce Geit, Avon Books, 959 Eighth Ave., New York, New York 10019, 1975, paperback, 156 pages, $2.95.

Growing A Green Thumb, by Lorraine Surcof, Barron's Educational Series, 113 Crossways Park Dr., Woodbury, New York 11797, 1975, paperback, 80 pages, $1.95

Growing Up Green, by Alice Skelsey and Gloria Huckaby, Workman Publishing Co., 231 East 51st St., New York, New York 10022, 1973, paperback, 240 pages, $4.95. An exceptional book.

Kid's Gardening, by Aileen Paul, Doubleday and Co., 245 Fifth Ave., New York, New York 10017, 1972, hardbound, 96 pages, $4.95.

Color magic

Start with a white flower, such as a carnation or daisy. Trim off the bottom one inch of stem and place the flower in a glass. Pour an inch or two of water into the glass, then add enough food coloring or dye to turn the water a dark color. Slowly, before your very eyes, the flower will magically become the same color as the water!

Next, repeat the experiment – only this time use a stalk of celery. The color will again travel up the stalk to the leaves. To learn how the dye travels from the glass to the leaves or flower, take the celery out of the water and slice off the bottom. You will actually be able to see the tubes that carry water and food up the stem of all plants, thus enabling the leaves and flowers to manufacture food and stay alive.

Terrarium

A child can easily construct his own terrarium to house a plant collection that seldom needs watering. All that is needed is a large, wide-mouthed clear glass bottle or jar (such as those used for large quantities of food for institutions and restaurants), some pebbles or gravel, sterilized potting soil, and small plants such as pileas, peperomias, iresine, miniature begonias, and ferns.

Procedure

1. Wash and rinse the jar well. Pour in a layer of pebbles or gravel, and then about 2 inches of potting soil. Carefully pour in enough water to moisten the soil slightly. You can use a kitchen baster or a spray bottle to control the amount and direction of water so the soil neither becomes soggy nor splashes onto the side of the jar. If you have added too much water, let the soil dry out for a day or two before you begin planting.

2. With your finger (or a spoon or stick if you wish), poke a hole in the soil and set one of the plants into it. Work carefully so you don't injure the delicate roots. Then pack the soil around the roots so the plant stands up by itself. Continue making holes and planting plants until you have an arrangement that pleases you. You can also form little hills and valleys with the soil, and add rocks, twigs, and ceramic animals to resemble nature. Finally, add a bit more water if the soil seems dry, and put the lid on the jar.

Terrarium care

Keep the terrarium out of direct sunlight, since the bottle will get too hot for the plants. Remove any dead or yellow leaves, and pinch back plants that grow too large. If too many water droplets form on the side of the jar, open it for awhile to allow the excess water to evaporate. Replace the lid, and repeat the procedure if many droplets form again. If no water at all condenses, the soil is too dry and you should replenish the water supply.

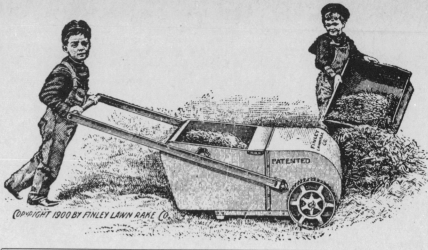

COPYRIGHT 1900 BY FINLEY LAWN RAKE CO.

Bean and potato vines

Beans (such as kidney and lima), potatoes, and sweet potatoes grow long, twining vines that you can train to curl up a pole, trellis, or around a window frame. Both beans and potato vines will grow for a while in plain water, but for longer-lasting plants, transfer them to potting soil soon after they sprout.

Potatoes: Fill a glass jar with water. Insert three toothpicks into the potato. Place the potato in the jar, resting the toothpicks on the rim so the bottom third of the potato is submerged. Keep the jar in an indirectly lit location and replace the water as it is used up. In a week or two the roots will begin to fill the jar and leaves will sprout on top.

Beans: Sprout beans in a glass jar for a clear picture of the growing process. Cut a piece of a blotter to fit inside the jar. Moisten the blotter with water, and place the beans between the blotter and the jar. Put the jar in a warm place, and soon the beans will sprout roots and many leaves.

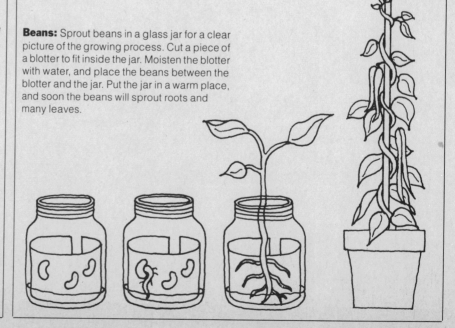

Supplies & equipment

Environmental educational resource materials are available from Chevron Chemical Company. Included are *A Child's Garden . . .A Guide for Parents and Teachers*, single copy 50 cents; *All About Trees . . .For A More Livable Environment*, single copy 50 cents; *Celebration of Life: Trees*, no charge; *Ecological Super Posters*, $3.00 per set of 6 full-color posters; *Growing Ideas Learning Kit*, $1.00. Rental films are also available.

For ordering or further information on any of the above resource materials, write:
**Public Relations
Chevron Chemical Company
Box 3744
San Francisco, CA 94119**

Green environment series for young children is a unique combination of colorful stories in a fold-out presentation and an involvement feature in the form of a mini-garden to be grown by the child. Titles include *Have You Ever Heard Of A Shy Flower?*, *Farmer Ed Takes Us Through His Green Factory*, *Exploring Roots and Leaves*, and *Exploring Seeds and Flowers*.

For information write:
**Berkshire Products
219 Ninth Street
San Francisco, CA 94103**

A quick and easy garden

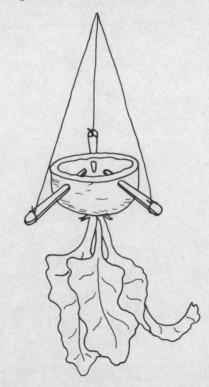

An easy, quick way to grow lots of greenery is by using the tops of root plants such as carrots, beets, turnips, radishes, and rutabagas. The most exciting, fascinating method is the upside-down basket technique. Large vegetables, such as turnips, beets, and rutabagas, are easiest to work with, but a nice fat carrot is another good choice.

With an apple corer, hollow out the center of the vegetable to form a little cup. Start at the bottom end, leaving the root end intact. If you are using a carrot, first trim off the pointed end, leaving a 2- or 3-inch carrot top.

Insert three toothpicks halfway into the hollowed-out vegetable and tie a length of string around each end for hanging. A single skewer, if you have one, could also be used. For a carrot, a single toothpick will do.

Knot the strings together at the top and hang the basket in a sunny location. Fill the carved-out cup with water to make the leaves of the vegetable grow. Since the water is used up quickly, check the supply several times a day and refill when necessary. Soon the vegetable basket will be covered with leaves.

The second method involves cutting off the top ½ inch of the vegetable and planting it in moist sand, perlite, or potting soil. Keep your fledgling plant in a sunny location and keep it well watered. It too will sprout new leaves.

Cooperative extension service

The Cooperative Extension Service is a nationwide system of educational agencies that involves a financial and administrative arrangement among three levels of government: federal, state, and county. This national system encompasses 69 land-grant universities and staffs in nearly all the United States counties.

Cooperative Extension serves people by working directly with those concerned with the human development and the quality of the human environment, agriculture and related industries, natural resources, consumer information, health and family well-being, environmental quality, effects of technology on food, clothing and shelter, and community development.

Cooperative Extension's mandate to "serve the people" is embodied in the Smith-Lever Act of 1914. This act states that "Cooperative Extension work shall consist of diffusing among the people useful and practical information on subjects relating to agriculture and home economics and subjects relating there to, and to encourage the application of the same."

Through each state, regional, and county staff, Cooperative Extension disseminates research-based information to the farm, rural nonfarm, and urban citizens across the United States. This system of rapidly transmitting information and new knowledge is usually not a feature of other public service agencies.

Although widely recognized as a provider of factual, unbiased information for solutions to practical problems, Cooperative Extension also serves people in a larger context through its adult educational and youth-oriented programs. Cooperative Extension stands alone as an agency designed to extend the educational resources of its land-grant colleges to those who wish to avail themselves of the opportunities for noncredit study in an informal out-of-school setting.

Cooperative Extension remains the only system with federal, state, and county governments forming a cooperative relationship which is dedicated to providing a link between the needs of the people and the knowledge and resources of the land-grant colleges.

In essence, Cooperative Extension is a continuing educational process based on the belief that human progress can be enhanced if the products of research are properly disseminated and translated for the purpose of quality decision making. To find your county Cooperative Extension office, look in the yellow pages under County Government.

Cooperative Extension serves each and every one of us, through its bulletins, pamphlets and booklets. Within each state an enormously wide range of topics is represented. These publications are practical, informative and easy to follow. To keep up with new publications, states put out a list each year for your convenience. These lists can be gotten by writing the state office address or by contacting your county office.

State cooperative extension service publications offices

Cooperative Extension Service
Auburn University
Auburn, Alabama 38630

Cooperative Extension Service
University of Alaska
Box 95151
Fairbanks, Alaska 99701

Cooperative Extension Service
University of Arizona
Tucson, Arizona 85721

Cooperative Extension Service
University of Arkansas
Box 391
Little Rock, Arkansas 72203

Public Service
University Hall
University of California
Berkeley, California 94720

Bulletin Room
Colorado State University
Fort Collins, Colorado 80521

Agricultural Publications
University of Connecticut
Storrs, Connecticut 06268

Mailing Room
Agricultural Hall
University of Delaware
Newark, Delaware 19711

Bulletin Room
Building 440
University of Florida
Gainesville, Florida 32601

Cooperative Extension Service
University of Georgia
Athens, Georgia 30601

Publications Distribution Office
Krauss Hall
University of Hawaii
2500 Dole Street
Honolulu, Hawaii 96822

Mailing Room
Agricultural Science Building
University of Idaho
Moscow, Idaho 83843

Agricultural Publications Office
123 Mumford Hall
University of Illinois
Urbana, Illinois 61801

Mailing Room
Agricultural Administration Building
Purdue University
West Lafayette, Indiana 47907

Publications Distribution Center
Printing and Publications Building
Iowa State University
Ames, Iowa 50010

Distribution Center
Umberger Hall
Kansas State University
Manhattan, Kansas 66506

Bulletin Room
Experiment Station Building
University of Kentucky
Lexington, Kentucky 40506

Publications Librarian
Room 192, Knapp Hall
Louisiana State University
Baton Rouge, Louisiana 70803

Department of Public Information
PICS Building
University of Maine
Orono, Maine 04473

Agricultural Duplication Services
University of Maryland
College Park, Maryland 20742

Cooperative Extension Service
Stockbridge Hall
University of Massachusetts
Amherst, Massachusetts 01002

MSU Bulletin Office
Box 231
Michigan State University
East Lansing, Michigan 48823

Bulletin Room
Coffey Hall
University of Minnesota
St. Paul, Minnesota 55101

Cooperative Extension Service
Mississippi State University
State College, Mississippi 39762

Publications
Whitten Hall
University of Missouri
Columbia, Missouri 65201

Extension Mailing Room
Montana State University
Bozeman, Montana 59715

Department of Information
College of Agriculture
University of Nebraska
Lincoln, Nebraska 68503

Agricultural Communications
University of Nevada
Reno, Nevada 89507

Mail Service
Hewitt Hall
University of New Hampshire
Durham, New Hampshire 03824

Bulletin Clerk
College of Agriculture
Rutgers University
New Brunswick, New Jersey 08903

Bulletin Office
Department of Agricultural Information
Drawer 3A1
New Mexico State University
Las Cruces, New Mexico 88001

Mailing Room, Building 7
Research Park
Cornell University
Ithaca, New York 14850

Publications Office
Department of Agricultural Information
Box 5037
North Carolina State University
Raleigh, North Carolina 27607

Department of Agricultural Information
North Dakota State University
Fargo, North Dakota 58102

Extension Office
Ohio State University
2120 Fyffe Road
Columbus, Ohio 43210

Central Mailing Services
Oklahoma State University
Stillwater, Oklahoma 74074

Extension Hall 118
Oregon State University
Corvallis, Oregon 97331

Sales Supervisor
230 Agricultural Administration Building
Pennsylvania State University
University Park, Pennsylvania 16802

Resource Information Office
16 Woodward Hall
University of Rhode Island
Kingston, Rhode Island 02881

Publications
Department of Public Relations,
Trustee House
Clemson University
Clemson, South Carolina 29631

Bulletin Room
Extension Building
South Dakota State University
Brookings, South Dakota 57006

Agricultural Extension Service
Box 1071
University of Tennessee
Knoxville, Tennessee 37901

Department of Agricultural Communications
Texas A & M University
College Station, Texas 77843

Publications Room
Agricultural Science Building
Utah State University
Logan, Utah 84321

Publications Office
Morrill Hall
University of Vermont
Burlington, Vermont 05401

Extension Division
Virginia Polytechnic Institute
Blacksburg, Virginia 24061

Cooperative Extension Bulletin Room
Publications Building
Washington State University
Pullman, Washington 99163

Mailing Room, Communications Building
Patterson Drive
West Virginia University
Morgantown, West Virginia 26506

Agricultural Bulletin Building
1535 Observatory Drive
University of Wisconsin
Madison, Wisconsin 53706

Bulletin Room
Box 3354, College of Agriculture
University of Wyoming
Laramie, Wyoming 82071

Decorating with plants

The addition of indoor plants can bring new beauty to your home. No matter how many plants you have or where you choose to grow and display them, the decorative arrangement you choose will make a tremendous difference in the look of both your home and your plants.

While a large single tree carefully placed as an accent plant can produce a certain visual excitement, one small plant alone on a windowsill is a dreary sight. So, the first thing to remember is that a sense of scale is important. As a rule, medium and small plants look and grow best when grouped together. However, plants should never be so closely placed that their leaves overlap preventing proper exposure to the light.

Foliage and floral colors can be coordinated to enhance existing color schemes. In addition, the forms of the plants can be used to complement or contrast with the design forms in your home. A sculptural-looking cactus or sansevieria looks smashing against the background of a city skyline, while a leafy plant in an austere setting can produce a wonderful balance. Or, you can simply mix various plant forms together. By grouping a single type of flowering or foliage variety together, you can achieve an impressive display. If the flower pots are to be seen, keep colors uniform to make the display more effective.

An arrangement of various height levels will improve the appearance. You can use upturned matching pots or mix various sized plants together. Clear plastic cylinders with rigid sides or glass bricks allow the light to filter through. Pipes, rods, or ladders can serve as hanging plant racks, with fishing line used to attach the hanging pots to the rack. This eliminates all those hooks and nails and also provides flexibility for the future.

With fluorescent lighting, we no longer need to depend exclusively on natural light. Plants can now be grown anywhere you want them. For instance, a boring entrance or hallway can be made exciting with a plant grouping, or planters can be used as room dividers. Bare fluorescents, used without a valance, always give the feeling of a supermarket or gas station. However, coverings like the commercially available parawedge or angle-flex louvers can be used so that the light source is invisible, with or without using a valance.

At night, show off an accent plant or plant grouping with spotlights. Lighting from above or below can produce interesting shadows and a dramatic look. Spotlights should be kept far enough away to avoid heat damage to the foliage.

When plants are displayed and grown in the same place, some form of waterproof container or trough should be placed underneath them. When the plants are watered, the surplus drains into the container supplying humidity through evaporation. There are many plastic containers for sale, or custom containers can be made from sheet metal or wood. These can be lined with heavy plastic sheets or a waterproof fiberglass resin. To raise the plants above the water, use stones, gravel, metal grills, or plastic egg crates.

With so many plant forms, colors, and textures to choose from, you can enhance the visuals in your home almost endlessly.

Madelyn Simon

Books

Decorating With Plants, by Rex Mabe, Potpourri Press, Box 10312, Greensboro, North Carolina 27404, 1975, 48 pages, paperback, $1.50.

Decorating with Plants and Flowers, Better Homes and Gardens, Creative Home Library, Meredith Corporation, 1716 Locust St., Des Moines, Iowa 50336, 1972, 123 pages, $4.95. A guide to coordinating your plants and flowers with your home environment. Includes advice on grouping and hanging plants, along with tips on arranging your flowers and dried plants for the most pleasing effect. Color photographs show how it's done.

Every Room A Garden, by Alice Skelsey and Cecile Mooney, Workman Publishing Company, 231 E. 51st St., New York, New York 10022, 1976, 336 pages, $6.95. How to decorate your home with plants; goes from the basics to harvesting kitchen crops to "devising special plant fantasies for the adventurous bed-

room." Complete with over 300 illustrations and a special guide to more than 600 plants.

Interior Decorating with Plants, by Carla Wallach, Collier Books (Macmillan), 866 Third Ave., New York, New York 10022, 1976, 239 pages, hardbound, $14.95; paperback $8.95.

Living With Plants, by William S. Hawkey, William Morrow and Co., 105 Madison Ave., New York, New York 10016, 1974, 119 pages, 26 color photographs, hardbound, $15.95.

Madelyn Simon is, by profession, an interior designer and has incorporated horticulture into her work. She has designed the interiors of major airports, business offices, working studios, and personal residences.

SILVER PLATEAU, WITH VASE AND CORNUCOPIE.

Displaying plants

Not too long ago, the indoor gardener who wanted to display his plants was pretty well restricted in his options. Some potted plants resting on a windowsill (if the exposure was right) and a low-light plant placed on the dining-room table pretty well exhausted the possibilities.

Many options available

Times have certainly changed. There are hundreds of possibilities now open to indoor gardeners when it comes to plant display. A ready-made plant shelf, equipped with a lighting unit, can make up a garden totally devoid of natural light. Ceiling hooks and standard nylon plant hangers can be used for hanging plants to screen a window; or an entire area of a room can become an easy-care garden of large plants potted in sleek, modern, self-watering containers.

For one indoor gardener, this room represents the ideal. Yours may have a totally different landscape but, whatever it is, chances are you can readily achieve your desired effect. Shop around before you begin; remember, it helps to know what's available. You may find that a type of plant display you have always discounted as being too costly or difficult is now well within your scope. Take a look at the products in this section and throughout the book. You'll find that wall brackets for plants are not limited to one or two types. There are multi-armed brackets, brackets with extra-long arms, corner brackets, and even brackets that come with their own self-contained lights. You'll find that plant stands needn't necessarily be made of metal or wood; they are available in wicker and many other materials as well. Many stands are ready-made and, on top of being available in many styles, may also come complete with their own fluorescent lights.

Among other plant display items, you'll find floor-to-ceiling poles (some are also scaled to fit windows) that snap into place; ceiling-mounted tracks that hold a multitude of hanging plants with a minimum of work. (Once the track is secured, you don't have to drill holes in your ceiling to secure the plants; you simply slip the hooks into the track.)

You'll find standard items like baskets that can be used to hold already potted plants, plus some surprise items like pots that are made of denim.

Today, plant display products range in cost (and complexity) from plant hangers that cost less than a dollar to a handsome environment-controlled unit that, complete with stand, commands a tidy $1,000. Along with the products themselves, you'll be constantly evolving new ideas that will help display your plants so they are seen at their very best.

Jill Munves

Hand-carved planters, pots, and totems made of fernwood dramatize the garden.

For catalog and mail-order information, write:
Tropical Plant Products
1715 Silver Star Road
Box 7754
Orlando, FL 32804

Metal plant stands with up and down adjustable arms are made by Home Plant Displayers. Available in freestanding and floor-to-ceiling pole models; heights range from 28 to 105 inches. Wall units, both lighted and regular, are also available, as are lighting fixtures for pole models.

For mail-order information write:
Home Plant Displayers
51 East 42nd Street
New York, NY 10017.

Group 6

Hand-wrought brass plant stands, cachepots, and planters complement any room decor and are available in a range of styles, shapes, and sizes. Custom orders to your design or specification are taken.

For mail-order information and brochures, write:
Antique Brass Ltd.
Box 4694
13023 Los Nietos Road
Santa Fe Springs, CA 90670

Driftwood—to create hanging and standing planters, window boxes, plant stands, bases for terrariums and flower arrangements—is available finished, "as found," or in kit form.

For catalog send 50 cents to:
The Driftwood Company
2329 California Avenue Southwest
Seattle, WA 98116.

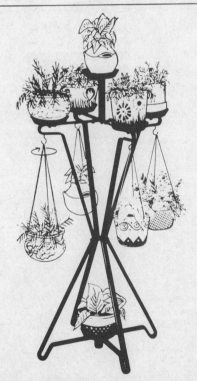

Flower centers are plant stands that can hold both standing and hanging flowerpots. Each unit is made of heavy-duty structural metal, finished with black or white baked enamel that will not rust, peel, or tarnish. The unit may be used indoors or out. All hanging hooks rotate to position plants for best sunlight exposure. Included are drip-proof flowerpot trays. Each unit requires only 2 square feet of floor space.

For catalog and mail-order information, send 50 cents to:
C.A. Gordon Associates
18 Church Street
Paterson, NJ 07505

The turtle is described by the manufacturer as a plant organizer. A domed stand for nesting small potted plants, the Turtle sits on the floor. It is made of a tough, durable white or earth-tone plastic. The stand is sold nationally in gift shops, specialty shops, and department stores.

No mail orders are accepted. For purchasing information and color catalog, write:
Ball Giftware
Box 591
Evansville, IN 47704.

Plant stands and étagères, made of walnut-stained hardwood, are featured by David Scott. A variety of styles are offered, all ready to assemble.

To obtain free brochures and mail-order information, write:
David Scott
Box 5621
Meridian, MS 39301.

Window garden shelf fits 16- to 24-inch windows and is held by pressure only; no nails or screws. Installs easily; removes easily, leaving no marks or holes. Made of white-enamelled steel, it is also available in large size to fit 24- to 38-inch windows.

Two-shelf window unit includes two 4-by-22-inch shelves that hang 10 and 20 inches below the center of the window. White.

For mail-order catalog, send 10 cents to:
Dorothy Biddle Service
DBS Buidling, Dept. TC
Hawthorne, NY 10532

Plant pedestals in transparent plastic come in three sizes and hold pots up to 6 inches wide. Each pedestal comes with a clear saucer.

For information write:
Opus
432 Boylston Street
Boston, MA 02116

Plant-display window shelf is made of heavy-gauge aluminum with baked-on white paint coated with clear plastic. Rustproof and stainproof, it is easily installed on any regular windowsill and is secure whether the window is opened or closed.

For mail-order information write:
Floral Window Display
50 Meadowbrook Road
Danbury, CT 06810

Plant Dolly is a rolling plant stand that lets you move heavy plants (up to 140 pounds) with ease. Constructed with a wood-grained, water resistant top, it comes in either 12-inch or 15-inch-wide models, 3½ inches high.

For free brochure and mail-order information write to:
Plant Dolly
Box 2551
Southfield, MI 48037

PS-6

Plant stands ranging from étagères to metal pushcarts, plus all types of fern and houseplant stands, are offered by the Koch Company. Most are made of brass or nickel plate; some are finished with white or black enamel. Sold by department stores, gift shops, and florists.

For buying information write:
George Koch Sons
Box 358
Evansville, IN 47744

Plant pedestals are adjustable from 24 to 36 inches in height. Made of heavy-duty steel, they are easy to assemble and each includes an 8-inch saucer, which revolves for balanced plant growth. Available in white, chrome, and black.

For buying information write:
Christen
59 Branch Street
St. Louis, MO 63147

1675   Page 5

Plant stands, veneer-finished and ready-to-assemble, are marketed by JS Permaneer. Among the models is a plant étagère finished in walnut and white vinyl veneer. It features a socket for a "grow light," adjustable glass shelves, and a lower storage closet. A plant cart and three-tier plant stand are also available.

These items are sold nationally in discount stores, drug chains, and department and hardware stores.

For free catalog sheets and buying information, write to:
JS Permaneer
201 Parkway
St. Louis, MO 63043

Three-step plant stand made of vinyl-cushioned steel is offered by Grayline. It is colored black, measures, 5 x 5⅛ x 15⅞ inches and doubles as an extra shelf.

For free catalog and buying information, write:
Grayline Housewares
1616 Berkley Street
Elgin, IL 60120

Adjustable tension poles, scaled for floor-to-ceiling or window installation, are marketed by Queen Manufacturing Company. All are chromium-or brass-plated, and all have adjustable arms for hanging or holding plants. Free-standing models with floor bases are also available. Some units come complete with a shaded grow light; separate grow lights are also available.

For additional information write:
Queen Manufacturing Company
1400 North Cicero Avenue
Chicago, IL 60651

Stepladder in clear plastic allows light to reach all plants. The unit requires very little floor space and is easily assembled. Available in two sizes, one holding up to 16 plants and the other holding up to 30 plants.

Old-fashioned fern stand in natural or enamel-painted wicker. The stand is 39 inches high and 10 inches in diameter at the top, which will hold a large potted fern or several smaller plants.

Wicker plant trees hold several plants. Available in walnut or white. Four-branch tree is 39 inches high; five-branch tree is 45 inches high.

For mail-order information write:
Halame Company
Charlevoix, MI 19720

"Lexington green"

Handcrafted planters, made of sugar pine and finished with water-resistant sealer and a semigloss lacquer, are available in kits or fully assembled.

For catalog and mail-order information, write:
E.X.I.T.
Box 201
Dracut, MA 01826

Posie Perch lets you use narrow windowsills as plant shelves. Measuring 12 x 20 inches, it can be installed in most windows without the use of tools. It is made of solid wood, decorated with a green leaf pattern, and will hold up to 50 pounds.

For mail-order information write:
Posie Perch
5958 North 83rd Street
Department T.C.
Scottsdale, AZ 85251

Plant Furniture is the perfect system for incorporating plants into today's interiors. Fine-quality hardwoods are expertly constructed into an assortment of pedestals, cylinders, and planters. Finished in natural or dark walnut, each piece is treated with Danish oil and hand-rubbed with steel wool.

For brochure and mail-order information, write:
Plant Furniture
Box 94
Waitsfield, VT 05673

Plant stands from Rubbermaid include: a two-shelf; a three-shelf; and a swing-shelf stand, which has four adjustable shelves that function as drip trays. The shelves are sold nationally at retail stores. No mail order, please.

For free catalogs and buying information, write:
Rubbermaid
147 Akron Road
Wooster, OH 44691

Klima-gro is a complete growing system that includes artificial lights, a temperature controlled soil bed, and an optional moisture sensor that tells when to add water. A complete instruction booklet is included. Three separate units are available, each with 100 percent solid state controls, and storage space for plant utensils.

For brochures and information write:
Care-Free General Aluminum Products
Charlotte, MI 48813

Phytarium is a controlled-environment growth chamber recommended for home, office, and classroom use. The 40-inch chamber has automatic timers and controls for providing proper lighting, carbon-dioxide levels, air circulation, and temperature. Water and plant food are supplied from reservoirs by wicks. Two fully assembled models, standard and deluxe, are offered. A do-it-yourself kit is also available.

For catalog and mail-order information, send 50 cents to:
Alprax Enterprises
Rotterdam Industrial Park, Bldg. #4
Box 2636
Schenectady, NY 12309

Dried flowers and plants

The lovely, vibrant-colored seasonal flowers can decorate your house the year round if you preserve them. In dried arrangements, you can combine flowers blooming at different times of the year. If you collect from your garden throughout the year, you will have a variety of colors, shapes, sizes, single, and clustered blossoms as well as foliage and seed pods. There are various techniques for drying or preserving. Some plants turn out better with one method than another. Whatever method you use for outdoor flowers, pick them on a sunny day after the dew has gone but before the flowers have wilted from the mid-day heat. Never pick flowers that are fully open because they open further as they dry. Drying also causes flowers to shrink and to darken in color slightly, so choose blossoms that are large and brightly colored. Treat the flowers immediately after picking with one of the following methods. Drying is something you can experiment with because there is no one fool-proof method.

Glycerine method

Glycerine is a good method for preserving foliage. Use one part glycerin to two parts water. Pour the mixture into a deep container. Crush or slit the bottom two inches of the stems (to speed up absorption) and stand the branches in the solution. (Only the bottom of the stems need to be in the solution.)

Keep them in the solution until the color changes to brown all the way to the tips of the leaves. This will take from three days to three weeks. Remove the stems, allow them to dry for a week to ten days, and then store them in a dark place. Cover the glycerine solution because it can be used again.

Air-drying method

To air dry flowers, strip all the foliage from the stems. With string, tie about 10 flowers of the same kind together. Hang them upside down in a cool place. You can hold several bunches on a wire coat hanger. The drying time will be from three to six weeks depending on the flower.

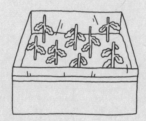

Silica-gel method

Silica gel is a chemical compound that is commercially available under different trade names at plant stores. It is expensive but provides a quick drying method that retains the flower's color. To use silica gel, first strip the foliage and cut the stems to 2 or 3 inches. Pour ½ inch of silica gel crystals into a container. Place the flowers upside down and far enough apart so they don't touch each other. Gently work the crystals around the petals until the flower heads are covered. Then make the container airtight by covering it with plastic and sealing it with tape. The drying takes from two to eight days depending on the flower.

When you buy silica gel, buy at least five pounds. This will last a long time because it can be reused. When the blue crystals have absorbed too much moisture to be effective, they will turn white or pink. Put them in a shallow pan in a 300-degree-F. oven until they turn blue again. Allow to cool before using, and store them in an air-tight container.

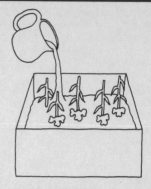

Cornmeal and borax method

Strip all the foliage from the stems. Combine ten parts of white cornmeal with three parts of borax and mix thoroughly. Pour 2 to 4 inches of the mixture into a box. Place the flowers upside down and move the mixture around and over until they are just covered. Place the flower heads so they do not touch or overlap. The stems do not have to be covered. Put only one layer in the box. Label the box with the name of the flower and the date, and store it in a dark, cool place. The drying time ranges from a few days to three weeks. To test the dryness, brush aside a little of the mixture and see if the petals are crisp to the touch. Sand can be used instead of cornmeal, but sand is heavier so you must be careful not to crush the flowers. Use sand that is fine and light in a mixture of one part borax to three parts sand.

Pressing method

Pressing is the method used for small flowers and autumn leaves. To press, place the flowers or leaves between several thicknesses of absorbent paper such as newspaper. Arrange them the way you want them to look when dry because you will not be able to reposition blossoms after they have dried. Then place the newspaper between two heavy books so the flowers are under pressure. The drying time will vary according to how thick the petals and leaves are, but check after ten days.

Linda Hetzer

Wiring stems

Pods: Trim off the stem. With a drill, awl, or large needle (depending on the pod), pierce a hole in the pod as shown. Thread a length of thin florist wire through the hole and fasten it by wrapping one end around the other.

Flowers and leaves: To lengthen or strengthen stems, reinforce with thin florist wire. Bend a piece of the wire, forming a loop, and place it on top of the existing stem. Hold the loop securely just under the base of the flower or leaf while you twist one end of the wire around the other and the stem. The wire and stem may be wrapped with florists' tape.

Cones: Remove the stem, if any, and pass a length of thin copper wire between the scales near the end of the cone. Fasten the wire by wrapping one end around the other.

Decorative wreath

To make a decorative wreath from dried plant materials, start with a chicken wire or styrofoam form (available at florists' shops). Wrap the wreath with raffia or half-inch strips of corn husk to disguise the form.

Prepare the flowers and foliage by using one of the drying methods described. If you would like to add pods or cones to the design, simply air dry them. Long-stemmed pods are best preserved by hanging them upside down. Dry small, short-stemmed ones on a flat, absorbent surface such as a shallow cardboard box. Turn them over every other day to aid drying. Cones are usually covered with a sticky sap; wash it off with soap and water. If the weather is warm and dry enough, air dry them outside (keep them out of direct sunlight or their colors will fade). Indoors, place the cones on a radiator or on top of a furnace to speed drying.

Add wire stems to the dried materials. Then attach them to the wreath by wrapping the wires around the form. Trim the finished wreath with a big ribbon bow.

Flowers and plants to dry

Air dry	Glycerine (foliage)
Baby's breath	Beech
Blue sage	Birch
Chrysanthemums	Peach
Coxcomb	Forsythia
Goldenrod	Canna
Hydrangea	Rhododendron
Pussy Willow	Barberry
Statice	Crab apple
Strawflowers	Plum
Yarrow	
Thistle	**Silica gel**
Chinese lantern pods	Marigolds
Cornmeal and borax	Carnations
Queen Anne's lace	Zinnias
Rose	Clematis
Blackeyed Susan	Lilacs
Dogwood	Roses
Milkweed	Chrysanthemums
Lilac	Dahlia
Marigolds	Aster

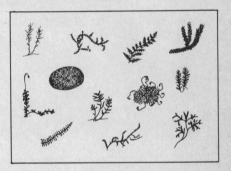

Double Indian Nasturtium

Ferns

Bird's nest fern

Rabbit's foot fern

Ferns have acquired the reputation of the fastidious prima donna – an unfortunate exaggeration. We live in sunny, warm, dry homes, and ferns simply prefer the cooler, more sober, behind-the-lace curtain atmosphere of great-grandmother's day. Far from being outdated, however, many species thrive with only minimal adaptation of room decor and plant care.

Most important for a contented fern are an evenly moist growing medium and a reasonably humid atmosphere. (Make no mistake – ferns cannot tolerate soggy soil as an alternative or as a boost to moisture in the air.) Add to these conditions regular balanced food for crisp foliage and texture, bright diffuse light, temperatures between 55 degrees and 70 degrees F., and a bit of gentle air movement. A plant confined to a pot is dependent on the grower for its needs. The fern asks only that you be consistently watchful.

A grouping of ferns is both attractive and pragmatic, the collection providing a microclimate with increased humidity in an otherwise dry living area – not the classic cool, moist, shady glen, but ferns will find it an accepta-

ble substitute. An inexpensive tray filled with moistened pebbles may provide humidity around an individual plant or a grouping. Hand misting is of momentary value to growing tips, but may be detrimental by rotting the tightly packed inside foliage. A house or room humidifier or even a small vaporizer placed near the plants during part of the drier daylight hours will add to the plants' comfort – and yours.

North, northwest, and northeast windowsills, a bit of morning or late afternoon sun through a nearby east or west window, or diffused light from a south window satisfies the fern's light requirements. Fluorescent tubes hidden under a shelf provide ideal light and a theatrical setting for an individual plant or a collection.

There are several decorative, readily available varieties likely to bring success to the beginner and to the enthusiast with limited time for plant care.

Among the most forgiving are the footed ferns, so named for the hairy, water-and-food-storing rhizome which resembles an animal's paw. Especially tolerant are *Polypodium*

aureum, and *P. aureum* "Mandaianum," the latter more ruffled, both with crisp, blue-green foliage. Daintier of foot and foliage are the various *Davallia fejeensis* cultivars, *D. mariesii, D. solida, D. trichomanoides,* and *Scyphularia pentaphylla* (formerly *D. pentaphylla). Aglaomorpha coronans*, with coarse foliage, forms a striking spreading crown. The footed ferns are especially suited to hanging baskets.

Asplenium nidus (bird's nest fern) with wide straplike, shiny fronds grows slowly with sculptural effect, first for table, then for floor accent. *A. bulbiferum* (mother fern), related to *A. nidus*, provides a filmy appearance for table or hanging pot.

Despite its fragile appearance, the climbing *Lygodium japonicum (L. scandens)* twines happily in diffused light in or near a window. Plants may be difficult to find, but spores are readily available.

Most readily available on the market are nephrolepis and pteris varieties, the Boston and table ferns. Try any of the numerous *N. exaltata* cultivars or *N. cordifolia*, the tasseled

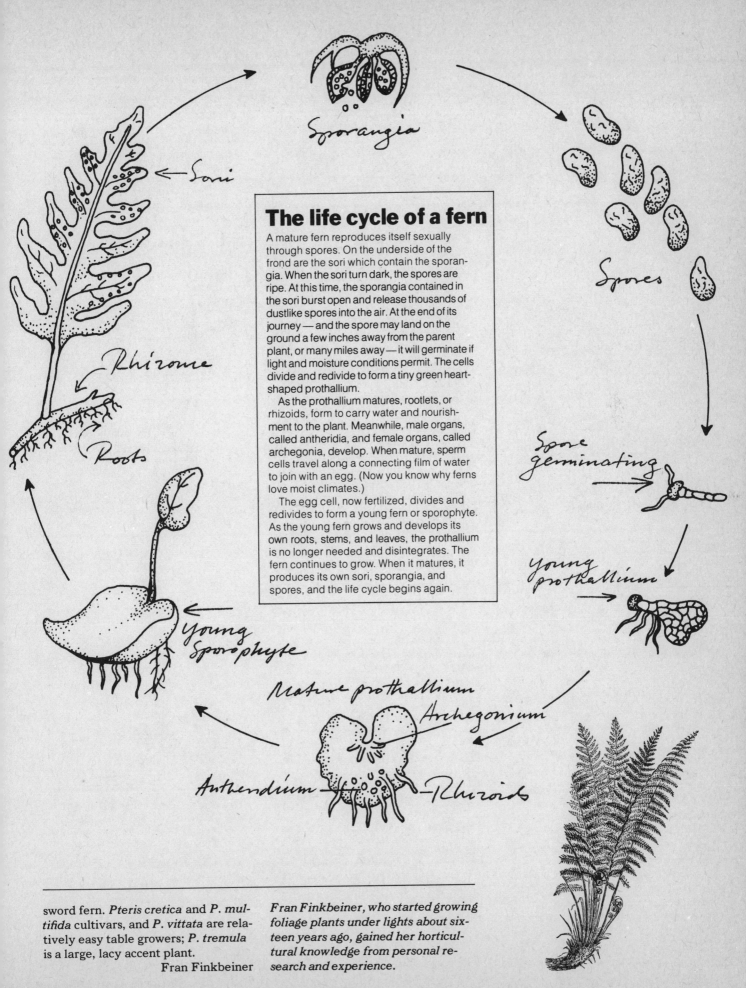

Sporangia

Spores

Sori

Rhizome

Roots

Spore germinating

young prothallium

Young Sporophyte

Mature prothallium

Archegonium

Antheridium — Rhizoids

The life cycle of a fern

A mature fern reproduces itself sexually through spores. On the underside of the frond are the sori which contain the sporangia. When the sori turn dark, the spores are ripe. At this time, the sporangia contained in the sori burst open and release thousands of dustlike spores into the air. At the end of its journey — and the spore may land on the ground a few inches away from the parent plant, or many miles away — it will germinate if light and moisture conditions permit. The cells divide and redivide to form a tiny green heart-shaped prothallium.

As the prothallium matures, rootlets, or rhizoids, form to carry water and nourishment to the plant. Meanwhile, male organs, called antheridia, and female organs, called archegonia, develop. When mature, sperm cells travel along a connecting film of water to join with an egg. (Now you know why ferns love moist climates.)

The egg cell, now fertilized, divides and redivides to form a young fern or sporophyte. As the young fern grows and develops its own roots, stems, and leaves, the prothallium is no longer needed and disintegrates. The fern continues to grow. When it matures, it produces its own sori, sporangia, and spores, and the life cycle begins again.

sword fern. *Pteris cretica* and *P. multifida* cultivars, and *P. vittata* are relatively easy table growers; *P. tremula* is a large, lacy accent plant.

Fran Finkbeiner

Fran Finkbeiner, who started growing foliage plants under lights about sixteen years ago, gained her horticultural knowledge from personal research and experience.

Mother fern

Ferns from Spores

Live ferns were collected and transported with difficulty beginning in the early 1600's. In 1699 a description of the phenomenon of spore reproduction was a boon to the collector and to the botanist of the eighteenth century who depended on slow sea travel. Although the twentieth century grower may not find shipment of live plants so chancey, collections may still be increased easily with spores, a mastery of the technique of spore propagation, and patience. Success rests most on a sterile, just-moist propagation medium and natural humidity or hand misting. The following method is calculated to provide these necessities with a minimum of care and effort.

1. Fill clean 3-inch clay pots to within an inch of the top with a mixture of 2 parts commercial African violet mix and 1 part fine or medium perlite. Place a woven cotton wick through the bottom two-thirds of the mix, and extend through the drainage hole about an inch.

2. Thoroughly moisten and drain the mix; then bake pots and mix for an hour at 250 degree F. Cool, and cover pots with sterile glass covers or 3½-inch squat plastic glasses.

3. Sink pots in an aluminum roasting pan containing damp vermiculite to the level of the growing mix, and moisten pots, mix, and vermiculite with boiled or distilled water.

Collecting spores

When the spore cases on the back of a fern frond begin to ripen and turn brown, remove the frond and place it on a piece of paper or in an envelope. In a day or so, the spores will be released; store these in a paper sack or envelope to dry for a week or so before planting.

Plant sources

Alberts and Merkel Brothers, 2210 South Federal Highway, Boynton Beach, Florida 33435. (305) 732-2071. Plant list 75 cents. Open Monday through Saturday 8:00 a.m. to 4:30 p.m. Adiantum, alsophilia, asplenium, blechnum, cyrtomium, davallia, nephrolepis, pityrogramma, polypodium, polystichum, pteris, psilotum, and selaginella are offered.

Antonelli Brothers, 2545 Capitola Road, Santa Cruz, California 95062. (408) 475-5222. Illustrated catalog. Open every day. Adiantum, dryopteris, pellaea, phyllitis, polypodium, polystichum, pteris, nephrolepis, humata, asplenium, dicksonia, and platycerium ferns are offered.

Arant's Exotic Greenhouses, Route 3, Box 972, Bessemer, Alabama 35020. (205) 428-1827. Catalog $1.50 (refundable with order). Open Tuesday through Saturday 9:00 a.m. to 5:00 p.m. Call before visiting. Adiantum, aglaomorpha, asplenium, davallia, nephrolepis, platycerium, polypodium, pteris, and many other unusual ferns.

Bolduc's Greenhill Nursery, 2131 Vallejo Street, St. Helena, California 94574. (707) 963-2998. Plant list available by sending a stamped, self-addressed envelope. Open Saturday and Sunday 10:00 a.m. to 4:00 p.m., or by appointment. Over 110 varieties of ferns are stocked, including hard-to-get species. Large selection of adiantum, nephrolepis, pteris, polystichum, and polypodium ferns.

Edelweiss Gardens, 54 Robbinsville-Allentown Road, Box 66R, Robbinsville, New Jersey 08691. (609) 259-2831. Plant list 35 cents. Open until 4:00 p.m. every day. Adiantum, asplenium, phyllitis, davallia, polypodium, cyrtomium, pellaea, dryopteris, nephrolepis, polystichim, pteris, and platycerium ferns are offered.

Jerry Horne, 10195 Southwest 70th Street, Miami, Florida 33173. (305) 270-1235. Plant list. Visitors welcome by appointment. Aglaomorpha, davallia, lycopodium, platycerium, polypodium, and pyrrosia ferns are offered.

Logee's Greenhouses, 55 North Street, Danielson, Connecticut 06239. (203) 774-8038. Catalog $2.00. Open daily 9:00 a.m. to 4:00 p.m. Visitors welcome. Adiantum, asplenium, cyclophorus, cyrtomium, davallia, humata, nephrolepis, pellaea, platycerium, polypodium, polystichum, phyllitis, and selaginella are offered.

Merry Gardens, Camden, Maine 04843. Pictorial handbook $1.00; list 50 cents. Visitors welcome Monday through Saturday 9:00 a.m. to 4:30 p.m. Asplenium, adiantum, cyrtomium, pteris, nephrolepis, davillia, platycerium, and others.

Geo. W. Park Seed Company, Greenwood, South Carolina 29647. Color catalog. Spores available for maidenhair, bird's nests, brake, and Boston ferns, plus mixtures of tender and hardy ferns. Fern plants are also available.

The Plant Room, 6373 Trafalgar Road, Hornby, Ontario LOP 1EO, Canada. (416) 878-4984. Open daily 10:00 a.m. to 4:00 p.m. (closed Wednesday). Visitors welcome. A wide selection of rare fern spores is available. Send a stamped, self-addressed envelope for availability list.

Thompson and Morgan, Box 24, 401 Kennedy Boulevard, Somerdale, New Jersey 08083. Color-illustrated catalog. Spores available of adiantum, asplenium, and dicksonia; also spore mixtures of tender and hardy ferns.

4. Prepare labels with species name and date.

5. Tap spores from smooth, once-folded paper as evenly as possible on cooled growing medium. Remove cover, and sow one pot at a time to minimize mixing of species. Label.

6. Place pan in diffuse light (or 8 to 10 inches from the fluorescent tubes), maintain 65 to 75 degrees F. and keep vermiculite moist.

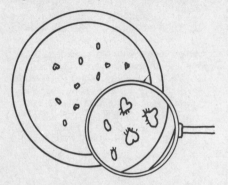

7. Germination may occur in a week or more. A green shadow on the growing medium (Act I) indicates that individual cells have formed and they eventually form oval or heart-shaped structures (prothallia). (A 10x hand lens will enable you to watch the process.) Tiny roots form to provide food for the prothallia, which mature and develop male and female organs.

8. If the growing medium does not contain nutrients, diluted fertilizer should be misted on the surface or added through the moistened vermiculite if the prothallia assume a yellow-green color.

9. Temperature changes in the sealed container provide condensation which enables the sperm to swim and fertilize the egg. If no natural condensation occurs, hand mist daily with distilled water.

10. The prothallia spread, and the first tiny fronds (sporophytes) appear—Act II of the two-part drama.

If few plants are desired, young sporlings should be thinned. If you want many plants, remove and transplant sections of prothallia under the same sterile conditions, and continue to keep the plugs covered. Young plants should be acclimatized by gradually removing the covering. The sporlings grow best when close together and should not be transplanted separately to 2½-inch pots until the plants are 2 or 3 inches tall. Sporlings should be transplanted into a just-moist potting medium, placed in diffuse light, and lightly covered (or placed at the ends of fluorescent tubes) for a few days until established.

Sterilization of the mix and container and a close-fitting cover should inhibit moss, algae, or fungi spores from blowing into the growing mix. The tight container provides natural condensation necessary to fertilize the egg.

A small amount of propagation mix may be sterilized with boiling water and put in a sterile glass-topped container with equal results. The method is flexible, if basic germination requirements are understood.

Common fern-shade with ornamental stand.

Maidenhair fern

Button fern

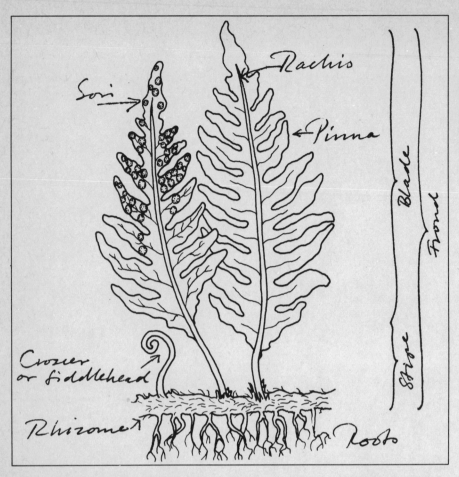

Soi

Rachis

Pinna

Blade

Frond

Crozier
or fiddlehead

Stipe

Rhizome

Roots

Books

Fern Growers Manual, by Barbara Jo Hoshizaki, Alfred A. Knopf, 201 E. 50 St., New York, New York 10022, 1975, hardbound, 256 pages, $15.00. The author, a professor of botany, has done extensive field work and has written the best book on ferns. The book has 8 color plates and 300 black and white photographs, plus drawings.

Ferns to Know and Grow, by F. Gordon Foster, Hawthorne Books, 260 Madison Ave., New York, New York 10016, 1976, paperback, 258 pages, $4.95. A revised and enlarged edition of *The Gardener's Fern Book*, this is an extremely practical guide to the study and culture of ferns.

Fern collections to visit

Longwood Gardens, Kennett Square, Pennsylvania.
Montreal Botanic Garden, 410 Sherbrook St. E., Montreal, Quebec, Canada.

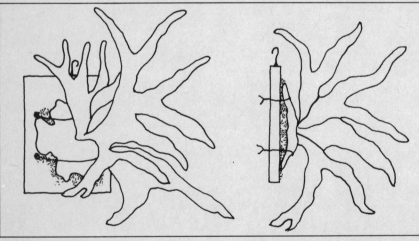

Slab mounting

A staghorn fern has a striking appearance which can be even more dramatic when mounted on a tree fern slab. To begin, drill four holes in the slab. Place the fern on the slab with a cushion of sphagnum moss in between. Secure the fern by passing pieces of plastic-coated wire through the holes and around the shield fronds of the fern. Twist the wire ends together at the back. Water the fern by immersing the slab in water for 15 minutes.

Societies

American Fern Society

Terry R. Webster
University of Connecticut
Storrs, Connecticut 06268
Membership dues are $5.00 a year and include a subscription to the quarterly *American Fern Journal*.

International Tropical Fern Society

8720 S.W. 34 Street
Miami, Florida 33165
The International Tropical Fern Society was founded in December 1975 in Coral Gables, Florida. There are now 2,000 members in 34 states and 17 foreign countries.

The purpose of the organization is to study ferns and related plants and to stimulate interest in these plants through meetings, lectures, programs, exhibits, field trips, workshops, and garden tours.

Members can attend meetings; participate in annual trips or fern forays into the tropical rain forests of the world; borrow books from the society's library; utilize the society's discount store; and obtain spores from the spore vault. Other benefits include visiting members' collections and participating in plant shows. All members also receive a free copy of the Society's monthly magazine, *The Rhizome Reporter*, which includes a bulletin of the chapters' activities and programs. A loose-leaf lesson accompanies each issue of the magazine.

Los Angeles International Fern Society

Wilbur W. Olson
2423 Burret Avenue
Redondo Beach, California 90278
The Los Angeles International Fern Society was founded in 1959 by Clyde Drummond. Its purpose is to further interest in ferns and to furnish information on the propagation of ferns and the conservation of ferns and all plants.

Benefits of membership in the Society include a subscription to its 28-page monthly magazine, *LAIFS*. In addition, members receive a monthly 2-page article or lesson on how to grow a specific fern. Membership is open to anyone interested in fulfilling the Society's goals; the fee is $5.50 per year.

Fertilizer

What is fertilizer?
Fertilizer is any substance containing one or more of the nutrients required by a plant to maintain growth, health, and vigor.

It is most commonly incorporated into the soil, where the nutrients become dissolved in water and are absorbed by the plant's roots. The nutrients are then transported throughout the plant and used in the various processes vital to the plant's existence.

The basic nutrients
The primary plant nutrients are nitrogen (N), phosphorous (P) and potassium (K). Plants require them in larger amounts than other nutrients. Fertilizers contain varying amounts of them, and the percentage of each appears on the package in a number form, such as 5-10-5, 15-15-15 or 23-19-17. The first number indicates the amount of nitrogen, the second phosphorous and the third potassium. Potassium is in the form of potash, a potassium compound.

Nitrogen is necessary for the growth of shoots and leaves and the formation of chlorophyll.

Phosphorous is important for the development of flowers and roots. It also helps a plant resist many diseases.

Potassium controls a plant's general growth.

Types of fertilizers
The best fertilizers for houseplants are the water-soluble types. These dissolve immediately in water, and the nutrients can then be readily taken up by the plant's roots. Water-soluble fertilizers are available under a wide variety of brand names in different formulations. They usually contain trace elements, as well as the three basic nutrients. The directions on each should be carefully followed to prevent harming the plant. A good way to avoid accidental root burn is to apply the fertilizer at half-rate and increase the frequency of application.

Slow-release or encapsulated fertilizers are gaining in popularity. These are designed to release nutrients to the plant at a gradual rate over a long period of time, eliminating frequent feeding. Since they release their nutrients a little at a time as the plant is watered, they are safe and convenient to use.

Secondary nutrients and trace elements
The other elements required by plants are known as secondary nutrients and trace elements, and include calcium, boron, manganese, iron, copper, molybdenum, sulphur, zinc, and chlorine. These are needed in much smaller quantities.

Granular garden-type fertilizer or slow-release plant food can be added when mixing potting soil, and thoroughly blended in at that time.

Acid-type fertilizers are available for acid-loving plants such as azaleas, gardenias and camellias.

Some people believe that plants prefer organic rather than chemical fertilizer, but this is not so. Since a plant absorbs a nutrient in its elemental form, it recognizes no difference between an organic and a chemical source.

How much and how often?
Although there is no one rule to follow when it comes to feeding house plants, there are some general rules that can be helpful.
- House plants require much less food than plants growing outdoors. Too much fertilizer is just as bad as too little.
- Check cultural instructions for feeding a particular plant.
- Don't feed a dormant or sick plant.
- Use little or no fertilizer in winter. Generally, the less light a plant receives, the less fertilizer is required.
- Under artificial light, fertilize about once a week, but water with plain water once a month to flush out salts.
- A newly potted plant may not require feeding for six months or more.

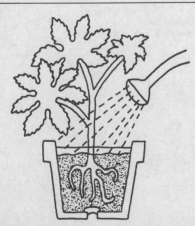

Water-soluble
To apply water-soluble fertilizer, first dissolve the powder, tablet, or concentrated liquid in water (this protects the delicate roots from fertilizer burn), and then apply the fertilizer solution. This is by far the most popular way to fertilize plants, and the most convenient.

Slow-release
Add a slow-release fertilizer to the soil directly from the package. Work fertilizer in powder or granule form into the surface of the soil. Bury sticks or tablets in the soil, close to the walls of the pot. Nutrients in this form of fertilizer are dissolved gradually each time you water the plant, which some people find convenient.

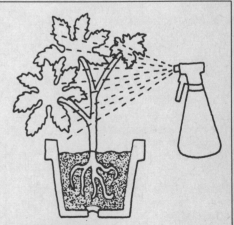

Foliar feeding
Use foliar feeding for certain plants such as bromeliads and citrus, and when a plant appears starved and needs to absorb nutrients immediately. Be sure to use a formula designated for this purpose — spraying ordinary, water-soluble fertilizer on leaves may sometimes cause harm.

- Flowering plants should be fed when buds form and just before bloom.
- Slow-growing plants, such as those with large foliage, require only two or three feedings a year.
- Don't feed any plant for at least two weeks after transplanting to allow for root development.
- Don't feed a plant while it's in bloom.

Symptoms of fertilizer problems

Nitrogen deficiency causes a plant's growth to be restricted, roots to become stunted and leaves to yellow and drop off. Too much nitrogen will cause excessive leaf and stem growth and little or no flowering. It can also burn the roots.

Lack of phosphorous will also cause leaves to darken or to yellow and drop off, or yellow edges to appear on the upper leaves.

Too little potassium will cause dry leaves and scorched leaf edges.

Over-fertilization can also be recognized by the presence of algae on the side of the pot, or white granules on the soil's surface.

David A. Pottinger

Gardening has been a personal, and sometimes professional, pursuit of David A. Pottinger for many years. He and his brother, George, are presently designing and developing a large-scale, commercial composting operation in Puerto Rico.

Worm castings provide an excellent source of nutrients for indoor plants. Castings are water soluble and immediately available to plants; also, they will not burn any plants. Available by the pint, quart, or gallon.

For mail-order information write:
Longmire's Worm Farm
Star Route, Ettersburg
Garberville, CA 95440

Organic supplies, including hybro-tite, rock phosphate, kelp meal, liquid seaweed, compost activator, composted poultry waste, agricultural lime, and corn cob mulch, are available from Sunnylawn Farm. Also included in their brocure are seed-starting pellets, potting mix, pots, hanging baskets, and flats.

For mail-order information write:
Sunnylawn Farm
Box 101
Steward, IL 60553

Supplies & equipment

Liquid fertilizer is an odorless, concentrated fertilizer that can be used in all gardens, indoors and out. It will encourage healthy growth in all plants, flowers, vegetables, trees, shrubs, and lawns. Can be used as a foliar feed. 5-10-5 analysis.

Fish emulsion plant food is an all-fish, organic fertilizer in a liquid concentrate form. A chelating agent is incorporated to activate iron uptake. Suitable for all types of plants.

Liquid seaweed provides extra growing power for germinating seeds, flowering plants, foliage plants, and vegetables.

For catalog and mail-order information, write:
The Hy-Trous Corporation
3 Green Street
Woburn, MA 01801

Maxicrop is made from seaweed and contains 55 trace elements. This natural, nontoxic product is harmless to plants, animals, and man. It is widely used on orchids as a feed for both cut flowers and potted plants. The maker also recommends it for African violets. For the indoor gardener, it is available in 8-ounce, quart, and gallon bottles.

For mail-order information write:
Maxicrop, U.S.A.
Box 964
Arlington Heights, IL 60006

Liquinox liquid fertilizers are made for lawns, dichondra, shrubs, flowers, and indoor plants. Products are available only through garden-supply stores and nurseries.

For a brochure write:
Liquinox Company
221 West Meats Avenue
Orange, CA 92667

Re-nu-erth is a 100 percent organic, highly concentrated worm-bed compost. This product is made from angle worms that live in a soil-free environment and are fed on a diet of pure vegetable matter. The maker, Mosser Lee Co., claims the resultant fertilizer is odorless and does not deteriorate. The company also offers a number of other fertilizers.

For information and the mail-order catalog, send 50 cents to:
Mosser Lee Company
Millston, WI 54643

Plant grower, a plant food and soil conditioner, is a 100 percent organic, natural product derived from seaweed. It contains minerals, trace elements, hormones, vitamins, carbohydrates, and chelating agents. It is supplied for use as a spray, or in granules that can be mixed in soil. Plant Grower is available at specialty plant stores, florists, and discount chains, primarily in the East and Midwest.

Distributed by:
J. Lindsay Company
Box 452
Westport, NY 12933

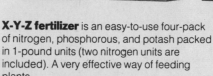

X-Y-Z fertilizer is an easy-to-use four-pack of nitrogen, phosphorous, and potash packed in 1-pound units (two nitrogen units are included). A very effective way of feeding plants.

Sea-power fertilizer is a completely organic liquified seaweed. It contains natural trace elements, minerals, and vitamins essential to good plant growth. One tablespoon makes one gallon of solution.

Free catalog is available. Also booklets: *The Good Earth Can Do You Dirt* (25 cents) and *The Organic Supplement* (50 cents). Send requests to:
Sudbury Laboratory
572 Dutton Road
Sudbury, MA 01776

Organic-based plant foods (seven types in all) are offered by A.H. Hoffman. Included are Super Manure, Cottonseed Meal, Cocoa Shell Mulch and Bone Meal. These feature natural, slow release of plant nutrients. No mail order, but products can be found in major chain stores, hardware stores, and garden centers.

Houseplant food is a timed-release fertilizer; one application lasts three to four months. It encourages healthier growth and strong root systems. 19-6-13 analysis.

African violet food encourages richer and more abundant blooms and greener, more supple leaves. Timed-release so one application lasts five to six months. 18-8-12 analysis.

All-purpose food is designed for both indoor and outdoor plants, flowers, and vegetables. It's safe to use with all plants; will not burn. Timed-release formulation makes one application last for three to four months. 14-14-14 analysis.

These and other indoor and outdoor timed-release plant foods are available in retail garden centers and nurseries. For information write:
Rainbird
7045 North Grand Avenue
Glendora, CA 91740

   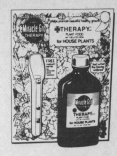

Liquid miracle-gro comes ready to use. Just put several drops on the soil; then water the plant. 8-7-6 analysis with chelated iron.

Miracle-gro is an all-purpose plant food in water-soluble crystal form. It stimulates growth and health in both indoor and outdoor plants. Instant action.

Miracid is a soil acidifier and plant food specifically designed for acid-loving plants, such as azaleas, camellias, and gardenias.

Therapy plant food is specifically designed for indoor use. Contains chelated iron. 10-8-7 analysis. Comes as a liquid concentrate to be mixed with water.

Available in nurseries and garden centers. For information and mail-order catalog, send 35 cents to:
Stern's Nurseries
Geneva, NY 14456

Peters soluble fertilizers are available in nine different formulas for the home gardener. All Peters fertilizers contain chelating agents, trace elements, and a penetrant for uniform penetration into the soil. They are also completely water-soluble, free of excess soluble salts, and noncorrosive to application equipment. All the fertilizers are non-burning when used as directed. For indoor use, there are houseplant, African violet, variegated African violet, and three orchid formulations.

For information write:
Robert B. Peters Company
2833 Pennsylvania Street
Allentown, PA 18104

Houseplant food is an easy-to-use fertilizer; just add drops to soil, and then water the plant. Balanced 5-10-5 formula contains organic material plus iron, manganese, and zinc.

Pot and planter food is a timed-release plant food; a single application feeds plants for four to six months. Important trace elements of iron, zinc, and manganese are included in this 5-10-5 fertilizer.

African violet food is a timed-release fertilizer; a single application feeds plants from four to six months. The analysis is 6-9-5, with iron, zinc, and manganese included.

Products are available nationally in retail outlets that handle indoor-plant products. For additional information write:
Chevron Chemical Company
Box 3744
San Francisco, CA 94119

Schultz-instant liquid plant food comes with a dropper for easy measuring. Designed to be used with every watering, it is safe for all types of plants; no burning. 10-15-10 analysis.

For mail-order information write:
Schultz Company
11730 Northline
St. Louis, MO 63043

Roto grow 9-9-9, a chemical fertilizer in tablet form, is useful for both indoor and outdoor plants. It contains the primary plant nutrients: nitrogen, phosphoric acid, and potash, plus mineral traces. The tablets are designed for periodic use—one application will last up to three months on indoor plants; more frequent applications are necessary for outdoor plants.

For retail availability and ordering information, write:
Roto Grow Company
Box 421
118 Monell Street
Penn Yan, NY 14527

Watch-us-grow liquid fertilizer can be used for all indoor and outdoor plants and vegetables. Economical; 1 quart makes 64 gallons. Also available in a pint size, which comes with a spray bottle.

For mail-order information write:
Bluestone Perennials
3500 Jackson Street
Mentor, OH 44060

Tender leaf plant starter contains Vitamin B1, which stimulates root growth. It is useful in minimizing transplant shock.

Tender leaf houseplant food has a 10-10-5 formulation. It also contains chelated iron, zinc, and manganese, plus a penetrant for uniform feeding.

Fishol fish emulsion is a 100 percent organic fish concentrate that can be used on a wide variety of plants. It may be applied to the soil or used for foliar feeding. Deodorized.

Dexol products are sold through distributors, but the company welcomes requests for catalogs and buying information. Write:
Dexol Industries
1450 West 228th Street
Torrance, CA 90501

The mini pill is a safe, easy way to keep your plants growing and healthy. The odorless tablets are just inserted in the soil; then the plants are watered normally.

Available in nurseries and garden centers. For information write:
The Dramm Company
Box 528
Manitowoc, WI 54220

Timed-release plant food by Unifeed is pre-measured for 6- to 9-inch pots and requires no mixing. Each feeding (there are 11 in each package) lasts three months. There are two formulations, one for leafy plants (14-7-7) and another for flowering plants (10-20-5). Included in each package is a "time to refeed" pot sticker. Available at retail outlets throughout the country.

Manufactured by:
Unifeed Division
Diamond Crystal Salt Company
Wilmington, MA 10887

Super-thrive is a complex of vitamins and hormones that many gardeners use to enhance the growth and overall appearance of their plants. While not a fertilizer, it promotes rapid plant growth and rooting, revives failing plants, and enhances plant color. Super-Thrive is available in a range of sizes, from 1/10 ounce (69 cents) to 90 gallons ($1,614). Each ounce makes up to 500 gallons of solution.

For brochure and mail-order information, write:
Vitamin Institute
5409-5415 Satsuma Avenue
Box 230
North Hollywood, Ca 91603

Hormex concentrate is a formulation of vitamins and hormones. It is useful in aiding general plant health, in keeping cut flowers fresh, and minimizing transplant shock. Look for Hormex in nurseries, garden centers, flower shops, and department stores.

For information write:
Brooker Chemical Corporation
Box 9335
North Hollywood, CA 91609

Houseplant food tablets provide fertilizer elements in a quick and easy form. Odorless tablets are just pushed into the soil. Will not burn even the youngest plants. 11-15-20 analysis.

African violet food is specifically formulated to produce healthy foliage and abundant flowers. 11-15-20 analysis.

Liquid houseplant food, a concentrate that readily dissolves in water, is an instant fertilizer. Suitable for all plants. 10-10-10 analysis.

Patio food can be used for all plants, flowers, and shrubs. Designed for the window-box gardener. Easy to use; just push tablets into soil. 13-26-13 analysis.

Plant marvel all-purpose plant food is a water-soluble fertilizer. It can be used with both indoor and outdoor plants and is suitable for foliar or root feeding. Dissolves quickly in water; goes to work immediately. 12-31-14 analysis.

Spring rain terrarium mist is a mineral-enriched, water-misting solution formulated for greener, more beautiful terrarium plants.

Spring rain indoor plant food is an all-purpose, ready-to-use fertilizer that produces healthy, balanced growth. No mixing is required; solution is poured directly into the soil. 1-3-1 analysis.

For free brochures and mail-order information, write:
**Plant Marvel Laboratories
624 West 119th Street
Chicago, IL 60628**

Osmocote and agriform are timed-release fertilizers in tablet form. Because of the slow release of nutrients, one tablet can feed a plant for three to eight months. Both products are available in nurseries and garden-supply centers.

For buying information write:
**Sierra Chemical Company
1001 Yosemite Drive
Milpitas, CA 95035**

Spoonit plant food is an all-purpose fertilizer in a highly concentrated form. It dissolves instantly in water and can be used on all types of plants, both indoors and out. Comes in re-sealable plastic container. 18-20-16 analysis with chelated iron.

Orchid spoonit is specifically designed for use with orchids grown in bark. It is a highly concentrated, water-soluble fertilizer. In re-sealable plastic container. 30-10-10 analysis.

For a free brochure and mail-order information, write:
**Plantsmith
1924 Plymouth Street
Mountain View, CA 94043**

Timed-release plant foods require no mixing and, when used correctly, eliminate the danger of overfeeding. In addition to a general-purpose plant food, and Precise timed-release African violet food, food for tomatoes, vegetables, flowers, and roses is available.

For information write:
**3M Company
Plant Care Systems
Box 33600
St. Paul, MN 55101**

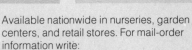

C-food is an organic plant food made entirely from sea fish. Easy to use; 1 tablespoon makes a gallon. 5-2-2 analysis.

Orchid food is a special 100 percent water-soluble plant food with a balanced 18-18-18 analysis, plus seven essential minor elements. One pound makes 100 gallons of orchid food.

Terrarium food is a special slow-release plant food, with one feeding lasting up to 12 months. Plants are fed safely, continuously. 18-6-12 analysis.

Aquarium plant food is a safe, easy way to make aquarium plants thrive without harming fish. 11-15-20 analysis.

Available nationwide in nurseries, garden centers, and retail stores. For mail-order information write:
**Plantabbs Corporation
Timonium, MD 21093**

Flower arranging

Arranging plant material in containers has been a pleasant means of decorating since the first colonial wives had homes in America. Most countries and eras have developed styles of arranging which reflect their customs, architecture, and the plants available.

In this country, flowers and foliage are arranged not only for special occasions and garden club shows, but also for the kitchen table. The latter type of arrangement, the casual, spontaneous bouquet, is probably enjoyed more than any of the others.

Arranging should be easy and natural. Much frustration can be prevented with the use of sturdy, sensible tools. The arranger should not be intimidated by rules. Rules should be only guidelines which suggest rather than dictate the methods and reasons behind most arranging.

Begin with small arrangements to get the feel of a variety of plant material. This practice builds confidence as well as the ability to make larger arrangements. Familiar plants that grow in the yard are the easiest to use since they can be gathered in any size and their growth habits can be understood.

Start with the easiest

The simplest arrangement is the one that does not appear arranged, such as a handful of the last fall flowers brought in from the garden before frost. Calendulas, a couple of gaillardias and a stem of chrysanthemums would be natural in a pottery vase with a narrow neck and no room for a holder. The beauty of these flowers can be emphasized if a little thought is used to place them in the vase. Sharp clippers or a knife would be the only equipment needed.

The stem of chrysanthemums probably would be the largest and fullest, so it should be first in the vase to hold the other stems. A few of the most branching stems might be cut off to prevent catching later additions. The calendulas and gaillardias could go in next, toward the center of the arrangement for a focal point. A few sprigs of goldenrod or grass might be placed in and around the few flowers to tie them together as a group. Taller spiked pieces of goldenrod or grass can provide height for this simple arrangement.

More complicated arrangements

The same techniques can be translated into larger arrangements. With more flowers and a vase with a wider mouth, a pinholder or frog would be needed to secure the plant material. The largest holder which will fit into a vase is the best, because it will not be as likely to move nor need to be fastened. Oasis is useful for glass bowls and arrangements that must travel. However, it is not easy to add fresh water to oasis or to place heavy stems into it.

The basic components of a large arrangement are the foliage plus at least three flower forms to avoid monotony. The three forms are the spike, the round massive flower, and the small filler flower.

Placing plant material in a vase should follow a logical order. Secure the heaviest and largest stems first. These are usually the foliage. Leafy material is fine for covering pinholders, for beginning to shape the arrangement, and for blending the flowers together.

Spiked flowers should be next, for they define height, width, and dimension. If the spikes are not placed in an outline shape, but at varying heights and throughout the arrangement, a pleasing sense of depth will be gained. Large rounded flowers should be more toward the center, and low for visual stability. Dark colors also give the feeling of weight. These round, dark colored flowers, if placed toward the center, will draw the eye there, creating balance.

The final touch to the arrangement are the filler flowers. A flower head made of many smaller flowers, placed throughout the other flowers, fills gaps and unifies, just as the foliage did. The size and color of the flowers should work with the room and the vase in which they are being placed. Flower colors can draw attention to paintings and fabrics in a room or clash with them. Unity and proper color use are easy to achieve if a few flowers are taken into the room before they are all cut.

If flowers are not available in the forms recommended, variety can be found in the various stages of maturity of one flower. Buds which are slender and slightly pointed can be substituted for a spike. A vase of bright yellow coreopsis can have as much variety and beauty as a mixture of larkspur, marigolds, day lilies, and Queen Anne's lace.

A home arrangement, no matter what size or style it is, should reflect the personality of the arranger. Choices of color, favorite flowers, and design of vases all combine to make an individual arrangement.

Arrangements go together with ease if plant material is fresh, if the proper equipment is at hand, and if thought has been given to location of the arrangement. Although, ideally, a good flower arranger would be a person with a knowledge of horticulture and art, any person who enjoys working with flowers becomes aware of these fields along with a growing enthusiasm and talent for arranging.

Libbey Hodges

Libbey Hodges is supervisor of the flower section at Colonial Williamsburg. She is responsible for dried materials, flower arrangements in the exhibition buildings, and special workshop demonstrations.

Books

Sheila McQueen's Encyclopedia of Flower Arranging, by Sheila McQueen, Faber and Faber, London, England, 1967. Out of print.

Flower Arranging, by Helen Chase, Octopus Books, 59 Grosvenor St., London, W1X 9DA, England, 1975, $5.98.

The Flower World of Williamsburg, by Joan Parry Dutton, Holt, Rinehart and Winston, 383 Madison Ave., New York, New York 10017, 1973, paperback, 128 pages, $5.95. A house-by-house, garden-by-garden tour of Colonial Williamsburg. Various colonial flower arrangements and an historical account of the flowers are included along with 40 color photographs.

The Complete Flower Arranger, by Amalie A. Ascher, Simon and Schuster, 630 Fifth Ave., Rockefeller Center, New York, New York 10020, 1974, hardbound, 288 pages, $9.95. A comprehensive view of flower arrangements in step-by-step photographs. Ranges from the basics of design to analyzing all the different techniques of floral arrangement. Also included are tips on arranging fruits and vegetables.

Designing with Flowers, Brooklyn Botanic Garden, 100 Washington Ave., Brooklyn, New York 11225. Order No. 80, $1.75 postpaid.

The basics of flower arranging

1. Spiked flowers are tall, and are used to establish height, width, and depth in an arrangement. Popular spiked flowers are delphiniums, larkspurs, gladiolus, snapdragons, and roses.

2. Massive flowers are usually placed toward the center for a focal point. Typical massive flowers are: chrysanthemums, carnations, poppies, dahlias, asters, and large daisies.

3. Filler flowers and foliage fill gaps. Most often used are: heather, baby's breath, French hyacinths, azaleas, trumpet grass, stephanotis, ferns, clover, and boxwoods.

History of flower arrangement

There is much evidence that flower arranging has been going on throughout the ages. In 3000 B.C., the Egyptians worshipped Ra, the Sun God. He was symbolized by a lotus that held the sun within its petals. Tomb paintings depict bowls of lotus used in decorative arrangements and carried by priests and maidens in processions. The Greeks and Romans used flowers in garlands and crowned victors with wreaths of laurel and flowers.

In sixth-century Japan, flower arranging took on importance as a priestly art. Closely associated with Buddhist religious practices, it remained in the temples for several hundred years. Later, in the fifteenth century, it spread from the priests to the aristocracy and commoners in the form of the tea ceremony, which was accompanied by a picture scroll and flower arrangement.

Nothing was heard of flower arranging in the Western world from the fall of Rome until the Italian Renaissance in the fifteenth century, when Italian gardens became famous for their beauty of design and lavish flower effects.

Flowers as art

After the Dark Ages, flowers became a theme for artists. Seventeenth-century Flemish painters were lavish in their now-famous flower paintings; eighteenth-century French painters featured a lighter, more airy effect. The French painters Fragonard and Watteau give us a clue to this elegant, romantic, and softly colored style.

If flowers on canvas were appreciated, so were living arrangements. Georgian silver bowls and epergnes, Waterford crystal, English, Delft, and Chinese porcelain provided containers for the elegant mass bouquets of the English great houses. The English style can still be seen at the restoration of Williamsburg, Virginia.

In the Victorian era, when flower arranging became a grand pastime, the nosegay bouquet was popular. Also in favor were massed flower arrangements in ornate containers.

Twentieth-century developments

Later, in twentieth-century Japan, the moribana, or nature-sketch flower arrangements, were developed. These are made in low containers and utilize the needlepoint holders now commonly used in America. After World War II, Japanese arrangers turned to modern abstract and semi-abstract designs. This was due to the introduction of modern Western art into the Japanese culture. Traditional flower masters did not relate to these designs, which make use of cut-off branches, criss-crossed stems and unnatural materials.

In today's Japan, both classical and modern forms survive—a happy occurrence for all who love beauty without having to label it.

In the early part of the twentieth century, the Western world suddenly discovered the art of Japanese flower arranging. Americans could not accept intact most of the symbolic Japanese design principles because

Flower arranging forms

Horizontal

L-Shape

Basic triangle

they had no meanings for them. New line designs were adapted, such as the L, crescent, hogarth, horizontal, vertical, and spiral. A new style, combining the line feeling of the Orient with some of the mass quality of the European arrangements, was created. This form can properly be called the mass-line style of flower arranging, a distinctly American style.

New casualness

A recent trend in American flower arranging is a style reminiscent of the eighteenth century, which features an overall bouquet effect. This style employs a variety of flowers and colors in a circular or oval bouquet which can be placed on a dining-room table, coffee table, or chest. The elegantly casual effect conveyed by this style of arranging fits beautifully into our present mode of living, because it blends with modern, traditional, or contemporary decor.

Americans are becoming more interested in using flowers as decorative accessories, and they will continue to be used, not only for their own loveliness, but to bring the beauty of nature indoors.

Raymond T. Fox

Raymond T. Fox is a professor of horticulture at Cornell University in Ithaca, New York. He teaches floral design classes, and has also written newspaper and magazine articles and extension bulletins on the subject.

Supplies & equipment

Flower arranging supplies from Dorothy Biddle Service include an assortment of needlepoint and hairpin holders, floral clays, florist's wire and tape, plus corsage supplies.

For mail-order catalog send 10 cents to:
Dorothy Biddle Service
DBS Building, Dept. TC
Hawthorne, NY 10532

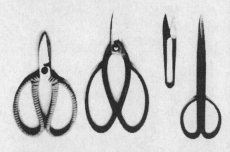

Floral Art's mail-order catalog features everything a flower arranger might need, from vases to bases, pruners, shears, and a selection of garden supplies. Also included: a very extensive list of flower-arranging and gardening books.

For the catalog send 50 cents to:
Floral Art
Box 1985
Springfield, MA 01101

Flower arranging supplies from Boycan include floral tape, clay, and wire. Also: bouquet holders, vases, baskets, oasis, wired picks, and corsage supplies.

For mail-order catalog send $1.00 to:
Boycan's Craft Supplies
Mail-Order Division
Box 897
Sharon, PA 16146

Pop-up vase, a silvery, shimmering foil cardboard vase, comes with a plastic liner and instantly folds together.

For mail-order information write:
Souhan Design
Box 36384
Dallas, TX 75235

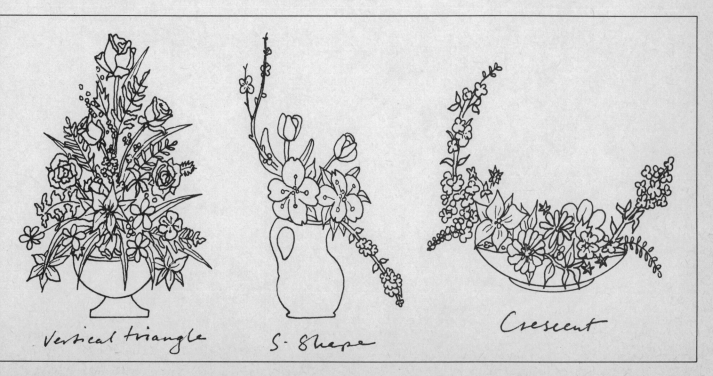

Vertical triangle

S- Shape

Crescent

Flowering gift plants

Flowering plants are always a welcome gift. Many of these plants have colorful flowers which last for days or even weeks, if given proper care. These plants make fine choices for offices, public buildings, and homes.

Make them last longer

You don't need a green thumb to make a blooming plant last a long time. Here are a few pointers to help give them proper care:

1. Give them bright light; direct sunlight is not needed.
2. Give them cool temperatures.
3. Keep them out of drafts.
4. Keep soil moist, but not soggy.

Most flowering plants require lots of light. Windows with east, south, or west exposures make excellent locations. Plants placed in low light or poor light will tend towards sunlight, if available. Turning plants weekly will help maintain a symmetrical growth.

Houseplants will do well if they are kept in a bright location with a temperature range of 65 to 75 degrees F. during the day and 50 to 55 degrees F. at night. Placing in a cool location at night will assure longer lasting flowers. Windowsill locations may have lower temperatures than the rest of the home.

Don't put your plant in a draft of hot or cold air such as those from hot air registers, radiators, or air conditioners. Air constantly moving past the plant dries it out faster than the roots can take up water, and the plant might suffer.

Flowering plants should have moderate soil moisture. Roots should not be allowed to get soggy. Plant roots must have air as well as water. Be careful that water is not standing in the bottom of the pot if it has no drainage hole.

Let the surface of the soil dry out between waterings; then apply enough water to soak the entire soil ball until the water runs through the drainage hole in the pot. Dunking the pot in a bucket or deep pan until the air bubbles stop is a quick way to replenish soil moisture. Allow all excess water to drain, and throw away this water. Don't let the pot sit in water.

Greenhouse conditions cannot be duplicated in the home. For most of the potted plants, it is probably best to discard them after they have flowered. The following cultural information is provided as a guide of how to buy and care for some common flowering florist plants.

James K. Rathmell

James Rathmell is a professor of horticulture at Pennsylvania State University. He has spent a good deal of time in England, researching and bringing back various plants for propagation and study.

Hydrangea plants require much water, especially when in bloom. The blooms last longer when the plant is kept cool at night. It does not need direct sunlight, but needs plenty of light.

Calceolaria and **cineraria** should be purchased with buds and open flowers. These plants require a bright location and abundant moisture. When given a night temperature of 50 degrees F., they will last for an extended period. Both of these plants are annuals and should be discarded after blooming.

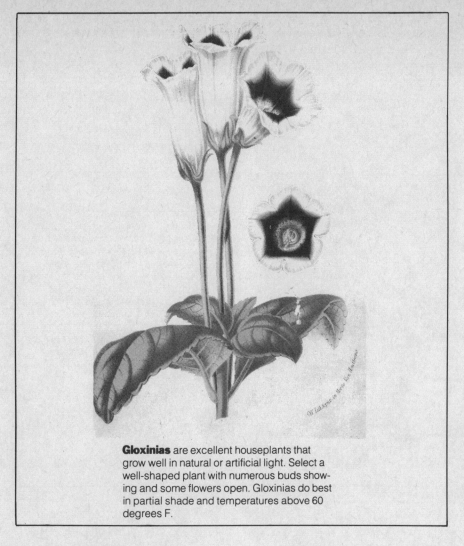

Gloxinias are excellent houseplants that grow well in natural or artificial light. Select a well-shaped plant with numerous buds showing and some flowers open. Gloxinias do best in partial shade and temperatures above 60 degrees F.

Easter lily selection should be based on a plant that has one or two flower buds that have opened. The remaining buds will open over a period of time. Remove the old flowers as they wilt.

Give the plant bright light and abundant moisture. A night temperature of 60 degrees F. is preferable. After the plant turns brown, cut it off at the soil line, and plant it outdoors when the ground warms up.

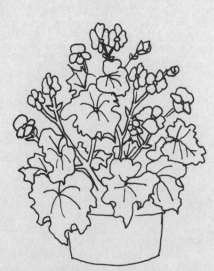

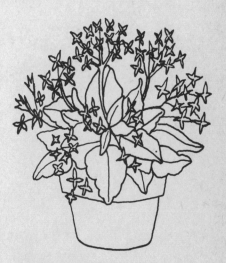

Rieger begonias, developed in Germany, are now available in all parts of this country. The large blooms provide vivid color over a very long flowering season. The plants should not be placed in direct sunlight. Watering should be moderate. This is an excellent houseplant.

Jerusalem cherry and **ornamental pepper** are purchased when the fruit is ripe. Keep the plants in full sun during the day and give them a night temperature of 55 degrees F. Do not allow the soil to dry out.

Kalanchoes are available year round in some areas of the United States. New varieties with pastel shades help make this an attractive pot plant. The plants should be kept in full sunshine, if possible. Allow the soil to dry out between waterings. The flowers are long lasting, especially when kept in a cool room.

Azaleas last longest if purchased with many buds and only a few open flowers. Bright light or direct sunlight and a constant moisture supply are preferred. Azaleas require large quantities of water, as often as twice a day. The soil ball should never be allowed to dry.

Plants should not be placed in too dark a location. No fertilization is needed during the flowering season. The plants will keep well and long if they are in the coolest part of the room. A majority of the florist azaleas are not hardy in the colder areas of the country.

Poinsettias are purchased when in full bloom. They are one of the most striking holiday plants. Many of the new cultivars will retain their colorful bracts for weeks.

Place plants in a warm sunny window, and do not allow the soil to dry out. Poinsettias are sensitive to sudden changes in temperature, improper watering, and low light intensities. Temperatures over 75 degrees F. will shorten the life of the blooms.

Cyclamen have hidden buds under the foliage. Select a plant that has many buds as well as some open flowers.

Do not overwater as it is sensitive to excess watering. If allowed to wilt at high temperatures, however, the foilage may turn yellow.

The cooler the cyclamen is kept, the longer it will last. If kept at 65 degrees F. or higher for an extended period of time, all the buds will flower in a very short time.

Gardenia is an attractive flowering and foliage plant. Select a well-budded plant that has some open blooms. The gardenia plant is a challenging plant to grow.

The key to an attractive plant in the home is high humidity. A gardenia grown in low humidity may form flower buds, but they will fall before opening. High humidity may be maintained by misting or placing the pot in a tray containing pebbles and water. The bottom of the pot should be above the water level.

Gardenias are very exacting in temperature requirements. If the night temperature is above 65 degrees F. the flower buds will drop. If below 60 degrees F. the foliage turns yellow.

Fragrant plants

Gardenia

Jasmine

Meyer's lemon

With many years spent in working at an institution for blind and deaf-blind pupils, and a lifetime of thinking and writing, lecturing and discussing, and gardening indoors and out, I am convinced that too few people are aware of the reactions and interactions of our five senses—sight, sound, touch, taste and smell. Other chapters in this book are discussing the beauty of houseplants, perhaps some are mentioning the pleasant sounds of rustling leaves of large palms and the like, while a discussion of cacti or velvety foliage may tell about touch, or another may discuss the houseplants useful for improving the taste of foods, but tying them all together, there should be fragrance.

With the fragrance which comes from our garden and indoor plant life, there are three basic values. First is the simple matter of pleasure, as an opening hyacinth in January overwhelms us, or the rosemary-laden spiciness of roasting meat tingles our nose. Next, and perhaps most valu-

able, is the nostalgia which comes over us as the sudden smell of one thing or another takes us back to childhood or some happy incident in our lives. And third is the therapeutic value of fragrances—something just being recognized by the medical profession.

From an experiment made in Texas a few years ago, the doctor made the observation that: "We established fairly accurately that when a pleasant odor was disseminated in the room, not only did the patient's mental attitude brighten and the appetite build up, but fuller cooperation in following routine instructions occurred."

And to this, as a recommendation for fragrant plants, one can simply observe the known value of fine perfumes for adding to the attractiveness of men and women, or the value of incense, long used by the most important religious faiths.

All of this is well said by the finest of English garden writers, Reginald Farrar, when he writes: "What folly to ignore the curative, the stimulant

powers of scent! I defy anyone to remain mumpish, groovy, or fanatical in a room full of primroses."

What, then, are the kinds of plants which may be grown in the house, or the small attached home greenhouse, to provide the fragrances which will achieve pleasure, nostalgia, and other effects on the mind and body?

First, for delight, would be a climbing shrub called the wax-plant, *Hoya carnosa,* and a second would be one of the several kinds of jasmine, *Jasminum grandiflorum* and others, all with a floral sweetness which needs to be taken *en passant* as close breathing of overpowering fragrances often quickly stifles the sense of smell. Another sweet climber would be *Stephanotis floribunda,* which I used to grow, when I was a florist, for making wedding bouquets.

Also make a place for the forcing of the fragrant "Dutch" bulbs. Potted in October, stored in a cold frame or refrigerator to make roots, and then brought to room temperatures, one can easily have a continuation for several months of flowers of fragrant narcissus, hyacinths, and freesias. The small-flowered French-Roman hyacinths are perhaps nicer than the huge heads of the regular type. My favorite member of the narcissus group is a variety called Cragford, with small white and scarlet flowers; then, too, there are the well-known "paper-whites."

One plant much desired by indoor gardeners is the gardenia. Another choice-scented thing is the common heliotrope.

Also, within the orchid family there are some that are fragrant; the fragrant varieties are usually noted in the orchid catalogs. Another plant with fragrant flowers is *Osmanthus fragrans*; while the true European myrtle, *Myrtus communis*, has pungent leaves.

Certainly essential for the home would be a plant each of rosemary and lemon verbena, which, whether for smelling or flavoring, are nice plants. Another I like is the pineapple sage, *Salvia rutilans*. And if you've a cool, sunny room, the common nasturtium is worth a trial, both for fragrant flowers and for tasty salad leaves.

All of the above are possibilities, but if I were to mention one group as being certainties, it would be the scented-leaved geraniums. Of course here we would have no notable flowers to sniff, but always the chance to please our nose with a crushed leaf. Certainly, most people know of geraniums as a bright summer flower, but not so many know about the scented ones (it is better to call them by their scientific name, the *pelargoniums*). There are a number of these, but some of the sweet ones are:

> *Pelargonium graveolens:*
> rose scented
> *Pelargonium quercifolium:*
> oak leaf
> *Pelargonium tomentosum:*
> peppermint
> *Pelargonium denticulum:*
> pine scented
> *Pelargonium fragrans:*
> strong scented
> *Pelargonium crispum:*
> lemon scented

From this list of the fragrant species you will find some, among the variations of each, which will be valuable not only for a quick sniff, but useful for culinary purposes. The nicely cut leaves of the rose geraniums are wonderful to use to flavor jellies (and are so used in my home for tomato jam), while the small leaves of the lemon-scented are nice for finger bowls. And any of the species are a good source for some quick-to-be-cut-foliage for a table bouquet.

In all of this, no mention has been made of roses, and yet there is today a rapidly improving list of really dwarf roses which, under some of the better indoor growing conditions, could make a good hobby for the plant lover, and would provide sweetness as well as the beauty for which the rose is famous. Investigate dwarf roses as you organize your indoor growing plants.

But if this is not possible, and you still want the fragrance for which the rose is famous, why not do what has been done for centuries before, and that is make a potpourri or rose jar. This is something to give you a summer garden objective when your houseplants are out-of-doors, and the winter results will be more than pleasing, as you open the jar for sweetening your home or showing off as an indoor decoration.

In reviewing all of these suggestions, it is regrettable that not more of our many houseplants are fragrant ones, but perhaps one would not want a conglomeration of fragrant plants around for the nasal confusion they might engender. Instead, choose only two or three to add a special dimension to your indoor plants.

Nelson Coon

Nelson Coon has worked throughout his long life as a florist, nursery owner, groundskeeper, and natural-history museum curator. He has written seven books, numerous articles for gardening magazines, and a column for The Boston Herald. *In recent years, he has also had a daily radio show devoted to gardening lore and advice. In 1973 he was honored for his career by the American Horticultural Society.*

Heliotrope

Potpourris

A potpourri is a mixture of dried flowers, herbs, and spices used to impart a subtle fragrance to a room or closet. You can place the mixture in an open container such as a glass bowl or straw basket. You can even make soothing scented pillows by stuffing them with a bulky (uncrushed) mixture. Smaller pillows, stuffed with crushed ingredients, can be used as sachets and tucked away in drawers or closets.

To make your own potpourri, combine several herbs, flower petals, and spices, choosing them for their colors and shapes as well as their fragrances.

Rose petals	Sweet bay
Rose geranium leaves	Thyme
Lavender flowers	Mint
Rosemary	Star anise
Crushed whole cloves	Sage
Cinnamon	Camomile
Allspice	Angelica
Verbena	Eucalyptus leaves
Marjoram	

Books

Fragrance and Fragrant Plants for House and Garden, by Nelson Coon, Diversity Books, Grandview, Missouri 64030, 1967, hardbound, 235 pages, $7.95. Directed at the senses, this book defines and classifies fragrances and fragrant plants. Included are descriptions of fragrant plants, shrubs and trees for the garden as well as the house. The book contains 30 photographs.

The Fragrant Year, by Helen Van Pelt Wilson and Leonie Bell, William Morrow and Co., 105 Madison Ave., New York, New York 10016, 1967, paperback, 306 pages, $4.95. Included in this book are classifications of different scents, what flowers smell sweetest in each season, and advice on growing and caring for fragrant flowers indoors and outdoors.

Potpourri, Incense and Other Fragrant Concoctions, by Ann Tucker, Workman Publishing Company, 231 E. 51st St., New York, New York 10022, 1972, paperback, 96 pages, $2.45. Includes a discussion on the nature of scent and the elements and ingredients of perfume, plus recipes for potpourri, sachets, toilet waters, incense, candles, and pomanders.

Free plants

Do you yearn for a roomful of lush, tropical plants—but your appetite is bigger than your pocketbook? Would you like a taste of adventure without leaving your armchair? Then put your eating habits to work by starting free plants from the cast-off parts of unsuspecting fruits and vegetables. Apples, mangoes, potatoes, pineapples, avocados, lemons, oranges, gooseberries, sunflowers, peanuts, grapes, papayas, and more—all are potential plants for a pittance.

Make no mistake: not all are as easy as plopping a relatively neglected avocado pit in a glass of water. Some seeds and pits must be washed, dried, and coddled as carefully as a newborn baby. Some can only be coaxed out of dormancy by exposure to low temperatures. And although some seeds will sprout in a few days or weeks, others require months, and some, for one reason or another, will never sprout at all.

But take heart. There's hope for the free-plant gardener. The authors of the books in this section have done most of the hard work for you, and perfected the art of getting something for nothing. Just follow their advice and you, too, will be pruning your own four-foot-high lemon tree down to a more manageable size, a firm believer that the best plants in life are free.

Nancy Bruning

Books

The After Dinner Gardening Book, by Richard W. Langer, Collier Books, Division of Macmillan Publishing Co., 866 Third Ave., New York, New York 10022, 1971, paperback, 198 pages, $1.50. For the indoor gardener, this book provides an easy step-by-step guide on how to grow your own plants from the pits and seeds of such common fruits as pineapples, avocados, artichokes, grapes, and bananas. Uncommon fruits included are papayas, loquats, and even coconuts.

The Avocado Pit Grower's Indoor How-To Book, by Hazel Perper, Walker and Co., 720 Fifth Ave., New York, New York 10019, 1965, hardbound, 64 pages, $3.95.

The Citrus Seed Grower's Indoor How-To Book, by Hazel Perper, Dodd, Mead and Company, 79 Madison Ave., New York, New York 10016, 1971, hardbound, 64 pages, $3.95.

The Indoor How-To Book of Oats, Peas, Beans, and Other Pretty Plants, by Hazel Perper, The Viking Press, 625 Madison Ave., New York, New York 10022, 1975, hardbound, 64 pages, $4.95.

Germinating fruit pits

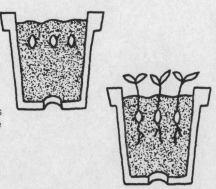

General procedure
Use 4- to 5-inch pots and standard potting soil for most plants. Depending on their size, plant one to four pits (well washed) per pot, burying them about twice as deep as the pits are long. For example, orange pits should be covered with ½ inch of soil. Place the pots in a warm (70 degrees F.) location with indirect light. When the pits send up shoots (3 to 4 weeks for most plants), move them to a brightly lit spot.

When the plants are 4 inches tall, transplant them into individual pots, being careful not to injure tender roots.

You can use almost any fruit pit to grow your own miniature version of the tree from which the fruit came. Those most often used are: oranges, lemons, grapefruit, limes, dates, litchis, mangoes, cherries, peaches, plums, pomegranates, apricots, nectarines, and apples. Just be sure you start with pits from fresh fruits; canned, cooked or dried fruit pits will usually not grow.

Pineapples

1. Slice off the top of the pineapple about two inches below the leaves.

2. Trim off the outer skin and fruit, up to the hard, stringy core. Let the fruit dry out for a few days to prevent rotting.

3. Insert the core in moistened, sterilized, fast-draining potting mix. Pineapples are bromeliads, so keep the plant in a warm (about 65 to 70 degrees F.), light location, and mist the leaves regularly. As it takes root, the leaves will come out from the center.

Avocados

1. Carefully slice the fruit open to avoid cutting into the pit. Remove as much skin as possible and wash the pit in plain water. Insert three or four wooden toothpicks and suspend

the pit over a glass of water. Make sure the bottom ½ inch of the pit (flat end) is under water. (You could also plant the pit directly into a 5-inch pot as described in Step 3, but this seems to slow down the germination.)

2. Place the glass in a warm, dimly-lit location. Replace the water as it evaporates. Soon you will see roots growing in the water; next, a stem with a few small leaves will appear at the top.

 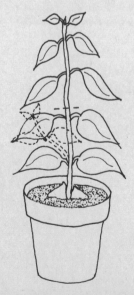

3. When the plant is 3 to 4 inches high, plant it in a 5-inch pot. Use a sandy potting mixture and leave one quarter of the pit sticking up out of the soil. At this point, move the plant to a sunny location.

4. To encourage bushiness, cut the stem in half when it reaches a height of 5 to 6 inches. The plant will send out more side shoots and take on a fuller appearance if you continue pinching out the growing tips.

Supplies & equipment

Ceramic avocado planter provides the perfect home for your avocado pit.

For mail-order information write:
Door 26
3131 Southwest Freeway
Houston, TX 77098

Sweet potato planter comes with a special container, sisal hanger, and bracket. All elements designed especially for growing a beautiful hanging plant. Complete with instruction folder.

For buying information write:
Christen
59 Branch Street
St. Louis, MO 63147

74

Gardening under lights

Raising plants in the home is becoming a way of life—part of the atmosphere and decoration—and has come a long way from the tired sansevieria on the kitchen windowsill or the dusty palm in a dark corner. Many types of plants do very well in the home with good natural light, but as plant growers learn more about plant culture, they develop more sophisticated tastes and long for the more unusual—the blooming or the harder-to-grow tropicals. These are becoming more easily available to the average grower, but success is not always that easy. The solution is simple, however, for fluorescent light will make your plants grow and bloom beautifully, and a light garden will also decorate your home.

The basic light garden

For a basic light garden all you need is a 2- or 4-foot industrial 2-tube fixture with a reflector and two fluorescent tubes—Deluxe Cool White and Deluxe Warm White (used on a 1 to 1 ratio) being the least expensive, most available, and completely satisfactory. Hang the fixture over a table or bench, or attach under a cupboard or shelf; then provide yourself with a waterproof tray the size of your fixture, and fill with fine gravel, coarse sand, or vermiculite, which is kept half-filled with water for humidity, which should be at least 50 percent; attach a timer to turn the lights on and off—a 14- to 16-hour day is recommended. Invest in a tiny fan to keep the warm, moist air circulating gently; add your plants and, providing you resolve to give the plants a proper watering and fertilizing program and keep them pest and disease free, you are growing under lights. It's as easy as that, and it's fun!

Which plants to grow?

Now, what can you grow? Anything—from carrots to orchids, from rhododendrons to pine trees. Of course you have to have the right environmental conditions for the types of plants you choose to grow. Rhododendrons will not thrive in your living room but will be easy to propagate in cool conditions under lights (with bottom heat of about 70 degrees F.), and vegetables and annuals can be started under lights to get a jump on spring. Non-hardy ornamentals, such as some varieties of camellias, can be grown in containers and brought in from the garden in the fall and grown under lights in a cool basement.

To grow most tropical blooming plants, such as all types of gesneriads, crossandra, oxalis, cuphea, begonias, some orchids, succulents of all kinds, and so forth, you will need a minimum of two tubes for every foot of bench or table depth, or 20 watts per square foot. If you wish to grow harder-to-bloom plants, four to six tubes may be needed.

Light fixtures need not be strictly utilitarian, as we have described above, for there are all types of commercially made fixtures available, ranging from handsome pieces of furniture to movable carts. Fixtures may be placed in bookcases, unused fireplaces, china cupboards, under tables or in north-facing bay windows. Vallances, or shields made of wood or a suitable material, are used to soften any glare that might reach a seated guest. Spotlights are attractive means to light foliage plants in dark corners, and an attractive hanging lamp may be used for supplemental light over a group of plants or a terrarium. Incandescent light—such as spot lights or regular light bulbs—maintains foliage plants but should only be used as supplemental light for most others.

Propagating new plants from seed or cuttings is easy and fast under fluorescent light. All you need to do is place the cuttings or seed in or on damp vermiculite in a covered plastic bread or shoe box and place close to the lights in your warmest spot. Most cuttings will root in two to three weeks, with seeds taking various times for germination. When cuttings are rooted or the seedlings are up, slowly harden them off by removing the cover a little bit every day.

Light gardeners have found that growing plants in a soilless mix is convenient and successful. The ingredients are easy to buy, easy to mix and, most important, sterile. Various combinations of sphagnum peat moss, horticultural vermiculite and perlite are combined according to the plant's needs. A regular fertilization program, using a very dilute solution (1/10 to 1/8 of the strength recommended on the bottle or can of fertilizer) with each watering, should be maintained.

Pat Morrison

Pat Morrison grows tropical plants—especially orchids, gesneriads, and begonias—both under lights and in the greenhouse. A chapter organizer and regional vice-president of the Indoor Light Gardening Society of America, Pat is founder of her local light gardening chapter.

A light garden in the kitchen

If you would like to increase your gardening space, but don't want to get involved in any construction, the lighting unit shown here provides an ideal solution. It consists of a reflector-type utility fixture, which comes complete with screwholes drilled in it, and two fluorescent tubes. By mounting the fixture to the underside of a cabinet and arranging your plants on a counter underneath, you can create an indoor garden in just a few hours. Two things to note, even in a garden this simple, are: 1. Put your plants on pebble-lined trays and keep the trays filled with water to just below the top layer of pebbles. This provides the humidity plants need without letting them sit in water. 2. Use a timer. Most plants need between 14 and 16 hours of light each day. A timer, set to turn the lights on and off, will forestall your forgetting to do this.

Garden courtesy of Mrs. Lew Egal

Build a light garden

When indoor gardeners dream of the ideal artificial light unit, it is one that is attractive as well as functional; one that can grow plants with varying light requirements; one that can be adjusted to accommodate growing plants; and finally, one that minimizes muss and fuss.

Mrs. Berland is a Manhattan gardener and her light garden fills the bill admirably on all counts. With a little planning, you can build a system like it, modifying it as you like to fit your own gardening needs.

The basic garden unit consists of three shelves. The top shelf rests on top of the unit. The adjustable middle shelf rests on expanding aluminum rods (available at hardware and plumbing-supply stores) and is illuminated by four fluorescent tubes attached to the underside of the top shelf. The bottom shelf rests on braces at the bottom of the unit and is lighted

by just two tubes, whose light is amplified by a reflector fixture.

Plants on the bottom two shelves rest on eggcrate louvers (from lighting-supply and plastic stores) set into plastic trays (sold at gardening-supply stores). When the plants are watered, the excess drains through the louvers to rest in the tray. This frees the gardener from the task of emptying out saucers, while providing the humidity level the plants need.

The unit is 51 inches wide to accommodate the fixtures for the 48-inch long tubes, and 19 inches deep to hold the four-tube fixture that lights the middle shelf. The Berlands used 1-by-2-inch lumber for braces. The shelves are ½-inch plywood edged with 1-by-2-inch strips. The basic frame was constructed with nails and reinforced with angle-iron braces.

Ready-to-assemble units

Elegant-but-easy indoor gardens are hard to come by. The unit shown at right is an exception to the rule. The secret lies in two factors. For one, the legs are actually snap-apart units that can be put together into any desired height (they are supplied in standard 12-, 18-, 22-, and 24-inch lengths). The second advantage is that the shelves are bought separately in any desired length and width. The result? A unit that can be assembled in very short order, but looks 100 percent custom-built.

The one shown here belongs to Mrs. Lew Egal of New York, who says it was literally a snap to put it together. At the lumberyard where she bought the shelves, she had them cut to size and drilled with holes for the legs (both services are standard at good

lumberyards). From there it was simply a matter of joining legs to shelves to establish the basic unit.

To turn it into a light garden proper, Mrs. Egal mounted two fluorescent tubes on the underside of each shelf. All the lights are plugged into a strip outlet that is placed on the middle shelf of the unit; the lights are turned on and off by a timer. In addition to the lights, Mrs. Egal added paneling to the front of the shelves to coordinate the unit with the room and to hide the light fixtures from view.

The snap-apart legs were purchased from Channel Lumber in New Jersey. Comparable units can be purchased at good lumber yards. Many garden centers also carry premade or ready-to-assemble units.

Gardening Indoors Under Lights, by Frederick H. Kranz and Jacqueline L. Kranz, The Viking Press, 625 Madison Ave., New York, New York 10022, 1971, hardbound, 259 pages, $7.95. The Kranzes were pioneers in the field, but, in spite of revision, the book is dated and makes light gardening seem much more difficult than it is.

The Complete Book of Gardening Under Lights, by Elvin McDonald, Doubleday and Co., 245 Park Ave., New York, New York 10017, 1965, hardbound, 204 pages, $6.95, paperback, $1.50. Good cultural information; however, information on lights and on the newer hybrids is dated.

The Complete Book of Houseplants Under Lights, by Charles Marden Fitch, Hawthorn Books, 260 Madison Ave., New York, New York 10016, 1975, hardbound, 260 pages, $9.95. An up-to-date, excellent source of information on all phases of light gardening and plants to grow under lights.

Fluorescent Light Gardening, by Elaine C. Cherry, Van Nostrand Reinhold Co., 450 W. 33rd St., New York, New York 10001, 1965, hardbound, 245 pages, $7.95. The very best of the early books; recently reprinted but not revised. Good plans for fixtures and light stands; excellent cultural information, but lamp information is dated. Still an excellent reference.

The Indoor Light Gardening Book, by George A. Elbert, Crown Publishers, One Park Ave., New York, New York 10017, 1973, hardbound, $10.95, paperback, $5.95. Excellent source of information on everything from fixtures to plants; includes plant sources and culture.

Learn To Grow Under Fluorescent Lights, by Pat Morrison, Indoor Light Gardening Society of America, 128 W. 58th St., New York, New York 10019, 1974, paperback, 22 pages, $1.50. A cultural bulletin published by the Indoor Light Gardening Society; includes good basic information for beginners.

Societies

The Indoor Lighting Society of America, 423 Powell Drive, Bay Village, Ohio 44140. The Society started in 1966 as a round-robin group with The Gloxinia Society. The major purpose of the Society is growing any type plant under lights and using lights in new endeavors in horticultural therapy.

Membership is $5.00 per year ($7.50 in foreign countries) and is open to anyone interested in the Society. Membership includes a subscription to the *Light Garden*, the Society's bimonthly magazine, access to cultural guides, seeds, and films.

A biannual convention is held in October in various cities across the United States.

Supplies & equipment

Shadegro, a fixture for use with 48-inch fluorescent tubes, has specially designed reflectors that deliver four times more light to plants than conventional fixtures. The fixture can be mounted on chrome-plated legs (optional) or hung from walls or ceilings.

Nitegro, a special high intensity lamp covering 4 x 8 feet, is for house gardeners or plant hobbyists lighting a larger than usual area.

For mail-order information write:
JD-21 Lighting Systems
1840 130th Avenue Northeast, Suite 7
Bellevue, WA 98005.

The Floralite Company stocks a wide range of equipment for growing plants with artificial light. They offer stands holding two, four, and eight trays, light fixtures, switches, and timers: tabletop and ceiling-hung reflectors; a full range of brand-name fluorescent tubes and incandescent bulbs.

For brochures and mail-order information, send a 13-cent stamp to:
Floralite Company
4124 East Oakwood Road
Oak Creek, WI 53154.

The Green House carries a complete line of indoor plant light equipment including plant stands and hanging and wall-mounted fixtures. The *Fun Sun* brand and their own *Gro-Cart* plant stands come in both stationary and movable models that feature adjustable lights, metal or wood construction, and various sizes and finishes.

For mail-order information and free brochure, write:
The Green House
9515 Flower Street
Bellflower, CA 90706.

Gro & Sho is a whole family of incandescent and fluorescent plant lights that can be used both to highlight your plants and to keep them growing. The incandescents are available as 50, 75, and 150-watt reflector floodlights and as a 60-watt bulb. The fluorescent tubes are available in 15-, 20-, 30- and 40-watt sizes.

Gro & Sho is manufactured by General Electric and is available in retail stores throughout the country. For a complimentary copy of *Listen To Your Plants*, a booklet of helpful advice on growing plants indoors, write:
General Electric Company
Department #1180.20PL, Nela Park
Cleveland, OH 44112.

Lite-Gro Indoor Garden Center, a complete four-shelf stand in brown wood finish, comes equipped with six 20-watt Naturescent grow lights. Waterproof plastic shelf liners are included to hold water and stone chips, to insure proper humidity. A Time-All automatic timer is included in the unit.

For free catalog and mail-order information, write:

Esmay Products
Department 6TCL1
Box 547
Bristol, IN 46507.

Plant Lite, an incandescent bulb containing the light waves essential to plant growth, can be installed in any ordinary light socket.

Vita-Lite, a full-spectrum fluorescent tube, nearly duplicates sunlight, and includes a controlled amount of ultra-violet light.

Vita-Lite Power Twist, another fluorescent, is designed with a spiraled construction to give greater light output.

Natur-escent is another fluorescent that is close to natural light, eliminating purple distortion. It is particularly recommended for germinating seeds and rooting cuttings.

Duro-Lite Lamps, Inc. manufactures these lamps specifically for plants and guarantees them for one to three years. All lamps are sold nationally through major chain and department stores and garden and electric supply stores.

Indoor Gardening Supplies features a variety of gardening tools and supplies, including fluorescent lighting fixtures, room dividers, and electronic timers.

Mail-order information can be obtained by writing:

Indoor Gardening Supplies
Box 40567
Detroit, MI 48240.

Verilux Tru-Bloom is a fluorescent tube for indoor gardening. The lamp is designed to produce a balanced natural light and is guaranteed to retain true color for a maximum of 12,000 hours. Available at retail outlets.

For mail-order information write:
Verilux
35 Mason Street
Greenwich, CT 06830.

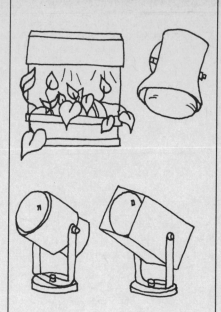

Modern-design plant lamps using fluorescent or incandescent bulbs are available in six styles. Colors available include white, black, chrome, yellow, brown, and orange. For brochure and mail-order information, write:

Lite Factory Ltd.
40-24 22nd Street
Long Island City, NY 11101

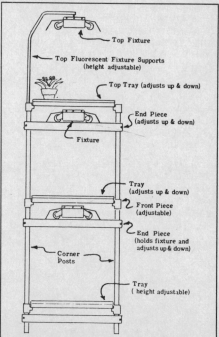

Shoplite Company specializes in fluorescent lighting for indoor growing. Timers, reflectors, growth units, and plant stands are a few of their products related to plant growth.

A catalog is available for 25 cents. For prices, other information, and mail orders, write:
Shoplite Company, Inc.
566 Franklin Avenue
Nutley, NJ 07110.

Agro-Lite Indoor Nursery, an indoor lighting unit, is 25 inches long, 24 inches high, and 10½ inches wide. Height is adjustable, and lighting is provided by two 20-watt Agro-Lite fluorescent lamps. It can be set up on the floor or a table, or used as a wall unit.

Contact a Westinghouse Sales Office for a dealer or write:
**Westinghouse Electric Corporation
Lamp Division
Bloomfield, NJ 07003.**

AGRO 220 Agro-Lite Indoor Nursery.
Contents: 1 Fixture, 2-F20T12/AGRO Lamps,
1"How To Grow" Folder.
Fixture Size: 24" long x 10⅜" wide x 21⅝" high.
Carton Size: 27½" long x 12½" wide x 3' deep.
Weight: 11 lbs.

FloraCart is a light unit constructed of corrosion-resistant 1¼-inch aluminum tubing. The three-shelf model stands 57 inches high, the two-shelf model, 37 inches. When a bracket is used to suspend an additional light fixture over the top shelf, it adds 14 inches to either height. Both models are 52 inches long and 19 inches wide. Molded fiberglass trays with provision for drainage are included. Units may be purchased with or without light fixtures. The fixtures available from the company utilize two 40-watt fluorescent tubes and two 25-watt incandescent bulbs. A plastic humidity tent is also available.

For mail-order information write:
**Tube Craft
1311 West 80th Street
Cleveland, OH 44102**

Plant guides available

The Indoor Light Gardening Society of America has a series of cultural guides for growing plants under fluorescent light. These include: *Learn to Grow Under Fluorescent Lights*, $1.50; *Ferns Under Fluorescents*, 50 cents; *Seed Propagation*, 50 cents; *Orchid Culture Under Lights*, 50 cents; *Flowering Plants for Light Gardens*, 75 cents; *Light Garden Primer*, $1.00; and *Begonias for Light Gardens*, 50 cents. Enclose a 13-cent stamp with all orders except for *Learn to Grow Under Fluorescent Lights*, which requires 26 cents in stamps. Make all checks payable to I.L.G.S.A., Inc. Mail to: James Martin, I.L.G.S.A. Librarian, 423 Powell Drive, Bay Village, OH 44140.

Spot-O-Sun Grow-Lite consists of a plant bowl with a laterally supported light reflector over it, made in avocado green.

Ripe-N-Grow Sun-Lite is a plant bowl on 3 legs with a center-mounted reflector; metal construction with avocado green enamel finish. Both units use a Wide-Spectrum Gro-Lux circline tube.

For free catalog sheets and mail-order information, write:
**Hall Industries
2323 Commonwealth Avenue
North Chicago, IL 60064.**

Spot-Gro is an incandescent light bulb designed for highlighting plants. It is available with a versatile beige-and-brown fixture that can be wall- or ceiling-mounted or placed on a shelf.

Hanging fixture is designed for use with hanging foliage and flowering plants. The fixture contains a Circline Gro-Lux lamp and is finished in gold-tone metal.

Plant grower features a single, high-intensity, 30-watt Gro-Lux lamp. Sturdy construction and fast, easy height adjustment.

Decorator-styled plant grower has two 20-watt Gro-Lux lamps. The all-metal frame assembles in minutes and the height is adjustable.

Indoor garden light is a utility-type fixture and includes two 4-foot Gro-Lux lamps. Comes with chains, S-hooks, and a bracket for hanging.

Fluorescent and incandescent plant-growth lamps are manufactured by Sylvania. Both wide-spectrum and standard fluorescent Gro-Lux lamps come in a range of wattages and lengths.

For more product information and a guide to indoor-garden lighting, write:
Mr. Russ Blauser
GTE Sylvania Lighting Center
100 Endicott Street
Danvers, MA 01923

SYLVANIA

Incandescent plant lights in spherically shaped reflector lamps provide style in lighting for your plants. Models are designed for use on table, shelf or wall.

For buying information, write:
Roxter Corporation
10-11 40th Avenue
Long Island City, NY 11101

Three-lamp show and grow light is a wall-mounted, walnut vinyl-finished fixture. Featured is parawedge louver shielding which concentrates light onto the plants and eliminates glare. Also offered is a wall-mounted garden tray, waterproofed with epoxy resin, and equipped with styrene grates for drainage and humidity. Both items are sold in 24-, 36-, and 48-inch lengths.

For mail-order information write:
Marko
94 Porete Avenue
North Arlington, NJ 07032

The Sunshine Center plant stand is equipped with Sylvania's Wide-Spectrum Gro-Lux fluorescent lamps. The stands are available in both floor and table models. They come in oak with a black frame and walnut with a tan frame. Both are sold nationally at retail stores. No mail order.

For catalogs and buying information, write:
Rubbermaid
1147 Akron Road
Wooster, OH 44691.

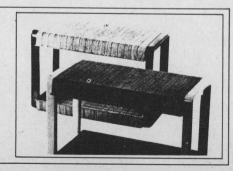

Gardens to visit

Indulge your interest in plants by visiting the botanic gardens and arboreta that are close to your home or by including them as part of your next vacation. These public gardens across the country offer both beauty and new gardening ideas. The concentration of plants in these gardens provides a surprisingly sensual delight, a feast for the eyes and other senses. Upon entering, one becomes a part of a world where both children and adults can share the wonder of discovering how nature is a part of their daily lives.

Public gardens are constantly changing, so plan to make several visits during the different seasons. Almost all offer special seasonal shows and exhibits. Most offer ongoing courses for all types of gardeners; one- or two-day courses can be taken advantage of if you're taking a "plant vacation."

At the gardens, you'll very possibly see plants you already own, but being raised differently — and perhaps more successfully. You'll also see plants you have never seen before. Some may have just been brought into cultivation from the far reaches of the world; others may be native to different climates; still others may simply have escaped your notice previously.

At public gardens you will see, as well as read about, how all these plants are grown. Information-filled pamphlets are available, as are verbal tips from experts who are often on hand. In these ways, public gardens offer instant and constant inspiration for your plant-growing efforts.

The following paragraphs describe some of the major public gardens in the United States and Canada. Some may be in your vicinity, others may lie en route to your next vacation spot. Either way, visit as many as you can. You — and your indoor garden — will be glad you did.

Gardens to visit

Alabama
Birmingham Botanical Gardens
2612 Lane Park Road
Birmingham, Alabama 35223
The gardens cover 67 acres and the greenhouse spans one-half acre. There are continuously changing flower shows year round. The greenhouse features special, permanent exhibits of cacti and orchids. Classes, which are open to the public at nominal fees, are offered several times a month during the spring and fall. The gardens are open 365 days a year from dawn to dusk. There is no charge for admission.

Arizona
Boyce Thompson Southwest Arboretum
Superior, Arizona 85273
Xerophytic plants—those species adapted to sustaining life with a minimum supply of water—are the mainstay of this arboretum. Spread over 30 acres of land, it offers two miles of trails, display greenhouses, and several special gardens. Cacti and other succulents are featured, along with plants of the genus *Eucalyptus* and plants native to the deserts of the American Southwest.

Guests are invited to make use of the garden's picnic grounds and the Visitor Center, where publications and xerophytic plants are offered for sale. All guests receive a complimentary pamphlet on growing succulents, produced by the Boyce staff.

The arboretum is open from 8:00 a.m. to 4:30 p.m. daily except for holidays. The admission fee is $.50 for adults. Children under 14 are admitted free of charge.

California
Botanical Garden
University of California
Berkeley, California 94720
Though its 32-acre site is small compared with other major botanical gardens, the garden at the University of California ranks with the world's leading gardens in the number of different plants it contains. Presently, there are approximately 8,000 different species. The largest collection is cacti and other succulent plants. Special collections include: herbs and spices, palms, rhododendrons, gymnosperms, ferns, carnivorous plants, orchids, and economically important species.

The garden is open to the public daily except Christmas from 9:00 a.m. to 5:00 p.m. In addition to the sale of booklets and pamphlets, an educational program is offered which includes instructional tours of the various plant collections. Membership is $5.00 for students, $10.00 for individuals, and $15.00 for families, and includes special tours and a quarterly newsletter.

Botanical Gardens – Herbarium
University of California
Los Angeles, California 90024
The collection currently contains approximately 3,500 species of plants. Special areas are devoted to native plants, succulents, palms, camellias, and conifers. There is also a fine representative collection of Australian plants. Tour guidebooks are available. Hours are 8:00 a.m. to 5:00 p.m., Monday through Friday, and 10:00 a.m. to 4:00 p.m., Saturday and Sunday. The gardens are closed on holidays. Admission is free.

Huntington Botanical Gardens
San Marino, California 91108
The parklike grounds of the Huntington Botanical Gardens contain more than 2,000 varieties of succulents, over 100 kinds of palms, and a large selection of cycads scattered throughout the grounds. Several specialized gardens are featured including the Shakespeare garden, a representative sampling of plants and flowers used in Elizabethan gardens; the rose garden, featuring the largest United States collection of tea roses; the palm garden; a 5-acre landscaped Japanese garden; a 6-acre camellia collection, the largest public collection in the world; and the desert garden, the largest outdoor collection of desert plants in the world. The garden is open to the public Tuesday through Sunday 1:00 p.m. to 4:30 p.m. Closed Monday, major holidays, and throughout October. Admission is free.

Quail Gardens
P.O. Box 5
Encinitas, California 92024
Administrated by the San Diego County Parks and Recreation Department, Quail Gardens is a refreshing and soothing collection of plants and shrubs, many of which are native to southern California. The garden also displays subtropical plants and the famous Mexican Montezuma cypresses. The grounds include pools, nature trails, and a designated bird sanctuary. Open free to the public 8:00 a.m. to 5:00 p.m. (6:00 p.m. in the summer).

The Santa Barbara Botanic Garden
1212 Mission Canyon Road
Santa Barbara, California 93103
The garden is devoted entirely to the study of flora native to California. A section of the garden is devoted to each geographic area of the state, including the deserts, Sierras, southern mountains, and offshore islands. Of special interest are the ceanothus section and the meadow section, plus the giant oaks, flowering shrubs, and an attractive water garden. Classes on horticulture and southern California plants are given annually; there are also Sunday lectures and an occasional one-day workshop. The grounds are open daily from 8:00 a.m. to sunset.

Sherman Foundation Education Program
Sherman Foundation Center
2647 East Coast Highway
Corona Del Mar, California 92625
The Sherman facilities provide an educational forum for people of all ages interested in horticulture and related areas, as well as a magnificent garden containing a wide variety of common, rare, and specimen plants. Classes include Propagation for the Home Gardener, Beginning Bonsai, Floral Design, and Hanging Your Own Plants. A set fee is charged, plus materials. The garden is open to the public daily from 10:30 a.m. to 4:00 p.m.

The Strybing Arboretum
9th Avenue and Lincoln Way
San Francisco, California 94122
Covering approximately 70 acres, the Strybing Arboretum is a veritable library of plants from around the world, all of which can be grown in the San Francisco climate. Special features include the Garden of Fragrance, a redwood trail for nature walks, a Japanese garden, and collections of dwarf conifers and native California trees and shrubs. Lectures on subjects like gardening, horticulture, and botany are open to the public; there are also special introductory classes for schoolchildren. Hours are 8:00 a.m. to 4:30 p.m., Monday through Friday and 10:00 a.m. to 5:00 p.m. Saturday, Sunday, and holidays. Admission is free.

Colorado
Denver Botanic Gardens
909 York Street
Denver, Colorado 80206
The gardens, which contain the only conservatory between St. Louis and San Francisco, consist of 11,500 square feet of tropical environment, housing over 600 kinds of tropical and subtropical plants. A 20-acre outdoor garden is under development; it will highlight plantings of spring bulbs, water lilies, and colorful annuals. Other points of interest include a vegetable garden, an herb garden, and a prize-winning rose garden. Educational courses in a variety of horticultural subjects are offered throughout the year and some are free.
Open daily from 9:00 a.m. to 4:45 p.m. Admission to all facilities is free.

Connecticut
The Connecticut Arboretum
Connecticut College
New London, Connecticut 06320
The arboretum's 415 acres house an extensive collection of native trees and shrubs, wildflower preserves, several demonstration areas in vegetation management, and two natural tracts for ecological research. Special points of interest include a native wildflower collection and an ornamental tree and shrub collection. Some classes and clinics are open to the public. There is no charge for admission.

Delaware
The Winterthur Gardens
The Henry Francis du Pont
Winterthur Museum
Winterthur, Delaware 19735
Situated on 60 acres, the Winterthur Gardens feature plants, displayed in natural settings, native to the Middle Atlantic States. Visitors can tour the gardens on their own, enjoying the colorful backdrop of such areas as the azalea woods, quarry, and sundial gardens, which roll on for 2½ miles. The gardens are open from mid-April through October; hours are 10:00 a.m. to 4:00 p.m., Tuesday through Sunday. Admission is $2.00 for adults and $.50 for children under 16 who are accompanied by an adult.

Florida
Thomas A. Edison's Winter Home Laboratory, Botanical Gardens, and Museum
2350 McGregor Boulevard
Fort Myers, Florida 33901
The inventor's own garden contains over 300 varieties of shrubs and trees from all over the world. Originally established as an experimental garden of unusual plants, it is now one of the most beautiful gardens in the country. Open from 9:00 a.m. to 4:00 p.m. Monday through Saturday and from 12:30 p.m. to 4:30 p.m. Sunday. Admission is $2.00 for adults and $1.00 for children and students.

Fairchild Tropical Garden
10901 Old Cutler Road
Miami, Florida 33156
This is the most comprehensive collection of tropical plants in the continental United States. Over 4,000 plants are represented in the garden's 83 acres. Outstanding collections include orchids, bromeliads, ferns, aroids, and colorful varieties of bougainvilleas and hibiscus. Adult education courses in horticulture and botany are offered several times a year. The garden is open daily year round from 10:00 a.m. to 5:00 p.m. Admission is $2.00 for adults; children under 16 are admitted free if accompanied by a parent.

Jungle Larry's African Safari and Caribbean Gardens
P.O. Box 7129, Fleischmann Boulevard
Naples, Florida 33940
Jungle Larry's showcases 3,500 species of subtropical and tropical plants and trees. Special features are a large collection of bromeliads and over 10,000 orchids thriving outdoors among trees. Guided tours, on foot or by train, are available. The gardens are open daily from 9:30 a.m. to 5:00 p.m. Admission is $3.50, but for $8.00 you can purchase a one year pass good for as many visits as you please.

The Orchid Jungle
Fennel Orchid Company
26715 S. W. 157th Avenue
Homestead, Florida 33030
This is a unique natural garden, with orchids, ferns, anthuriums, bromeliads, and other rare tropical plants growing as they would in the wild. There are three main display areas. The *Fennel Orchid News* and an orchid catalog are published biannually. The Orchid Jungle is open daily from 8:30 a.m. to 5:30 p.m. Admission is $2.00 for adults and $1.00 for children. Special groups rates are available.

Vizcaya
3251 S. Miami Avenue
Miami, Florida 33129
Operated by the Dade County Department of Parks and Recreation, Vizcaya has acres of formal gardens surrounding the stately manor of the late industrialist James Deering. The gardens are both colorful and magnificently designed in the Italian Renaissance style. The collection includes flowering plants from all over the world. Open from 9:30 a.m. to 4:45 p.m. every day except Christmas. Admission to both the house and the gardens is $3.00 for adults and $1.00 for children.

Georgia
Sears Garden – Civic Center
3012 Bacon Road
Columbus, Georgia 31906
Use of the center's facilities is available to all garden clubs and civic organizations free of charge. There is an auditorium for club-spon-

sored programs. A small library of donated books and magazines is maintained. The center is open Monday through Friday from 10:00 a.m. to 9:00 p.m.

Hawaii
Harold L. Lyon Arboretum
University of Hawaii at Manoa
3860 Manoa Road
Honolulu, Hawaii 96822
The Lyon Arboretum, which covers 124 acres in Upper Manoa Valley, is a unit of the University of Hawaii devoted to research, instruction, and public service. Facilities include greenhouses, nursery area, research building, herbarium, and reference library. There are collections of native Hawaiian plants and plants of ethnobotanical and economic importance. Classes and lectures, open to the general public, are offered in practical botany, horticulture, plant crafts, and ethnobotany. The arboretum publishes an annual magazine covering subjects related to the Pacific area and an occasional series of technical papers. Guided tours of the grounds and facilities are conducted free of charge at 1:00 p.m. on the first Friday of every month. Memberships are available.

Waimea Arboretum
Waimea Falls Park
59-864 Kamehameha Highway
Haleiwa, Oahu, Hawaii 96712
Located in the magnificently beautiful Waimea Falls Park, this arboretum showcases tropical plants and flowers in their natural environment. The Waimea Arboretum is unparalleled in color and beauty. There are 32 collections of plants from all over the tropics. The arboretum is open all year round. Admission is $2.00 for adults and $1.00 for children 10 to 15; children under 10 are admitted free.

Illinois
Chicago Botanic Garden
715 Dundee Road
Glencoe, Illinois 60022
The garden is run by the Chicago Horticultural Society and features a home landscape center, a demonstration vegetable garden, a Braille nature trail, an education center, and a greenhouse complex. The grounds are landscaped with woody trees and shrubs ideal for northern climates. Educational classes are offered in a variety of horticultural topics and are open to the public. A catalog of classes and fees is available from the society. The garden is open to the public daily from 9:00 a.m. to 6:00 p.m.

The Morton Arboretum
Lisle, Illinois 60532
Originally established for the purpose of evaluating the suitability of woody plants for northeastern Illinois, the arboretum now contains 1,500 acres of cultivated plants and natural vegetation. The collections include both native and introduced plants, with such popular features as a hedge garden, a lilac collection, ericaceous collection, and even a Japanese garden. There are lectures on plant identification, propagation, landscaping, botanical illustration, and many other topics. All programs are listed in the *Program of Educational Activities,*

which is available on request. The grounds are open every day from 8:00 a.m. to 5:00 p.m. and from 8:00 a.m. to 7:00 p.m. during daylight savings time. There is an admission fee of $1.00 per car, but pedestrians are admitted free.

Indiana
Hayes Regional Arboretum
801 Elks Road
Richmond, Indiana 47374
Hayes, one of the few regionalized arboretums, is devoted exclusively to trees, shrubs, vines, and plants native to the immediate area – the Whitewater River Drainage Basin. In addition to its collection of native trees and shrubs, the arboretum has the first solar-heated greenhouse in Indiana, in which woody plants are grown for research, education, and exhibition. A primary purpose of this greenhouse is to demonstrate that solar heating is a practical source of energy for Indiana and also to prove that it is relatively easy to obtain materials for constructing and operating solar-heated buildings. Classes are offered in nature studies and wood crafts throughout the year. The facilities are open daily from 1:00 p.m. to 5:00 p.m., year round except Mondays. The arboretum is closed the first two weeks of September. Admission is free.

Kentucky
Bernheim Forest
Clermont, Kentucky 40110
These 10,000 scenic acres of Kentucky woodlands offer wilderness trails, a wildlife preserve, two arboretums with countless varieties of plants, a nature museum, and a large planting of hollies native to America and Japan. Open daily between 9:00 a.m. and sundown, from March 15 through November 15.

Louisiana
Live Oaks Gardens, Ltd.
on Jefferson Island
P.O. Box 284
New Iberia, Louisiana 70560
Covering 20 acres on beautiful Jefferson Island, this subtropical garden is a series of "gardens within a garden," including a replica of the famous knot garden at Hampton Court in London. There are over 1,000 species of flowering and tropical foliage plants scattered through the grounds, which have been carved out of a woodland of live oaks. Admission is $2.25 for adults, $1.00 for children over 4.

Longue Vue Gardens
Number 7 Bamboo Road
New Orleans, Louisiana 70124
The eight acres of gardens are divided into various landscaped areas, each with its own color scheme and design. Hundreds of different plant varieties are presented, but the emphasis is on roses, azaleas, camellias, and trees and shrubs native to Louisiana. Membership in the Friends of Longue Vue is open to the general public. The group, which meets regularly, conducts programs and clinics and sponsors exhibits. Membership fees, which include a subscription to the garden's newsletter, start at $7.00 per year. Longue Vue is open daily, be-

tween 1:00 p.m. and 5:00 p.m. with the following exceptions: Mondays, national holidays, and the period from July 15 through September 14. Admission is $2.00 for adults and $1.00 for children and students.

Rosedown Plantations and Gardens
P.O. Drawer M
St. Francisville, Louisiana 70775
Points of special interest at Rosedown include a camellia collection, an herb garden, a garden of medicinal herbs, and a flower garden. The grounds are open daily, except Christmas, from 9:00 a.m. to 5:00 p.m. from March through November and from 10:00 a.m. to 4:00 p.m. from December through February. Admission is $2.00, but children under 12 are admitted free.

Maine
University of Maine at Orono
Department of Botany and Plant Pathology
Deering Hall
Orono, Maine 04473
The gardens, used primarily as a study area for the university's students, cover 5 acres and feature some 200 species of native trees and shrubs. The public is welcome to visit the grounds. Classes, clinics, and tours are offered free of charge. The gardens are open daily. Admission is free.

Maryland
Cylburn Wildflower Preserve and Garden Center
Cylburn Park
4915 Greenspring Avenue
Baltimore, Maryland 21209
The center is a wilderness area of more than 176 acres, consisting of 12 nature trails, with a variety of native flora, an arboretum, and several gardens containing assorted plants, including herbs. The center, activities, and workshops are open to the public throughout the year.

Harvey Smith Ladew Topiary Gardens
Monkton, Maryland 21111
This topiary garden specializes in trimmed and sculptured shrubbery and flowers. The extensive outdoor gardens are supplemented with an expanding greenhouse collection. Four short courses on various gardening subjects are offered each year. Open from April 1 to November 1. Hours are 10:00 a.m. to 5:00 p.m., Monday through Saturday, and noon to 5:00 p.m. Sunday. Admission is $2.00 for adults, $1.00 for students, and $.50 for children.

Massachusetts
The Arnold Arboretum
Jamaica Plain, Massachusetts 02130
The Arnold Arboretum spans 265 acres and contains some 6,000 varieties of ornamental trees and shrubs from everywhere in the North Temperate Zone. Plants capable of being grown in the Boston area are the feature at various times of the year: for example, honeysuckles, azaleas, and lilacs in late May; native witch hazel and autumn color during October

and November. Classes are offered in such subjects as bonsai, pruning, plant identification, and landscaping for an average fee of $10.00 to $20.00. The grounds are open to pedestrians daily, from sunrise to sunset, year-round. Visitors who wish to drive through the arboretum must obtain a permit, available on weekdays only, at the Administration Building. There is no charge for admission.

Berkshire Garden Center
Routes 102 and 183
Stockbridge, Massachusetts 01262
The center presents seasonal exhibits and demonstrations of popular plants, along with several permanent collections of roses, dwarf conifers, perennials and assorted tropical plants, including banana plants, coffee trees, and sugarcane. The center offers an annual youth program that introduces almost 4,000 children to the importance and pleasures of gardening. The center also has workshops and lectures on horticulture and related areas and arranges field trips to other gardens and exhibits of special interest. The grounds are open at all times from April through October. There is no charge for admission.

The Botanic Garden of Smith College
Northampton, Massachusetts 01060
The garden, which features several greenhouses, herb gardens, and an arboretum, is versatile in both approach and collections. The greenhouses contain displays of some 1,200 labeled species of plants. Arranged according to climate, they provide the visitor with a representative view of plants from around the world. Courses in botany and horticulture are offered as part of the college curriculum. The facilities are open daily from 8:00 a.m. to 4:00 p.m. Admission is free.

Isabella Stewart Gardner Museum
2 Palace Road
Boston, Massachusetts 02115
The greenhouses of the museum are used for growing the plants which are placed in the museum courtyard. A wide range of flowering and foliage plants are featured. Group tours of the greenhouses can be arranged by requesting permission from the head gardener or the director.

Michigan
Iva Doty Native Flower Trail
Bellevue, Michigan 49021
The Iva Doty Native Flower Trail is a nature trek, where visitors can enjoy over 30 species of plants and flowers native to Michigan, including mayapples, violets, wild roses, Michigan lilies, asters, and aspens. The trail is divided into 10 sections and is open in spring, summer, and fall. Admission is free.

Garden Center
Grand Rapids Public Museum
54 Jefferson S.E.
Grand Rapids, Michigan 49502
The facilities of the garden center, which is located in the museum's East Building, include a library, lounge, conference room, and adjoining auditorium. A greenhouse is devoted to the growth of common and exotic houseplants. The center maintains a collection of scheffleras, hibiscus, crotons, Norfolk Island pines, and

birds-of-paradise. A wide variety of activities are available to the public, including classes, lectures, demonstrations, workshops, garden shows, plant society shows, and two annual shows featuring the combined talents of various garden clubs. There is no fee for these activities. Two indoor garden plant societies and an African violet club belong to the garden center. The center also sponsors tours and trips with a nominal charge to cover the chartering of a bus. Garden center memberships start at $1.00. Hours are 10:00 a.m. to 5:00 p.m. Monday through Friday. Admission is free.

Hidden Lake Gardens
Michigan State University
Tipton, Michigan 49287
Hidden Lake Gardens, occupying over 670 acres of countryside, contains more than 2,000 different plant species and cultivars representing over 150 genera. Collections and plantings include flowering cherries, hawthorns, junipers, lilacs, magnolias, azaleas, shrub roses, and primroses. The most recent addition is a new, large glass conservatory. Classes are taught in gardening, landscaping, and nature appreciation. Hours are 8:00 a.m. to 30 minutes before sundown Monday through Friday, April to October, and 8:00 a.m. to 4:30 p.m. Monday through Friday, November through March. The conservatory opens when the gardens do but closes at 7:00 p.m. April through October. Admission is $.75 for a car and its driver and $.25 for each passenger.

Matthaei Botanical Gardens
The University of Michigan
1800 North Dixboro Road
Ann Arbor, Michigan 48105
The gardens are located on 250 acres, and house an extensive greenhouse complex. Special features include a medicinal and herb garden, an indoor conservatory of tropical and temperate plants, and four nature trails, containing some 700 different species of native plants. Educational programs at the gardens are offered through the University of Michigan. The gardens are open every day from sunrise to sunset; the conservatory is open daily from 10:00 a.m. to 4:30 p.m. Closed Thanksgiving, Christmas, and New Year's Day.

Minnesota
Como Park Conservatory
1224 North Lexington
St. Paul, Minnesota 55103
A 3-acre complex offers a variety of areas and collections including formal gardens, a tropical wilderness, aromatic fruit trees, a palm house, and a fern room. The conservatory holds four annual flower shows – the Spring Flower Show (March–April); the Summer Show (starting in May and running throughout the summer); the Fall Chrysanthemum Show; and the Winter Flower Show. The conservatory also offers Saturday workshops and, through the city's libraries, weekly programs. All are free to the general public; the only fee is for materials. The conservatory is open daily from 10:00 a.m. to 4:00 p.m. in winter; from 10:00 a.m. to 8:00 p.m. in summer.

The Minnesota Landscape Arboretum
3675 Arboretum Drive
Chaska, Minnesota 55318
These 560 acres of rolling hills, open fields, two natural lakes, and several marshland areas are the home of over 4,000 species and cultivars of ornamental plants, trees, and shrubs. Included among the collections are dahlias, dwarf conifers, roses, irises, lilies, perennials, and an herb garden. Tours are conducted; classes in gardening and related areas are offered through the University of Minnesota's General Extension Division. The grounds are open from 8:00 a.m. to sunset. A $1.00 admission is charged. (This fee is subject to change as of April, 1977.)

Missouri
The Missouri Botanical Garden
2345 Tower Grove Avenue
St. Louis, Missouri 63110
With over 79 acres of picturesque indoor and outdoor exhibits, this botanical garden is ranked among the best in the world. At different times of the year it features roses, spring bulbs, orchids, annuals, perennials, and a varied selection of trees and shrubs. Its internationally famous dome-shaped structure, the Climatron, contains a wide assortment of exotic plants, representing the tropical regions of the world. There is also a desert house exhibiting cacti and succulents from the world's desert regions. Affiliated with the garden is the Arboretum and Nature Reserve at Grey Summit, 35 miles southwest of St. Louis. The reserve contains 10 miles of trails and a seemingly endless supply of forest, meadows, ponds, and brooks. The botanical garden offers educational workshops for teachers, and classes and lectures on horticulture, botany, and natural history for the general public. Hours are 9:00 a.m. to 6:00 p.m. from May through October and 9:00 a.m. to 5:00 p.m. from November through April. The garden is open daily except Christmas. Admission is $1.50 for adults and $.50 for children aged 6 to 12; children under 6 are admitted free.

New Jersey
Skyland
Ringwood State Park
P.O. Box 1304
Ringwood, New Jersey 07456
Skylands has over 13 garden areas featuring a wide variety of hardy plants. There are 4 greenhouses of tropical and temperate plants, which are used to decorate the nearby Ringwood and Skyland manors. Collections include azaleas, roses, lilacs, rhododendrons, annuals, perennials, and a wildflower garden. The grounds are open year round.

New Mexico
Living Desert State Park
Carlsbad, New Mexico
The Living Desert State Park, consists of 48 acres on a hillside overlooking Carlsbad, New Mexico. It has 2 miles of walkways, which visitors can enjoy along with 2,500 cacti and succulents and about 1,500 houseplants representing some 200 varieties and species. In the

propagation house are some 2,000 rare plants from desert regions as far away as Africa. This is one of the most extensive collections in the country. Open during the winter from 9:00 a.m. to 5:00 p.m., and during the summer from 8:00 a.m. to 10:00 p.m. Admission is $1.00 for adults and $.50 for school-age children; non-school-age children are admitted free. Membership is $5.00 per year.

New York
Brooklyn Botanic Garden
1000 Washington Avenue
Brooklyn, New York 11225
In existence since 1910, the Brooklyn Botanic Garden is a 50-acre, green oasis in the midst of New York City. Over 12,000 different plants are represented. The extensive collections include over 400 rhododendron species, 5,000 roses, lilies, azaleas, native flora, and dwarf plants. A conservatory contains countless species of tropical plants from around the world, cacti and succulents, flowering plants and bulbs, and many others. Short courses in horticulture and related areas are offered year-round. Course fees are nominal. From May through August, the grounds are open from 8:00 a.m. to 6:00 p.m. on weekdays and from 10:00 a.m. to 6:00 p.m. on weekends and holidays. From September through April, the grounds are open from 8:00 a.m. to 4:30 p.m. on weekdays and from 10:00 a.m. to 4:30 p.m. on weekends and holidays. Conservatory hours are 10:00 a.m. to 4:00 p.m. on weekdays and 11:00 a.m. to 4:30 p.m. on weekends and holidays, year round. Admission to the grounds is free.

The Cloisters
The Metropolitan Museum of Art
Fort Tryon Park
New York, New York
This medieval monastery, situated on top of a hill in New York's Fort Tryon Park, attracts visitors from all over the world. It is noted both for its collection of medieval art and for the serenity and peacefulness of its surrounding gardens. A walk through this very special place is indeed a pleasure. Hours are 10:00 a.m. to 4:45 p.m. Tuesday through Saturday, and 1:00 a.m. to 4:45 p.m., Sunday and holidays. From May through September, Sunday hours are noon to 4:45 p.m. Admission is whatever you wish to contribute.

The Cornell Plantations
Cornell University
100 Judd Falls Road
Ithaca, New York 14853
The grounds feature collections of a variety of woody plants, especially conifers, viburnums, and rhododendrons. Also on the grounds are a comprehensive herb garden, an annual and perennial garden, a rose species collection, and a poisonous plants garden. Evening classes covering such topics as bonsai, propagation, and houseplant culture are offered during the spring and fall and are open to the public. Fees range from $10.00 to $25.00. The grounds are open every day from sunrise to sunset. Tours may be arranged by appointment. Admission is free.

The New York Botanical Garden
Southern Boulevard and 200 Street
Bronx, New York 10458
The garden's many features include the greenhouses of the Main Conservatory, with their varied plant collections; the museum building, featuring changing educational exhibits on themes related to ecology, environmental studies, botany, and horticulture; and numerous specialized gardens. Courses are offered in botany, gardening, landscape gardening, crafts and nature studies. There are also field trips, flower shows, lecture series, nature walks, and college-level instruction. Memberships start at $20.00 a year and include a subscription to *Garden Journal,* the garden's official bimonthly publication. The grounds are open daily from 8:00 a.m. to 7:00 p.m., June through September, and from 10:00 a.m. to 5:00 p.m., October through May. Admission is free.

Old Westbury Gardens
P.O. Box 430
Old Westbury, New York 11568
Spread over more than 100 acres, the Old Westbury Gardens are a series of elaborately landscaped formal gardens and linden-filled allées. Flowering bushes, fruit trees, and primroses dot the grounds; fern paths, rose gardens, thousands of tulips, and a special display of daisies, grown in greenhouses from carefully selected strains, are a few of the surprises. In addition, there is the lovely, stately lilac walk, the English bluebell walk, and the spectacular walled Italian garden bordered by a pool of water lilies and lotus.

Open to the public Wednesday through Sunday (and on all holidays) from early May through late October, 10:00 a.m. to 5:00 p.m. Admission to the gardens is $1.50 for adults and $.50 for children 6 to 12. (There is a separate admission to Westbury House).

The Parrish Art Museum Arboretum
Southampton, New York
The Parrish Arboretum, established in 1897, contains over 250 trees and shrubs representing nearly 100 species collected from around the world. Collections include Japanese umbrella pines, feathery bamboo, pine and red oaks, magnolias, Norway spruces, 15 separate species of maples, and many, many more. There are also some indoor plants, including a giant white bird-of-paradise. There is no charge for admission.

Planting Fields Arboretum
Planting Fields Road
Oyster Bay, New York 11771
The Planting Fields Arboretum is known primarily for its rhododendron and azalea collections, containing over 600 different species and regarded as one of the finest in the East. It also has a magnificent camellia collection. All the collections come to full bloom from mid-May through mid-June. In addition, there are greenhouses displaying orchids, hibiscus, begonias, and countless other tropical plants and fruit, including bananas, citrus, and coffee. Open daily throughout the year. Hours are 10:00 a.m. to 5:30 p.m. from mid-April through mid-October and 10:00 a.m. to 4:30 p.m. from

mid-October through mid-April. Greenhouses are open daily from 10:00 a.m. to 4:30 p.m. in fall and winter and 10:00 a.m. to 5:30 p.m. in spring and summer. An admission fee is charged.

Queens Botanical Garden
43-50 Main Street
Flushing, New York 11355
This garden contains 15 acres of colorful trees, plants, and shrubs. Exhibits are presented throughout the year featuring tulips, rhododendrons, roses, petunias, zinnias, and many other flowers. Courses are offered on Tuesday nights during the fall, winter, and spring months; special day and evening classes are scheduled throughout the year. Open from 9:00 a.m. to dusk, Wednesday through Sunday. Admission is free.

The Root Glen
Hamilton and Kirkland Colleges
Clinton, New York 13323
The Root Glen is a 10-acre natural area. One of its unusual attractions is a large, hemlock-enclosed formal garden. There are also 2 miles of red shale paths. The beauty of the gardens is enhanced by a large assortment of primroses, peonies, clematis, iris, lilies, and azaleas. The Glen stream, which flows through the grounds, becomes an interesting landscape feature due to seven bridges. Open from dawn to dusk year round. Admission is free.

The Stroll Garden of The Hammond Museum
North Salem, New York
A part of Japanese culture has been transplanted to North Salem. Visitors can walk through the tranquil and serene atmosphere of the Stroll Garden, complete with waterfalls, mountains, reflecting pools, stone bridges, and 15 beautifully designed gardens. The garden is open from the end of May to the end of October. Hours are 11:00 a.m. to 5:00 p.m., Wednesday through Sunday. Admission is $1.00 for adults and $.75 for children under 12. Visitors are advised to wear low-heeled shoes. Not recommended for children under 10.

Wave Hill Center for Environmental Studies
675 W. 252 Street
Bronx, New York 10471
Wave Hill, which is easily accessible to New York residents, offers 28 acres of cultivated and woodland beauty. There are three greenhouses and a palm house. Greenhouses contain a collection of over 1,000 species of cacti and succulents and a varied selection of tropical plants, many suitable for indoor gardening. Of special interest are the Perkins Gardens, which feature a rose garden, an English-style wild garden, an aquatic garden, and an herb garden. There are classes and other programs open to the public, including workshops, lectures, nature walks, and field trips. Tours of the grounds and facilities are given. Anyone can become a member for as little as $10.00 per year. Members receive a quarterly calendar of events. Wave Hill is open daily from 10:00 a.m. to 4:00 p.m. There is no charge for admission.

North Dakota
International Peace Garden
Dunseith, North Dakota 58329
Bossevain, Manitoba, ROK OEO, Canada.
The International Peace Garden, designed as a tribute to peace and understanding between the United States and Canada, is also a magnificent and colorful park straddling the two countries. The flower collection is remarkably beautiful and unparalleled in this part of the continent. Open to the public free of charge.

Ohio
Canton Garden Center
1615 Stadium Park N.W.
Canton, Ohio 44718
The Canton Garden Center, which is maintained by the city's park department, is unique for the themes of its gardens and its approach to educating the public. There is an indoor patio with a new display of plants for each season, designed to appeal to all five senses, and a Japanese garden with a bell tower. Among the educational programs provided by the center are a weekly flower-arranging course for inmates at the State Hospital and a monthly therapy class to teach shut-ins plant-related projects. Courses in horticulture and botany are open to the general public. Open Tuesday through Friday from 10:00 a.m. to noon and from 1:00 p.m. to 4:00 p.m.

Cox Arboretum
6733 Springboro Pike
Dayton, Ohio 45449
The Cox Arboretum, a reserve of the Dayton-Montgomery County Park District, covers 160 acres. The outdoor collection includes deciduous shrubs and trees, coniferous trees and shrubs, herbs, and a rock garden. There are also greenhouse collections of ferns, begonias, ivies, geraniums, and cacti and succulents. The arboretum's Annual Fall Open House emphasizes houseplants. There are monthly educational programs (open to the public free of charge) on horticulture and nature subjects. Memberships are $12.50 a year. There is a quarterly newsletter for members and plant-related brochures. The grounds are open daily from 8:00 a.m. until dark; the greenhouses are open from 8:30 a.m. to 4:30 p.m., Monday through Friday, and from 1:00 p.m. to 4:00 p.m. on Sunday. Admission is free.

The Dawes Arboretum
R.F.D. 5
Newark, Ohio 43055
These 950 acres of restful woods are the home of many fine collections of trees, shrubs, and assorted plants from around the world. Special features include a Japanese garden, complete with native Japanese plantings. A wide variety of classes and workshops, on topics like bonsai, terrariums, and children's gardening, are open to the public for a fee. Open daily during daylight hours year round. Admission is free.

The Garden Center of Greater Cleveland
11030 East Boulevard
Cleveland, Ohio 44106
This is the oldest civic garden center in the country. The center is known for its magnificent plant shows; many are produced by local plant

societies and presented on a rotating basis throughout the year. The center also offers an outstanding horticultural library of 10,000 volumes, and there are herb, rose, and reading gardens. In the spring and during the Christmas season, special displays are open to the public free of charge. Classes, lectures, and exhibits relating to indoor gardening are offered throughout the year and are open to all. Hours are 9:00 a.m. to 5:00 p.m. Monday through Friday and 2:00 p.m. to 5:00 p.m. on Sunday. Admission is free.

The Holden Arboretum
9500 Sperry Road
Mentor, Ohio 44060
The Holden Arboretum is a veritable museum of woody plants. It contains 6,000 varieties of species and cultivars along its many wilderness trails. Classes and activities are scheduled throughout the year and are open to the public unless otherwise specified. Open daily except Monday. Hours are 10:00 a.m. to 7:00 p.m. April through October and 10:00 a.m. to 4:00 p.m. from November through March. Admission is $1.00 for adults and $.50 for children aged 6 to 15. Annual membership is $18.00.

Kingwood Center
900 Park Avenue West
Mansfield, Ohio 44906
The Kingwood Center, set on 47 scenic acres, is an educational institution with a special interest in horticulture, gardening, nature, and related subjects. Twelve gardens highlight such plants as chrysanthemums, daffodils, dahlias, lilies, roses, and tulips. Various educational programs are offered throughout the year and all are open to the public free of charge. The gardens, greenhouse, and nature area are open daily from 8:00 a.m. to 5:00 p.m. Admission is free.

Irwin M. Krohn Conservatory
Board of Park Commissioners
950 Eden Park Drive
Cincinnati, Ohio 45200
The conservatory consists of greenhouses covering approximately ¾ acre. They house collections of tropical and semitropical plant materials, notably ferns, tropical fruits, palms, a general assortment of other tropical foliage plants, cacti, succulents, and orchids. Tours and slide and lecture presentations are available on request. Hours are 10:00 a.m. to 5:00 p.m., Monday through Saturday, and 10:00 a.m. to 6:00 p.m. Sunday, with special night time hours during the seasons of Easter and Christmas. Admission is free.

Secor Park
Route 1
Berkey, Ohio 43504
Secor Park covers approximately 500 acres, including a 200-acre arboretum, a nature center, and a greenhouse. Tours of the park's facilities and other related programs are available through the park district and its staff of naturalists. A quarterly publication on the park's programs is available. (Write: Wildwood Metro Park Preserve, 5120 Central Ave., Toledo, Ohio 43615.) The grounds are open year round; the nature center and greenhouse

are open daily from 9:00 a.m. to 5:00 p.m. during the summer months and from noon to 5:00 p.m. Sunday only, during the winter months. Admission is free.

Secrest Arboretum
Ohio Agricultural Research and Development Center
Wooster, Ohio 44691
The Secrest Arboretum is designed to test and display trees and shrubs ideal for the climate in the Wooster area. The first planting took place in 1903, and now the 85-acre grounds boast more than 2,000 species, not only from Ohio but from around the world. There is a sizeable collection of boxwoods as well as a dwarf evergreen display, rhododendron and holly display gardens, and examples of hardwoods and pines. Walking trails crisscross the grounds. Open free to the public during daylight hours throughout the year.

Oregon
International Rose Test Garden
400 S.W. Kingston Street
Portland, Oregon 97201
Located in Portland's Washington Park, this garden contains over 8,000 roses that represent 400 different varieties, including miniature roses. There are six different gardens to wander through, and one sees not only roses but a year-round display of bulbs, trees, shrubs, and flowering plants. There is also a Japanese garden, and an American Rose Society Miniature Rose Test Garden. The garden is open 365 days a year from sunrise to midnight. There is no admission charge.

Pennsylvania
Arboretum of the Barnes Foundation
Merion, Pennsylvania 19066
Although dedicated to the growing of woody plants, this arboretum also has an extensive herb garden with approximately 200 species of 87 genera from 32 families. If you are seriously interested in herbal gardens, this is a place to visit. Open Monday through Saturday from 9:00 a.m. to 4:00 p.m. by appointment only. Closed on Sundays. There is no charge for admission.

Bowman's Hill State Wildflower Preserve
Washington Crossing State Park
Route 32, River Road
Washington Crossing, Pennsylvania 18977
Established as a memorial to the veterans of Washington's army, these gardens contain many of the most notable native Pennsylvania trees, shrubs, vines, and flowering plants, as well as examples of outstanding introduced plants. The preserve covers 100 acres with over 26 trails centered around the Pidcock Creek Valley. Lectures, classes, and guided tours are provided to the public free of charge. The park is open daily from 8:00 a.m. to dusk. Admission is free.

Gardens of Japan
Swiss Pines
R.D. 1
Malvern, Pennsylvania 19355
Special features include collections of herbs, heathers, ground covers, rhododendrons, a

wildflower trail, and a crab apple grove. There is also a teahouse with its own garden. Hours are 10:00 a.m. to 4:00 p.m., Monday through Friday, and 9:00 a.m. to noon on Saturday. The gardens are closed from December 15 through March 15 and holidays. Admission is free.

Longwood Gardens
Kennett Square, Pennsylvania 19348
Longwood has many permanent collections, including palms, ferns, roses, orchids, slow-growing conifers, desert plants, plants of economic importance to man, and representatives of all tropical and subtropical plant families. Other features of special interest are a collection of bonsai trees, an outstanding collection of tropical water lilies and aquatic plants, an azalea house, an herb garden, a wildflower area, a topiary garden, and a heather garden, plus some of the most beautifully designed formal gardens in the country. Courses are offered in such horticultural subjects as botany, plant propagation, pressed-plant design, wildflowers, and various phases of gardening. Longwood also presents a series of evening lectures on a variety of horticultural subjects. Educational exhibits in Longwood's conservatories deal with subjects like solutions to common landscaping problems and the care of containerized houseplants and vegetables. Tours of the gardens are available. Longwood is open from 10:00 a.m. to 5:00 p.m. Admission is $3.00 for adults and $2.00 for children.

The Morris Arboretum
9414 Meadowbrook Avenue
Philadelphia, Pennsylvania 19118
The arboretum's grounds and greenhouses feature oaks, beeches, conifers, hollies, and azaleas. There is a collection of tropical ferns, and there are gardens devoted to roses, cacti, and medicinal herbs and other healthful plants. An outstanding variety of educational programs are offered. For children, there are nature discovery tours and summer gardening and crafts programs. For high school students, there are independent work-study programs. For adults, there are courses, lectures, and workshops on horticultural subjects and the artistic use of plants. Teachers may take advantage of graduate courses and in-service training. Plant professionals are invited to use the arboretum's resource center, international seed exchange, and computerized national plant records service. Morris Arboretum will train volunteers for greenhouse and gardening work, to act as guides, and to work as library assistants. Memberships start at $15.00 per year; a membership includes a free subscription to the arboretum's informative newsletter, *Woodchips*. The grounds are open from 9:00 a.m. to 5:00 p.m.; during the winter months, the closing hour is 4:00 p.m. Admission is $.50 for adults and $.25 for children. Members are admitted free of charge.

South Carolina
Brookgreen Gardens
Murrills Inlet, South Carolina 29576
This botanical garden and arboretum is devoted to the flora of the southeastern United States. In the summer hanging baskets are displayed outside, and there are guided nature

walks during the warm months. The garden publishes the *Brookgreen Bulletin*, a quarterly magazine with news of the garden's activities, its history, and additions to its collections. Memberships are available starting at $25.00 a year. Hours are 9:30 a.m. to 4:45 p.m. daily. Admission is $1.50 for adults and $.50 for children. Children under 6 are admitted free.

Tennessee
Tennessee Botanical Gardens and Fine Arts Center
Cheekwood
Nashville, Tennessee 37025
Cheekwood, once one of the South's most beautiful estates, now features botanical gardens, greenhouses, streams, forests, and trails. The Japanese sand garden inspires meditation; there are also pools, a large wildflower garden, and azalea walkways. The grounds are a combined art and garden center with constantly changing botanical exhibits. Open Tuesday through Saturday, 10:00 a.m. until 5:00 p.m.; Sunday, 1:00 p.m. until 5:00 p.m. Closed Mondays, Christmas Eve, Christmas Day, New Year's Day and Thanksgiving Day. Admission is $1.00; members and children under 12 free.

The University of Tennessee Institute of Agriculture
Agricultural Experiment Station
Forestry Stations and Arboretum
901 Kerr Hollow Road
Oak Ridge, Tennessee 37830
This 250-acre forested area is devoted mainly to the cultivation of trees and shrubs for scientific and educational purposes. Besides an abundance of Virginia pine and shortleaf pine, there is a collection of native plant groups emphasizing ecological points of interest. There is a reflecting pond with a small dam and waterfall. A marshy area provides a habitat for moist-site and stream-site plants. Major collections include hollies, pines, willows, and dwarf and unusual conifers. The grounds are open to the public from 9:00 a.m. to 4:30 p.m. Monday through Friday. Admission is free.

Virginia
Norfolk Botanical Garden
Airport Road
Norfolk, Virginia 23518
Covering some 175 acres, the gardens are known for their colorful year-round displays of blooms, including extensive collections of rhododendrons, azaleas, and other plants and flowers. The emphasis is on outdoor plants. Courses are offered in horticulture and topics like indoor plant care and greenhouse construction. Open Monday through Friday from 8:30 a.m. to 5:00 p.m. and Saturday, Sunday, and holidays from 10:00 a.m. to 5:00 p.m. Admission is $.50 per person; children under 5 are admitted free if accompanied by a parent.

Washington
The Finch Arboretum
W. 3404 Woodland Boulevard
Spokane, Washington 99204
The arboretum, which covers about 65 acres, contains native and ornamental trees and

shrubs adapted to a northern environment. Major collections include maples, conifers, crab apples, lilacs, and rhododendrons. There is also a special nature trail with signs in Braille. During the summer, the arboretum sponsors plant clinics (usually held one day a week). During the spring and fall, there are shows, usually featuring flower arrangements. Occasional classes are conducted, primarily related to outdoor gardening. A quarterly newsletter, *Arbor Notes,* describes activities at the arboretum and features gardening tips. The grounds are open daily during daylight hours. Admission is free.

Seymour Conservatory
P.O. Box 7014
Tacoma, Washington 98406
This is the sixth largest conservatory in the United States. Of special interest are the fine collections of orchids, palms, and native and exotic ferns. The Tacoma Metropolitan Park District (of which the conservatory is a part) offers a number of services free of charge, including a plant clinic, a program for schools in and out of the district, and speakers for local garden clubs. The conservatory is open daily from 8:00 a.m. to 4:20 p.m.

The University of Washington Arboretum
Seattle, Washington 98195
The two major points of interest at this arboretum are the beautiful Japanese garden, designed in Japan and constructed under the supervision of Japanese landscape architects, and the waterfront trail, where many species of water plants may be viewed. The arboretum numbers among its collections 4,400 different woody plants, including rhododendrons, hollies, and maples. A collection of indoor plants is also maintained. Open daily 10:00 a.m. to sunset during spring and autumn months; 10:00 a.m. to 7:30 p.m. during summer months. During winter months, the facilities are open from 10:00 a.m. to 4:00 p.m. on Saturdays and Sundays only. Admission is free.

Washington, D.C.
United States Botanic Garden
Washington, D.C. 20024
The garden houses collections of bromeliads, orchids, cacti and succulents, cycads, ferns, palms, and many other tropical and subtropical plants. Short courses on horticultural subjects, mostly dealing with indoor plants, are offered throughout the year and are free to the general public. The garden holds several plant and flower shows each year, and its facilities are also available to Washington-area garden clubs for their shows. All are open to the general public. Tours of the garden are available by appointment only. Hours are 9:00 a.m. to 5:00 p.m. daily. There is no charge for admission.

U.S. National Arboretum
United States Department of Agriculture
Washington, D.C. 20002
Besides the arboretum's fern valley trail, visitors can enjoy the national bonsai collection and collections of azaleas, rhododendrons, dogwood, dwarf conifers, many familiar trees, wildflowers, and much more. Educational

programs include tours, nature walks, horticultural demonstrations, flower shows, lectures, and art displays. There are also classes administered by the Department of Agriculture's Graduate School, but held at and coordinated by the National Arboretum. From April through October, the arboretum is open from 8:00 a.m. to 7:00 p.m., Monday through Friday, and 10:00 a.m. to 7:00 p.m., Saturday and Sunday. From November through March, the hours are 8:00 a.m. to 5:00 p.m., Monday through Friday, and 10:00 a.m. to 5:00 p.m., Saturday and Sunday. There is no charge for admission.

West Virginia
West Virginia University Arboretum
West Virginia University
Morgantown, West Virginia 26506
The West Virginia University Arboretum features several hundred trees and shrubs native to the state, including silver maples, boxelders, and black willows. The 75-acre tract has 3½ miles of wooded nature trails ranging from half-hour walks to four-hour hikes. Walking through the arboretum, one may notice fox squirrels, chipmunks, and many kinds of birds. Open to the public dawn to dusk free of charge.

Wisconsin
Boerner Botanical Gardens – Whitehall Park
5879 S. 92nd Street
Hales Corner, Wisconsin 53130
The gardens, administered by the Milwaukee County Park Commission, are well known for their internationally recognized group of formal and informal gardens. The gardens include two malled perennial gardens, a unique bog garden, a nationally famous rose garden, an herb garden, and a peony display. There are also woody plant collections, hiking trails, and a "trial" garden which specializes in dwarf shrubs, dahlias, and hedges. Numerous species of birds and various small animals live in natural communities in lagoons, restoration prairies, and meadows, which are distinctive features of the park. Open from 8:00 a.m. to sunset during the growing season and from 8:00 a.m. to 4:30 p.m. in the winter.

Mitchell Park Horticultural Conservatory
524 S. Layton Boulevard
Milwaukee, Wisconsin 53215
The conservatory, run by the Milwaukee County Park Commission, is unique for its three-dome structure: a show dome, which features six major plant shows each year, a tropical dome, and an arid (desert) dome. The conservatory, considered one of the finest in the world, contains plants ranging from those of the tropical rain forests of South America to those of the deserts of North Africa. Hours are 9:00 a.m. to 5:00 p.m. on Monday and 9:00 a.m. to 9:00 p.m. Tuesday through Sunday. Admission is $.50 for adults and $.25 for children; Milwaukee County residents are admitted free of charge from 9:00 a.m. to 10:30 a.m. with I.D. Senior citizens over 60 admitted free at all times with County I.D.

University of Wisconsin Madison Arboretum
The University of Wisconsin at Madison
Madison, Wisconsin 53706
The major plant communities of the Midwest prairies, woodlands, marshes, ponds, and lakes are well represented in this arboretum. The arboretum also includes a 60-acre area containing collections of ornamental woody plants suitable for landscape use in this part of the country. Free public tours are held most Sundays throughout the year; for a fee, guided tours are available at other times. The facilities are open year-round.

Virgin Islands
Saint Thomas Gardens
The Orchidiarium
6-37 Constant
St. Thomas, Virgin Islands 00801
The outstanding feature of these gardens is an orchid collection, but there is also a fine collection of tropical plants. Tours of the gardens are available, and there are plant clinics open to the public. Hours are 9:00 a.m. to 5:00 p.m. Monday through Saturday. There is no admission charge.

Water Isle Botanical Garden
P.O. Box 570
St. Thomas, Virgin Islands 00801
Water Isle concentrates on tropical plants that can be grown indoors, so this is a place of special interest to indoor gardeners. There are special, featured collections of orchids, bromeliads, cacti, and showy ornamental trees and plants. A hydroponic garden is also maintained. Tours are given, but you *must* make an appointment. Water Isle is open daily from 9:00 a.m. to 2:00 p.m. There is no charge for admission.

Canada
The Butchart Gardens
Postal Station A, P.O. Box 4010
Victoria, British Columbia
Canada
This is one of the world's leading show gardens. There is a continuous display of flowers, beginning in April with spring bulbs and lasting until the frosts of October. The emphasis is on masses of annuals, but there is also a generous representation of rhododendrons in May and June and of other trees and shrubs throughout the seasons. An outstanding feature is the Sunken Garden. Admission charges vary from $1.00 to $4.00, depending on the season.

The Morgan Arboretum
Macdonald Campus of McGill University
St. Anne de Bellevue, Quebec
Canada
The Morgan Arboretum is devoted entirely to outdoor plants and trees. It includes some 400 acres of natural forest and features native Canadian trees, a 2,000-tree sugar maple grove, and a nursery in which ornamental trees and shrubs are grown. Tours are conducted throughout the year, as are classes in various aspects of forest ecology and resource conservation. There is a $.50 admission fee.

The Niagara Parks Commission School of Horticulture
P.O. Box 150
Niagara Falls, Ontario L2E 6T2
Canada
Located about 5 miles north of the Canadian Niagara Falls, this school is renowned for its gardens, which contain hundreds of different plant and flower species. Its 100 acres feature an arboretum, informal ponds, greenhouses, nurseries, and gardens devoted to roses, alpine plants, lilacs, cacti, vegetables, edible fruits and more. The facilities are open all year. Admission is free.

Royal Botanical Gardens
P.O. Box 399
Hamilton, Ontario L8N 3H8
Canada
Located on a 2,000-acre tract in western Ontario, the gardens display thousands of species of plants. The RBG is also an educational institution, offering courses in such topics as: Indoor Plant Propagation, Fundamentals of Indoor Plant Culture, Flowering Plants for Indoors, Hanging Gardens, and just about any other topic related to indoor or outdoor gardening. In addition, there are plant clinics, nature walks and studies, and exhibits all year round. For further information on classes, contact Out-Reach Department, Royal Botanical Gardens, P.O. Box 399, Hamilton, Ontario, L8N 3H8, Canada.

The University of British Columbia Botanical Garden
6501 Northwest Marine Drive
Vancouver, British Columbia V6T 1W5
Canada
The U.B.C. Botanical Garden is one of those rare and lovely places that has something for everyone. Situated on 110 acres of land, it boasts a number of special gardens in addition to its greenhouses and nursery. Among them are the rose garden, a garden of plants native to British Columbia, and an alpine garden. It also has a beautiful Japanese garden, complete with a ceremonial tea house and pagoda.

The garden runs extensive educational programs which are open to the community at large. These range from specialized courses on topics like pruning and care of the home greenhouse to houseplant workshops.

The greenhouses are open Monday to Friday, from 8:00 a.m. to 4:00 p.m. Various gardens have different schedules, so visitors are advised to write ahead of time. Admission is free except for a nominal charge for visiting the Japanese Garden.

University of Guelph Arboretum
Guelph, Ontario N1G 2W1
Canada
The arboretum is a natural woodland containing over 2,000 different kinds of plants. Special features include collections of trees, shrubs, and woody vines seen very few places in the world. Tours are available; educational services are aimed primarily at regional schools. The arboretum is open to the public from 8:30 a.m. to 5:00 p.m., Monday through Friday. Admission is free.

General sources

Plant, supply and equipment sources

Alberta Nurseries and Seeds, Bowden, Alberta, TOM OKO, Canada. (403) 224-3362. Color-illustrated catalog. Open Monday through Friday from 9:00 a.m. to 5:00 p.m. Selection of vegetable seeds (including herbs) and many annual and perennial flowers. Also some flowering bulbs, trees, and shrubs, as well as rock garden plants. Garden supplies, from special click-on, click-off hoses to seed sowers.

J. Herbert Alexander, Dahliatown Nurseries, Middleboro, Massachusetts 02346. (617) 947-3397. Plant list. This small family operation specializes in mail-order blueberry bushes, ornamental plants, viburnums, vegetables, grapes, and lilac plants for outdoor culture.

Applewood Seed Company, 833 Parfet Street, Lakewood, Colorado 80215. (303) 233-1611. Catalog. Unique collection of seeds: wildflowers, culinary herbs mentioned in Shakespeare's writings, 18 ornamentals for dried arrangements, an herbalist collection for teas, tonics, salads, seasonings and potpourri, and some seeds for indoor plants. Packets come with full growing instructions. Owners' book, *Water, Light and Love*, is a guide to growing plants from seeds ($4.25 including postage).

Armstrong Nurseries, Box 4060, Ontario, California 91761. (714) 986-5114. Color-illustrated catalog. In addition to their extensive regular rose and fruit tree listings, Armstrong also offers miniature tree roses, gold-flowered gardenias, dwarf avocados, kiwi fruit plants, orchids, bromeliads, loquat trees, dwarf citrus trees, and some unusual houseplants.

Bonavista, 807 Van Buren Street, Douglas, Wyoming 82633. Color-illustrated catalog, price lists. Open Monday through Saturday 8:00 a.m. to 5:00 p.m. Wide selection of flower seeds including begonias, coleus, browallia, geranium hybrids, petunias, portulacas, snapdragons. Also vegetable seeds and some spring-blooming bulbs.

W. Atlee Burpee, Warminster, Pennsylvania 18974. Color-illustrated catalog. For visiting hours, directions, and other information, write nearest office: Warminster, Pennsylvania 18974; Clinton, Iowa 52732; Riverside, California 92502. World-famous flower and vegetable seed distributors. Extensive listings of garden vegetables, fruits, flowers, shrubs. Also nursery stock, bulbs, greenhouses, garden and household aids. Established 1876.

DeGiorgi Company, Council Bluffs, Iowa 51501. (712) 323-2372. Catalog 50 cents. Included are hundreds of seeds of vegetables, annuals, perennials, lilies, herbs, and some greenhouse plants and houseplants. Seed-starting pellets and pots are also available.

J.A. Demonchaux Company, 225 Jackson, Topeka, Kansas 66603. (913) 235-8502. Catalog. This unusual company specializes in French gourmet garden seeds featuring European varieties of vegetables, herbs, and berries. They also offer French gourmet foods. The catalog has a Gourmet Gardener Glossary in English, French, and Spanish.

Farmer Seed and Nursery Company, 818 Northwest 4th Street, Faribault, Minnesota 55021. (507) 334-6421. Catalog. Started in 1888 in Chicago, this seed company now has up to 14 nursery outlets. Wide range of seeds, nursery stock, and related items.

Far North Gardens, 15621 Auburndale Avenue, Livonia, Michigan 48154. (313) 422-0747. Illustrated catalog 50 cents. Open by appointment only. This very thorough and specialized company offers primroses from England and the Oregon coast, and rare flower seeds from all over the world. The descriptive, illustrated catalog gives a history of Barnhaven primroses as well as growing instructions.

Ferndale Gardens, Faribault, Minnesota 55021. Color-illustrated catalog and occasional supplements. A potpourri of garden plants, from exotic anthuriums, shrimp plants, and Hawaiian ti logs to berries and lavenders. Many unusual plants suitable to indoor or greenhouse culture. Also garden supplies, including rubber boots!

Henry Field Seed and Nursery Company, 407 Sycamore Street, Shenandoah, Iowa 51602. (712) 246-2110. Catalog. Shenandoah Garden Center, Hwy. 59, open Monday through Saturday 8:30 a.m. to 6:00 p.m., Sunday 10:00 a.m. to 5:00 p.m. (hours vary from month to month). General selection of flower and vegetable seeds, plants, fall bulbs, nursery stock, and related gardening supplies such as tools, hoses, sprayers, pots, fertilizers, and sprinklers.

Dean Foster Nurseries, Hartford, Michigan 49057. (616) 621-4480; 621-4738. Color-illustrated catalog. Open to visitors. Dean and Ruth Foster, carrying on a long family tradition, grow and breed a wide variety of strawberries, including the climbing and hanging hybrids. Also other fruits, dwarf fruit trees, some vegetables, roses, ornamental trees and shrubs, hardwood and nut trees, flower bulbs, and a selection of houseplants. They also offer planting mix and an indoor greenhouse climate-controlled garden unit. Established in 1837, this nursery claims to be "America's oldest and largest strawberry-plant nursery."

Gardens of the Blue Ridge, Box 10, Pineola, North Carolina 28662. (704) 756-4339. Illustrated catalog. Nursery is located 1 mile north of Pineola on US 221; open Monday through Friday 7:30 a.m. to 4:00 p.m. and Saturday until 2:00 p.m. Wildflower plants and shrubs native to the area are offered, including perennial flowers, ferns, and aquatic and bog plants.

Greer Gardens, 1280 Goodpasture Island Road, Eugene, Oregon 97401. Catalog. Rhododendrons, related plants, dwarf conifers, and maples; good source of bonsai material.

Gurney's Seed and Nursery Company, 2nd Street and Capitol Avenue, Yankton, South Dakota 57078. (605) 665-4451. Catalog 35 cents. Gurney's unusual catalog is really a how-to-grow-it book filled with information on planting everything from *Aloe vera* indoors to a time chart for planting fall bulbs. Wide range of plants from outdoor shrubs to vegetable seeds and indoor plants. Excellent houseplant information guide on the back.

The Chas. C. Hart Seed Company, 304 Main Street, Box 169, Wethersfield, Connecticut 06109. (203) 529-2537. Illustrated catalog. Open Monday through Friday 8:00 a.m. to 5:00 p.m., Saturday 8:00 a.m. to noon (closed Sunday). Established in 1892 this company offers vegetable and flower seeds, lawn seeds, field seeds, asparagus roots. onion sets, fertilizers, pesticides, and miscellaneous garden supplies.

Jackson and Perkins, 1 Rose Lane, Medford, Oregon 97501. (503) 776-2000. Color-illustrated catalog. Wide selection of plants and seeds, flowers, vegetables, berries, roses, dwarf fruit trees, and a few houseplants. Also, collection of many different varieties of tulips, daffodils, crocuses, and hyacinths. Seed-starter kits and fertilizer available also.

Johnny's Selected Seeds, Albion, Maine 04910. (207) 437-4303. Catalog 50 cents. Specialists in vegetable, fruit, and herb seeds, most of which are organically grown and untreated; some farm and garden implements. Descriptive catalog includes planting and maturity information, recipes, and some publications.

J.W. Jung Seed Company, Randolph, Wisconsin 53956. (414) 326-3121. Color-illustrated catalog; *Jung's Nursery Guide* 25 cents, *Garden Guide* 25 cents. This general seed and nursery company offers a wide selection of flowers, fruits, and vegetables, as well as trees, shrubs, and some houseplants. Many seeds and some small plants and seedlings. Jung has two excellent culture guides with detailed planting instructions for trees, shrubs, bushes, fruits, and vines (*Nursery Guide*) and instructions for growing vegetables and flowers from seeds (*Garden Guide*). Complete line of garden supplies.

Kelly Brothers Nurseries, Dansville, New York 14437. (716) 335-2211. Color-illustrated catalog. Their store on Maple Street is open from 8:00 a.m. to 5:00 p.m. daily. Selection of fruit trees, berries, grapes, hybrid tea roses, climbing vines, shrubs, trees, perennial flowers, bonsai plants, ginseng, flower bulbs, a few houseplants, miniature roses, tuberous begonias, herbs, and supplies.

Lakeland Nurseries, 340 Poplar Street, Hanover, Pennsylvania 17331. (717) 637-2271. Color-illustrated catalog (new customers pay $1.00 for a 2-year subscription). Mail order only. Large selection of fruit, vegetable, flowering, and foliage plants, including many specialized, rather unusual items; also, many gardening supplies and equipment and some houseplants.

The Lehman Gardens, 420 Southwest Tenth Street, Faribault, Minnesota 55021. (507) 334-8404. Catalog. Retail greenhouses open weekdays 9:00 a.m. to 6:00 p.m. and Sunday noon to 6:00 p.m. Mum fields are open for viewing daily during the fall season. Garden chrysanthemum plants.

Le Jardin du Gourmet, Box 88, West Danville, Vermont 05873. Catalog 25 cents. Open daily, May through October. This charming, snow-bound seed company is open for visitors from late spring to fall when the roads are passable. Specializing in French herbs, especially all kinds of shallot bulbs, rocambole, garlic, egyptian onions, leeks, jerusalem artichokes, and many unusual herb seeds. Recommended books on growing herbs and cooking with herbs; brochure with recipes. Also related French fancy-food items.

Earl May Seed and Nursery Garden, North Elm Street, Shenandoah, Iowa 51603. (712) 246-1020. Color-illustrated catalog. 49 garden centers in five states. Varied nursery stock of flower and vegetable seeds, bulbs, and plants. Unusual source for large selection of more-or-less standard items. Some gardening equipment (seed-starting paraphernalia, books, potting soil, planters, plant stands, fertilizers, light units, and pots.

Mellinger's, 2310 West South Range Road, North Lima, Ohio 44452. (216) 549-9861. Catalog. Open daily except Sunday from 9 a.m. to 5 p.m. A large variety of plants and gardening supplies, including: standard and novelty pots, wick planters, hanging baskets, fertilizers, pesticides, potting mixes, books, bonsai plants, pots, tools, shrubs, ferns, trees, foliage and flowering houseplants, dwarf plants, fruit and vegetable seeds, and cacti and succulents.

The Natural Development Company, Box 215, Bainbridge, Pennsylvania 17502. (717) 367-1566. Color-illustrated catalog. Vegetable and fruit seeds for the organic gardener. Some flower seeds. Complete line of organic garden supplies including Fertrell plant food, compost maker, and mulcher. Also natural organic foods (soup mixes, butters, jams, grains, and flours).

Nature's Garden, Route 1, Box 488, Beaverton, Oregon 97005. (503) 649-7155. Catalog. Visitors by appointment only. Woodland and rock garden plants and bulbs.

Nichols Garden Nursery, 1190 North Pacific Highway, Albany, Oregon 97321. Illustrated catalog. Open daily except Sundays and holidays from 9:00 a.m. to 5:00 p.m. Nichols' offers novelty, gourmet, and oriental vegetable seeds for outdoor gardens and for container planting; plants such as miniature roses, sempervivums, sedum, and cyclamen; gardening supplies such as misting cans, seed-starter pots, and yogurt-makers. Also available are herb seeds and plants, dried herbs and spices, herb teas, and books on gardening.

L.L. Olds Seed Company, Box 7790, Madison, Wisconsin 53707. (608) 249-9291. Illustrated catalog. Stores at 2901 Packers Avenue and 2358 Fish Hatchery Road in Madison. Open Monday through Saturday 8:00 a.m. to 5:30 p.m.; also open on Sunday, April through December. Wide variety of seeds, including annuals and perennials, houseplants, and dwarf vegetable varieties adapted to container gardening. Also offers bulbs, books, seed-starter supplies, fertilizers, an artificial light unit, potting mixes, and pesticides.

Palette Gardens, 26 West Zion Hill Road, Quakertown, Pennsylvania 18951. Catalog 50 cents. Deciduous and evergreen trees and shrubs, bamboo, hardy cactus, ornamental grasses, and perennials.

Geo. W. Park Seed Company, Box 31, Greenwood, South Carolina 29647. (803) 374-3341. Color-illustrated catalog. Open Monday through Friday from 8:00 a.m. to 4:30 p.m. The Park family has been supplying gardeners for over 100 years. Their big, colorful catalog lists seeds, bulbs, and some plants for a wide range of flowers, foliage plants, cacti, garden vegetables, herbs, and fruit. They also have a complete line of garden supplies including: seed-starter kits, soil testers, artificial light units, pots, fertilizers, and potting mixes.

Redwood City Seed Company, Box 361, Redwood City, California 94064. Illustrated catalog 25 cents; supplemental list of rare or seasonal plants, 25 cents or four for 75 cents. Vegetable, herb, fruit, nut, berry, and flower seeds. Many unusual listings: Chinese broccoli, burdock, Oriental and European cabbage, guava, jujube, various dye plants, wild lettuce. Catalog provides plant description and brief culture information for each plant. Book list.

Clyde Robin Seed Company, Box 2855, Castro Valley, California 94546. (415) 581-3467. Color-illustrated catalog $1.00. Unusually extensive collection of seeds including wildflowers, trees, herbs, terrarium plants, plants for bonsai, and many rare species. Some organic vegetable seeds and vacuum-packed seeds. Also, gardening supplies and books. Extremely helpful catalog gives general culture for sowing seeds.

Roswell Seed Company, Box 725, Roswell, New Mexico 88201. (505) 622-7701. Catalog. Store at 115-117 South Main Street, Roswell; open Monday through Saturday 8:00 a.m. to 5:30 p.m. Varied selection of vegetable seeds from asparagus to watermelons. Also many field seeds including alfalfa, millet, rye, sorghum grains, and various other grasses. Complete line of gardening supplies, pesticides, peat moss, pots, weed killers, and fertilizers.

Savage Farm Nurseries, Box 125 ML, McMinnville, Tennessee 37110. (615) 668-8902. Plant list. Open daily September through May. Specializing in flowering shrubs and trees, shade trees, and dwarf fruit trees. Also some berry plants, vines, wildflowers, and bulbs.

F.W. Schumacher, Sandwich, Massachusetts 02563. (617) 888-0659. Catalog. Seeds for flowering and foliage trees and shrubs, including many that can be grown indoors plus some bonsai; books and booklets including one on how to grow seedlings of trees and shrubs. Separate listing of vegetable seeds.

R.H. Shumway Seedsman, 628 Cedar Street, Rockford, Illinois 61101. (815) 964-7243. Color-illustrated catalog. Large selection of flower and vegetable seeds, plants, and nursery items; many roses and fruit trees. Variety of plant and garden supplies. Catalog is a mixture of modern photographs and old-fashioned engravings.

Spring Hill Nurseries, 110 Elm Street, Tipp City, Ohio 45371. (513) 667-2491. Color-illustrated catalog. Open 7:30 a.m. to 4:30 p.m. everyday except holidays. Mail and phone orders, retail. Plants and seeds of every variety: fruit and nut trees, vegetables, foliage and flowering plants, houseplants, bonsai trees and shrubs, and herbs.

Stark Brothers Nurseries and Orchards, Louisiana, Missouri 63353. (314) 754-5511. Color-illustrated catalog. The Stark family has been associated with quality fruit trees since 1816. Today their trees are hand-grafted or budded. In addition to apple, peach, pear, cherry, plum, nectarine, nut and dwarf trees, they offer berries, grapes, vegetable seeds, ornamental and flowering trees and shrubs, and some growing aids.

Stokes Seeds, 37-39 James Street, St. Catharines, Ontario, L2R 6R6, Canada. (416) 685-4255. Color-illustrated catalog. Open Monday through Friday 8:30 a.m. to 5:30 p.m.; farm on Martindale Road open daily during the summer; warehouse tours available at 34 Page Street in St. Catharines. USA address: Box 548, Main Post Office, Buffalo, New York 14280. Large selection of flower and vegetable seeds. Extensive listings include culture information on sowing seeds and maintaining plants. Complete line of garden supplies and books.

Thomas Seeds, Winthrop, Maine 04364. (207) 377-6724. Catalog. Thomas deals primarily in vegetable seeds, but also offers houseplants, nut and fruit trees, cactus, buckwheat, flower and herb seeds, grape vines, berries, flowering trees and shrubs, and some growing supplies and equipment.

Thompson and Morgan, Box 24, 401 Kennedy Boulevard, Somerdale, New Jersey, 08083. Illustrated color catalog. World-famous seed company has been supplying the world's gardens since 1855. Founded by a friend of Charles Darwin, the company admits to carrying on a tradition of controversy. For example, the organic theme runs through their catalog, and they mention the nutrient and fiber content for many of their vegetables. Thompson and Morgan offers seeds for vegetables, annuals, Chinese vegetables, bonsai trees and shrubs, houseplants, herbs, and seeds and beans for sprouting. They also have books and kitchen supplies.

Otis S. Twilley, Salisbury, Maryland 21801. (301) 749-3245. Catalog. Visitors welcome. Varied choice of selected seeds grown and bred in their own gardens.

Vesey's Seeds, York, Prince Edward Island, COA 1PO, Canada. (902) 894-8844. Color-illustrated catalog. Open to visitors. Wide variety of vegetable and flower seeds. Gardening supplies. Handy vegetable-planting chart in catalog indicates how and when to sow seeds.

Wayside Gardens, Hodges, South Carolina 29695. (803) 374-3387. Color-illustrated catalog $1.00. Open Monday through Friday 8:00 a.m. to 4:30 p.m. Miniature roses, annuals and perennials, succulents, ferns, begonias, caladiums, and bulbs. Some gardening equipment.

World Seed Service, J.L. Hudson, Seedsman, Box 1058, Redwood City, California 94064. Catalog 50 cents. Mail order only. Hudson claims to offer the largest selection of seeds available to the public, and warns that some seeds listed in the catalog may lack descriptions because they are so recently discovered that no English descriptions are available. Inventory consists of thousands of varieties of trees, shrubs, flowers, herbs, palms, ferns, cacti, vegetables, edible and beverage plants, and medicinal and fragrant plants.

Supply and equipment sources

American Science Center, 5700 Northwest Highway, Chicago, Illinois 60646. Catalog (50 cents) displays a wide range of scientific apparatus that includes a "plant chime" to monitor a plant's response to its environment, an indoor humidity gauge, thermometers, and unusual experimental devices—Kirlian photography and Galvanic Skin Response machines. The gardening section features a moisture and light meter and an indoor plant lamp.

Dorothy Biddle Service, Dept. TC, Hawthorne, New York 10532. A 10-cent catalog lists houseplant aids, window shelves, trays, plant stands and brackets, flower holders, and many other items. The service was started in 1936 to provide gardening tools and accessories to student lovers of flower and plant arranging.

Carefree Garden Products, Box 383, West Chicago, Illinois 60185. Products include several types of easy-to-use starter kits combining seeds, pots, and tray; Jiffy-Pots and Strips made of expandable peat; miniature greenhouses; soil supplies; pots; and even a Plant Keeper to keep your plants moist while you are on vacation. The products can be purchased nationally through garden centers, hardware and department stores, chain and discount stores. No mail order; product information queries welcomed.

Charley's Greenhouse Supplies. 12442 Northeast 124th Street, Kirkland, Washington 98033. Catalog ($1.00, refundable) lists a variety of products for gardening, including books, Sudbury soil-test kits, accessories, plant lights, and so forth.

Edmund Scientific Company, 1006 Edscorp Building, Barrington, New Jersey 08007. Catalog 50 cents. Wide assortment of scientific equipment. Of particular interest to gardeners

are the thermometers, hygrometers, plant response monitors, pH testers, soil-test kits, and other unusual items.

Fischer Greenhouses, Dept. 4, Linwood, New Jersey 08221. The mail-order catalog (50 cents) includes a full range of the indoor gardening aids that a plant lover might need (such as plant stands and lights, foggers, a water wand for watering hard-to-reach hanging plants) as well as a selection of orchids, African violets, bromeliads, and anthuriums.

Gardening Goodies, Box 5081-T, Beverly Hills, California 90210. The free catalog is filled with unique and practical items. Both indoor and outdoor accessories are available, including items for watering, displaying, and caring for your plants. Also featured is a "you asked for it" section, devoted to helping readers locate hard-to-find items.

Golden Earth Enterprises, 512 Lambert Road, Brea, California 92621. Free catalog (specify retail), featuring one of the widest assortments of containers available by mail order. In addition, the company carries decorator accessories and houseplant and greenhouse supplies. Included are hangers, markers, potting soil, fertilizers, and much more.

Mosser Lee Company, Millston, Wisconsin 54643. Send 50 cents for catalog of unusual gardening aids and also receive a booklet on using sphagnum moss, an instruction sheet on air layering, and a sample packet of Beefsteak tomato seeds. Catalog includes components for soil mixes, fertilizers, pesticides, pots, seed-starting equipment, and other gardening supplies and equipment.

Walter F. Nicke, Box 667G, Hudson, New York 12534. The Garden Talk catalog (25 cents) is chock full of handy items for the gardener, such as British pruning shears and "trug baskets," solo sprayers and sprinklers, watering cans, soil testers, plant trays, as well as sturdy

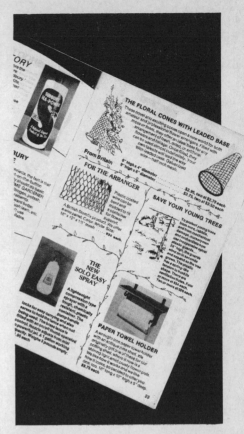

multipocketed aprons and thatched-roof birdhouses from England.

Rheinfrank and Associates, 5414 Sierra Vista Avenue, Los Angeles, California 90038. Free mail-order catalog features a selection of garden supplies useful to the orchid grower. Included are pots, insecticides, hangers, humidity indicators, and watering devices.

Mail-order book sources

The Book Chest, 19 Oxford Place, Rockville Centre, New York 11570, publishes catalogs several times a year. Many books are rare or out-of-print; among the books offered are those on orchids, growing mushrooms, pruning, flower arranging, natural history and plant lore, alpines, bulbs, hydroponics, herbs, miniatures, and ancient plants. To obtain a catalog, send $1.00 and specify botanical subjects. (The Book Chest also offers zoological subjects.)

Warren F. Broderick—Rare Books, 695 4th Avenue, Lansingburgh, New York 12182, publishes a free catalog annually, offering 250 new gardening books. Many of these are not in print or readily available in the United States. Subjects covered are garden history and lore, herb and vegetable gardening, exotic plants, indoor and greenhouse gardening, alpine and rock gardening, plus books about gardening that make especially good reading. Mr. Broderick also deals in used books (both rare and general out-of-print), and offers a free search service for new and rare titles.

H. Lawrence Ferguson, Box 5129, Ocean Park Station, Santa Monica, California 90405, publishes his catalog three times a year. Included are listings on all topics relating to botan-

ical subjects, gardening, and landscaping. A current catalog features 820 listings, divided into such general interest areas as: azaleas, camellias, rhododendrons, begonias, cacti, botany, soils, terrariums, and light gardening.

Garden Way Publishing, Charlotte, Vermont 05445, specializes in books about gardening, how-to methods, and subjects related to self-sufficient living, such as building your own stone house or raising livestock. An annual catalog features books on food gardening, alternate energy sources, low-cost house building, storing foods, homesteading, and home crafts.

HHH Horticultural, 68 Brooktree Road, Hightstown, New Jersey 08520, lists, in its own words, "almost every gardening title in print in English." Most of the books listed are kept in stock. Twenty-five cents (in stamps, coin, or check) will bring their current flyers or lists with a $1.00-off coupon good on any purchase. Lists are issued every 6 to 8 weeks and offer titles about indoor and outdoor gardening, including greenhouse annuals, trees, shrubs, and vines, as well as related arts like flower arranging.

Horticultural Books, Box 107, Stuart, Florida 33494, publishes an annual list specializing in books for warm regions. The company also stocks many books from foreign publishers; among its offerings are horticultural books about tropical Africa, the West Indies, and Cuba. Some of the subjects covered are fruits

and nuts, cacti, succulents, bromeliads, landscaping and gardening, and wildflowers of the United States.

Mother's Bookshelf, Box 70, Hendersonville, North Carolina 28739, publishes an extensive catalog of books that can be ordered by mail. Titles listed cover such topics as building, gardening, crafts, livestock, energy, homesteading, cooking, wild foods, herbs, stocking up, nature, environment, body and soul, camping, homemade music, home business, and children's books.

Pomona Book Exchange, Rockton, Ontario LOR 1XO, Canada, publishes a free catalog two to three times a year. The catalog lists a minimum of 750 titles (they have more in stock), and includes books on wildflowers, forestry, botany, pomology (fruit science), entomology, and other phases of horticulture, agriculture, and related natural history. Although the emphasis is on rare and out-of-print books, important new books are included.

Elisabeth Woodburn Booknoll Farm, Hopewell, New Jersey 08525, has 12,000 books on horticulture in stock. Ms. Woodburn specializes in old books with a number of better quality new books. All can be ordered from catalogs issued several times a year to regular customers; each catalog specializes in a particular area and offers between 300 and 800 items. To obtain a catalog, send $1.00.

Supplies & equipment

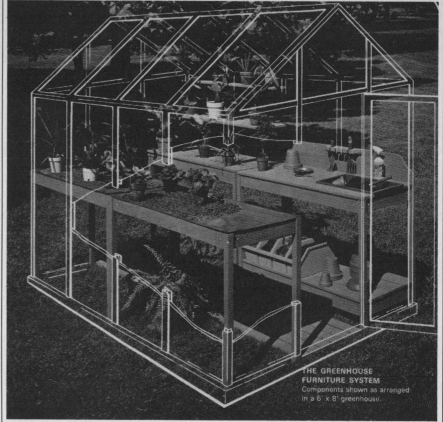

THE GREENHOUSE FURNITURE SYSTEM
Components shown as arranged in a 6' x 8' greenhouse.

Stainless-steel houseplant set includes a trowel and a gardening fork. Both are useful in planting, top dressing, and generally caring for your plants. Imported from England.

A widger, that most classic of gardening tools, is available in highly polished stainless steel. Useful for loosening the top crust of soil and transplanting seedlings.

Fine-point trowel is designed for gardening tasks that require a delicate touch, particularly useful in the cultivation of houseplants. Highly polished stainless steel, fitted with a polyvinyl-chloride grip. Part of the extensive line of pruners, knives, cultivators, and shears manufactured by Wilkinson Sword of England.

For buying information write:
British-American Marketing Services Ltd.
251 Welsh Pool Road
Lionville, PA 19353

Plant Care Center is a modular furniture system made of rough-sawn red cedar, and is suitable for use indoors, outdoors, and in greenhouses. It includes a potting table, planting table with evaporation tray, potting bench with mixing sink, storage bins, tool holder, plant-display riser, and a floor system. Components are approximately 48 inches long by 24 inches wide by 36 inches high.

Kits are easy to assemble and include precut and predrilled wood parts and all hardware. Available in hardware and department stores, garden supply stores, and many merchandising chains.

For buying information write:
Christen
59 Branch Street
St. Louis, MO 63147

Trowels—light, heavy, wide, narrow, short- and long-handled; all are well designed, heavily plated, with sharp cutting edges, and made of heavy-gauge steel with plastic handle grip.

For free catalog and mail-order information, write:
Wilcox All-Pro Tools and Supply
Montezuma, IA 50172

Plant guide is a color wheel of sixty-four houseplants, containing photographs, information on names, and proper amount of light, water, and humidity.

For buying information write:
Berkshire Products
219 Ninth Street
San Francisco, CA 94103

Magi-tag is a metal tag that is easily marked with only a ballpoint pen. It will not corrode and is 1 by 3 inches in size.

For sample and mail-order information, send 25 cents to:
Gaye Gifts
101 Virginia Street
Clearfield, PA 16830

Gardening guide wheels provide fingertip accessibility to information regarding planting seasons, plant ailments, and general care. Gardening wheels are available in six categories: flowers, herbs, vegetable gardens, houseplants, flowering houseplants, and foliage plants.

For mail-order information write:
Chesterfield Shop
14416 Marmont Drive
Chesterfield, MO 63017

Copper lamps with attached planters for hanging plants are lovingly handmade. Heavy, 16-ounce copper sheets are formed into six unique and unusual designs. Each lamp is hand-polished to a bright lustre, with an antique patina finish optional. All lamps are designed to be used with special plant lights.

For catalog and mail-order information, send 50 cents to:
Hosking Lamp Works
RFD 1, Box 136
Accord, NY 12404

Kelly green t-shirts in 100-percent cotton bear plant-oriented slogans in large felt letters. Suggested slogans are available, or you can have your own personalized messages applied. Small, medium, large, and extra-large sizes available. Prices depend on extent of lettering.

Send stamped, self-addressed envelope for mail-order information to:
Pedal On
371 Tampa Avenue
Pittsburgh, PA 15228

Illustrations of popular houseplants, printed on fine paper stock, are available in a series of 64 4-by-6-inch cards. Plant history and care information are on the back of each card.

Wall prints, gift tags, and note cards featuring illustrations of houseplants are also available.

For free catalog and mail-order information, write:
Dandeleau Productions
Box 11115
San Francisco, CA 94101

Four-color poster (24 x 36 inches) has complete plant care information and illustrations of 36 popular foliage plants. Available nationally at hardware, horticultural, and department stores and mass merchandising outlets.

For where-to-buy information write:
Christen
59 Branch Street
St. Louis, MO 63147

Plant persons' aprons, which are made from cotton duck, are available with a variety of plant-related phrases. Each apron has three large pockets and an adjustable neck strap. Each apron is 20 by 22½ inches.

For mail-order information write:
New Humor Company
Box 29033
Dallas, TX 75229

Sphagnum-filled totem-pole supports for climbing plants are among the many indoor gardening aids supplied by the Mosser Lee Company.

For mail-order catalog and literature, send 50 cents to:
Mosser Lee Company
Millston, WI 54643

Indoor plant-care chart uses a series of coded symbols to provide basic information on fifty plants, which are listed and illustrated. Included are plant requirements in terms of temperature, light, soil type, and frequency of watering. A die-cut adhesive-backed unit is provided for transfering coded labels to pots.

For mail-order information write:
Aleph Company
Box 522
Capitola, CA 95010

Houseplant chart has growing instructions for 48 foliage and flowering houseplants. Included is information on water and light requirements, temperature ranges, soil mixtures, and ease of growth.

For mail-order information write:
Plantabbs Corporation
Timonium, MD 21093

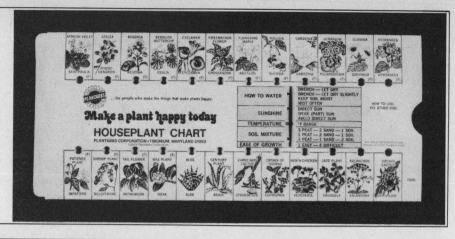

Questers nature tours offer more than 30 tours to Europe, Asia, Africa, Oceania, Australia, and the Americas. The tours are designed for the natural history buff interested in plants and animals, plus culture and customs. Each tour, led by an expert naturalist, also emphasizes art, architecture, and archeology.

For brochures and information write:
Questers Tours and Travel
257 Park Avenue South
New York, NY 10010

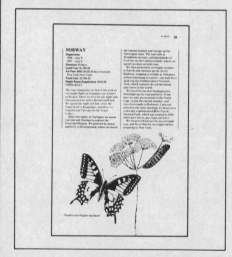

Pot bloomers easily dress up your favorite houseplants. Just slip the elasticized fabric covers over your flower pots. They come in three sizes and in calico, gingham, or solid.

For a brochure and buying information, write:
Calico Critters
Box 308
Pine Brook, NJ 07058

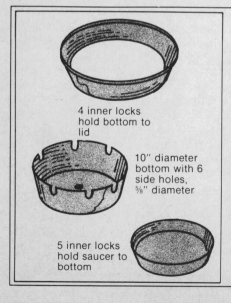

4 inner locks hold bottom to lid

10″ diameter bottom with 6 side holes, ⅝″ diameter

5 inner locks hold saucer to bottom

Plastic flower pots and bedding plant containers for starting plants indoors are available in bulk quantities or by the unit. Of special note is the unique Belden Hanging Pot that lets you create a hanging garden with the planting spaces in the side.

For catalog and mail-order information, write:
Flor-L-Pot
11550 Larch Street
Minneapolis, MN 55433

Geraniums

Miniature geraniums

Geraniums are plants for all seasons and for all people. It is the beauty of the flowers and the diversity of the plants which make them so appealing. The blossoms range from small yellow ones to medium-sized, deep-pink ones to large, snowy-white ones. The foliage can be deep, forest-green, trailing leaves or tricolored fancy leaves. Some plants grow to five feet in height, while others are miniatures. Every plant lover can find a favorite among the geraniums.

Name confusion

Why do we say the common geranium sold by florists and plant shops is botanically named a pelargonium? The reason is that when these plants were first brought from South Africa to Europe in the 1700s, it was thought that they were the same genera as a native, hardy plant named geranium, since the seed pods were similar. It wasn't until years later, when botanists discovered that the genetics of the South African plants were different, that they changed the name to pelargonium, meaning "stork's bill,"

Ivy-leaf geranium

and in both cases these names refer to the shape of the seed pod. Unfortunately, people continued to call the South African plants geraniums. As a result, when speaking of the native

geraniums of the northern hemisphere, we say "true geraniums" and when we say geraniums, we mean pelargoniums.

Infinite variety

Eventually, hundreds of species were introduced, and hybridizers were quick to crossbreed, forming thousands of cultivars. Geraniums were also found to sport or mutate readily, and many were crossed by natural means. Species and hybrids varied greatly so that a number of groupings were formed to make identification easier. The most popular florist type belongs to the zonal (*Pelargonium hortorum*) group. Here we find the single- and double-flowered bedding geraniums, including the colored-leaved and dwarf varieties. Other groups include ivy-leaf and regal, or Lady Washington (*Pelargonium domesticum*), geraniums. Scented-leaf types comprise many different species and hybrids, all with fragrant leaves of various scents. Among them, the most popular are rose, lemon, peppermint, and nutmeg, but there are strawberry, coconut, orange, lime, apple, and others.

The great variety of colors of geranium blossoms and their continuous blooming habits make them one of the most popular flowering plants. Colors include orange, red, pink, purple, white, and various combinations. The bronze, black and pastel-colored flowers of the regal geranium are not seen in any other group.

Culture and care

Geraniums are easy to care for but, like all plants, have certain cultural requirements. These are:

Light: They like full sun in the garden. Potted plants need shade from the mid-day sun in summer and full sun in winter. Indoors, most geraniums do not set buds without help from artificial light.

Temperature: Geraniums grow best at nighttime temperatures of 50 to 60 degrees F., but they tolerate higher or lower temperatures. Some types of geraniums, such as the regals and scented varieties, will not set buds unless night temperatures are below 60 degrees F. Therefore, their season of bloom is late winter and spring, with only scattered blooms in summer and fall and only where summers are cool.

Water: In spring, summer and fall, water the plants before they become dry. In the winter, and in periods of cloudy, wet weather, withhold water until the soil is quite dry; then water thoroughly.

Soil: Use regular potting soil. A good mix consists of equal parts of loam, peat moss, and perlite or sand. Add one cup of a high phosphorous fertilizer such as 4-12-4, or a slow release type, and one cup of dolomitic limestone per bushel of mix.

Potting: When a plant has outgrown its original pot, repot in the next size pot; don't overpot.

Feeding: Do not overfeed. When plants are in active growth, a monthly feeding, half-strength, of any good, well-balanced fertilizer should be given. When new leaves become lighter in color than is normal for the variety grown, it is a good indicator that the plant needs fertilizer.

Mary Ellen Ross

Zonal geranium

Books

The Joy of Geraniums, by Helen Van Pelt Wilson, William Morrow and Co., 105 Madison Ave., New York, New York 10016, paperback, 146 pages, $4.45. Includes many black-and-white illustrations and line drawings. An excellent book for the beginner.

Miniature Geraniums, by Harold Bagust, John Gifford Ltd., 125 Charing Cross Rd., London WC2, England, hardbound, 98 pages.

Perlargoniums, by Derek Clifford, Blandford Press, 167 High Holborn, London, WC1V 6 PH, England, hardbound. This book includes many illustrations with 15 color plates and 83 black-and-white photographs.

Perlargoniums, by Henry J. Wood, Faber and Faber Ltd., 24 Russell Square, London, England, hardbound, 164 pages. A fine book for the beginner which contains 30 color plates and 11 line drawings.

Societies

International Geranium Society, 11960 Pascal Ave., Colton, California 92324. Founded in 1953, the Society's purposes are to disseminate knowledge and promote the use of geraniums. In addition, the Society provides an information exchange for people interested in geraniums and maintains a clearinghouse where geranium fanciers can obtain seeds. Membership is open to anyone interested in joining, and it entitles members to a subscription to the quarterly magazine *Geraniums Around the World.* Dues are $4.00 per year. An annual meeting is held in June; the annual geranium show takes place in Los Angeles in May and is open to the public.

Making a tree geranium

Geraniums, which are normally low, bushy plants, can be trained to grow tall and tree-like. A year or two of careful pruning will result in a spectacularly dramatic tree, with a ball-shaped crown of foliage and flowers resting atop a long, trunklike stem. It's best to begin training in early spring.

Procedure

1. Begin with a well-rooted, 4- or 5-inch stem cutting (see Stem Cuttings, in *Propagation*). Pinch or cut off all side shoots and leaves, leaving just one growing tip. Then plant it in a 3-inch pot. (You might like to work with several cuttings, in separate pots, to ensure success.)

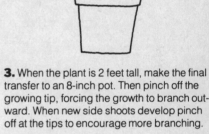

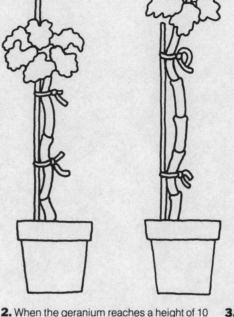

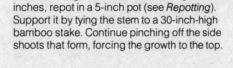

2. When the geranium reaches a height of 10 inches, repot in a 5-inch pot (see *Repotting*). Support it by tying the stem to a 30-inch-high bamboo stake. Continue pinching off the side shoots that form, forcing the growth to the top.

3. When the plant is 2 feet tall, make the final transfer to an 8-inch pot. Then pinch off the growing tip, forcing the growth to branch outward. When new side shoots develop pinch off at the tips to encourage more branching.

Plant sources

Caprilands Herb Farm, North Coventry, Connecticut 06238. (203) 742-7244. Plant list. Scented geraniums. Also herbs.

Carobil Farm, Church Road, R.D. 1, Brunswick, Maine 04011. Catalog. Open 9:00 a.m. to 5:00 p.m. daily. Visitors welcome. Carobil offers one of the most comprehensive selections of geraniums available. Some of the ones offered are: Hartsook hybrids, Deacon and Stellar varieties, bird's egg, carnation-flowered, rosebud species, miniature, and dwarf, as well as regals, zonals, fancy- and ivy-leaf, and scented geraniums. General cultural information is included.

Carroll Gardens, 444 East Main Street, Westminster, Maryland 21157. (301) 848-5422. Catalog. Open Monday through Friday 8:00 a.m. to 5:00 p.m. and Saturday and Sunday 9:00 a.m. to 5:00 p.m. Closed on Sunday from July 11 to September 12. Scented geraniums.

Cook's Geranium Nursery, 712 North Grand Street, Lyons, Kansas 67554. Catalog 35 cents. Visitors welcome. Cook's offers a comprehensive selection of geraniums. Stellar and Deacon varieties are available as well as an assortment of double and single zonals, miniatures, and dwarfs. Also offered are rare, unusual, and odd varieties and species plus fancy-leaved zonals and scented, ivy-leaf, and regal varieties. General cultural instructions given.

Hilltop Herb Farm, Box 1734, Cleveland, Texas 77327. Restaurant open to visitors with advance reservations. Scented geraniums; herbs.

Howe Hill Herbs, Camden, Maine 04843. List with descriptions 35 cents. Scented, miniature, dwarf, and rosebud geraniums available individually or in collections. Also herbs.

Kartuz Greenhouses, 92 Chestnut Street, Wilmington, Massachusetts 01887. (617) 658-9017. Catalog $1.00. Open Tuesday through Saturday 9:00 a.m. to 5:00 p.m. Visitors welcome. Dwarf and scented geraniums.

Logee's Greenhouses, 55 North Street, Danielson, Connecticut 06239. (203) 774-8038. Illustrated catalog $2.00. Open daily 9:00 a.m. to 4:00 p.m. Visitors welcome. Scented, fancy-leaf, dwarf, cactus, tuberous-rooted, rare, and other types of geraniums are available.

Merry Gardens, Camden, Maine 04843. Pictorial handbook $1.00; list 50 cents. Open Monday through Saturday 9:00 a.m. to 4:30 p.m. Single and double zonals, miniature, dwarf, odd and rare, ivy-leaf, fancy-leaf, scented, and regal geraniums are offered.

The Plant Room, 6373 Trafalgar Road, Hornby, Ontario LOP 1EO Canada. (416) 878-4984. List $1.00. Open daily 10:00 a.m. to 4:00 p.m. (closed Wednesday). Visitors welcome. Miniature, dwarf, fancy-leaf, and scented geraniums.

Rutland of Kentucky, 3 Bon Haven, Maysville, Kentucky 41056. List with cultural information. Scented geraniums; also herbs.

Sunnybrook Farms Nursery, 9448 Mayfield Road, Chesterland, Ohio 44026. (216) 729-7232 or 729-9838. Catalog 50 cents. Open Tuesday through Saturday 8:30 a.m. to 5:00 p.m. and Sunday 1:00 p.m. to 5:00 p.m. Visitors welcome. Wide assortment of geraniums, including miniature, dwarf, fancy-leaf, ivy-leaf, scented, pansy, odd, rare, and single types.

Taylor's Herb Garden, 1535 Lone Oak Road, Vista, California 92083. (714) 727-3485. Catalog 25 cents. Open daily from 8:00 a.m. to 5:00 p.m. Conducted tours the first Sunday of every other month at 11:00 a.m. Scented geraniums. Also herbs.

Wilson Brothers Floral Company, Roachdale, Indiana 46142. (317) 596-3455. Color-illustrated catalog. Open daily 8:30 a.m. to 5:00 p.m. Greenhouses located on US 231, 5 miles west of Roachdale. Visitors welcome. Single and double zonals plus ivy-leaf, scented, regal, miniature, fancy-leaf, novelty, and unusual geraniums are offered by this company founded in 1918.

Yankee Peddler Herb Farm, Department TC, Highway 36N, Brenham, Texas 77833. (713) 836-4442. Catalog $1.00 (refundable). Open daily from 9:00 a.m. to 5:00 p.m. Visitors welcome. Scented geraniums; also herbs.

Gesneriads

Columnea hybrid

The gesneriads (guess-nair-ee-ads) are a family of plants which flower so easily indoors that they are fast becoming one of the best plant groups to try. In the *Gesneriaceae* (the botanical name for the family) there are all sizes and shapes, from the 1-inch high sinningias to tree-sized cytandras; some are trailers and others are upright growers. The varieties of form, color, and texture are limitless. Most gesneriads have such beautiful foliage that they are a joy to look at even when not in bloom.

The best-known ones

African violets (saintpaulias), gloxinias (sinningias), flame violets (episcias), lipstick vines (aeschynanthus), goldfish plants (columnea), candy corn (nematanthus), cape primrose (*Streptocarpus rexii* hybrids), and nautilocalyx are probably the best known.

They can be found in any plant store even if the sales people, or the public, don't know their names. In the *Gesneriaceae* there are 135 genera and over 2,500 species. It is impossible to count hybrids, cultivars, or varieties.

All gesneriads require good light to flower. The growing medium must be porous, draining quickly but holding moisture, and with a good organic content. Fertilize regularly with a high-analysis liquid formula and keep the pH near neutral.

Velvet bells

After the African violet, probably the florist gloxinia is the next most popular. All colors and patterns can be found in upright bells or nodding blossoms of velvet. They come with either a single or double flower. Modern American hybridizers have brought the naturally large leaves down to a

more manageable size, softer in texture, with less leaf curl and bud loss. With proper care of the tuber during dormancy, they can last many years.

Bright foliage

Peacocks in a basket would be a more apt description of the episcias than flame violets. They are really grown for their beautifully colored and patterned foliage rather than their tiny flowers, which often clash with the leaf colors. To grow episcias with large lush leaves, it is necessary to pinch out the stolons (runners) as they appear, until the desired leaf size has been obtained. Most people permit too many stolons to grow, giving the plant a stringy appearance. The exceptions are with the small-leaved varieties, Such as *Episcia dianthiflora*, where the dense carpet effect is preferable. Episcia 'Cleopatra' is lovely but tem-

Sinningia species

Kohleria hybrid

Episcia dianthiflora

peramental, with pink, green, and white foliage, and is best when kept in a terrarium.

Several hanging types

Aeschynanthus is often called lip-stick vine. The common name comes from watching the crimson flower emerge from its tubelike calyx. Plants are best grown in hanging planters.

Columneas have been called the goldfish plant because the red-orange flowering varieties look very much like goldfish in motion. Most of the columneas for sale are basket plants because the upright growers produce stiff stems and are rarely graceful. There are many easy, ever-blooming hybrids which are best for house culture. Yellow-orange Early Bird, red Robin, and yellow Butterball, will give a variety of color. The frequently sold, small-leaved species require a cold period to set buds.

Nematanthus is a large genus with many basket beauties. Only *Nematanthus wettsteinii* has gotten wide attention because the tiny blossoms look just like, and are about the size of, candy corn. They peek out from behind small, dark green, shiny leaves. Any one of the new hybrids, mainly available through mail-order sources, would be excellent. Examples are Bambino, Bijou, Black Magic, Cameo, Cherrio, Green Magic, Sambo, and Tropicana.

Special new hybrids

Streptocarpus rexii hybrids are fast overtaking the florist gloxinia (*Sinningia speciosa*) in popularity. It, too, has large, trumpet-shaped flowers in various colors. Most frequently seen are the Nymph series. Colors range from purple through blue, rose, and white; many have throat markings. There is another member of this genus that is excellent in hanging baskets. *Streptocarpus saxorum* has small, fuzzy leaves and pale blue, trumpet-shaped flowers.

The shrublike gesneriad most often seen is *Nautilocalyx lynchii*, and sometimes *N. forgetii*. The first has dark red stems and leaves with creamy yellow flowers covered with red hairs appearing in the axils. The second has quilted green leaves with dark red veining and yellow flowers. They are best used as a shrub in a tub. For maximum potential, they need lots of light.

Ruth Katzenberger

Streptocarpus saxorum

Plant sources

Alberts and Merkel Brothers, 2210 South Federal Highway, Boynton Beach, Florida 33435. (305) 732-2071. Plant list 75 cents. Open Monday through Saturday 8:00 a.m. to 4:30 p.m. Episcia, nautilocalyx, aeschynanthus, columnea, and nematanthus.

Antonelli Brothers, 2545 Capitola Road, Santa Cruz, California 95062. (408) 475-5222. Illustrated catalog. Open daily. Sinningia, achimenes, streptocarpus, and smithiantha.

Buell's Greenhouses, Box 218, Weeks Road, Eastford, Connecticut 06242. (203) 974-0623. Descriptive list 25 cents, plus long, stamped, self-addressed envelope. Open Monday through Saturday 8:00 a.m. to 5:00 p.m. Aeschynanthus, agalmyla, boea, chirita, codonanthe, columnea, episcia, gesneria, nematanthus, nautilocalyx, petrocosmea, sarmienta, streptocarpus, achimenes, diastema, gloxinia, koellikeria, kohleria, seemannia, smithiantha, chrysothemis, and sinningia.

Edelweiss Gardens, 54 Robbinsville-Allentown Road, Box 66R, Robbinsville, New Jersey 08691. (609) 259-2831. List 35 cents. Open until 4:00 p.m. daily. Aeschynanthus, columnea, episcia, nematanthus, and nautilocalyx.

Fischer Greenhouses, Linwood, New Jersey 08221. Visitors are welcome at the greenhouses located one block west of Route 9, at Oak and Central Avenues in Linwood. Episcia, columnea, nematanthus, and aeschynanthus.

Harborcrest Nurseries, 4634 West Saanich Road, Victoria, British Columbia, V8Z 3G8, Canada. Aeschynanthus, columnea, episcia, nematanthus, and streptocarpus.

Heavenly Violets, 9 Turney Place, Trumbull, Connecticut 06611. Plant list 25 cents. Visitors welcome by appointment. Episcia.

Hewston Green, Box 3115, Seattle, Washington 98114. Plant list 50 cents. Aeschynanthus, codonanthe, columnea, episcia, kohleria, mitraria, nematanthus, neomortonia, petrocosmea, and streptocarpus.

Kartuz Greenhouses, 92 Chestnut Street, Wilmington, Massachusetts 01887. (617) 658-9017. Catalog $1.00. Open Tuesday through Saturday 9:00 a.m. to 5:00 p.m. Achimenes, aeschynanthus, agalmyla, alloplectus, boea, chirita, chrysothemis, codonanthe, columnea, corytoplectus, dalbergaria, diastema, drymonia, episcia, gesneria, gloxinia, koellikeria, kohleria, lysionotus, moussonia, nautilocalyx, neomortonia, nematanthus, niphaea, paradrymonia, pearcea, petrocosmea, rufodorsia, sinningia, smithiantha, streptocarpus, and trichantha.

Lauray of Salisbury, Under Mountain Road, Salisbury, Connecticut 06068. (203) 435-2263. Catalog 50 cents. Open daily 10:00 a.m. to 5:00 p.m. Aeschynanthus, alloplectus, boea, chirita, codonanthe, columnea, drymonia, episcia, gesneria, nautilocalyx, nematanthus, paradrymonia, streptocarpus, achimenes, diastema, gloxinia, koellikeria, kohleria, lysionotus, niphea, seemania, chrysothemis, and sinningia.

Lyndon Lyon, 14 Mutchler Street, Dolgeville, New York 13329. List with descriptions. Open daily 8:00 a.m. to 6:00 p.m. Visitors welcome. Gloxinia, sinningia, columnea, and episcia.

The Plant Room, 6373 Trafalgar Road, Hornby, Ontario, LOP 1EO, Canada. (416) 878-4984. List $1.00. Open daily 10:00 a.m. to 4:00 p.m. (closed Wednesday). Visitors welcome. Aeschynanthus, columnea, episcia, sinningia, achimenes, chrysothemis, codonanthe, gesneria, koellikeria, kohleria, nautilocalyx, nematanthus, seemania, and smithiantha.

San Francisco Plant Company, Box 575, Colma Station, Daly City, California 94014. Catalog 25 cents. Episcia, columnea, streptocarpus, and other gesneriads.

Wood's African Violets, Proton Station, Ontario, NOC 1LO, Canada. (519) 923-6123. List with descriptions 25 cents. Open daily 10:00 a.m. to 7:00 p.m. Located 5 miles north of Dundalk and 1 mile off Highway 10. Visitors welcome. Rooted clumps of episcia; supplies.

Societies

American Gloxinia/Gesneriad Society, Mrs. Wm. J. Rowe, P.O. Box 174, New Milford, Connecticut 06776. The American Gloxinia and Gesneriad Society, a nonprofit organization, was founded in 1951. It has grown to include members in every state, and from Canada and many other countries.

How to Know and Grow Gesneriads, a handbook mailed to all new members, and *The International Gesneriad Register* are both published by the Society, as is a bimonthly magazine, *The Gloxinian*.

Privileges of membership (the fee is $7.00 per year) include judged flower shows with awards, round-robin letters, a seed fund, and access to local chapters and a library of slides and books. All who wish to can meet at the annual convention, which is generally held in May or June.

Books

The Miracle Houseplants – The Gesneriad Family, by Virginie F. Elbert and George A. Elbert, Crown Publishers, One Park Ave. New York, New York 10016, 1976, 242 pages, $6.95. This book is entirely devoted to gesneriads, which number among their members the African violet and florist gloxinia. It is an easy to understand, well-written guide to raising these beautiful, blooming indoor plants. Information is provided on the types of soil to use, how much and when to water, proper temperature, frequency of fertilization, cuttings and leaf propagation.

African Violets and Relatives, Handbook of the Brooklyn Botanic Garden, 1000 Washington Ave., New York, New York 11225, order No. 53, $1.75 postpaid.

More gesneriads

A few other gesneriads to look for that are a joy to grow and easily obtained from the specialists:

With rhizomes:
Achimenes 'Crimson Beauty'
Diastema vexans
Gloxinia sylvatica
Koellikeria erinoides
Kohleria 'Connecticut Belle'
Smithiantha zebrina hybrids

With tubers:
Sinningia cardinalis, canescens, hirsuta, 'Bright Eyes,' 'Cindy,' 'Dollbaby,' 'Minarette,' and 'Snowflake.'

Fibrous rooted:
Alloplectus calochlamys
Boea hygroscopica

Greenhouses

Every sort of indoor gardening has its own rewards, but the pleasures of a greenhouse are in a class of their own. When we lure nature indoors and coax her into stretching the seasons for us, we create a living environment vastly more satisfying than the most luxuriant windowsill garden.

It's a more demanding environment, too, for the right conditions don't just happen; they come from thoughtful planning and watchful maintenance. A good greenhouse is one that suits the taste, the budget, and the energies of a grower. It harmonizes with its surroundings, has rugged, durable construction, and is flexible enough to change with expanding interests and seasonal cycles. Those gardeners who do their homework before buying— or building— their first greenhouse will be well rewarded for their efforts.

Many options available

Probably the most bewildering part of selecting a greenhouse is the enormous range of styles available. There are simple even-spans, elegant gothic arches, lean-tos, geodesic domes, A-frames, and greenhouses shaped like Mongolian yurts, gazebos, and quonset huts. They may be covered with glass, fiberglass, polyethylene, vinyl, mylar, acrylic, or a combination of several materials. Frameworks

may be wood, aluminum, steel, or tubular vinyl. Whatever *your* inclinations, look for durability. Wood supports must be either a rot-resistant species, such as redwood or cedar, or specially treated to withstand weathering. If you're considering a metal-framed house, a galvanized finish is far superior to painted metal, or something that vaguely claims to be rust-resistant. Better to skimp on the glazing, if you must, and get a framework that will still be in good shape when you can afford a better covering.

Style and location

As a general rule-of-thumb, the closer a greenhouse is to your home, the more it should harmonize in line, materials, and color. If your greenhouse is destined for a distant corner of the yard, you can indulge in something more exotic. Just don't put it so far away that midwinter maintenance becomes a burdensome chore.

Before you set up your greenhouse, check your site for the best possible winter sun, adequate air circulation, and, if possible, some shelter from strong winds. A good location might be one with an evergreen screen against the prevailing winter winds and a scattering of deciduous trees elsewhere. These will also moderate the winter wind, without blocking precious sunlight, and their summer shade will

help keep your greenhouse from turning into a giant vegetable steamer.

There are a number of good books available for greenhouse gardeners, and we have included some suggestions below. Use them to investigate the fine points of fiberglass versus acrylic, to learn about utility hookups, and most of all, to profit from the experience of knowledgeable growers. Send for all the manufacturers' literature you can get your hands on, visit showrooms, talk with greenhouse owners. If your budget is rather limited, you will get a feel for which features have top priority. As in most things, the best quality is the least expensive in the long run. Yet there is hardly such a thing as a bad greenhouse; the most inexpensive model can give you enormous satisfaction. Enjoy your garden under glass.

Noreen Mooney

Noreen Mooney is an amateur horticultural enthusiast. Foliage plants, vegetables, and miniatures in the greenhouse are her favorites.

Books

Build Your Own Greenhouse, by Charles D. Neal, Chilton Book Co., Chilton Way, Radnor, Pennsylvania 19089, 1975, hardback, 130 pages, $9.95. Probably the most complete book of its kind available.

The Complete Book of Greenhouse Gardening, by Ian G. Walls, Quadrangle Books, 10 E. 53rd St., New York, New York 10022, hardbound, 447 pages, $14.95. This book is concerned in detail with the design and maintenance of greenhouses and growing plants within them. Includes an in-depth look at site and greenhouse selection, environmental control, equipment, and care of various plants in the greenhouse. Very informative reading.

Gardening Under Glass, by Jerome A. Eaton, MacMillan, 866 Third Ave., New York, New York 10022, 1973, hardbound, 306 pages, $8.95. This book covers all aspects of greenhouse gardening, from selection to building and growing plants. The hows and whys of day-to-day maintenance of plants are expressed in layman's terms.

Greenhouse Gardening, Sunset Books, Lane Publishing Co., Menlo Park, California 94025, 1976, paperback, 95 pages, $2.45. Aimed at the person taking up greenhousing as a hobby, this book concentrates on the anatomy of a greenhouse. Included are tips on pest control, specialty plants, and a list of greenhouse manufacturers.

Greenhouse Gardening For Fun, by Claire L. Blake, William Morrow and Co., 105 Madison Ave., New York, New York 10016, 1967, 256 pages, hardbound, $6.95, paperback, $2.95. An excellent guide with all the practical shortcuts to make gardening under glass more joy than work. Deals with the basics to aid the beginner who hopes to make his greenhouse hobby pay off.

Greenhouse Gardening as a Hobby, by James U. Crockett, Doubleday and Co., 245 Park Ave., New York, New York 10017, 1961, $6.95. Excellent for ornamentals, especially orchids. A good monthly calendar helps in planning for year-round bloom.

Greenhouse–Place of Magic, by Charles H. Potter, E. P. Dutton and Co., 201 Park Ave. S., New York, New York 10003, 1976, paperback, 251 pages, $3.95. Essentially aimed at the person who is taking up greenhousing as a hobby. Included in this book is information on how to buy, build, equip, and maintain your own greenhouse. In addition, there are tips on all aspects of choosing and using a greenhouse.

Greenhouse Gardening Made Easy, by Jack Kramer, Bantam Books, 666 Fifth Ave., New York, New York 10019, 1976, paperback, $1.95. A concise and informative introduction to greenhouse gardening.

Greenhousing for Purple Thumbs, by D. X. Fenton, 101 Productions, 834 Mission St., San Francisco, California 94103, 1976, paperback, 186 pages, $4.95. Readable, attractive, with plans for building your own greenhouse. Also included is a month-by-month guide to using the greenhouse.

The Handmade Greenhouse from Windowsill to Backyard, by Richard Nicholls, Running Press, 38 S. 19th St., Philadelphia, Pennsylvania 19103, 1975, 128 pages, $4.95. Building plans for all types of greenhouses are included as well as information for utilizing your greenhouse.

How to Build Your Own Greenhouse, by Elvin McDonald, Popular Library, 600 Third Ave., New York, New York 10016, 1976, paperback, 318 pages, $1.50. A step-by-step guide to building your own greenhouse. Contains many photographs, descriptions, and assessments of all major greenhouse models. Also includes tips on what plants can be grown in the greenhouse and how to properly care for them.

Organic Gardening Under Glass, by George and Katy Abraham, Rodale Press, 33 E. Minor St., Emmaus, Pennsylvania 18049, 1975, hardbound, 308 pages, $8.95. This book was written by two well-known greenhouse owners. Topics include fruits, vegetables, and ornamentals in the greenhouse. It's useful for both organic and non-organic gardeners and includes many charts and tables which are helpful for growing edibles under glass.

The Underground Gardener, by Jack Kramer, Thomas Y. Crowell, 666 Fifth Ave., New York, New York 10019, paperback, $4.95. For the energy-conscious gardener; the book includes ways to take advantage of natural insulation and cut heating costs.

Winter Flowers in Greenhouse and Sun-heated Pit, by Kathryn S. Taylor and Edith W. Gregg, Charles Scribner's Sons, 597 Fifth Ave., New York, New York 10017, 1969, paperback, 281 pages, $7.50. This book supplies all the necessary information for setting up your own greenhouse or sun-heated pit. Included are instructions for year-round maintenance as well as the cultivation of plants which can be grown under these energy-saving conditions.

Your Homemade Greenhouse and How to Build It, by Jack Kramer, Cornerstone Library, 630 Fifth Ave., New York, New York 10020, paperback, $2.95. Even if you have no intention of building a greenhouse, this book would be a great help in evaluating kits and pre-fabs. Also includes good ideas on arranging your greenery.

Information sources

Under Glass – The Home Greenhouse Gardener's Magazine. A bimonthly publication, devoted entirely to greenhouse and window greenhouse gardening. Contains information on what to grow, when and how to grow it, along with listings of new products, sources of supply, new plant varieties, and so forth. Sold by subscription only. Write to *Under Glass*, P.O. Box 114, Irvington, New York 10533. Subscription rates are $2.75 for one year and $4.00 for two years.

For advice on the different types of greenhouses, location, design, construction, frames and various accessories, there is an excellent, inexpensive government bulletin which will help you make the necessary decisions. Send 25 cents to Superintendent of Documents, U.S. Government Printing Office, Washington, D.C. 20402, and request Building Hobby Greenhouses, Agricultural Information Bulletin No. 357.

Societies

Hobby Greenhouse Association, Box 695-F, Wallingford, Connecticut 06492. The Hobby Greenhouse Association is a nonprofit organization devoted to popularizing greenhouse gardening as a healthy recreation.

Membership includes access to a plant-swap service, a library that lends books by mail, and written round robins in which members share their experiences on specific greenhouse gardening topics, such as growing a specific type of plant. The $5.00 annual membership fee includes a subscription to *The Planter*, a publication containing advice about greenhouse gardening.

Energy-saving greenhouses

It's rather ironic that as home greenhouses are becoming more popular, less expensive, and easier to set up and maintain, they are becoming more costly to heat. These enchanting perpetual gardens are, after all, artificial worlds. And as the cost of fossil fuels rises, more and more gardeners will be asking themselves if they can—or should—continue to heat them with electricity, oil, or gas.

Happily, the current push for alternative energy sources is generating ideas useful for greenhouses as well as homes. One of the simplest is a revival of an old horticultural technique: the growing pit. Basically a greenhouse sunk into the ground some 4 feet, the traditional pit depends entirely on the sun as a source of heat. At night, its glass wall is covered with some thick sort of matting, but it really depends upon its earth walls to retain solar heat. It's possible, of course, to supplement the heat artificially, and some growers now do this.

It's easy to see how the basic principles of the pit can be applied to modern greenhouse design. If the foundation cannot be sunk into the earth, then the earth can be brought up around the foundation walls of the greenhouse—an effective and inexpensive type of insulation already being used for solar-heated homes. For some good ideas on earth-insulated greenhouses, look at

Winter Flowers in Greenhouse and Sun-heated Pit, by Kathryn S. Taylor and Edith W. Gregg (Scribners), and *The Underground Gardener*, by Jack Kramer (T.Y. Crowell).

Once you begin to see the need—and possibilities—for energy-efficient greenhouses, you will begin to discover all sorts of new techniques that can be adapted for greenhouse heating. Admittedly, solar collectors, methane digesters, and wind-powered generators are not weekend projects, but modest heat-storage walls using water and rocks are within the scope of amateur builders. Two useful books which come to mind are *Energy, Environment and Building* by Philip Steadman (Cambridge) and *Producing your Own Power*, edited by Carol Stoner (Rodale). Both have good bibliographies. *The Mother Earth News* is a good source for current experiments, and can lead you to more specialized publications.

You will enjoy, also, *The Provident Planner*, by Roger Rasbach (Walker). This is an intriguing, visionary blueprint for a new kind of architecture in which both indoor and outdoor gardening are a unified part of home design. It's rather exciting to think of a future in which gardening under glass will no longer be an energy debit, but will contribute energy *and* greenery to our microenvironments. Best of all, we can begin, now, in our own backyards.

Energy, Environment, and Building, by Philip Steadman, Cambridge University Press, 32 E. 57th St., New York, New York 10022, 1975, hardcover, 287 pages, $16.95.

Producing Your Own Power, edited by Carol Stoner, Rodale Press, 33 E. Minor St., Emmaus, Pennsylvania 18049, 1974, hardcover, 322 pages, $8.95.

The Provident Planner, by Roger Rasbach, Walker and Company, 720 Fifth Ave., New York, New York 10019, 1976, hardcover, $12.95, paperback, $6.95.

The Underground Gardener, by Jack Kramer, Thomas Y. Crowell, 666 Fifth Ave., New York, New York 10019, 1976, 192 pages, hardcover, $9.95, paperback, $4.95.

Winter Flowers in Greenhouse and Sun-heated Pit, by Kathryn S. Taylor and Edith W. Gregg, Charles Scribner's Sons, 597 Fifth Ave., New York, New York 10017, 1969, paperback, 281 pages, $7.50.

The Mother Earth News, P.O. Box 70 Hendersonville, North Carolina 28739. A bimonthly magazine focusing on alternative lifestyles, ecology, working with nature, and doing more with less. Subscriptions are $10.00 for 1 year, $18.00 for 2 years, $26.00 for 3 years, and $200.00 for forever.

Supplies & equipment

Automatic ventilating system for the greenhouse stabilizes greenhouse temperature regardless of outside weather. In case of power failure, the roof sash closes instantly to keep heat in the greenhouse until electricity is restored.

For free catalog and mail-order information, write:
Gleason-Avery Division
Box 635, Department T.C.
Auburn, NY 13021

Solar Technology Corporation offers solar design, consulting, and engineering services. Plans, solar materials, and do-it-yourself kits are also available. Solera, a walk-in solar collector, is easily adaptable to already existing structures. By adding Solus collector panels to Solera, thermal performance is increased, making possible solar furnace, water heating, and sauna applications. Solar Garden components transform Solera into a solar greenhouse that supplies supplemental heat and humidified air to attached homes. Also offered is a complete package for energy conservation and solar heating of new and existing greenhouses.

For brochure and more information, write:
Solar Technology Corporation
2160 Clay Street
Denver, Colorado 80211

Hansen WeatherPort features four home greenhouse models. These are freestanding, Quonset-style models with galvanized steel frames and laminated polyethylene covering. All four models are 7 feet high and 12 feet wide. They are available in lengths of 10, 15, 20, and 25 feet. If you need a larger model, Hansen WeatherPort has other sizes available. The largest measures 30 by 120 feet.

WeatherPort greenhouses are shipped ready for easy assembly and include several special features as standard equipment: a 16-inch exhaust fan with automatic shutters, a steel-framed fiberglass door with a shuttered ventilating unit, and a forced air blower (included in the price of a double cover) which insulates the greenhouse by maintaining a constant air pressure between the two layers. The greenhouses are guaranteed.

For brochures and mail-order information, write:
Hansen WeatherPort
313 North Taylor
Gunnison, CO 81230

Semisphere offers a line of greenhouses featuring geodesic construction. The greenhouses are partially assembled Plexiglas triangles already fitted into the wood sections. A wood-bladed overhead fan is available, as is a curved, two-level slatted growing table. Semispheres' geodesic greenhouses come in a variety of sizes, ranging from 8 feet to 48 feet in diameter.

For brochure and mail-order information, write:
Semispheres
Box 26273
Richmond, VA 23260

National Greenhouse Company offers a line of hobby greenhouses plus accessories. The greenhouses come in four models, including freestanding and lean-to styles. Freestanding models are from 8½ to 32 feet long, and from 7½ to 17 feet wide. The lean-tos range from 8½ to 32 feet long, and from 5 to 8 feet wide. (All measurements are approximate.) These greenhouses feature aluminum frames; commercial quality, double-strength glass; continuous roof ventilation; and a glassed-in aluminum door with screen. All units are prefabricated, and come with complete instructions for easy, do-it-yourself assembly.

The new Quonset-shaped, Econolite models—priced to fit almost any budget—are made of arched, galvanized conduit frames and covered with two layers of air-inflated plastic.

For brochure and information, write:
National Greenhouse Company
Box 100
Pana, IL 62557

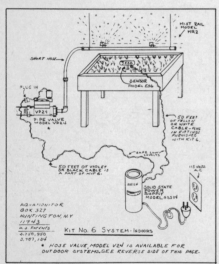

Aquamonitor offers a full line of misting and watering devices for the greenhouse. Kit No. 6 comes complete with a sensor, power supply, and valve. It supplies the correct minimum and optimum of water for climatized controlled mist propagation. Thirty-day warranty; detailed instructions included with each kit. Mist rails to use with Kit No. 6 are also available. Kit No. 7 is a drip, or trickle, irrigation system. It consists of a power supply, sensor, tank measure, and valve. The system applies water instantly to completely balance soil-evaporation and plant-transpiration losses.

For brochures and mail-order information, write:
Aquamonitor
Box 327
Huntington, NY 11743

Burpee greenhouses are available in free-standing and lean-to models. The framework is aluminum with a white enamel finish, and the covering is double-strength, tempered glass. A sliding glass door and ventilators are included in the easy-to-assemble kit.

For brochure and mail-order information, write:
W. Atlee Burpee Company
300 Park Avenue
Warminster, PA 18974

Ezyrected greenhouses are available in a wide range of styles and sizes from Texas Greenhouse Company. All are constructed of double-strength glass, or fiberglass, and rust-resistant materials, such as kiln-dried redwood, aluminum, brass, and galvanized steel. Most are available in either standard or glass-to-ground construction. The greenhouses are prefabricated; all parts are precut and predrilled and are shipped with illustrated instructions. Redwood-frame styles are constructed of 2-foot sections, each with its own roof vent for ventilation. (Additional sections can be ordered to increase the length.) Those with aluminum framing have a continuous ventilating sash on each side of the ridge. The smallest greenhouse is approximately 8 feet wide, 7 feet high, and 10½ feet long, and requires no foundation. At the other end of the spectrum are models up to 54 feet long for commercial growers. Texas Greenhouse also offers lean-tos in both aluminum and redwood framing. All greenhouses carry a one-year warranty.

Texas Greenhouse can also supply you with these greenhouse accessories: cooling, heating, and ventilating devices, watering and humidifying equipment, plant benches, hydroponic systems, timers, vinyl shading, light units, fertilizer, heating cables, mulch shredders, and soil sterilizers.

For catalog and mail-order information, write:
Texas Greenhouse Company
Box 11219
Fort Worth, TX 76110

Greenhouse equipment and accessories are available through Equipment Consultants and Sales. Among the items offered are automatic watering systems, propagating and seed-germinating equipment, heating units, thermostats, thermometers, hygrometers, misting, shading, and cooling devices.

For brochures and mail-order information, write:
Equipment Consultants and Sales
2241 Dunwin Drive
Erin Mills
Mississauga, Ontario L5L 1A3 Canada

Plantworks has three different greenhouses available. Two are freestanding models, available alone or with a specially designed growing system. The latter includes a push-button environmental control center that provides automatic heating, cooling, humidity, ventilation, louver control, and an exhaust system. An automatic hydroponic-gardening system can also be supplied with either of these greenhouses. The third model, a lean-to, is not currently available with these systems.

Of the freestanding greenhouses, one is a traditional arched model with a 16-gauge metal frame and 5-ounce fiberglass panels. It measures 9 feet wide, 12 feet long, and 9½ feet high. For maximizing the length, 34½-inch extensions are available. More unusual is the modern geodesic-style greenhouse, made entirely of preformed fiberglass. Its translucent surface is impervious to the elements, and it is structurally designed to withstand heavy snow loads and strong winds. This model is 10 feet 9 inches wide, 14 feet long, and 8 feet high. Additional extensions can be ordered.

The lean-to greenhouse is made with a heavy-duty metal frame and fiberglass panels. It measures 7 feet wide, 9 feet long, and 9 feet high.

For brochures and mail-order information, write:
The Plantworks
145 Weldon Parkway
Maryland Heights, MO 63043

Lord and Burnham, the oldest and largest greenhouse company in the country, manufactures freestanding, even-span, and lean-to greenhouses, constructed of aluminum and glass. The greenhouses are available in a wide variety of styles and sizes (from 7 to about 20 feet wide, and from 8 feet 6 inches to over 51 feet long). The Orlyt and Imperial models come in standardized lengths based on modular sections; additional sections may be attached at any time to increase the length. Colors (baked enamel finish) cost extra. Lord and Burnham green-

houses can be assembled in a few weekends, and all carry a one-year warranty.

Lord and Burnham offers many greenhouse accessories, including planting benches; glass shelves; vent screens; shades; heating, cooling, ventilating, and humidifying devices; a wick-watering system; and books on greenhouse gardening.

For catalog and mail-order information, write:
Lord and Burnham
Dept. HC
Irvington, NY 10533

Greenhouse Growing Systems offers five different freestanding greenhouses. They range in style from a traditional rectangular model to an A-frame and a semicommercial model with center benches and double aisles. They range in size from 8 by 6 feet to 14 by 43 feet. All greenhouses are constructed of prefabricated redwood and glass. Greenhouse Growing Systems will install greenhouses for local residents (installation fees are quoted for each model). Orders will also be taken for custom-made greenhouses, including window models.

For a brochure and further information, write:
Greenhouse Growing Systems
Box 988
5248 North Sereno Drive
Temple City, CA 91780

Santa Barbara Greenhouses sells two types of greenhouses, a freestanding model and a lean-to. Each model is 7 feet wide and is available in four lengths: 4, 8, 12, and 16 feet. Frames are of kiln-dried redwood, bolted together with rust-resistant galvanized hardware. The vertical siding is hail- and shatter-resistant fiberglass that is guaranteed for 15 years.

Greenhouses are sold as kits ready for home assembly. No foundation is necessary. All models include Dutch doors pre-assembled and ready for hanging and four sets of fiberglass vents as standard equipment. Benches, fiberglass sunscreens, and other accessories are available.

For brochures and mail-order information, write:
Santa Barbara Greenhouses
390 Dawson Drive
Camarillo, CA 93010

AirCap is a transparent, flexible plastic insulating material that is especially useful for both glass and fiberglass greenhouses. Entrapped air bubbles in the plastic greatly reduce heat loss in winter. AirCap comes in regular and heavy weights and can be taped or stapled in place.

For free catalog sheets and buying information, write:
Sealed Air Corporation, Marketing
19-01 State Highway 208
Fair Lawn, NJ 07410

Reliable Greenhouses is the exclusive United States distributor of Baco aluminum greenhouses. There are five models—three freestanding and two lean-to. The lean-to models are both 7 feet 8 inches high (ridge height, no base). The smaller model is 8 feet 3 inches long by 6 feet 4 inches wide. The freestanding models are all 6 feet 8 inches high (ridge height, no base) and the base sizes range from approximately 6 by 8 feet to approximately 8 by 12 feet.

Standard equipment differs from one model to the next, but in all cases includes: numbered aluminum parts, precut glass, nuts and bolts, special glazing strips, integral gutters, a sliding or hinged door, and assembly instructions. Many optional accessories are available. All materials are guaranteed for 25

years against normal corrosion and faulty workmanship.

For further information write:
Reliable Greenhouses
Box G, Route 53
Norwell, MA 02061

Everlite aluminum greenhouses include four lean-to and four freestanding models, all with straight sides and full-length ventilation of roof areas. Each model comes in a standard size, though the company will make greenhouses to specific dimensions. For do-it-yourselfers, the standard models can be increased (in length) with add-on sections. Most can also easily be increased or reduced in height.

The smallest lean-to model is 3 feet 10 inches wide and is available in 8-foot 7-inch-long sections. The largest lean-to is 8 feet 7 inches wide and is available in 10-foot-long sections. The freestanding models range from 7½ to 17 feet in width and from 8 feet 7 inches to 10 feet in length.

The price of each greenhouse includes all parts needed for assembly, except foundation. (Free foundation sketches will be provided on request.) The standard equipment includes corrosion-resistant aluminum extrusions and castings, vent machinery, precut double-strength glass, glazing compound, and assembly tools. All parts carry a one-year guarantee.

Many greenhouse accessories are also available.

For brochures and mail-order information, write:
Aluminum Greenhouses
14615 Lorain Avenue
Cleveland, OH 44111

Solarvent is a solar-powered automatic greenhouse vent. The unit can be used with most aluminum or wood greenhouses and is easily adaptable to cold-frame sashes or other applications.

The automator waters and feeds plants, mulches the surrounding soil, and provides heat in cold spells. It furnishes more than a half gallon of water to plant root systems with each filling.

For mail-order information write:
**Dalen Products
201 Sherlake Drive
Knoxville, TN 37922**

Greenhouse climate-control equipment is manufactured by the Acme Engineering and Manufacturing Corporation. The company offers a wide selection of ventilating fans, fan-and-pad cooling and ventilating systems, and a perimeter heating system to eliminate cold floors.

For brochures and buying information, write:
**Acme Engineering and Manufacturing Corporation
Box 978
Muskogee, OK 74401**

Standard humidifiers utilize the principle of centrifugal force to atomize water into a fog-like vapor. The shaft of each unit contains a ball-bearing motor.

Different size models are available. The small model, for use in small greenhouses, vaporizes up to 2 quarts of water per hour and will provide 55 to 65 percent relative humidity in a space of approximately 2,000 cubic feet.

For information and catalog write:
**Standard Engineering Works
289 Roosevelt Avenue
Pawtucket, RI 02860**

Greenhouse Specialties has a budget-priced greenhouse with support tubing that extends into the ground, eliminating the need for costly foundations. The prefabricated parts are constructed of heavy-gauge galvanized steel and special greenhouse sheeting.

The company also offers a new, more expensive greenhouse with a galvanized steel frame and fiberglass walls and roof.

Accessory equipment is also available for use with the fiberglass, such as exhaust fans, heating units, and timers. The company also supplies plans for construction of a 14- by 14-foot greenhouse.

For information write:
**Greenhouse Specialties Company
9849 Kimker Lane
St. Louis, MO 63127**

Greenhouses designed for small spaces, such as patios, terraces, or balconies, are offered by Casaplanta. The framework is made of extruded plastic tubing; molded plastic fittings let you join the parts without tools. The shatterproof, heavy-duty vinyl covering is resistant to heat, cold, and ultra-violet light. Redwood benches and built-in vents are included. Two sizes are available. One has a base measurement of 4 by 6 feet and is 7½ feet high; the other is 3 feet by 4 feet 10 inches and 7 feet high. Extension units are available for the larger model. Optional equipment (humidifier, cooler, heater, screen, water hose, and mister) is sold separately. One-year warranty.

Casabella is a mini-greenhouse designed to be used indoors. Unbreakable vinyl plastic covers the tubular plastic frame. Six plastic trays are provided to hold plants; a ventilator is built in. The overall size is 39 inches wide, 20 inches deep, and 60 inches high.

For brochures and mail-order information, write:
**Casaplanta
16129 Runnymede Street
Van Nuys, CA 91406**

Freestanding greenhouses with aluminum frames and safety-glass coverings are offered by Edward Owen Engineering. Four models are available; each is 8 feet 5 inches wide, with a ridge height of 7 feet 11 inches. Lengths range from 6 feet 5 inches to 12 feet 6 inches. Features include commercial-strength ridge, patented glazing system, extra-large vents, aluminum base wall, sliding door, gutters and downspouts, and aluminum benches, among others. Available as a kit with a fully illustrated, step-by-step assembly manual.

For brochure and mail-order information, write:
**Edward Owen Engineering
Snow Shoe, PA 18764**

Sturdi-Built Manufacturing Company produces greenhouses in a great variety of styles, ranging from traditional to unique. All have natural redwood frames and are available with your choice of glass or hail-proof fiberglass. (Both clear and self-shading fiberglass are offered.) Models are available in a variety of sizes, ranging from a junior model that is 5½ feet by 9 feet to a unit 10 feet wide and adaptable to whatever length you want, via 10-foot connector sections plus 2-foot extensions.

Designs include such unusual models as circular and gazebo-type greenhouses. More traditional models are available in either free-standng or lean-to adaptations.

All greenhouses are factory preassembled, and shipped in large wall, roof, and door sections for easy installation, and all doors are pre-hung. Hardware and built-in vents are included with all models, and redwood benches are included with most.

Sturdi-Built also sells greenhouse accessories, such as heating, cooling, ventilating, and humidifying equipment.

For brochures and ordering information, write:
**Sturdi-Built Maufacturing Company
11304 Southwest Boones Ferry Road
Portland, OR 97219**

Sunglo greenhouses are offered in free-standing and lean-to models. All have extruded aluminum frames covered with high-impact acrylic. The double-wall construction acts as dead-air insulation, minimizing heat loss. Aluminum benches and vents are included with all models. Control systems kits are available. All models are easy to assemble, with instructions included. Sunglo greenhouses are distributed on the West Coast in garden centers and nurseries.

For buying information write:
Sunglo Greenhouses
3714 South Hudson Street
Seattle, WA 98118

Sun-Lite greenhouses feature aluminum frames and double-strength glass. The three models available are all 8 feet wide and 7 feet high; lengths are 8½ feet, 10 feet, and 12 feet. (All measurements are approximate.) Extensions up to 12 feet 2¾ inches are available. Standard features include: sliding door with tempered glass, condensation channels, eaves, and gutters. The new standard feature is a solar-powered automatic ventilating system with two roof vents that open and close gradually as the internal temperature rises and falls. Available in kit form, with illustrated assembly instructions.

For brochure and mail-order information, write:
Weber Systems Incorporated
P.O. Drawer L
New Hope, AL 35760

The stairhouse greenhouse is specifically designed to be attached directly to a house wall on top of a cellar passageway. It is equally adaptable, however, to ground-level exits where no stairs are involved. This is the only greenhouse offered by the Verandel Company, and it comes in one size: width, 5 feet 4¼ inches; length, 6 feet 2¼ inches; and height, 7½ feet. For easy home assembly, the Stairhouse is made of prefabricated aluminum. It is shipped complete with bolts and nuts, precut double-strength glass, an outward-swinging aluminum door, and assembly instructions. Optional equipment, available at extra cost, includes: jalousie or fan ventilation, an electric heater, shading material, and shelves.
For a brochure and mail-order information, write:
Verandel Company
Box 1568
Worcester, MA 01601

Archway greenhouses are available in five standard sizes, ranging from 8 by 10 to 16 by 20 feet; the minimum height is 8 feet. All are sold either in easy-to-assemble kits or delivered and installed. Other sizes may be requested on special order.

On all models, the frame is kiln-dried yellow pine, which has been treated against rot and termites and carries a 20-year guarantee. The fiberglass covering has a 12-year guarantee. All models feature aluminum storm doors fitted with safety glass, and ventilating shutters are included. Screw-shank nails, weather-stripping, and neoprene washers are included with the kits. Fans, heaters, thermostats, a cooling system, lights, and wood benches are available separately.

For further information or estimate, write:
Archway Greenhouses
Box 246
Duck Hill, MS 38925

Environmental Dynamics has greenhouse kits available. All of their Sunglow greenhouses feature heavy-duty steel frameworks, an aluminum door, clear plastic front panels, and nylon-reinforced Filon fiberglass coverings.

The Plant Starter is Environmental's smallest greenhouse, one specifically designed for germinating seeds and giving plants a head start on the growing season. The unit is 5 feet long, 4 feet wide, and 6½ feet high, and is available with polyethylene, vinyl, or fiberglass covering. All plants are within reach from the outside of the greenhouse.

For brochure and mail-order information, write:
Environmental Dynamics
Box 996
Sunnymead, CA 92388

J. A. Nearing sells freestanding, even-span, and lean-to greenhouses in nine different designs. (The company also carries one window model.) Each prefabricated aluminum greenhouse is available with straight or curved eaves, and can be ordered glass-to-ground or for placement on built-up masonry walls. The smallest model is a freestanding greenhouse, 4 by 8½ feet at the base and 7½ feet high; the largest is an even-span greenhouse, 21 feet wide, 9½ feet high and available in lengths ranging from 21 to 51 feet. (All measurements are approximate.) With most models, additional section lengths can be ordered.

Greenhouses include all hardware, vents (automatic ventilation is available at extra cost), swing-out doors, and in most cases, a choice of glass or fiberglass. All parts are covered by a one-year warranty.

Nearing sells many greenhouse accessories, including heaters, automatic controls, watering equipment, and shades.

For brochures and mail-order information, write:
J. A. Nearing Company
10788 Tucker Street
Beltsville, MD 20705

Vegetable Factory offers freestanding and lean-to greenhouses which require no foundations. The lean-to models come in two standard width and lengths: 5½ feet and 8½ feet wide, and 8 and 12 feet long. The freestanding models are also available in two standard widths and lengths: 8 and 11 feet wide, and 8 and 12 feet long. Add-on sections make it possible to extend all models at any time. One or more extensions, combined with any of the models, produce greenhouses with approximate lengths of 16 feet, 20 feet, 24 feet, and so forth.

Greenhouses are shipped in ready-to-assemble sections that consist of two layers of rigid, fiberglass-reinforced acrylic, permanently bonded to aluminum support frames. The shatterproof panes are separated by a thermal air space. The only tools needed are a screwdriver and drill. The entire greenhouse is guaranteed for five years.

For brochures and mail-order information, send 35 cents to:
**Vegetable Factory
Department TCC
Box 2235, Grand Central Station
New York, NY 10017**

Plantation greenhouses have aluminized high-strength steel frames and are available covered with either plastic or fiberglass. There is a choice of two designs, traditional and gothic arch. Twelve-foot-wide models come in four lengths, and 20-foot-wide models come in five lengths. Only ordinary household tools are needed for assembly, and complete installation instructions are included. There is a seven-year warranty on exteriors and a ten-year warranty on the main structure. Optional equipment includes lighting, heating, ventilating, solar heating, and cooling systems.

For brochure and mail-order information, write:
**Enclosures Incorporated
80 Main Street
Moreland, GA 30259**

McGregor greenhouses are made of 4-ounce Filon fiberglass and have a bolt-together frame of precut redwood. There are six models to choose from: four freestanding and two attached models. All of the models have vertical sides to maximize growing space, and all are 6 feet 10 inches wide and 8 feet high. The freestanding models are available in 4-, 8-, 12-, and 16-foot lengths, while the attached models come in 4- and·8-foot lengths. (All measurements are approximate.) Greenhouses can be easily enlarged with 4- or 8-foot bolt-on extensions, which can be ordered any time.

McGregor also offers a special budget kit. It includes all materials except the redwood frame, in case you want to save money by buying your lumber locally. Both the budget and regular kits include free plans for winterizing your greenhouse.

For brochures and mail-order information, write:
**McGregor Greenhouses
1195 Thompson Avenue
Santa Cruz, CA 95063**

Cloud Company offers a budget-priced greenhouse with no frills that measures approximately 7 by 7 by 7 feet. It is available in a kit that includes high-quality precut lumber, plastic covering material (which must be replaced yearly), and step-by-step instructions for assembly. You provide the nails. Directions (but not materials) for constructing the floor are also supplied. The design, by David Brock, allows for maximum flexibility, and the Cloud Company will provide suggestions for shelves and other additions upon request.

For brochure and mail-order information, write:
**Cloud Company
1318 28th Street Southeast
Auburn, WA 98002**

Filon fiberglass-reinforced panels, specifically made for do-it-yourselfers, can quickly be turned into a backyard greenhouse. These shatterproof panels transmit more light (and lose less heat) than glass. They are available in standard corrugated sheets that are 26 inches wide and 8, 10, or 12 feet long, as well as in flat sheets, sold in 50-foot rolls that are 48 inches wide.

A brochure, with plans for an 8- or 12-foot greenhouse, can be obtained by mail or from lumberyards and home-improvement centers. Also included are tips on foundations, location, and equipment.

For brochure and buying information, write:
**Filon Home Greenhouse
Hawthorne, CA 90250**

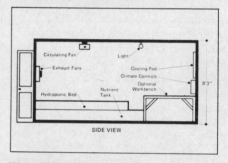

SIDE VIEW

Water Works GardenHouses offers a variety of high-quality greenhouses. Models range in size from 8 by 12 feet to 8 by 24 feet; each is 8 feet 3 inches high.

The basic greenhouse consists of a redwood frame with Filon fiberglass covering, rust-resistant hardware, a prehung door, and an installation manual. Two special models are also available: climate-controlled and hydroponic. Both maintain safe greenhouse temperatures regardless of climate. Climate-controlled greenhouses include an evaporative cooling unit, exhaust fan, heating unit, fan, light, and a control panel. The hydroponic model includes these features, plus all equipment necessary for hydroponic gardening: plastic-lined redwood growing beds, a nutrient storage tank and an automatic nutrient-pumping system, a control panel, and an operating manual.

Accessories include slat-type redwood benches, a hydroponic planter that automatically feeds and waters plants, hydroponic nutrients, pH tester, seed-starting cubes, hygrometers, minimum-maximum-temperature thermometers, and several greenhouse books.

For catalogs and ordering information, write:
**Water Works GardenHouses
Box 905
El Cerrito, CA 94530**

Hanging plants

Big, lush, fluffy Boston ferns are what probably come first to your mind when hanging baskets are mentioned. But don't stop there: innumerable other plants look great when hung, and there are an equal number of imaginative ways to display them.

Generally, plants that cascade or trail look best in hanging baskets. You can grow just one plant in a basket or a combination of plants with similar cultural needs.

Take care to choose plants that will thrive in the conditions you can easily provide. Matching plants and cultural conditions is the key to success. If you're unexpectedly given a hanging plant, find out its environmental needs before choosing its permanent location.

Almost anything can grow in front of a bright window, since you can always hang the plant a few feet back or install a translucent shade if the light is too strong. But a dim window will only support low-light tolerant plants, unless supplemental electric lighting is added. One trick is to plant a combination basket with sun-loving plants facing the window and shade-lovers facing into the room. Or hang a plant from a swivel hook so that it can be turned. In windowless rooms, use the circline fluorescent light units with their own pots made especially for hanging plants.

Temperature is usually only a consideration where extremes are involved, but you should keep in mind that hot air rises—right up to where your hanging baskets are! If your situation is extreme, choose only warmth-loving plants. On the other hand, be aware of how close your baskets are to cold winter windowpanes. Some people solve this by hanging plants from swinging brackets that allow plants to be near windows by day, swung away at night.

If your baskets are in the kitchen or bathroom, there will probably be ample air moisture. For drier rooms, choose plants noted for their ability to withstand low humidity. The hot air that rises to hanging basket height is dry air, while cooler, moister air stays near the floor.

Because the air surrounding them is warm and dry, hanging baskets need frequent watering. There are plastic squeeze bottles available with tall curved spouts made especially for watering hanging baskets, and indoor hoses that reach up high, also. But to see what you're doing, you'll need to lower the plant. Some people hang plants with pulley arrangements for this purpose.

Since some provision for drainage must be made anyway, many people find it easiest to simply carry plants to a sink for watering. If your plant will be watered in place, use a saucer, emptying it if it remains filled 30 minutes after watering.

Because of frequent watering, hanging plants may need a little more fertilizing than other potted plants, as the fertilizer tends to wash away.

The only special consideration regarding soil for hanging plants is that it be lightweight. For this reason, soil-less potting mixes are often used.

The weight of the container, too, is a consideration. Plastic is lightest. But since the container of a hanging plant is often quite visible, you may want to use the pot (of whatever material) that most appeals to you and complements the plant. Just be sure your method of attachment to the ceiling or wall is strong enough.

Last thoughts: for safety, hang baskets where no one will bump his head; for beauty, use your imagination in combining plants, containers, and decorative hangers, and hang them as high or as low as you wish, singly or in multi-plant hanging gardens.

Wendy Schrock Dreyzin

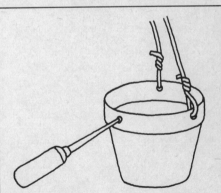

Wendy Schrock Dreyzin has put her journalism training at the University of Washington to use through editing and freelance writing, with a specialty in indoor gardening.

She is a member of the Garden Writers Association of America.

Books

Container and Hanging Gardens, Ortho Books, Chevron Chemical Co., Ortho Division, 200 Bush St., San Francisco, California 94101, 1975, paperback, 97 pages, $3.98. This book is mostly about outdoor containers and hanging baskets, but many of the unique planting ideas could be easily adapted for indoor use.

Fun with Hanging Plants, by Julie Hogan, Ideals Publishing Co., Milwaukee, Wisconsin 53201, paperback, 64 pages, $2.25. Beautiful color photographs grace this book, which is mainly concerned with indoor plants.

Gardening in Hanging Baskets, by Rex Mabe, Potpourri Press, Box 10312, Greensboro, North Carolina 27404, 1973, paperback, 46 pages, $1.50. The hanging basket beginner will find this a handy primer. Both foliage and flowering plants for indoor baskets are discussed.

Hanging Plants for Home, Terrace and Garden, by John P. Baumgardt, Simon and Schuster, 630 Fifth Ave., New York, New York 10020, 1974, paperback, 128 pages, $2.95. All about hanging plants—cascading from boxes, spilling down from baskets, trailing from urns, or dangling from posts, this book gives all the methods as well as helpful hints on where to hang your plants for the best possible effect, suggestions on what plants to grow and how to keep them growing, advice on where to buy plants and accessories.

Ideas for Hanging Gardens, Sunset Books, Lane Publishing Co., Menlo Park, California 94025, 1974, paperback, 80 pages, $2.45. This is the most complete book on hanging baskets, covering both indoor and outdoor plantings in a thorough manner.

Do-it-yourself hanging planter

An easy, if somewhat odorous way to convert an ordinary plastic pot into one that you can hang is with a hot ice pick. Mark the position of the holes with a felt-tipped pen, spacing them equidistantly. Then heat the ice pick over an open flame, and melt the holes in the pot. Insert cords, wires, or chains with S-hooks into the holes for hanging.

Hardware sampler

A hanging plant, when watered, can weigh as much as 50 pounds or more. So, for safety's sake, choose your hardware carefully. In most cases, you will need to drill a test hole in your wall or ceiling to determine its construction.

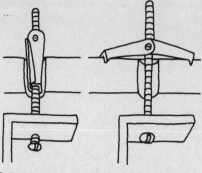

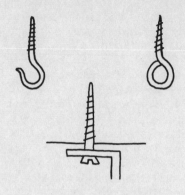

4. Toggles are also used for hollow construction, but bear heavier weights than mollies. Drill a hole the diameter of the closed toggle wings. Insert the toggle and the bolt, eye bolt, or bolt hook, and tighten. The wings will open on the other side of the wall to hold the bolt in place.

1. Wood screws, screw eyes, and screw hooks are used for solid wood or for wood studs behind plasterboard. Simply make a pilot (starter) hole with an awl and hammer or a drill, insert the screw (with the bracket in place if you are using one), and tighten.

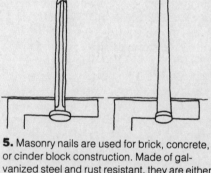

5. Masonry nails are used for brick, concrete, or cinder block construction. Made of galvanized steel and rust resistant, they are either finely ridged or square-edged to grip the masonry. Simply use a heavy hammer to drive them into the wall.

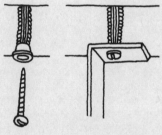

2. Fiber, plastic, or lead plugs and screws are used for plaster construction, which would crumble if screws were used alone. Drill a hole the same diameter as the plug. Tap the plug into the hole, insert the screw (with bracket in between) and tighten.

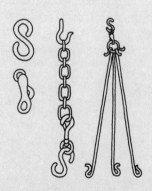

6. S-hooks, swivels, chain, and wire are used to suspend pots once the fasteners are in the wall or ceiling. S-hooks connect wire or chain lengths to fastener or pot; link several together to lengthen wire or chain and so lower a plant. Swivels enable you to rotate plants without unhooking them. Chain and wire are sold by the foot in hardware stores. Wire comes in many gauges; chain is available in many weights, styles, and finishes.

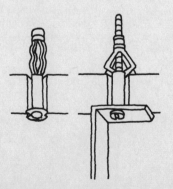

3. Mollies are used for hollow construction (usually plasterboard). Drill a hole the diameter of the anchor. Insert the bolt and tighten. The metal shoulders spread open and grip the other side of the wall.

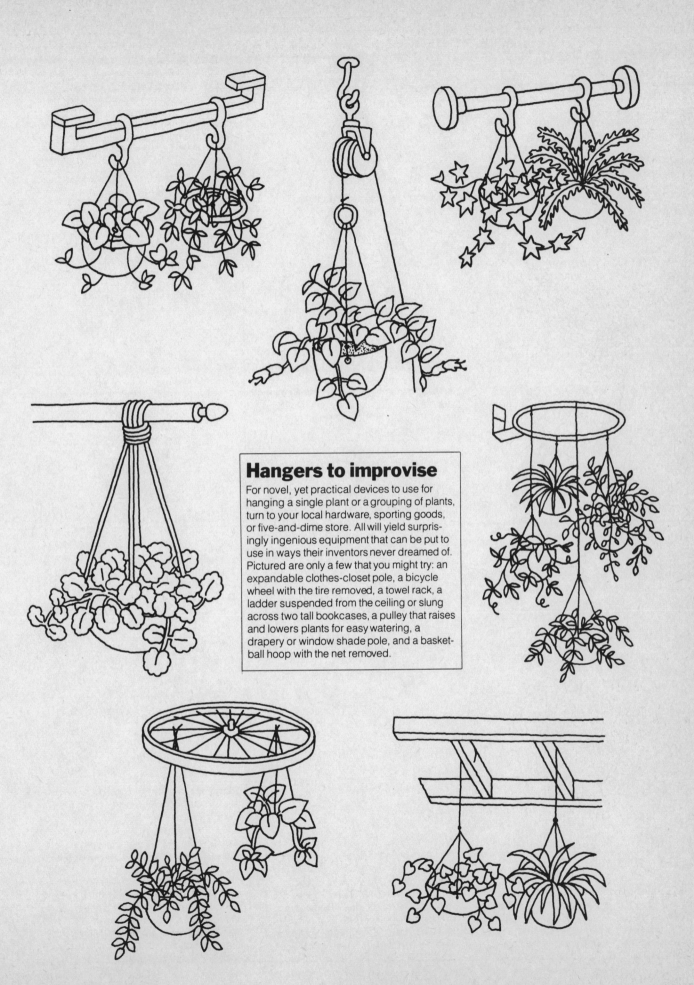

Hangers to improvise

For novel, yet practical devices to use for hanging a single plant or a grouping of plants, turn to your local hardware, sporting goods, or five-and-dime store. All will yield surprisingly ingenious equipment that can be put to use in ways their inventors never dreamed of. Pictured are only a few that you might try: an expandable clothes-closet pole, a bicycle wheel with the tire removed, a towel rack, a ladder suspended from the ceiling or slung across two tall bookcases, a pulley that raises and lowers plants for easy watering, a drapery or window shade pole, and a basketball hoop with the net removed.

Macramé hanger

Even beginners can make an attractive macramé hanger, since it requires only the overhand knot. The more experienced can add additional cords and beads, and tie more elaborate knots. There's no worry about the pot fitting the hanger—this design expands and/or contracts to fit just about any size and shape. To calculate the length the cords should be, multiply the desired finished length by four. If you want a 3-foot-long hanger, start with 12-foot-long cords. Any cord, even leather lacing, works. But thin cord will rot quickly due to watering; so jute or nylon cord is recommended.

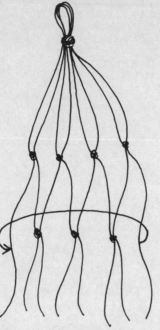

3. Make a row of alternate knots by joining strands from each adjacent pair. Make the knots 3 to 5 inches below the first row, depending upon the size of the pot.

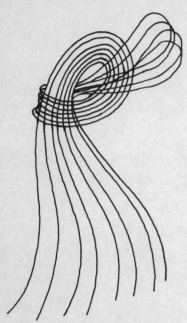

1. Gather the four cords together with the ends even. Fold the group in half, and tie an overhand knot 2 inches below the fold. This forms the loop for hanging.

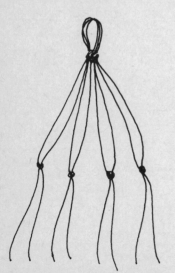

2. Catch the loop over a door knob or drawer knob to steady your work. About 5 inches above where the top of the pot will be, tie the cords together in pairs. Make sure all knots are the same distance from the top knot.

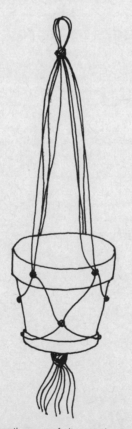

4. Make another row of alternate knots in the same way, again 3 to 5 inches below the previous row. Gather all 8 strands together, about 3 inches below the last row of knots. Tie a single overhand knot with all 8 strands, forming a tassel. Insert the pot in the hanger, and trim the tassel ends evenly.

Supplies & equipment

Pot suspenders come either ruffled or beaded. The ruffled version has three separate variations. Each has a ruffle which surrounds the pot and is suspended by fabric cording that matches the ruffle. The beaded version comes in either calico or gingham prints. Wooden beads give a macramé look to the hanger. Both are adjustable to fit most hanging plants.

For brochure and buying information, write:
Calico Critters
Box 308
Pine Brook, NJ 07058

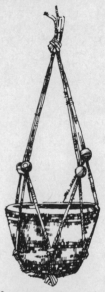

Gingham hangers, which come in 34- or 42-inch lengths, are made from gingham tubing and are adjustable to fit almost any size pot.

For mail-order information write:
New Humor Company
Box 29033
Dallas, TX 75229

Plantrac is a ceiling-mounted plant-hanging system that includes multi-level hanging tracks, large tiering rings, and hooks. Plants can be rotated 360 degrees for even, healthy growth. Plant-Rail is a simpler version.
Hang downs allow for hanging two, three, four, or more planters from a single 15-inch-long hook (50-pound capacity). Available nationally in garden supply, hardware, chain, and department stores.

For mail-order information write:
Plantrac Corporation
38 West Mall
Plainview, NY 11803

Hanging planters range from 6 to 14 inches in diameter. All sizes come with three lengths of chain and an S-hook. Two of the smaller planters have snap-on drip trays. All are made of weather-resistant, lightweight, high-impact plastic in a variety of colors.

Wall or **ceiling brackets** are for hanging planters, lamps, terrariums, or bird cages. Filigree-designed and molded of high-impact, weather-resistant plastic, the brackets support up to 40 pounds. In black and white. Both planters and brackets are sold in garden centers, chain stores, and florists.

For free catalog, write:
Mr. Chain
1805 Larchmont Street
Troy, MI 48084

Hanging planter assortment including ceramic pots with wrought-iron supports and wooden tubs with macramé; also slatted cedar boxes, woven rattan, and plastic holders. Available in department, hardware, and horticultural stores, as well as many merchandising chains.

For buying information write:
Christen
59 Branch Street
St. Louis, MO 63147

Upper bracket, a swivel hook and wood bracket assembly, has a 25-pound capacity. It is available in walnut or natural tone wood, complete with hardware and mounting instructions. A concealed bar mount with an adjustable ring allows for variable positioning.

For information write:
Opus
437 Boylston Street
Boston, MA 02116

Spiral planter has four 4-inch saucer and hanger units to hold four potted plants. Made of epoxy-coated heavy-gauge steel, it comes complete with hardware for hanging. Available in black, white, or green.

For information write:
Berkshire Products
219 Ninth Street
San Francisco, CA 94103

Kangaroo pouch planter has a built-in drainage system. An inner plastic pouch, containing soil and the plant, fits into a plastic reservoir pouch; it in turn is encased in decorative hanging or standing pouches of denim, burlap, leatherette, or other materials in assorted colors. Lightweight, nonbreakable.

For catalogs and mail-order information, write:
Adam Jay
Box 459
Worchester, MA 01613

Macrame plant-hanger kits can help you enhance your garden in short order. One has an 11-inch metal ring and stained wood; another is complete with glass planter, seed, soil, and cord; a third includes shells and bamboo. Instructions provided. Available nationally at mass merchandisers, craft stores, and department stores.

For mail-order information write:
**Avalon Industries
95 Lorimer Street
Brooklyn, NY 11206**

Hardwood brackets and **plant holders** are available from David Scott. The units are box-shaped in design, and each can hold one plant.

For brochures and mail-order information, write:
**David Scott
Box 5621
Meridian, MS 39301**

Green trak is a three-foot ceiling track with six removable swivel hooks for hanging plants. The unit can be mounted in multiples and comes with all installation hardware.

For 50-cent catalog and mail-order information, write:
**C.A. Gordon Associates
18 Church Street
Paterson, NJ 07505**

Hanging garden is a clear plastic planter that can be used as a terrarium, flower vase, cutting rooter, or just as a hanging planter. Durable and fun to look at.

For brochures and mail-order information, write:
**CalMil Plastic Products
6100 Lowden Lane
Carlsbad, CA 92008**

Natural sheet moss has many uses for the home gardener. Since it comes in large, rolled sheets, you can simply cut it to the size you need. In general, it is both decorative and functional. (Sheet moss promotes plant growth by helping soil retain moisture.) Specifically, it is perfect for lining wire hanging baskets, covering the topsoil in planters, and double potting.

For mail-order information and catalog, send 50 cents to:
**Mosser Lee Company
Millston, WI 54643**

Decorative wall hanging devices include a lucite wall bracket that holds up to 10 pounds, a 6-inch open top lucite cube, and monofilament-cord sets in three lengths. Also available is a lucite ceiling hook for wood or hollow ceilings.

For ordering information write:
**Souhan Design
Box 36384
Dallas, TX 75235**

Slide-a-plant is a cast metal, corrosion resistant, ceiling-mounted track. Sliding swivel hooks let you hang plants wherever you want along its length. Plant Curtain is similar, but in addition to hooks, has sliding pulleys for hoisting plants to desired level. Both items available in 4- and 6-foot lengths, complete with necessary hardware. Also available are chains and swivel hooks for hanging single plants from hollow walls or ceilings. Available nationally at mass merchandisers, chain stores, and nurseries.

For free catalog and mail-order information, write:
**Hang-Em-All Products Corporation
11 Ralph Avenue
Copiague, NY 11726**

Macramé plant light, constructed of jute with dark brown beads, is 5 feet long and 15 inches in diameter. Fully wired with porcelain socket and a frosted white globe, the wicker basket will hold a large plant or several small ones.

Round pot in the square hole consists of white pine sections fitted together. Each of the three recesses holds a 4½-inch pot, giving a flower-box appearance.

Ring around the plant is a 28-inch-long wrought-iron hanger with a 5-inch shelf. It holds a pot up to 4½ inches in diameter.

Other wrought-iron products available are hooks in five different styles and a 9-inch wall bracket for heavier plants.

For catalog send 25 cents to:
**Vermont Crafts Market
West Hill, Box 17
Putney, VT 05346**

Hanging planters made of polished aluminum can be used for direct-planting both indoors and out. There are six styles, ranging from 8 to 12 inches in diameter. Each comes with its own hanging wire. Looks great wherever used.

For mail-order information write:
**Wall Designs, Ltd.
199 East Post Road
White Plains, NY 10601**

Plant springer ends messy spills and drips by securing saucers to hanging pots. Each one consists of a tripod base attached to three wire springs. All are constructed of sturdy, rustproof materials.

For more information write:
**In Motion Product Industries
Box 34039
San Francisco, CA 94134**

Handy hooker has three swinging hooks made of cushion-coated steel.

For free catalog and buying information, write:
**Grayline Housewares
1616 Berkley Street
Elgin, IL 60120**

Earth lamp, a planter with its own light source, can be hung from wall brackets or ceiling. Three plastic-coated chains suspend the planter beneath a white cylindrical light fixture. The bulb included stimulates plant growth in addition to providing illumination.

For mail-order information write:
**Syntropics
Box 2587
Sarasota, FL 33578**

Skyfold free-form planter bowls come in clear lucite for hanging singly and in pairs. Clear lucite hanging trays for displaying potted plants are also available. Hang them on lucite brackets with nylon monofilament, or place them on tables and shelves. Available nationally in some garden centers, department stores, and gift shops.

Send 25 cents for a catalog to:
**Akko
Dundee Park
Andover, MA 01810**

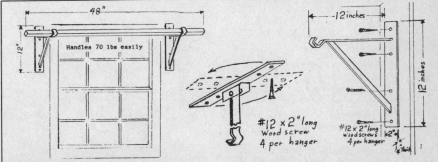

Plant brackets and **bracket-and-bar assemblies** (for hanging multiple plants with one installation) are constructed of heavy steel throughout. These units can support over 200 pounds depending on the structure on which they are mounted. Instructions and mounting materials are included. The mounting plates are 12 inches long by 2 inches wide by ¼ inch thick, with predrilled ¼-inch holes. A matching cross bar of 5, 6, 7, or 8 feet is also available.

For further information and a brochure, write:
**Alcestis Distribution Company
Box 29
Grantville, PA 17028**

Herbs

A sprig of dill in the hand prevents epilepsy; coriander conjures spirits; and basil is a sure-fire cure for over-weight ladies. In the not-too-distant past, every good herbalist knew these things and a thousand and one other bits of herb lore. Nowadays, herb gardeners may smile skeptically at such nostrums. But their smiles for their gardens are pure affection: few things are as nice as being able to harvest your own herbs from your kitchen windowsill or patio garden.

Flavor and fragrance

Beyond being useful to the cook, herbs are pretty and many are delightfully fragrant. Add to this the fact that they are among the easiest plants to cultivate, and it's easy to see the reason for their lasting popularity. Herbs can be grown indoors or out, and there is an almost limitless variety to try.

Growing your herbs

Wherever you grow your herbs, they require bright light, a fairly cool temperature (50 to 60 degrees F. is optimal), frequent watering (the soil should be kept moist but not soggy), good drainage, and a high humidity level.

If your indoor garden doesn't have adequate natural light, supplement it with artificial light. Two 40-watt fluorescent tubes should be adequate, even for an extensive garden. The less sun you have, the longer the lights should be left on. In a dark room, you will need to leave them on 16 hours a day.

Small pots, plastic-lined boxes, hanging baskets, and plant trays that provide drainage all make good herb containers. You can grow each herb separately or group several in one container. Use a general potting mixture that has good drainage.

Nutrients and pests

Herbalists at one end of the spectrum say that insecticides and fertilizer are necessary; those at the other end eschew both. How you play it is really up to you. If your plants take on a weak and straggly look, fertilizer certainly should help. Frequently washing the herbs' foliage with soapy water is generally beneficial and in most cases will control insects. If you find a plant infested with aphids or spider mites despite this treatment, you may want to turn to an insecticide. If you do, be sure to use one of the *non-toxic* brands on the market. Since even a mild insecticide may affect the taste of the harvested plant, you may decide simply to forego it and begin a new plant.

Harvesting

Different herbs take different times to mature, but you can begin mini-harvests as soon as they are big enough not to miss a few leaves. This type of harvesting should be done frequently, as it automatically provides the pruning and pinching back that keeps plants healthy and full.

Once a plant reaches its prime, all the usable parts should be cut; otherwise the plant's flavor will be lost. For harvesting leaves, the best time is just

when the plants are beginning to bloom. When you are harvesting seeds, as with dill and coriander, cut the whole seed head from the stem after the seeds turn brown, but before they fully ripen.

Don't worry about waste. Any excess can be dried or frozen and placed in tightly-sealed glass or metal containers. An interesting way to utilize parsley is to moisten and roll it into a "cigar", wrap with aluminum foil and place in a freezer. When needed, slice off the amount desired, reseal, and place back in the freezer.

George and Katy Abraham

George and Katy Abraham are the originators of the syndicated gardening column, "The Green Thumb," which appears in over 125 newspapers.

Societies

The Herb Club, 7 Greenbriar Drive, Savannah, Georgia 31406. The purpose of the Herb Club is to give gardeners information on herbs. In addition to pragmatic instructional information, the Club strives to keep alive the folklore surrounding herbs and their traditional uses.

All members receive the bimonthly newsletter *The Herb Patch,* which carries articles on herbs and lore and gives members a place to trade seeds and plants plus ask questions. The Club also publishes a bimonthly lesson on growing and using a particular herb. Membership is open to anyone interested in herbs; dues are $4.00 per year.

Magazines

The Herbalist. A monthly magazine available by subscription and at newsstands, devoted entirely to the furtherance of herbal knowledge and the art of healthful living. Features include profiles of herbs and scientific research on their use, as well as growing information. Articles are written by scientists and experts from around the world. "Educational, motivational, entertaining reading for all herbalists." Subscription rates are $6.00 for 12 issues, 75 cents a copy at newsstands. For subscriptions, write *The Herbalist,* Box 62, Provo, Utah 84601. For a sample copy, send 75 cents to the above address.

Herb vinegars

Add fresh herbs to give plain jug vinegar exciting new flavor.

Equipment and ingredients
–Empty bottles or jars (wine bottles are ideal)
–Screw caps or corks to fit bottles or jars
–white wine or cider vinegar [red wine vinegar may be used, but only for herbs that are starred (*)]
–Fresh herbs
–Ribbons and wax (optional)
–Labels and felt-tipped pen

How to seal with wax
Melt sealing wax or candle scraps in a tall tin can by placing it in a pan of water over a low flame. Run a short length of ribbon over the neck, as shown, and glue it to the cork. Dip the bottle top in the melted wax. To unseal the bottle, just lift up the ribbon.

Suggested herbs
Tarragon*	Thyme
Sage*	Salad burnet
Oregano*	Shallots
Garlic* (peeled and crushed or skewered)	Chives
	Marjoram
Basil	Dill
Chervil	Savory
Mint	Parsley

Procedure
1. For each quart of herb vinegar, you will need ¼ to ½ cup of one or more herbs. For example, about 6 garlic cloves, 5 sprigs of mint or tarragon (or one sprig each of parsley, chives, chervil, and tarragon). Bruise the herbs slightly to release their flavor, and place in a jar or bottle.

2. Fill the container with vinegar and close with a cap or a cork. For a special touch, seal it with wax. Label each for identification and tie it with a pretty bow if it is to be a gift.

3. Let stand for 2 or 3 weeks to allow the flavor to develop fully.

Herb butter

Herb butter is delicious spread on bread, or melted on meat, fish, eggs, and vegetables. Try tarragon butter on chicken, steak, or broiled fish. Spread garlic butter on French bread, or oregano butter on broiled tomatoes. Herb butter should be made ahead of time to allow the flavor to develop. Stored in the refrigerator, it keeps for up to two weeks.

Procedure
1. Have the butter at room temperature for easy blending. Chop fresh herbs finely, crush garlic, or pound dry herbs with a mortar and pestle. Use 2 tablespoons of fresh herbs for each ½ cup of butter.

2. Whip butter and herbs in a blender or cream them together by hand.

Herbal teas or tisanes

Some people drink herbal teas for their medicinal qualities; others because they enjoy the exotic taste. If you would like to try making tea from herbs, be sure to use a non-metallic container for brewing. A crockery pot that you can reserve solely for this purpose is ideal. Your everyday teapot could taint the more delicate flavors of an herbal tea. Sweeten the tea with a little sugar or honey.

Procedure
1. Bring water to a boil. Rinse out the teapot with a little boiling water to warm it.

2. Using about 1 teaspoon dried herbs or 2 teaspoons of fresh, put the tea directly into the teapot or a metal tea ball (crushing the tea leaves slightly will help release their flavor).

3. Pour freshly boiling water over the tea and let it steep for seven to ten minutes. If the tea is not strong enough, add more tea leaves next time; do not increase the brewing time, since this will merely make the tea bitter not more flavorful.

Suggested herbs
Almost any culinary herb, or combination of herbs, can be used to make tea. What follows is a list of the most popular.

Lemon balm	Thyme
Lemon verbena	Angelica
Mint	Bergamot
Rosemary	Chamomile
Sage	Marjoram

CARAWAY (*Carum Carui*, L., Fig. 155—
Pentandria Digynia, L.; Umbelliferæ, D.C.;

CORIANDER (*Coriandrum sativum*, L., Fig. 157—Pentandria Digynia, L.; Umbelliferæ,

Bouquet garni

Bouquet garni is a French term for a small bunch of fresh herbs, tied together and used to flavor stews, ragouts, and meat casseroles. To make a bouquet garni, tie the herbs together with string, leaving a long tail at one end. Place the bundle in the pot, letting the tail hang over the side so you can remove the bouquet once the flavors have entered the dish. The basic bouquet garni consists of:

    1 bay leaf
    1 sprig thyme
    several sprigs parsley

If you have dried herbs, use little squares of muslin or cheesecloth to make little sacks. Again, use string for tying, and leave a long tail for easy removal. In this method, you can add other herbs and spices such as allspice, peppercorns, and cloves.

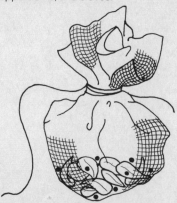

Harvesting, drying, and storing herbs

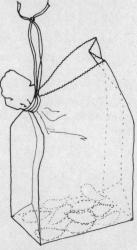

Harvesting
To harvest fresh herbs for immediate use, simply snip or pinch off as much as you need. Drying them (for later use or to give as gifts) requires a bit more planning and effort. For best results, harvest herbs just before or when they begin to flower, and in the morning when their flavor oils are the strongest.

Drying
For small-leaved herbs such as thyme, savory, and tarragon, fasten a bunch of freshly harvested herbs together by wrapping a rubber band around their stems. Hang them upside down in a dry, well-ventilated area away from direct sunlight.

    For large-leaved herbs such as mint, sage, and basil, strip the leaves from the stems and place them in a plain brown paper bag. Do not fill the bag; allow enough room for air to circulate. Leave the bag open at the top and suspend it so the bottom does not touch the ground.

    Drying time varies from herb to herb and according to the humidity in the air. Test the herbs every other day; when they are crisp and brittle to the touch, they are ready for storing.

Storing
Place the dried herbs in airtight containers such as plastic bags or sealed jars. Try to leave the leaves uncrushed, since this retains the flavor. Store in a cool, dry place and replace herbs once a year.

For poultry or rabbit:
Thyme
Tarragon
Parsley
Chervil
Sage
Peppercorns

For beef or game:
Rosemary
Parsley
Basil
Marjoram
Whole allspice
Peppercorns
Bay leaf
Sage

For lamb:
Rosemary
Peppercorns
Tarragon
Marjoram
Savory

For seafood:
Thyme
Bay leaf
Dried lemon rind
Chervil

For tomato dishes:
Cloves
Bay leaf
Basil
Tarragon
Parsley

Books

Herb Gardening In Five Seasons, by Adelma Grenier Simmons, Hawthorne Books, 260 Madison Ave., New York, New York 10016, 1971, 353 pages, $7.95. Concerns indoor and outdoor herb gardens, associating different herbs for each season (using Christmas as the fifth). Includes advice on every aspect of herb culture from planning and planting to harvesting and drying. Also offered is an herbal dictionary, taking an in-depth look at 50 different herbs.

Herbs To Grow Indoors: For Flavor, For Fragrance, For Fun, by Adelma Grenier Simmons, Hawthorne Books, 260 Madison Ave., New York, New York 10016, 1969, 146 pages, $5.95. Intended for those who wish to grow herbs under average home conditions, this book is filled with information ranging from where to place and group plants, general care, making stem cuttings and transplanting, to how you can spruce up your meals with homegrown herbs. With 22 pages of illustrations.

The Rodale Herb Book—How To Use, Grow and Buy Nature's Miracle Plants, Edited by William H. Hylton, Rodale Press, 33 E. Minor St., Emmaus, Pennsylvania 18049, 1974, 653 pages, $12.95. This book provides insight not only to the herbal newcomer, but also provides a new outlook for those already familiar with herbs. Contains a history of names, folklore, medicinal value of certain herbs, and of course how to grow, care for, and use the herbs. Also included are more than 50 detailed descriptions of the most significant herbs, complete with photographs of each.

Herbs For The Kitchen, by Irma Goodwich Mazza, Little, Brown and Co., 34 Beacon St., Boston, Massachusetts 02106, 1975, hardbound, 366 pages, $8.95. A factual and interesting book; makes good reading because it has many bits of folklore. Good for those who may know something about herbs but want to know more; includes recipes.

A Garden of Herbs, by Eleanour Sinclair Rohde, Dover Publications, 180 Varick St., New York, New York 10014, 1969, 300 pages, $2.50. This book is jam-packed with historical descriptions, recipes for puddings, drinks, and all kinds of ideas not found in other books. This book is a delight for anyone interested in herbs.

Herbs and Savory Seeds, by Rosetta E. Clarkson, Dover Publications, 180 Varick St., New York, New York 10014, 1972, 369 pages, $3.00. Contains a storehouse of useful information. Good index, up to date and interesting.

Grow Herbs In Pots, by John Burton Brimer, Simon and Schuster Co., 630 Fifth Ave., New York, New York 10020, 1976, 206 pages, $6.95. Presents information on growing kitchen herbs on the windowsill, patio or under lights. Over 100 tempting recipes.

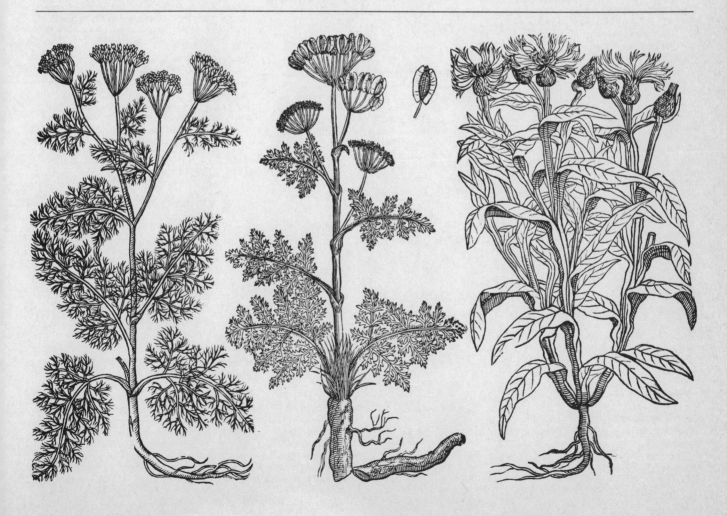

Plant sources

ABC Nursery and Greenhouse, Route 1, Box 313, Lecoma, Missouri 65540. (314) 435-6389. List. Open Monday through Friday from 8:00 a.m. Farm is located 2 miles south and 3 miles west of Lecoma on Highway OO. Large selection of herbs with suggested culinary uses; especially large selection of thyme plants.

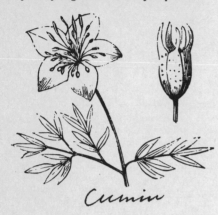

Cumin

Borchelt Herb Gardens, 474 Carriage Shop Road, East Falmouth, Massachusetts 02356. Seed list; plants sold at garden only. Open Tuesday through Saturday 11:00 a.m. to 5:00 p.m. Extensive list of over 185 potted plants with abbreviated descriptions from agrimony to string of hearts. Many seeds with cultural information on each packet are available by mail order.

Capriland's Herb Farm, Silver Street, Coventry, Connecticut 06238. (203) 742-7244. Plant list. Open 9:00 a.m. to 5:00 p.m. April through December; 1:00 p.m. to 5:00 p.m. January through March. Visitors welcome. Herbal luncheon programs by Adelma Simmons (reservations required). Many basic herbs sold in 2- and 4-inch pots, herb and herbal flower seed packets, and several herb-related items such as teas, fragrances, and oils. Outstanding herb farm, noted for the lectures and presence of Adelma Simmons, distinguished herb horticulturalist and author of numerous volumes on herb growing. Books available from the farm.

Marjoram

Carroll Gardens, 444 East Main Street, Westminster, Maryland 21157. (301) 848-5422. Catalog. Open Monday through Friday 8:00 a.m. to 5:00 p.m.; Saturday and Sunday 9:00 a.m. to 5:00 p.m. Closed on Sundays from July 11 to September 12. Extensive assortment of hardy perennial herbs for cooking and fragrance.

Arnica

Casa Yerba, Star Route 2, Box 21, Days Creek, Oregon 97429. Catalog 50 cents. Visitors by appointment. Extensive seed offerings with plant description, use, and sowing times. Rare, old-fashioned, and modern herbs, from mercury and Good King Henry to the newly popular ginseng root. Also many plants and tubers. Brief book list plus chatty newsletter advertising tidbits.

Fennel

Hemlock Hill Herb Farm, Hemlock Hill Road, Litchfield, Connecticut 06759. (203) 567-5031. Illustrated catalog 50 cents. Open May 1 through August 31, 10:00 a.m. to 4:00 p.m.; closed Sunday, Monday, and holidays. Highly readable catalog lists culinary, medicinal, and fragrant herbs from A to Z; it also provides description, growing tips, and average growing height for most. Catalog also features a map and directions for driving to the farm and to nearby historic Litchfield.

Dill

The Herbary and Potpourri Shop, Box 543, Childs Homestead Road, Orleans, Massachusetts 02653. (617) 255-4422. Brochure. Plants sold at gardens only. Open Monday through Saturday 9:00 a.m. to 5:00 p.m. Guided tours available by appointment. Mail-order brochure lists dried herbs, seeds, potpourris, and sachets; herbs, scented geraniums and houseplants available at nursery only.

Herb Shop, Box 362, Fairfield, Connecticut 06430. (203) 255-4004. Business address is 15 Sherman Street, Fairfield. Brochure 50 cents. Open Monday through Saturday 9:00 a.m. to 5:30 p.m. Seed packages mostly of culinary and sachet herbs. Plants sold at the store only. Brochure includes large variety of dried herbs, herbal teas, oils, candles, potpourris, and earthworms by the pint, quart or gallon—"as insurance for a successful garden!"

Rosemary

Herbs 'N Honey Nursery, Route 2, Box 205, Monmouth, Oregon 97361. (503) 623-4033. Plant list. Open Monday through Friday 8:00 a.m. to 4:00 p.m. Weekends by appointment. Visitors welcome. A list of 132 culinary, medicinal, and garden herbs with a particularly large selection of onions, artemisias, scented geraniums, lavenders, mints, sages, berries, thymes, and violets. Also miniature rose plants. Herbal book written by the owners, describing how to plant, propagate, harvest, store, and use herbs, is sold for $4.95.

Hickory Hollow, Route 1, Box 52, Peterstown, West Virginia 24963. Brochure 25 cents. Seeds and plants—ordinary cooking herbs as well as herbs for teas. The owner, Bonnie Fischer, is author of *Herbs for Everyone*, and in addition to brief discussion of uses, the brochure offers a book list on herb growing, herbal teas, sachets, dressings, and herb jellies.

Hyssop

Hilltop Herb Farm, Box 1734, Cleveland, Texas 77327. (713) 592-5859. Catalog 50 cents. Visitors welcome. Lunch and dinner served with advance reservations. Whimsical collection of plants and herb-related goodies from jellies, teas, vinegars, salts, and herbal soaps to books. Plants are listed according to ye old use: "table-olfactory"—chives, lemon balm, rosemary; dye plants—agrimony, elecampane, St. John's wort; and border or ground covers—alkanet, wormwood, sweet woodruff, thymes. Also a variety of herb and herbal flower seed packages are sold.

Howe Hill Herbs, Camden, Maine 04843. Plant list 35 cents. Specializing in herbs and geraniums; 2- to 3-inch potted plants sent. A choice of 90 different herbs (mostly perennials) and a limited number of seeds.

Anise

Sweet Basil

Logee's Greenhouses, 55 North Street, Danielson, Connecticut 06239. (203) 774-8038. Illustrated catalog $2.00. Open daily 9:00 a.m. to 4:00 p.m. Visitors welcome. Unusual and varied selection of herbs.

Bene

Penn Herb Company, 603 North Second Street, Philadelphia, Pennsylvania 19123. (215) 925-3336. Catalog 25 cents. Open from 8:30 a.m. to 5:00 p.m. Monday through Friday, 8:30 a.m. to noon Saturday. Basically specializing in dried herbs and herbal products, this medicinal herb house offers a limited collection of herb seeds for planting, from angelica to yucca (31 in all). Interesting catalog for herb lovers.

Sage

Raphael Ranch, Box 1647, Sequim, Washington 98382. (206) 457-9211. Brochure. Open Monday through Friday 9:00 a.m. to 5:00 p.m. Visitors welcome. This herb farm sells herbal wreaths and sachets made from the herbs grown in its own garden — all natural scents and foliage.

Otto Richter and Sons, Box 26, Goodwood, Ontario LOC 1AO Canada. (416) 294-1457. Catalog 50 cents; seeds only. Open 9:00 a.m. to 4:00 p.m. winter; 8:00 a.m. to 5:00 p.m. spring, summer, and fall; plants available at nursery. Over 150 seeds, many very unusual, including an extensive list of dye herbs with their colors. Also, exotics like the South American maté used to make tea. The catalog gives general plant description, use, and sowing times plus information on seed sowing and raising seedlings. Some books on herbs.

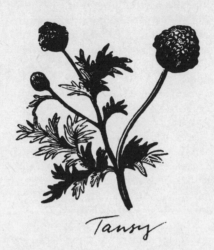

Tansy

Rutland of Kentucky, Herb Specialists, 3 Bon Haven, Maysville, Kentucky 41056. Plant list 50 cents. Extensive offerings of herbs listed by botanical name according to their modern-day use: culinary herbs, dyer's art herbs, apothecary herbs, historical herbs, and fragrant herbs. Catalog includes suggested bedding arrangements, cultural information, recommended books, and potpourri and pomander ingredients. Owner Mary Peddie plans gardens, lectures, and has conducted an "herb school" sponsored by the Living Arts and Science Center in Lexington, Kentucky.

Lavender

Sunnybrook Farms Nursery, Box 6, 9448 Mayfield Road, Chesterland, Ohio 44026. (216) 729-7232. Catalog 50 cents. Open Tuesday through Saturday 8:30 a.m. to 5:00 p.m.; Sunday 1:00 p.m. to 5:00 p.m. Visitors welcome. Wide range of herbs, scented geraniums, exotic houseplants, cacti, succulents, and other novelty plants. Special colonial herb garden package with planting instructions. General culture notes in the catalog. Plants sent in 2¼-, 3-, or 4-inch pots, depending on their sizes.

Taylor's Herb Garden, 1535 Lone Oak Road, Vista, California 92083. (714) 727-3485. Additional stores at 2649 Stingle Avenue, Rosemead, California 91770, (213) 280-4639; 3038 Mohawk Lane, Phoenix, Arizona 82050, (602) 992-7967. Plant list 25 cents with self-addressed, stamped envelope. Stores open every day, 8:00 a.m. to 5:00 p.m. Visitors welcome. Over 125 common and unusual herbs from culinary to fragrant foliage plants. The catalog is full of interesting descriptions of old-time and present uses: cooking, medicinal home-remedies, dyes, garden display. Large selection of mints, thymes, sages, lavenders, and scented geraniums. Additional unlisted varieties upon request.

Caraway

Well Sweep Herb Farm, Mt. Bethel Road, Port Murray, New Jersey 07865. (201) 852-5390. Catalog 25 cents. Open by appointment only. Included in the catalog are scented geraniums, a wide variety of dried flowers, and herb plants. Herb seeds and products are also available.

Yankee Peddler Herb Farm, Department TC, Highway 36 North, Brenham, Texas 77833. (713) 836-4442. Catalog $1.00 (refundable upon plant purchase). Open daily 9:00 a.m. to 5:00 p.m. Over 700 herbs (seeds and plants) listed by common and botanical names. Full description of plant, including size, whether annual, biennial, or perennial, and use. Many rare old-time species along with modern-day plants as well as herbal leaves, teas, roots, and barks. Includes excellent list of approximately 350 books on herb growing and cooking.

Horticultural careers

If the plants you grow intrigue you—if you have ever wondered at the forces behind a salmon-pink flower or asked yourself why some plants need a certain period of darkness in order to blossom—you're a step beyond being a hobbyist. And if, like most of us, you have wondered how to not only make a living, but enjoy it, you might want to take a serious look at a career in horticulture. It is an area that has literally blossomed in the past few decades and the reasons aren't very hard to find.

Unlike most fields, horticulture offers a working knowledge of a field that is at once esoteric (it touches on the mystery of life itself) and practical (with as little as a year of training, a horticulturist can put his knowledge to work in a paying job). Moreover, this is one of the few fields that is equally open to men and women, young and old alike. In fact, many horticulturists are hobbyists who became professionals in their late years. It offers a variety of job choices that is astounding in its breadth. Possible careers range from having your own nursery or plant shop to working at a botanical garden to doing pure scientific research. And beyond all of this, there is the sheer pleasure of working with living things.

If all this sounds good, there are a few basics you should know before you choose a specific program—or even career—within the field.

Training in this field is as varied as the areas which horticulture encompasses (fruit and vegetable crops, flowers and ornamental plants, turf grass, and landscaping). Basically, there are one-, two-, and four-year programs available through government agencies and at various colleges. Technical schools, botanical gardens, and some private gardens connected with nearby universities also offer programs.

One-year programs teach the basic skills required of, say, a greenhouse, nursery, or landscape-maintenance-firm employee. They are not usually designed for those who wish to enter management.

Two-year programs can lead to management positions, but this varies from program to program. There are about 150 to 200 programs in two-

year schools for those interested in areas such as nursery work and landscaping. Many of the people entering the nursery industry come from junior colleges and technical programs. Often they augment their formal education with on-the-job training or in some job-related program. Says one nurseryman, "A college degree is not always the criterion for getting hired."

Four-year programs most often lead to positions in management. For example, some recent graduates of the University of Wisconsin own and operate retail flower shops and greenhouses. Many of those who work for florists actually manage the business. Some work at botanical gardens and arboretums, and a number hold extension positions, teaching positions, or are involved in research.

There's no doubt that this explosion in horticultural careers is having a positive carry-over effect. "The more people we have working in this field," says one industry man, "the more we'll all learn and the better off everybody will be."

Penny Girard

Educational programs

Institutions offering horticulture as a major field for baccalaureate or advanced degrees, as well as institutions offering training below the baccalaureate level, are indicated below as B (Bachelor), M (Masters), P (PhD), AAS (Associate in Applied Science), AS (Associate in Science), AA (Associate in Arts), T (credits are transferable), N (credits are non-transferable), C (Certificate), D (Diploma), CC (correspondence course), WS (work study).

The range of horticultural specialization is wide and varies considerably among these schools. For detailed information, write to the Director of Admissions of the college or university being considered at the addresses given below. Several institutions offer landscape architecture—a list of those accredited by the American Society of Landscape Architects is available from ASLA, 1750 Old Meadow Road, McLean, Virginia 22101.

Degree-granting

Alabama

Alabama A & M University
Department of Natural Resource and Environmental Studies
Normal, Alabama 35762
B, M, T

Auburn University
Department of Horticulture
Auburn, Alabama 36830
B, M

Arizona

Arizona State University
Department of Horticulture
Tempe, Arizona 85281
B, M, T, D

University of Arizona
Department of Horticulture and Landscape Architecture
Tucson, Arizona 85721
A.E. Thompson, Head
B, M, P, T, D

Arkansas

Arkansas State University
Department of Horticulture
State University, Arkansas 72467
Dr. A.J. Langlois
501-972-2085
B

Petit Jean Vocational-Technical School
Highway 9 North
Morliton, Arkansas 72110
M

University of Arkansas
Department of Horticulture
Fayetteville, Arkansas 72701
B, M

California

California Polytechnic State University
Department of Horticulture
San Luis Obispo, California 93407
B, AAS, T, C, D

California State Polytechnic University
Ornamental Horticulture Department
Pomona, California 91768
B

California State University
Department of Plant Science
Fresno, California 93740
B, M, T, D

California State University-Chico
Department of Plant and Soil Sciences
Chico, California 95929
B. M, T

University of California
Department of Ecology and
Evolutionary Biology
Irvine, California 92717
B, M, P

University of California
Environmental Horticulture Department
Davis, California 95616
B, M, P, T, D

Colorado

Colorado State University
Department of Horticulture
Fort Collins, Colorado 80523
B, M, P

Connecticut

University of Connecticut
Consumer Horticulture Center
Plant Science Department
College of Agriculture and Natural Resources
Storrs, Connecticut 06268
B, M, P, D, C

Delaware

University of Delaware
Plant Science Department
College of Agricultural Sciences
Newark, Delaware 19711
B, M, P, AAS, AS, T

Florida

Florida Southern College
Citrus Institute
Lakeland, Florida 33802
Thomas B. Mack, Director
B, T, D

University of Florida
Department of Ornamental Horticulture
105 Rolff Hall, IFAS
Gainesville, Florida 32611
B, M, P

Georgia

University of Georgia
Department of Horticulture
Athens, Georgia 30602
J. Denton Jones, Jr.
404-542-2471
B, M, P, T, D

Hawaii

University of Hawaii
Department of Horticulture
Honolulu, Hawaii 96822
B, M, P, T

Iowa

**Iowa State University of
Science and Technology**
Department of Horticulture
Ames, Iowa 50011
B, M, P, T, D

Illinois

Illinois State University
Department of Agriculture
Normal, Illinois 61761
M, T

Southern Illinois University
Department of Plant and Soil Science
Carbondale, Illinois 62901
B, M

University of Illinois
Department of Horticulture
Urbana, Illinois 61801
B, M, P

Indiana

Purdue University
Department of Horticulture
Lafayette, Indiana 47907
B, M, P, T, D

Kansas

Kansas State University
Department of Horticulture
Manhattan, Kansas 66506
B, M, P, T, C

Kentucky

Eastern Kentucky University
Department of Horticulture
Richmond, Kentucky 40475
Dr. W.A. Householder, Chairman
B, AAS, T, D

Murray State University
Horticulture Section
Department of Agriculture
Murray, Kentucky 42071
B, M, AS, T, D

University of Kentucky
Department of Horticulture
Lexington, Kentucky 40506
B, M, P, T, D

Louisiana

**Louisiana State University
and A & M University**
Department of Horticulture
Baton Rouge, Louisiana 70803
B, M, P

Louisiana Technical University
Department of Horticulture
Ruston, Louisiana 71270
B, T

McNeese State University
Department of Horticulture
Lake Charles, Louisiana 70601
B, T, D

Southeastern Louisiana University
Department of Agriculture
Hammond, Louisiana 70402
A.D. Owings
B, T, D

University of Southwestern Louisiana
Department of Horticulture
Lafayette, Louisiana 70501
J.A. Foret
318-233-3850
B, T, D

Maine

University of Maine
Dept. of Plant and Soil Sciences
Orono, Maine 04473
B, M, P, AS, T, D

Maryland

University of Maryland
Department of Horticulture
College Park, Maryland 20742
B, M, P, T

Massachusetts

University of Massachusetts
Department of Plant and Soil Sciences
Amherst, Massachusetts 01002
B, M, P, AS, T

Michigan

Michigan State University
Institute of Agricultural Technology
Department of Horticulture
East Lansing, Michigan 48823
B, M, P, AS, T, C, D

Minnesota

University of Minnesota
Department of Horticultural Science and
Landscape Architecture
St. Paul, Minnesota 55108
B, M, P, T

Mississippi

Mississippi State University
Department of Horticulture
State College, Mississippi 39762
B, M, P, T

Missouri

Lincoln University
Department of Agriculture and Natural
Resources
Jefferson City, Missouri 65101
B, T

Northwest Missouri State University
Department of Horticulture
Maryville, Missouri 64468
B, T, D

Southwest Missouri State University
Department of Horticulture
Springfield, Missouri 65802
B, T, D

University of Missouri
Department of Horticulture
Columbia, Missouri 65201
B, M, P, T, D

Montana

Montana State University
Department of Horticulture
Bozeman, Montana 59715
B, M, P, T, D

Nebraska

University of Nebraska
Department of Horticulture
Lincoln, Nebraska 68503
B, M, P, T, N

Nevada

University of Nevada
Max C. Fleischmann College
of Agriculture
9th and Valley Road
Reno, Nevada 89507
R.L. Post, Asst. Prof. of Hort.
B, M, AS, T, N, C, D

New Hampshire

University of New Hampshire
Department of Plant Science
Durham, New Hampshire 03824
B, M, P

New Jersey

Rutgers – The State University
Department of Horticulture
New Brunswick, New Jersey 08903
B, M, P, T, D

New Mexico

New Mexico State University
Department of Horticulture
Las Cruces, New Mexico 88003
B, M, T, D

New York

Cornell University
Department of Floriculture and Ornamental
Horticulture
Ithaca, New York 14850
C.F. Gortzig, Chairman
B, M, P, T, D

North Carolina

North Carolina Agricultural and
Technical University
Department of Horticulture
Greensboro, North Carolina 27411
B

North Carolina State University
Department of Horticulture
Raleigh, North Carolina 27607
B, M, P, T, D

North Dakota

North Dakota State University
Department of Horticulture
Fargo, North Dakota 58102
B, M, AS, T, N, C, D

Ohio

Ohio State University
Department of Horticulture
Columbus, Ohio 43210
B, M, P, T, D

Oklahoma

Oklahoma State University
Department of Horticulture
Stillwater, Oklahoma 74074
Grant Best, Head of Department
405-624-5414

Oregon

Oregon State University
Department of Horticulture
Corvallis, Oregon 97331
Leslie H. Fuchigama
B, M, P, T, D

Pennsylvania

Delaware Valley College of Science
and Agriculture
Department of Horticulture
Doylestown, Pennsylvania 18901
B, T, D

Pennsylvania State University
Department of Horticulture
103 Tyson Building
University Park, Pennsylvania 16802
R.W. Hepler
B, M, P, N, C, D

Puerto Rico

University of Puerto Rico
Department of Horticulture
College Station
Mayaguez, Puerto Rico 00708
B, M, T, C, D

Rhode Island

University of Rhode Island
Plant and Soil Science Department
Woodward Hall
Kingston, Rhode Island 02881
B, M, P, T, D

South Carolina

Clemson University
Department of Horticulture
Clemson, South Carolina 29631
B, M, P, T, D

South Dakota

South Dakota State University
Department of Horticulture-Forestry
Brookings, South Dakota 57006
B, T, D

Tennessee

Middle Tennessee State University
Department of Horticulture
Murfreesboro, Tennessee 37130
B

Tennessee State University
Department of Horticulture
Nashville, Tennessee 37202
B, T, C

Tennessee Technological University
Department of Horticulture
Cookeville, Tennessee 38501
B, T

University of Tennessee
Department of Ornamental Horticulture and
Landscape Design
Knoxville, Tennessee 37916
B, M, T

Texas

Sam Houston State University
Department of Horticulture
Huntsville, Texas 77340
V.A. Amato
B, M, T, D

Texas A & I University
Department of Horticulture
Kingsville, Texas 87363
Leo L. Bailey
B, AAS, AS, T

Texas A & M University
Department of Horticulture
College Station, Texas 77843
B, M, P, T

Texas State Technical Institute
James Connally Campus
Department of Plant and Soil Science
Waco, Texas 76705
Dr. George Teresh Kovich
B, AS, T, C

Texas Tech University
Department of Horticulture
Lubbock, Texas 79407
B, M

Utah

Brigham Young University
Department of Horticulture
Provo, Utah 84601
B, M, T, D

Utah State University
University Extension UMC 50
Department of Horticulture
Independent Study Division
Logan, Utah 84322
B, M, P, AAS, T, C, D

Vermont

University of Vermont
Department of Plant and Soil Science
Burlington, Vermont 05401
B, M, P, T, D

Virginia

**Virginia Polytechnic Institute
and State University**
Department of Horticulture
Blacksburg, Virginia 24061
Dr. C.L. McCombs
703-951-5451
B, M, P, WS, T, D

Washington

Washington State University
Department of Horticulture
Pullman, Washington 99164
Orrin E. Smith, Chairman
B, M, P, T, D

Wisconsin

University of Wisconsin-Madison
Department of Horticulture
1575 Linden Drive
Madison, Wisconsin 53706
Malcolm N. Dava, Chairman
B, M, P, T

Canada

Laval University
Plant Science Department
St. Foy
Quebec City, Canada
B, M, AAS, T, C

University of Alberta
Horticulture Division
Department of Plant Science
Edmonton, Canada
Wm. T. Andrew, Professor of Horticulture
B, M, D

University of British Columbia
Department of Plant Science
Vancouver 8, B.C., Canada

University of Guelph
Horticultural Science Department
Ontario, Canada
B, M, P, T, D

University of Manitoba
Department of Plant Science
Winnipeg, Manitoba, Canada R3T 2N2
B, M, P, T, D

University of Saskatchewan
Department of Horticulture Science
Saskatoon, Saskatchewan, Canada S7N OWO
B, M, T

Certificate or associate degree-granting (Including correspondence courses)

Arizona

Mesa Community College
Department of Horticulture
1833 W. Southern Avenue
Mesa, Arizona 85201
J. D. Claridge, Chairman, Agriculture
AA, T, D

Arkansas

Southern Arkansas University
Department of Horticulture
Magnolia, Arkansas 71753
AS, T, D

California

American River College
Department of Horticulture
4700 College Oak Drive
Sacramento, California 98541
AA, T, C

Antelope Valley College
Agriculture Department
3041 West Avenue K
Lancaster, California 93534
Jos. B. Randolph, Agriculture Department
AS, T, N, C, D

Bakersfield College
Department of Ornamental Horticulture
1801 Panorama Drive
Bakersfield, California 93305
AS, T, C, D

Butte Junior College
Department of Horticulture
Route 1-Box 183 A
Oraville, California 95965
Frank Hutchinson, Chairman
AAS, T, C, D

College of the Desert
Department of Horticulture
43-500 Monterey Avenue
Palm Desert, California 92260
Jeffrey W. Place, Instructor
AA, T, C

College of the Redwoods
Department of Horticulture
Eureka, Caifornia 95501
AA, T, C, D

College of San Mateo
Department of Horticulture
1700 W. Hillsdale Boulevard
San Mateo, California 94402
AAS, T, C

College of the Sequoias
Department of Horticulture
915 S. Mooney Boulevard
Visalia, California 93277
AA, T, D

Foothill College
Department of Horticulture
Los Altos Hills, California 94022
AS, T, C

Fullerton College
Department of Horticulture
321 E. Chapman
Fullerton, California 92634
AA, T, N, C, D

Hartnell College
Department of Horticulture
156 Homestead Avenue
Salinas, California 93901
Jerry Mailman
AS, T, C, D

Los Angeles Pierce College
Department of Horticulture
6201 Winnetka Avenue
Woodland Hills, California 91364
R. W. South, Professor of Horticulture
AS, T, N, C, D

Merced Community College
Department of Horticulture
3600 M Street
Merced, California 95340
Richard Dodson, Agriculture Division
AA, T, C, D

Merritt College
Ornamental Horticulture
12500 Campus Drive
Oakland, Caifornia 94619
AS, AA, T, C, D

Mira Costa College
Department of Horticulture
Barnard Drive
Oceanside, California 92054
Wm. H. Thompson, Agriculture Instructor
AS, T, C

Modesto Junior College
Department of Horticulture
College Avenue
Modesto, California 95350
AS, T, C, D

Modesto Junior College
Yosemite Junior College District
Department of Horticulture
835 Glenn Avenue, Box 4065
Modesto, California 95352
D.D. Waits
AS, T, C, D

Monterey Peninsula College
Department of Horticulture
980 Fremont Street
Monterey, California, 93940
AS, T, C, D

Moorpark College
Department of Horticulture
7075 Campus Road
Moorpark, California 93021
AS, T, C, D

Mt. San Antonio College
Department of Horticulture
1100 N. Grand Avenue
Walnut, California 91789
AS, T, C, D

Napa Community College
Department of Horticulture
2277 Napa Vallejo Highway
Napa, California 94558
Joe Davis, Horticultural Science
AS, T, C

Orange Coast College
Department of Horticulture
2701 Fairview Road
Costa Mesa, California 92626
AA, T, C

San Bernardino Valley College
Department of Horticulture
701 S. Mt. Vernon Avenue
San Bernardino, California 92403
AS, T, C, D

San Diego Mesa College
Department of Nursery and
Landscape Technology
7250 Artillary Drive
San Diego, California 92111
AS, C

San Joaquin Delta College
Department of Horticulture
5151 Pacific Avenue
Stockton, California 95207
AS, T

Santa Rosa Junior College
Department of Horticulture
Santa Rosa, California 95401
Robert H. Cannard
AAS, T, C, D

Shasta Community College
Department of Horticulture
Highway 299, E. Old Oregon Trail
Redding, California 96001
AAS, T, C

Sierra Community College
Landscape Horticulture
5000 Rocklin Road
Rocklin, California 95677
AS, AA, T, C, D

Ventura College
Department of Horticulture
4667 Telegraph Road
Ventura, California 93003
AS, T, C

Colorado
Community College of Denver
Department of Horticulture
1001 East 62nd Avenue
Denver, Colorado 80216
J. V. O'Shea
AA, T, C, D

Mesa Junior College
Department of Horticulture
Grand Junction, Colorado 81501
AS, T, D

Northeastern Junior College
Department of Horticulture
Sterling, Colorado 80751
AAS, T, C

Connecticut
University of Connecticut
Plant Science Department
Ratcliffe Hicks, School of Agriculture
Storrs, Connecticut 06268
T, C

Florida
Broward Community College
Department of Horticulture
3501 Southwest Davie Road
Fort Lauderdale, Florida 33314
AS, T, D

Daytona Beach Community College
Department of Horticulture
Box 1111
Daytona Beach, Florida 32015
C

Manatee Area Vo-Tech Center
Department of Horticulture
Bradenton, Florida 33505
C

Miami Dade Community College
Department of Horticulture
11011 S.W. 104th Street
Miami, Florida 33176
AS, T, N, C, D

Pinellas Vocational-Tech Institute
Department of Horticulture
6100 154th Avenue North
Clearwater, Florida 33520
C, D

Polk Community College
Department of Horticulture
999 Avenue H, N. E.
Winter Haven, Florida 33880
AS, T, D

Polk Vo-Tech Center
P. O. Box 720
Eaton Park, Florida 33840
C, D

**Suwanee-Hamilton Area Voc-Tech
and Adult Center**
Department of Horticulture
Live Oak, Florida 32060
AS

Georgia
**North Georgia Technical and
Vocational School**
Ornamental Horticulture Department
Clarksville, Georgia 30523
D

Hawaii
Hawaii Community College
Department of Horticulture
1175 Manono Street
Hilo, Hawaii 96720
AS, N, C, D

Leeward Community College
Division of Math and Science
Pearl City, Hawaii 96782
Ala Ike
AS, T, C, D

Pacific Tropical Botanical Garden
Apprentice Gardeners Program
P. O. Box 340
Lawai, Kauai, Hawaii 96765
C

Idaho
Boise State College
Department of Horticulture
1907 Campus Drive
Boise, Idaho 83701
N, D

Illinois
Belleville Junior College
Department of Horticulture
Carlyle Road
Belleville, Illinois 62221
Charles Giebeman
AAS, T, C

College of Lake County
Department of Ornamental Horticulture
19351 West Washington Street
Grayslake, Illinois 60030
AAS, AS, C

Danville Junior College
Department of Ornamental Horticulture
2000 Main Street
Danville, Illinois 61832
AAS, T, N, C, D

DuPage Horticultural School
Greenhouse Management and
Operation Training
P. O. Box 342
West Chicago, Illinois 60185
N, C

Joliet Junior College
Department of Horticulture
1216 Houbolt Avenue
Joliet, Illinois 60436
AAS, AS, T, D

Kishwaukee College
Department of Horticulture
Malta, Illinois 60150
AAS, T, C

McHenry County College
Department of Horticulture
Crystal Lake, Illinois 60014
AAS, T, C

Sauk Valley College
Department of Horticulture
Route 1
Dixon, Illinois 61021
N, C

Wright College
Department of Horticulture
N. Austin Avenue
Chicago, Illinois 60634
T, C

Indiana

Vincennes University
Department of Horticulture
Vincennes, Indiana 47591
AS, T, N, D

Iowa

Hawkeye Institute of Technology
Department of Horticulture
Box 8015
Waterloo, Iowa 50704
AAS, N, D

Kirkwood Community College
Department of Horticulture
P. O. Box 2068
Cedar Rapids, Iowa 52406
Mel Essex
AAS, T, D

Kansas

Central Kansas Area Vocational Technical School
Department of Horticulture
Hutchinson Community Junior College
Hutchinson, Kansas 67501
AAS, T, C, D

Friends University
Department of Horticulture
Wichita, Kansas 67213
B

Kaw Area Vocational Technical School
Department of Horticulture
5724 Huntoon
Topeka, Kansas 66604
John Tonkin
N, C

Kentucky

Jefferson State Vocational Agri Business Center
Department of Ornamental Horticulture
2219 Lakeland Road
Anchorage, Kentucky 40223
C, D

Louisiana

Delgado College
Department of Horticulture
615 City Park Avenue
New Orleans, Louisiana 70119
P. R. Kurtzweil, Assistant Professor
AS, T, C, D

Maine

Southern Maine Vo-Tech Institute
Department of Horticulture
Portland, Maine 04104
AAS, T, C, D

Maryland

Chesapeake Community College
Department of Horticulture
Easton, Maryland 21601
T, C

Howard Vo-Tech Center
Department of Horticulture
19020 Route 108
Ellicott City, Maryland 21043
T, D

J. Millard Tawes Vocational Center
Department of Horticulture
P. O. Box 189
Westover, Maryland 21871
Robert S. Fitzgerald
D

University of Maryland
Institute of Applied Agriculture
College Park, Maryland 20742
T, C

Massachusetts

Norfolk County Agricultural High School
Department of Horticulture
460 Main Street
Walpole, Massachusetts 02081
C

Springfield Technical Community College
Department of Horticulture
Armory Square
Springfield, Massachusetts 01105
AS, T

University of Massachusetts
Stockbridge School of Agriculture
Department of Horticulture
Amherst, Massachusetts 01002
John W. Denison, Director
AS, T, D

Michigan

Kalamazoo Valley Community College
Kalamazoo, Michigan 49009
AAS, C

Oakland Community College
Auburn Hills Campus
Department of Horticulture
2900 Featherstone Road
Auburn Heights, Michigan 48057
AAS, T, D

Southwestern Michigan College
Department of Horticulture
Cherry Grove Road
Dowagiac, Michigan 49047
AAS, AS, T, C, D

Minnesota

Brainerd Area Vo-Tech Institute
Department of Horticulture
300 Quince Street
Brainerd, Minnesota 56401
D

Dakota County Vo-Tech School
Department of Horticulture
P. O. Drawer K
Rosemount, Minnesota 55068
T, C, D

Landscape Career Center Anoka Area Vo-Tech Institute
Department of Horticulture
Box 191
Anoka, Minnesota 55303
C, D

**University of Minnesota
Technical College**
Agriculture Division
Department of Horticulture
Crookston, Minnesota 56716
AAS, T

**University of Minnesota
Technical College**
Agriculture Division
Department of Horticulture
Waseca, Minnesota 56093
AAS, T, D

916 Vo-Tech Institute
Department of Horticulture
3300 Century Avenue
White Bear Lake, Minnesota 55110
C, D

Mississippi
Hinds Junior College
Department of Horticulture
Raymond, Mississippi 39154
AS, T

Missouri
Meramec Community College
Department of Horticulture
11333 Big Bend Boulevard
Kirkwood, Missouri 63122
AAS, T, C

Nebraska
**Central Technical Community
College**
Department of Horticulture
Box 1024
Hastings, Nebraska 68901
AAS, T, C, D

University of Nebraska
School of Technical Agriculture
Department of Horticulture
Curtis, Nebraska 69025
AAS, T, D

New Hampshire
University of New Hampshire
Thompson School of Applied Science
Department of Horticulture
Durham, New Hampshire 03824
AAS

New Jersey
**Mercer County Community
College**
Department of Horticulture
1200 Old Trenton Road
P. O. Box B
Trenton, New Jersey 08690
AAS, AS, T, C, D

New York
New York Botanical Garden
Bronx Park
Bronx, New York 10458
C

**State University of New York
Agricultural and Technical College**
Department of Horticulture
Alfred, New York 14802
AAS, T, C

**State University of New York
Agricultural and Technical College**
Plant Science Department
Cobleskill, New York 12043
AAS, T, C

**State University of New York
Agricultural and Technical College**
Department of Horticulture
Delhi, New York 13753
Dr. E.L. Metcalf, Associate Professor
AAS, T

**State University of New York
Agricultural and Technical College**
Department of Horticulture
Farmingdale, New York 11735
AAS, T, C

**State University of New York
Agricultural and Technical College**
Department of Horticulture
Morrisville, New York 13408
AAS, T

North Carolina
**Catawba Valley Technical
Institute**
Department of Horticulture
Highway 64-70
Hickory, North Carolina 28601
AAS, T

Lenoir Community College
Department of Horticulture
Box 188
Kinston, North Carolina 28501
AAS, T, N

Sandhills Community College
Landscape Gardening Department
Route 3, Box 182-C
Carthage, North Carolina 28327
AAS, T, C, D

Wayne Community College
Department of Horticulture
Drawer 1878
Goldsboro, North Carolina 27530
Curtis Shivar
AAS, N

North Dakota
North Dakota State University
Department of Horticulture
Bottineau Branch and
Institute of Forestry
Bottineau, North Dakota 58318
Gerald C. Carlson
AS, C

Ohio
Clark Technical College
Department of Natural Science
P.O. Box 869
570 E. Leffels Lane
Springfield, Ohio 45501
AAS, T

Cleveland Technician School
Department of Horticulture
4600 Detroit Avenue
Cleveland, Ohio 44102
T, N, C

**The Ohio State University
Agricultural Technical Institute**
Division of Horticultural Industries
Wooster, Ohio 44691
AAS, T, D

Oklahoma
Eastern Oklahoma State College
Department of Forestry,
Ornamental Forestry Option
Wilburton, Oklahoma 74578
Earl R. Hutchinson, Instructor
AS, T, N, D (Arboriculture)

Northeastern Oklahoma A & M College
Department of Horticulture
Miami, Oklahoma 74354
AAS

Northern Oklahoma College
Department of Horticulture
Tonkawa, Oklahoma 74653
AS, T

Oregon
Clackamas Community College
Department of Horticulture
19600 S. Molalla Avenue
Oregon City, Oregon 97045
AS, T, N, C

Mt. Hood Community College
Department of Horticulture
2600 S.E. Stark Street
Gresham, Oregon 97030
AA, T, N, C, D

Treasure Valley Community College
Department of Horticulture
650 College Boulevard
Ontario, Oregon 97914
AS, N

Pennsylvania
Temple University
Ambler Campus
Department of Horticulture
Meetinghouse Road
Ambler, Pennsylvania 19002
AS, T, D

Williamsport Area Community College
Department of Horticulture
1005 W. 3rd Street
Williamsport, Pennsylvania 17701
AAS, T, D

South Carolina

Columbia Technical Education Center
Department of Horticulture
West Columbia, South Carolina 29169
Stephen F. Angelo
704-796-8401
C

Horry-Georgetown Tech Education Center
Department of Horticulture
P.O. Box 317
Conway, South Carolina 29426
AS, T

Spartanburg Technical College
Department of Horticulture
Interstate 85
Spartanburg, South Carolina 29301
AAS, T, D

Trident Technical College
7000 Rivers Avenue
Charleston, South Carolina 29405
Mack Fleming
AAS

Tennessee

Austin-Peay University
Department of Horticulture
Clarksville, Tennessee 37040
AS

Jackson State Community College
Department of Horticulture
Jackson, Tennessee 38301
AS, T

University of Tennessee at Martin
The School of Agriculture
Martin, Tennessee 38238
H.J. Smith, Dean, School of Agriculture

Texas

Blinn College
Department of Horticulture
900 College Avenue
Brenham, Texas 77833
AAS, T

Cisco Junior College
Department of Horticulture
Cisco, Texas 76437
Robert H. Donovan, Chairman
AAS, AS, T, D

Richland College
Department of Horticulture
12800 Abrams Road
Dallas, Texas 75231
Hank Griffith
AAS, T

Tarrant County Junior College-NW
Department of Horticulture
Fort Worth, Texas 76179
AAS, T, D

Virginia

Norfolk Botanical Gardens
Airport Road
Norfolk, Virginia 23518
Mr. George W. Baker, Curator
804-855-0194
AAS

Northern Virginia Community College
Horticultural Technology
1000 Harry Flood Bird Highway
Sterling, Virginia 22170
703-323-4576
AAS, T

Virginia State College
Department of Plant and Soil Science
Petersburg, Virginia 23803
Dr. W.L. Watson

Washington

Bellevue Community College
Department of Horticulture
3000 145th Place, S.E.
Bellevue, Washington 98007
AS, T, C, D

Centralia Community College
Department of Horticulture
Centralia, Washington 98531
AAS, AS, T, D

Clover Park Vo-Tech School
Department of Horticulture
4500 Steilacoon Boulevard S.W.
Lakewood Center, Washington 98499
T, C, D

Edmonds Community College
Department of Horticulture
20000 68th W.
Lynnwood, Washington 98036
AA, T, C

Skagit Valley Community College
College Way
Mt. Vernon, Washington 98273
AAS, C

Spokane Community College
1810 Green Street
Spokane, Washington 99207
Charles Parsons, Instructor of Horticulture
T, C

Wenatchee Valley College
Department of Horticulture
1300-5th Street
Wenatchee, Washington 98801
AAS, T, D

Yakima Valley College
Department of Horticulture
Yakima, Washington 98901
AAS, T, D

Wisconsin

Gateway Technical Institute
Department of Horticulture
3520 30th Avenue
Kenosha, Wisconsin 53140
AAS, T, D

Wyoming

University of Wyoming
Department of Horticulture
P.O. Box 3354
University Station
Laramie, Wyoming 82071
T

Canada

Algonquin College of Applied Science and Technology
Horticultural Division
P.O. Box 4501, Station E
Ottawa, Ontario, Canada K1S 5G2
Herbert S. Ransom, Coordinator, Horticulture Program
T, D

Humber College of Applied Art and Technology
Humber College Boulevard
Rexdale, Ontario, Canada
Richard Hook, Chairman
C, D

Institut de Technologie Agricole de St-Hyacinthe
3230 Rue Sicotte
St. Hyacinthe, PQ, Canada J2F 2M2
T, D

Niagara Parks Commission School of Horticulture
Box 747
Niagara Falls, Ontario, Canada
T, D

Nova Scotia Agriculture College
Department of Plant Science
Truro, Nova Scotia, Canada B2N, 5E3
J.S. Bubar
T, D

Nova Scotia Department of Agriculture and Marketing
Horticultural and Biological Services Branch
Truro, Nova Scotia, Canada B2N 5E3

Ryerson Polytechnical Institute
Landscape Architecture Dept.
50 Gould Street
Toronto 2, Ontario, Canada
AS, D

University of Guelph
Correspondence Study
Office of Continuing Education
Guelph, Ontario, Canada
D, CC

Reprinted by permission from the *Directory of American Horticulture*, Revised Edition, American Horticultural Society, Mt. Vernon, Virginia 22121, 1977, paperback, 118 pages, $5.00 plus 50 cents postage and handling. A useful and complete guide to professional associations, plant societies, conservation organizations, government programs, gardens and other reference material.

Houseplants

Today, it seems, plants are everywhere. Businessmen are mixing their own soils and coping with scale and spider mites. African violets are no longer the sole domain of white-haired grandmothers. Boston ferns and spathiphyllum have come off their pedestals and out of Victorian parlors. Greenhouses are no longer the exclusive property of the well-to-do. Virtually every city block and small town now has a plant shop. Florists, too, have joined the bandwagon and increased the number of plants they sell. And plant and garden societies have thousands of members.

Reasons are various

Some people claim the plant boom is part of the back-to-nature movement. Others say they are just plain bored with plastic philodendrons, and appreciate the touch of warmth and life a real plant imparts to a room. Still others believe it satisfies a creative need. Whatever the reasons, the consensus is clear: The plant world is in full bloom—the dusty, static world of plastic plants has all but succumbed to the mighty challenge of the living leaf.

In some respects, growing plants has become easier, primarily because of new growing aids, hardier strains, better fertilizers, and increased knowledge. But there is more to growing plants than that, for an indoor garden is an individual's own choice—and challenege—where pleasure and success are not measured by size or prize.

Different plants for different people

You can choose plants to blend with your decor, match the size of a plant to an empty corner, or buy plants to meet almost any lighting situation. The type of plant you choose should also match your own lifestyle and interest. For instance, even if you cannot devote a tremendous amount of time to your garden, there are scores of plants that are easy to grow yet will still impress others—and possibly even you. And if you are more ambitious, there are other varieties whose successful growth and glorious blooms will be a direct reflection of your attention and devotion.

Personal taste

Another point that is often ignored is the role that personal taste plays in successful gardening. No matter how perfectly suited a plant may be to your lighting situation, decor, or habits, you must like it too; somehow a plant that is loved seems to do better than one that is not. And oftentimes, it is the small occurrences which bring the biggest thrills. Perhaps you've finally gotten a pot of baby's tears to grow after the first four pots died, or a Christmas cactus that was your grandmother's suddenly bloomed after five lackluster years. In the end, it isn't *what* you grow that measures your success; it's how much pleasure it brings.

Penny Girard

Books

The Apartment Gardener, by Florence and Stanley Dworkin, Signet Books, The New American Library, 1301 Avenue of the Americas, New York, New York 10019, 1974, paperback, 400 pages, $1.50. Covers all aspects of indoor gardening.

The Avant Gardener, by Thomas and Betty Powell, Houghton-Mifflin Co., 2 Park St., Boston, Massachusetts, 02107, 1975, 264 pages, hardbound $12.95, paperback $6.95. A compilation of the Powell's informative newsletter.

Beyond the House Plant, by Jack Kramer, Ballantine Books, 201 E. 50th St., New York, New York 10022, 1976, paperback, $3.95. Extend your present garden with the step-by-step ideas for window, rooftop, balcony, loft, greenhouse, porch, and patio gardens given in this book. Included are construction tips and suggestions of plants for the various areas.

The Complete Book of Houseplants and Indoor Gardening, Consulting Editor, Edwin M. Steffek, Crown Publishers, One Park Ave., New York, New York 10016, 1976, 252 pages, $16.95. A comprehensive and beautifully illustrated reference work edited by a former editor of *Horticulture* magazine.

The Complete Indoor Gardener, edited by Michael Wright and Dennis Brown, Random House, 210 E. 50th St., New York, New York 10022, 1975, 256 pages, hardbound, $15.95, paperback, $7.95. This is a book packed with unusual and creative ideas. In addition to descriptions and cultural information on many houseplants, there are also sections on container and water gardening, bonsai, miniature gardens, free plants, children's gardening, food growing, and much more.

Exotic Houseplants, by Alfred Byrd Graf, Roehrs Co., East Rutherford, New Jersey 07073, 1974, hardbound, $8.95. A small version of the *Exotic Plant Manual*.

Exotic Plant Manual, by Alfred Byrd Graf, Roehrs Co., East Rutherford, New Jersey 07073, 1974, hardbound, 840 pages, $37.50. A comprehensive listing of exotic plants; contents include science of plants, cultivation and propagation, present-day usage, along with 4200 illustrations and growing information. A must for any serious indoor gardener.

Exotica III: Pictorial Encyclopedia of Exotic Plants, by Alfred Byrd Graf, Roehrs Co., East Rutherford, New Jersey 07073, 1974, hardbound, 1,834 pages, $78.00. *The* reference

Ixora javanica

work on exotic plants and the most comprehensive means of visual plant identification.

Garden In Your House, by Ernesta Drinker Ballard, Harper and Row Publishers, 10 E. 53rd St., New York, New York 10022, 1971, hardbound, $8.95. Covers 500 plants for indoor growing, each personally grown by the author; descriptions of the plants are given with any special care requirements. Also excellent sections on the basic principles involved with growing plants.

Grow It Indoors, by Richard W. Langer, Saturday Review Press, E. P. Dutton and Co., 201 Park Ave. S., New York, New York 10003, 1975, hardbound, $9.95. In the most readable and entertaining of styles, over 250 plants, grouped by family, are discussed. Included are specific details on cultural requirements. Also included are chapters on overall care, buying a plant, soil mixes, pest control, propagation and much more.

Hortus Third—A Concise Dictionary of Plants Cultivated in the United States and Canada, by the staff of the L.H. Bailey Hortorium, Cornell University, Macmillan Publishing Co., 866 Third Ave., New York, New York 10022, 1976, hardbound, 1304 pages, $99.50. Thirty-five years of research has produced this standard reference work on the cultivated plants of North America; 23,979 entries with correct botanical name, complete botanical description, common names, and uses and culture.

House Plants for the Purple Thumb, by Maggie Baylis, 101 Productions, 834 Mission St., San Francisco, California 94103, 1973, 192 pages, hardbound, $7.95, paperback, $4.95. A charmingly written and illustrated book that covers the basics of growing, caring, and living with houseplants. Also included are descriptions and care instructions for a large assortment of plants.

Making Things Grow: A Practical Guide for the Indoor Gardener, by Thalassa Cruso, Alfred A. Knopf, 201 E. 50th St., New York, New York 10022, 1973, hardbound, 257 pages, $7.95. A manual on growing and keeping your plants healthy. Deals with such basic problems as: watering, type of soil needed, training and pruning, along with suggestions on how to hang your plants.

Planters: Make Your Own Containers for Indoor and Outdoor Plants, by Jack Kramer, Ballantine Books, 201 E. 50th St., New York, New York 10022, 1977, paperback, 128 pages, $3.95. Learn how to make unusual, colorful, and inexpensive pots to showcase your plants and accent your room or landscape. Clear, concise, simple-to-follow instructions are illustrated with photographs and drawings for a variety of containers, stands, pedestals, and terrariums.

Plant Parenthood, by Maggie Baylis, 101 Productions, 834 Mission St., San Francisco, California 94103, 1975, 192 pages, hardbound, $7.95, paperback, $4.95. This book is written in a witty, intelligent manner with the author delving deeply into the problems of feeding and caring for your house plants. Included are case histories of 118 plants under such categories as: plants for tall people and tall ceilings, bedrooms and dull dining rooms, and decorative plants to "fernish" a bath. Good reading.

Plants At A Glance (flip file), by E.T. Henke, Plants-At-A-Glance Corp., Box 273-P, Pleasantville, New York, 1975. 109 index cards containing information on selecting, growing, potting, and propagating 78 different household plants. Quick, concise, and indexed.

Plants That Really Bloom Indoors, by George and Virginie Elbert, Simon and Schuster, Rockefeller Center, 630 Fifth Ave., New York, New York 10020, 1974, hardbound, 222 pages, $7.95. A guide to the growing of flowering plants: on windowsills, in terrariums, and under artificial lights. Included are chapters on light and plant problems, how tropical plants grow, as well as advice on where to buy house plants, seeds, and supplies.

Simon and Schuster's Complete Guide To Plants and Flowers, edited by Frances Perry, Simon and Schuster, Rockefeller Center, 630 Fifth Ave., New York, New York 10020, 1974, paperback, 522 pages, $6.95. For both the indoor and outdoor gardener, this book provides a wealth of information on all kinds of plants including houseplants as well as shrubs, vines, roses, and lilies. Over 500 plants and flowers are discussed in detail, with descriptions, use, and tips on planting and care as well as a color photo of the plant itself.

The Time-Life Encyclopedia of Gardening: Flowering House Plants, by James U. Crockett and the Editors of Time-Life Books, Time Life Books, 777 Duke St., Alexandria, Virginia 22314, 1972, hardbound, 160 pages, $6.95. This volume, one of a highly respected series authored by a noted gardening personality, is divided into two major sections; the first, illustrated with color photographs and drawings, deals with tips on decorating your home, advice on raising orchids, instructions on prop-

agation, information on light and water as well as help in choosing the right soil and pots. The second section, an A to Z encyclopedia of 145 of the most popular flowering houseplants, gives specific directions on the raising and care of each plant. Included are temperature, light, water, soil, and humidity requirements, along with colorful paintings of the plants. Informative and beautifully produced.

The Time-Life Encyclopedia of Gardening: Foliage House Plants, by James U. Crockett and the Editors of Time-Life Books, Time-Life Books, 777 Duke St., Alexandria, Virginia 22314, 1972, hardbound, 160 pages, $6.95. This volume, one in the gardening series by Time-Life, is divided into two major sections devoted to foliage plants for the home. The first section concerns itself with general information. Useful instructions for growing foliage inside bottles is included with a special chapter on succulents and cacti. This book is illustrated with both color photographs and drawings. The second section is an A to Z encyclopedia of 239 varieties of the most popular indoor foliage.

The Total Book of House Plants, by Russell C. Mott, Delacourt Press, 1 Dag Hammarskjold Plaza, New York, New York 10017, 1975, hardbound, 208 pages, $16.95. A comprehensive guide to over 350 plants covering almost every facet of indoor gardening. Included are an A to Z guide to almost 400 houseplants giving specific information on light, temperature and moisture requirements, as well as advice on propagation, potting, and fertilizer. Contains 350 beautiful color paintings with 120 line drawings and diagrams. Well done.

The Treasury of Houseplants, by Rob Herwig and Margot Schubert, Macmillan Publishing Co., 866 Third Ave., New York, New York 10022, 1976, hardbound, 368 pages, $12.95. Contains most of what one needs to know about selecting, growing, and caring for over 1,000 kinds of houseplants. Tips on plant watering, insect and disease prevention, temperature control, and positioning your plants are given. In addition, there are special sections on hydroponics, plants grown under fluorescent light, and a glossary of commonly used gardening terms.

The World Book of House Plants, by Elvin McDonald, Funk and Wagnalls, 666 Fifth Ave., New York, New York 10019, 1975, hardbound, $8.95. An easy-to-follow guide to indoor gardening, offering advice on such common questions as: when you should water your plants, what kind of containers are best, how much light and humidity your plant needs, along with recommendations on what to do for an ailing plant. Also included is an illustrated encyclopedia of more than 700 plants.

Schlumbergera hybrid

Calathea makoyana

Brassaia actinophylla

Peperomia obtusifolia 'Variegata'

Foliage plants

Plant name	Temperature	Moisture	Light
Acalypha godseffiana (copperleaf)	warm	moist	high
Acorus gramineus variegatus (variegated Japanese sweet flag)	cool	moist	medium
Adiantum species (maidenhair fern)	warm	moist	medium
Adromischus species (pretty pebbles, plover eggs, etc.)	warm	dry	medium
Agave species (century plants)	warm	dry	high
Aglaonema varieties (Chinese evergreen)	warm	dry	low
Aloe species (aloe)	warm	dry	high
Araucaria heterophylla (Norfolk Island pine)	cool	moist	high
Asparagus densiflorus 'Sprengeri' (asparagus fern)	warm	dry	medium
Asparagus setaceus (asparagus fern)	warm	dry	medium
Aspidistra elatior (cast-iron plant)	warm	moist	low
Asplenium nidus (bird's nest fern)	warm	moist	low
Aucuba japonica variegata (gold dust plant)	cool	dry	medium
Bambusa species (bamboo)	cool	moist	high
Begonia masoniana (iron cross begonia)	warm	moist	medium
Begonia rex cultorum hybrids (painted leaf begonia)	warm	moist	medium
Brassaia actinophylla (schefflera)	warm	dry	medium
Buxus sempervirens (boxwood)	cool	moist	high
Caladium hortulanum (fancy-leaved caladium)	warm	moist	medium
Calathea makoyana (peacock plant)	warm	moist	medium
Caryota mitis (fishtail palm)	warm	moist	medium
Cephalocereus senilis (old man cactus)	warm	dry	high
Chamaedorea elegans (parlor palm)	warm	moist	medium
Chlorophytum comosum (spider plant)	warm	moist	medium
Cissus antarctica (kangaroo ivy)	warm	dry	medium
Cissus rhombifolia (grape ivy)	warm	moist	medium
Codiaeum variegatum pictum (croton)	warm	moist	high
Coleus blumei (coleus)	warm	moist	high
Colocasia esculenta (elephant's ear)	warm	moist	medium
Cordyline terminalis (ti plant)	warm	moist	medium
Costus malortieanus (stepladder plant)	warm	moist	medium
Crassula argentea (jade plant)	warm	dry	high
Cryptanthus bromeloides tricolor (earth star)	warm	dry	medium
Cyanotis kewensis (teddy bear plant)	warm	dry	high
Cyanotis somaliensis (pussy ears)	warm	dry	high
Cyathea arborea (tree fern)	warm	moist	medium
Cycas revoluta (sago palm)	warm	dry	medium
Cyperus alternifolius (umbrella plant)	warm	moist	medium
Davallia fejeensis (rabbit's foot fern)	warm	moist	medium
Dichorisandra reginae (queen's spiderwort)	warm	dry	medium
Dieffenbachia varieties (dumb canes)	warm	dry	medium
Dizygotheca elegantissima (false aralia)	warm	moist	medium
Dracaena varieties (cornstalk plant, gold dust dracaena, etc.)	warm	moist	medium
Echeveria species (painted lady, Mexican snow-ball, plush plant, etc.)	warm	dry	high
Echinocereus dasyacanthus (rainbow cactus)	warm	dry	high
Euonymus fortunei (winter creeper)	cool	moist	high
Euonymus japonicus (evergreen euonymus)	cool	moist	medium
Euphorbia species (spurges)	warm	dry	medium
Fatshedera lizei (miracle plant)	warm	moist	medium

Foliage plants, cont.

Plant name	Temperature	Moisture	Light
Fatsia japonica (Japanese aralia)	cool	moist	medium
Ficus benjamina (weeping fig)	warm	dry	high
Ficus elastica (rubber plant)	warm	dry	high
Ficus lyrata (fiddleleaf fig)	warm	dry	medium
Fittonia verschaffeltii (nerve plant)	warm	moist	medium
Gasteria x hybrida (oxtongue plant)	warm	dry	medium
Geogenanthus undatus (seersucker plant)	warm	moist	medium
Grevillea robusta (silk oak)	warm	dry	high
Gynura aurantiaca (velvet plant)	warm	moist	medium
Gynura sarmentosa (purple passion vine)	warm	moist	high
Haworthia species (haworthia)	warm	dry	medium
Hedera canariensis 'Variegata' (Algerian ivy)	warm	moist	high
Hedera helix (English ivy)	cool	moist	high
Helxine soleirolii (baby's tears)	warm	moist	medium
Howeia belmoreana (sentry palm)	warm	moist	medium
Howeia forsteriana (paradise palm)	warm	moist	medium
Hoya carnosa (wax plant)	warm	dry	medium
Hypoestes sanguinolenta (freckle face)	warm	moist	medium
Kalanchoe daigremontiana (devil's backbone)	warm	dry	high
Kalanchoe marmorata (penwiper plant)	warm	dry	high
Kalanchoe tomentosa (panda plant)	warm	dry	high
Laurus nobilis (bay laurel)	cool	moist	high
Ligularia tussilaginea aureo-maculata (leopard plant)	warm	moist	medium
Ligustrum lucidum 'Texanum' (wax-leaf privet)	cool	dry	high
Livistonia chinensis (Chinese fan palm)	warm	moist	medium
Lobivia aurea (golden lily cactus)	warm	dry	high
Lotus berthelotii (coral gem)	warm	dry	high
Mammillaria species (bird's nest, powder puff, snowball, pincushion cacti)	warm	dry	high
Maranta leuconeura kerchoveana (prayer plant)	warm	moist	medium
Monstera deliciosa (Mexican bread fruit)	warm	moist	medium
Myrtus communis microphylla (myrtle)	cool	dry	high
Nepenthes maxima (pitcher plant)	warm	moist	medium
Nephrolepis exaltata bostoniensis varieties (Boston fern)	warm	moist	medium
Nerium oleander (oleander)	cool	dry	high
Nicodemia diversifolia (indoor oak)	warm	moist	medium
Notocactus species (ball cactus)	warm	dry	high
Olea europaea (olive tree)	warm	dry	high
Opuntia species (prickly pear cactus)	warm	dry	high
Osmanthus fragrans (sweet olive)	cool	moist	high
Pachyphytum varieties (moonstones)	warm	dry	high
Pandanus veitchii (variegated screw pine)	warm	dry	medium
Pellaea rotundifolia (button fern)	warm	moist	medium
Pellionia daveauana (trailing watermelon begonia)	warm	moist	medium
Pellionia pulchra (satin pellionia)	warm	moist	medium
Peperomia varieties (peperomia)	warm	dry	medium
Philodendron varieties (philodendron)	warm	moist	medium
Phoenix roebelenii (dwarf date palm)	warm	moist	medium
Pilea varieties (aluminum plant, panamiga, etc.)	warm	moist	medium
Pittosporum tobira 'Variegatum' (variegated mock orange)	warm	dry	medium
Platycerium species (staghorn fern)	warm	moist	medium

Dracaena compacta

Tolmiea menziesii

Pilea involucrata

Fatshedera lizei variegata

133

Jacobinia velutina

Fittonia verschaffeltii argyroneura

Fatsia japonica

Pilea cadierei

Foliage plants, cont.

Plant name	Temperature	Moisture	Light
Plectranthus australis (Swedish ivy)	warm	dry	medium
Pleomele reflexa (Malaysian dracaena)	warm	moist	medium
Podocarpus macrophyllus 'Maki' (Southern yew)	warm	moist	high
Polypodium aureum 'Mandaianum' (blue fern)	warm	moist	medium
Polypodium polycarpon 'Grandiceps' (fish-tail fern)	warm	moist	medium
Polyscias varieties (ming aralia)	warm	dry	medium
Pteris cretica (table fern)	warm	moist	low
Pteris ensiformis 'Victoriae' (victoria fern)	warm	moist	low
Rhapis humilis (slender lady palm)	warm	moist	medium
Rhoeo spathacea (Moses-in-the-cradle)	warm	moist	medium
Sansevieria trifasciata (snake plant)	warm	dry	medium
Saxifraga stolonifera (strawberry geranium)	warm	dry	high
Scindapsus aureus (devil's ivy)	warm	dry	medium
Sedum species (burro's tail, carpet sedum, jelly beans, etc.)	warm	dry	high
Senecio mikanioides (German ivy)	warm	moist	medium
Sparmannia africana (African hemp)	cool	moist	high
Strobilanthes dyerianus (Persian shield)	warm	moist	low
Syngonium podophyllum (arrowhead vine)	warm	moist	medium
Tetrapanax papyriferus (rice paper plant)	cool	moist	high
Tolmiea menziesii (piggyback plant)	warm	moist	medium
Tradescantia albiflora 'Albo-vittata' (giant white inch plant)	warm	dry	medium
Tradescantia blossfeldiana (flowering inch plant)	warm	dry	high
Tradescantia fluminensis 'Variegata' (variegated wandering jew)	warm	dry	medium
Yucca elephantipes (yucca)	warm	dry	high
Zebrina pendula (wandering jew)	warm	dry	high

Flowering plants

Plant name	Temperature	Moisture	Light
Abutilon x hybridum (flowering maple)	warm	moist	high
Acalypha hispida (chenille plant)	warm	moist	medium
Achimenes varieties (magic flower)	warm	moist	medium
Aechmea fasciata (silver vase plant)	warm	dry	medium
Aeschynanthus varieties (lipstick vine)	warm	moist	medium
Agapanthus africanus (blue African lily)	warm	moist	high
Allamanda species (golden trumpet)	warm	moist	high
Allophyton mexicanum (Mexican foxglove)	warm	moist	medium
Ananas comosus (pineapple plant)	warm	dry	high
Angraecum varieties (angraecum orchid)	warm	moist	medium
Anthurium scherzerianum (flamingo flower)	warm	moist	low
Aphelandra squarrosa (zebra plant)	warm	moist	medium
Ardisia crispa (coral berry)	warm	moist	medium
Azalea varieties (azalea)	cool	moist	medium
Begonia semperflorens (wax begonia)	warm	dry	medium
Beloperone guttata (shrimp plant)	warm	dry	high
Billbergia species (queen's tears)	warm	dry	high
Bougainvillea varieties (paper flower)	warm	dry	high
Brassavola nodosa (lady-of-the-night orchid)	warm	dry	medium
Brassia caudata (spider orchid)	warm	moist	medium
Browallia speciosa major (sapphire flower)	warm	moist	medium
Brunfelsia calycina floribunda (yesterday, today and tomorrow)	warm	moist	high

Flowering plants, cont.

Plant name	Temperature	Moisture	Light
Calceolaria herbeohybrida 'Multiflora nana' (pocketbook flower)	cool	dry	medium
Calliandra emarginata (powder puff)	warm	moist	high
Camellia japonica (camellia)	cool	moist	medium
Campanula isophylla alba (white Italian bellflower)	cool	moist	high
Capsicum annum conoides (ornamental pepper)	warm	moist	high
Carissa grandiflora (Natal plum)	warm	moist	high
Cattleya varieties (cattleya orchid)	warm	dry	medium
Cestrum nocturnum (night jessamine)	warm	moist	high
Chirita sinensis (silver chirita)	warm	moist	medium
Chrysanthemum frutescens (marguerite)	cool	dry	high
Chrysanthemum morifolium (florist's chrysanthemum)	warm	dry	high
Citrus varieties (orange, lime, lemon)	warm	dry	high
Clerodendrum thomsonae (glory bower)	warm	moist	medium
Clivia miniata (Kafir lily)	warm	dry	medium
Coffea arabica (Arabian coffee)	warm	moist	medium
Columnea varieties (goldfish plant)	warm	moist	medium
Crimun 'Ellen Bosanquet' (red angel lily)	warm	moist	high
Crocus varieties (crocus)	cool	moist	high
Crossandra infundibuliformis (firecracker flower)	warm	moist	medium
Cuphea hyssopifolia (elfin herb)	warm	moist	high
Cuphea ignea (cigar plant)	warm	moist	high
Cyclamen persicum giganteum (cyclamen)	cool	moist	medium
Cymbidium hybrids (cymbidium orchid)	warm	moist	medium
Daphne odora 'Marginata' (variegated winter daphne)	cool	moist	medium
Dendrobium nobile (dendrobium orchid)	warm	dry	medium
Dipladenia x amoena (dipladenia)	warm	dry	medium
Dyckia brevifolia (miniature agave)	warm	moist	medium
Epidendrum cochleatum (clamshell orchid)	warm	dry	medium
Epiphyllum hybrids (orchid cacti)	warm	dry	medium
Episcia varieties (peacock plant)	warm	moist	medium
Eranthemum nervosum (blue sage)	warm	moist	medium
Ervatamia coronaria (butterfly gardenia)	warm	moist	high
Eucharis grandiflora (Amazon lily)	warm	moist	medium
Euphorbia pulcherrima (poinsettia)	warm	dry	high
Euphorbia splendens (crown of thorns)	warm	dry	medium
Exacum affine (Arabian violet)	warm	moist	medium
Felicia amelloides (blue marguerite)	warm	moist	high
Fortunella margarita (nagami kumquat)	warm	moist	high
Freesia x hybrida (freesia)	cool	dry	medium
Fuchsia x hybrida (fuchsia)	warm	moist	medium
Gardenia jasminoides 'Veitchii' (gardenia)	warm	moist	high
Gazania rigens (gazania)	warm	dry	high
Gelsemium sempervirens (Carolina jessamine)	warm	moist	high
Gloriosa rothschildiana (glory lily)	warm	dry	high
Gloxinera 'Rosebells' (gloxinera)	warm	moist	medium
Guzmania varieties (guzmania)	warm	moist	medium
Haemanthus katherinae (blood lily)	warm	moist	high
Heliotropium arborescens (common heliotrope)	warm	moist	medium
Hibiscus rosa-sinensis (Chinese hibiscus)	warm	moist	high
Hippeastrum hybrids (amaryllis)	warm	dry	high
Hyacinthus orientalis (hyacinth)	cool	moist	high

Peperomia caperata

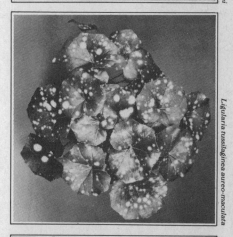

Coleus blumei

Ligularia tussilaginea aureo-maculata

Pentas lanceolata

Codiaeum 'Aucubaefolium'

Browallia speciosa major

Monstera deliciosa

Flowering plants, cont.

Plant name	Temperature	Moisture	Light
Hydrangea macrophylla (common hydrangea)	warm	moist	high
Impatiens walleriana (patient Lucy)	warm	moist	high
Ipomoea tricolor (morning glory)	warm	moist	high
Ixora species (flame-of-the-woods)	warm	moist	high
Jacobinia species (jacobinia)	warm	moist	medium
Jasminum species (jasmine)	warm	moist	high
Kalanchoe blossfeldiana (Christmas kalanchoe)	warm	dry	high
Lachenalia aloides (tricolor cape cowslip)	cool	moist	high
Laelia species (laelia orchid)	warm	dry	medium
Laeliocattleya varieties (laeliocattleya orchid)	warm	dry	medium
Lantana camara (lantana)	warm	dry	high
Lilium longiflorum (Easter lily)	warm	dry	high
Lobularia maritima (sweet alyssum)	warm	moist	high
Malpighia coccigera (miniature holly)	warm	dry	high
Malvaviscus penduliflorus (Turk's-cap)	warm	moist	high
Manettia inflata (firecracker vine)	warm	moist	high
Maxillaria tenuifolia (maxillaria orchid)	warm	moist	medium
Miltonia hybrids (pansy orchid)	warm	moist	medium
Muscari armeniacum (grape hyacinth)	cool	moist	high
Narcissus hybrids (daffodil, narcissus)	cool	moist	high
Nematanthus varieties (candy corn)	warm	moist	medium
Neofinetia falcata (neofinetia orchid)	cool	moist	medium
Neomarica gracilis (apostle plant)	warm	moist	medium
Nicotiana alata grandiflora (flowering tobacco)	warm	moist	medium
Nidularium species (nidularium)	warm	moist	medium
Odontoglossum pulchellum (lily-of-the-valley orchid)	cool	moist	medium
Oncidium flexuosum (dancing doll orchid)	warm	dry	medium
Ornithogalum caudatum (false sea onion)	warm	dry	high
Osmanthus fragrans (sweet olive)	cool	moist	high
Oxalis purpurea (grand duchess oxalis)	warm	dry	high
Paphiopedilum 'Maudiae' (paphiopedilum orchid)	warm	moist	medium
Passiflora x alato-caerulea (passion flower)	warm	moist	high
Pelargonium hortorum (geranium)	warm	dry	high
Pentas lanceolata (Egyptian star cluster)	warm	moist	high
Petunia x hybrida (petunia)	warm	dry	high
Phalaenopsis amabilis (moth orchid)	warm	moist	medium
Primula malacoides (fairy primrose)	cool	moist	medium
Punica granatum nana (dwarf pomegranate)	warm	moist	high
Quesnelia liboniana (Grecian vase plant)	warm	moist	medium
Rodriguezia venusta (rodriguezia orchid)	warm	moist	medium
Rosa chinensis minima (miniature rose)	warm	moist	high
Rosmarinus officinalis (rosemary)	warm	dry	high
Ruellia macrantha (ruellia)	warm	moist	medium
Russelia equisetiformis (coral plant)	warm	dry	high
Saintpaulia varieties (African violet)	warm	moist	medium
Schizocentron elegans (Spanish shawl)	warm	moist	medium
Schlumbergera hybrids (Christmas cactus)	warm	dry	medium
Scilla peruviana (Peruvian squill)	warm	moist	medium
Senecio confusus (Mexican flame vine)	warm	moist	medium
Senecio cruentus (cineraria)	cool	moist	medium
Sinningia cardinalis (cardinal flower)	warm	moist	medium
Sinningia speciosa (gloxinia)	warm	moist	medium

Flowering plants, cont.

Plant name	Temperature	Moisture	Light
Smithiantha cinnabarina (temple bells)	warm	moist	medium
Solanum pseudocapsicum (Jerusalem cherry)	warm	dry	high
Sophrolaeliocattleya hybrids (sophrolaeliocattleya orchid)	warm	dry	high
Spathiphyllum varieties (spathiphyllum)	warm	moist	medium
Sprekelia formosissima (Aztec lily)	warm	dry	high
Stephanotis floribunda (stephanotis)	warm	moist	high
Strelitzia reginae (bird of paradise)	warm	dry	high
Streptocarpus rexii hybrids (cape primrose)	warm	dry	medium
Streptosolen jamesonii (orange streptosolen)	warm	moist	medium
Thunbergia alata (black-eyed-Susan vine)	warm	moist	high
Tillandsia cyanea (tillandsia)	warm	moist	medium
Trachelospermum jasminoides (star jasmine)	warm	dry	medium
Trichocentrum tigrinum (trichocentrum orchid)	warm	moist	medium
Tropaeolum majus (common nasturtium)	cool	dry	high
Tulbaghia fragrans (fragrant tulbaghia)	cool	moist	high
Tulip varieties (tulips)	cool	moist	high
Vallota speciosa (Scarborough lily)	warm	moist	high
Veltheimia viridifolia (veltheimia)	warm	moist	medium
Vriesia species (painted feather)	warm	dry	medium
Zantedeschia aethiopica 'Compacta' (dwarf white calla)	warm	moist	high
Zephyranthes grandiflora (rain lily)	warm	dry	high

This plant is no bargain, regardless of price. It shows sparse, leggy growth, and few flowers or buds.

Key to chart

Temperature
Warm: 72-degree F. day-time temperature, with variations from 65 to 85 degrees F.
Cool: 60-degree F. daytime temperature, with variations from 45 to 65 degrees F. *Nighttime temperatures should be 5 to 10 degrees lower.*

Moisture
Dry: Allow the top layer of the soil to dry before drenching the soil thoroughly; plants usually have thick roots.
Moist: Maintain uniform moisture throughout the soil without letting the plant stand in water; plants usually have fine, delicate roots.

Light
High: Highest light intensity possible indoors; usually a south window.
Medium: Bright, indirect sun, such that a shadow is barely visible; usually an east or west window.
Low: Diffused light; shady areas away from the sun; a north window.

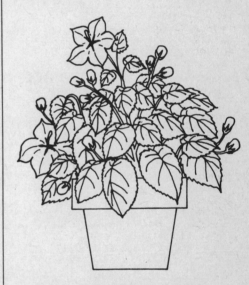

This plant's full, bushy growth and vigorous appearance indicate it's in good health. The large number of buds means that it will bloom for a long time to come.

How to buy healthy plants

The prospective plant buyer of today faces a problem that would have seemed laughable ten years ago: an overabundance of plant sources, coupled with a puzzling variety of prices. It is possible, however, to buy high-quality, healthy plants at low prices—if the buyer knows what to look for:

Roots and soil: The root system of a healthy plant has not outgrown its pot. If the proprietor will allow it, knock the plant out of its pot to examine the roots. (Do so carefully to avoid damaging the plant.) If the roots are thick and matted, have practically replaced the soil in the pot, and grow around and around in a circular pattern at the bottom of the pot, the plant is pot-bound (or root-bound). The roots may also be visible on the soil surface, or be poking out the drainage holes at the bottom of the pot. A pot-bound plant can be repotted in a larger pot when you get home. But if the roots have been cramped for too long, depriving the plant of air and nourishment, it may have suffered irreparable damage that will show up in a few weeks, regardless of how healthy the foliage appears to be when you buy it. Roots should show no sign of decay, and the soil should have no unpleasant odor. Soft, mushy roots indicate a chronically overwatered plant; dried, shrivelled roots mean chronic underwatering. Avoid plants with a white crust on the pot or on the soil surface. Such an accumulation of fertilizer salts can prove toxic. Check, too, for evidence of insect invasion or disease (see *Insect Pests* and *Ailments*).

Stems and leaves: Most plants should have a bushy, compact appearance. Leaves should be of a uniform size; when some leaves are much larger than others, the plant has been overfertilized. Sparse, small leaves on spindly stems often indicate a light-deprived plant. Both stems and leaves should be firm and upright. Hanging plants should appear perky, not droopy. Leaves should not be yellow, weak, damaged, wilted, or brown-edged. Inspect the foliage to make sure it is free of pests and diseases.

Flowers: Flowering plants are best purchased at the stage when they have some unopened buds as well as opened blooms. This way, you will enjoy the flowers for an extended period of time.

Plant sources

Alberts and Merkel Brothers, 2210 South Federal Highway, Boynton Beach, Florida 33435. (305) 732-2071. Plant list 75 cents. Open Monday through Saturday 8:00 a.m. to 4:30 p.m. Varied selection of tropical plants including many species of aglaonemas, anthuriums, aralias, cacti, calatheas, dracaenas, ferns, gesneriads, palms, cycads, bromeliads, gingers, heliconias, ixoras, platyceriums, and sansevierias. Special orchid collection and orchid gardening supplies available as well as book and general-purpose gardening aids.

Arthur Eames Allgrove, 281 Woburn Street, North Wilmington, Massachusetts 01887. (617) 658-4869. Catalog. Open by appointment. Specializing in terrariums and partridge berry bowls, Allgrove offers a variety of woodsy microenvironmental plant kits, including plants such as rattlesnake plantain (*Goodyera pubescens*), walking fern (*Camptosorus rhizophyllus*), striped and common pipsissewa (chimaphila), Venus flytrap (*Dionea muscipula*), and butterwort (*Pinguicula vulgaris*). Beginners kits range from bottles to bowls and terrariums. He also carries some native wildflowers, orchids, ferns, and groundcovers. Booklets on terrariums are available.

Aloha East, 217 South King Street, Honolulu, Hawaii 96827. (808) 537-1793. Catalog 25 cents. Limited collection of ti plants and logs; anthuriums; red, blue, and white ginger plants; a few cattleya and dendrobium orchids; coconut palms; and other Hawaiian tropical plants. Also special hanging shell planters available.

Antonelli Brothers, 2545 Capitola Road, Santa Cruz, California 95062. (408) 475-5222. Illustrated catalog. Open every day except major holidays. Specialists in tuberous begonias; other offerings include many foliage and flowering houseplants, such as ferns, miniature begonias, African violets, gloxinias, calla lilies, fuschias, and philodendrons. Also some growing information and gardening aids (plant food, fungicide, mister).

Arant's Exotic Greenhouses, Route 3, Box 972, Bessemer, Alabama 35020. (205) 428-1827. Catalog $1.50 (refundable with order). Open Tuesday through Saturday from 9:00 a.m. to 5:00 p.m.; Monday by appointment (always call before visiting). Specializing in ferns, bromeliads, orchids, cacti, succulents, and assorted tropical plants. Extensive listings and choice of many species for most plants. Cuttings or pot plants available. Catalog contains some growing hints on soil, light, water, and various fertilizers.

Baumer, 9900 North Michigan Road, Carmel, Indiana 46032. (317) 873-4647. Plant list. Specialists in rooted cuttings of carnations and chrysanthemums, especially for the hobby greenhouse. They offer fourteen different carnations (including miniature, or spray, varieties), and eight varieties of chrysanthemums.

John Brudy's Rare Plant House, Box 1348, Cocoa Beach, Florida 32931. Catalog $1.00 (refundable with order). Mail order only. This seed company specializes in tropical and semitropical trees, shrubs, philodendrons, bonsai, exotic edibles, annuals, perennials, and herbs. Also available are palm seedlings, aralia cuttings, and dwarf schefflera plants. All seeds listed come with descriptions and growing instructions.

Burgess Seed and Plant Company, Box 5000, Galesburg, Michigan 49053. (616) 665-7079. Color-illustrated catalog. This company caters to general indoor gardening. Wide selection, from trees, vegetables, and bulbs to ivies, ferns, begonias, bromeliads, carnivorous plants, fruits, and exotics. Complete line of indoor gardening supplies.

C.A. Cruickshank, 1015 Mount Pleasant Road, Toronto, Ontario M4P 2M1, Canada. (416) 488-8292. Color-illustrated catalogs issued spring and fall, plus special bulletins. Open Monday through Saturday 9:00 a.m. to 5:00 p.m. (closed on Saturday from June through September). An excellent selection of bulbs, plants, books, supplies, and equipment for indoor growing.

Deedee's Tropical Seeds, Box 416, Menlo Park, California 94025. Catalog. Offers seeds for over 60 tropical plants suitable for pots, terrariums, hanging baskets, and bonsai, such as: aralia, papaya, ardisia, carissa, ficus, jasmine, and bird of paradise.

Edelweiss Gardens, 54 Robbinsville-Allentown Road, Box 66R, Robbinsville, New Jersey 08691. (609) 259-2831. Plant list 35 cents. Open until 4:00 p.m. daily. Large assortment of begonias, bromeliads, cacti and succulents, carnivorous plants, ferns, gesneriads, orchids, and houseplants. Tree fern pots, logs, rafts, totems, and chunks are available.

Jim Fobel, 598-T Kipuka Place, Kailua, Hawaii 96734. (808) 261-1264. Catalog $1.00 (2 seed packets included). A varied collection of tropical plant seeds including bird of paradise, plumeria, shell ginger, areca palm, pink trumpet, a few orchids, and other exotics. Seeds are gathered in Hawaii by the family.

Fran's Dab Shop, 13351 32nd Avenue, Seattle, Washington 98168. Plant list with descriptions. A selection of rare and unusual exotic plants from South Africa is offered. Each has been started from seed by Fran. Care and feeding instructions are sent with the plants.

The Garden Spot, 4032 Rosewood Drive, Columbia, South Carolina 29205. Send stamped, self-addressed envelope for plant list. Open to visitors. Specialists in ivies. Over 100 hedera species, varieties and cultivars grown in quart tin cans for shipping.

Greenland Flower Shop, Route 1 (Stormstown), Port Matilda, Pennsylvania 16870. Catalog 25 cents. Visitors welcome. Large selection of plants for indoors including hanging, terrarium, miniatures, ferns, and begonias.

Green of the Earth, 1295 Lownes Place, Pomona, California 91766. (714) 623-7809. List 50 cents. This family-run business specializes in the most popular houseplants, including rare and unusual begonias.

Grow Your Own, Inc., Route 2, Fruitville Road, Sarasota, Florida 33577. (813) 371-3818. Catalog. Open daily to visitors, 9:00 a.m. to 5:00 p.m. Gardening kits of tropical plants and cacti come as preseeded growing blocks. Plant supplies are also available.

Robert B. Hamm and Associates, 2951 Elliott Street, Witchita Falls, Texas 76308. (817) 691-1295. Plant list 25 cents. Visitors welcome by appointment. This nursery specializes in begonias (including Reigers), gesneriads, unusual house and greenhouse plants, and plants for growing under lights. Supplies for the home grower including soils, fertilizers, and pots.

Hana Gardenland, Honokalani Farm, Box 177, Hana, Maui, Hawaii 96713. (808) 248-8073. Catalog and price lists. Visitors by appointment only. Located in a remote area deep in the tropical rain forest on the east Maui coast, this nursery specializes in tropical plants and novelty items such as anthuriums, plumeria, and tree ferns as well as ti logs, air plants, and some seeds. Many rare Hawaiian plants. Seeds, rooted cuttings, plants (all sizes).

Harborcrest Nurseries, 4634 West Saanich Road, Victoria, British Columbia, V8Z 3G8, Canada. (604) 479-1333. Catalog 25 cents. Open daily 9:00 a.m. to 4:00 p.m. A wide selection of tropical houseplants, including many hybrids and miniature varieties. They offer a particularly large group of African violets, gesneriads, cacti and succulents, fuschias, and orchids.

Hart and Tagami, 47-754 Lamaula Road, Kaneohe, Hawaii 96744. (808) 239-8146. List 35 cents. Open Sundays and Tuesday mornings by appointment. Rare and exotic tropical plants such as xanthosoma, water canna, rice plant, heliconias, calatheas, ferns, dieffenbachias, anthuriums, and dracaenas. The owners, a potter and an artist, also maintain a gallery where they exhibit plants, pottery and paintings.

Hewston Green, Box 3115, Seattle, Washington 98114. Plant list 50 cents. Varied selection of cacti and succulents, ferns, flowering plants, vines and basket plants, indoor trees and shrubs, miniatures. Offerings of streptocarpus 'Blue Boy,' and other recent introductions.

Hidden Springs Nursery, Route 3, Rockmark, Georgia, 30153. Brochure 25 cents. Open Friday and Saturday 8:00 a.m. to 6:00 p.m. Selection of fuchsias, houseplants, dwarf evergreens for bonsai, sempervivums, and herbs. Special brochure for sedum culture.

Jerry Horne, 10195 Southwest 70th Street, Miami, Florida 33173. (305) 270-1235. Catalog. Visitors by appointment only. This small family-run nursery tries to grow and import the more unusual and rare plants not handled by other greenhouses. They specialize in bromeliads, tropical ferns, unusual foliage plants, palms, and cycads. New variegated bromeliad varieties are available.

Hurov's Tropical Seeds, Box 10387, Honolulu, Hawaii 96816. (808) 735-1909. Plant lists. Extensive offerings of tropical seeds of especially unusual plants gathered from numerous expeditions to New Guinea, Southeast Asia, and other tropical areas. Plants available include Chinese dwarf ginger, Chinese pygmy date, and other dwarf tropical trees. Also Chinese orchid bulbs. Listings have descriptions, general culture notes, place of origin, and uses for plants.

International Growers Exchange, Box 397, Farmington, Michigan 48024. (313) 474-1827. Catalog $3.00. An extensive selection of rare and unusual bulbs and plants for both indoors and out. Included in the listings are anemones, anthuriums, begonias, clivia, cacti, dahlias, lilies, ginger, orchids, carnivorous plants, native wildflowers, herbs, perennials, and others.

Kartuz Greenhouses, 92 Chestnut Street, Wilmington, Massachusetts 01887. (617) 658-9017. Color-illustrated catalog $1.00. Open Tuesday through Saturday 9:00 a.m. to 5:00 p.m. Specializing in distinctive, colorful, flowering plants, Kartuz offers a selection of over 50 genera, including gesneriads, begonias, geraniums, succulents, terrarium plants, miniatures, and other foliage and flowering houseplants. Plants listed in the catalog are keyed according to their culture requirements.

Kuaola Farms, Box 1140, Hilo, Hawaii 96720. (808) 964-1746. Plant list. Nursery located at Panaewa Farm Lots, West Mamaki Street near Hilo. Open Monday through Friday 7:00 a.m. to 3:30 p.m. Visitors welcome. This company specializes in *Anthurium andreanum* with red, white, or pink flowers.

Lauray of Salisbury, Undermountain Road, Salisbury, Connecticut 06068. (203) 435-2263. Catalog 50 cents. Open daily 10:00 a.m. to 5:00 p.m. Varied stock of exotic plants ranging from cacti and succulents to African violets, ferns, orchids, begonias, fuchsias, gesneriads, some miniatures and dwarfs, and other houseplants. A family-run operation so that it is advisable to call ahead before visiting.

Lehua Anthurium Nursery, 80 Kokea Street, Hilo, Hawaii 96720. (808) 935-7859. Plant lists. Specializing in *Anthurium andreanum*, plus novelty varieties and hybrids. New dracaena cultivars, ferns, ficus, gingers, heliconias, maile, calathea, and some orchids, palms, and other tropical plants.

Loadholtz Ferneries, Box 45, Seville, Florida 32090. (904) 749-2665. Catalog $1.00. Open Monday through Friday 8:00 a.m. to 5:00 p.m. Growers of tropical foliage plants and ferns, including hanging plants and indoor trees. Sizes range from 3-inch to 10-gallon containers.

Logee's Greenhouses, 55 North Street, Danielson, Connecticut 06239. (203) 774-8038. Illustrated catalog $2.00. Open daily 9:00 a.m. to 4:00 p.m. Visitors welcome. Fibrous-rooted, rex, wax, and rhizomatous begonias (many their own hybrids) are offered. In addition, there is a wide selection of rare and unusual houseplants, miniatures, ferns, cacti and succulents, herbs. Recommended book list for cultivation included in the catalog.

Loyce's Flowers, Route 2, Box 11, Granbury, Texas 76048. Plant list with descriptions 50 cents. Large choice of hoya varieties; new plants constantly added to these listings. Also many bougainvillea species. General culture instructions included.

Merry Gardens, Box 595, Camden, Maine 04843. Pictorial handbook $1.00; list 50 cents. Open Monday through Saturday 9:00 a.m. to 4:30 p.m. Extensive collection of foliage and flowering houseplants including numerous vine and hanging basket plants, cacti and succulents, ivies, fuchsias, ferns, begonias (fibrous-rooted, rhizomatous, semperflorens, trailing), many geraniums (particularly rare, scented, and dwarf species).

Orinda Nursery, Bridgeville, Delaware 19933. Color-illustrated catalog 50 cents. Open 10:00 a.m. to 4:30 p.m. Thursday, Friday, and Saturday in September, October, December, February to June. Extensive offerings of camellias and rhododendrons including standard and rare varieties.

Pacific Bamboo Gardens, Box 16145, 4754 Vista Lane, San Diego, California 92116. (714) 282-8426 or 283-6141. Catalog $2.00; price list 25 cents. Visitors welcome; please call first. This company offers the largest selection of bamboos available in the country. Catalog includes culture and major characteristics of the plants available.

The Plant Room, 6373 Trafalgar Road, Hornby, Ontario, L0P 1E0, Canada. (416) 878-4984. Plant list $1.00. Open daily 10:00 a.m. to 4:00 p.m. Large selection of exotic plants including many varieties of African violets, gesneriads, orchids, miniature roses, geraniums, begonias, and other flowering and foliage plants. Complete line of accessories for indoor growing; also many gardening books are offered.

C.G. Robinson Nursery, 56 North Georgia Avenue, Mobile, Alabama 36604. List. Large selection of camellias; plants are sold singly and in one-dozen lots and in a variety of sizes.

Alvim Seidel, Box 1, Rua Roberto Seidel, 1981, 89280, Corupa, Santa Catarina, Brazil. Color-illustrated catalog. Correspondence in English, German, Portuguese, French, and Spanish. Huge selection of bromeliads, orchids, maranta family members, palms, and tropical foliage plants and seeds.

Shadow Lawn Nursery, 637 Holly Lane, Plantation, Florida 33317. (305) 587-4792. Plant list with descriptions 50 cents. Mail order only. Foliage and flowering plants, ornamental trees and shrubs, succulents, hanging plants, seeds, cuttings, and bulbs. Over 1,000 rare and unusual plants geared for the plant connoisseur are offered.

Spruce Brook Nursery, Box 925, Litchfield, Connecticut 06759. (203) 482-5229. Catalog $2.00 (refundable on $10.00 order). Nursery on Route 118; open daily 9:00 a.m. to 5:00 p.m.; closed on Sunday from January 2 through 27th. Unusual and hard-to-find greenhouse plants. Many dwarf and rare species; also clivia.

Sunnybrook Farms Nursery, 9448 Mayfield Road, Chesterland, Ohio 44026. (216) 729-7232 or 729-9838. Catalog 50 cents. Open Tuesday through Saturday 8:30 a.m. to 5:00 p.m. and Sunday 1:00 p.m. to 5:00 p.m. Visitors welcome. Extensive selection of both common and unusual houseplants. Included are gesneriads, begonias, bromeliads, ivies, and many more. Also, geraniums, cactus and succulents, and herbs.

Thomasville Nurseries, Box 7, Thomasville, Georgia 31792. (912) 226-5568. Illustrated catalog. Nursery at 1842 Smith Avenue is open Monday through Saturday 8:30 a.m. to 5:30 p.m.; Sunday from 2:00 p.m. to 5:00 p.m. November through May. Specialists in roses; also have azaleas and camellias.

Mrs. R.C. Welsh, Route 3, Box 181, Madison, Florida 32340. Catalog 15 cents. Visitors welcome any time, any day. Mrs. Welsh runs a one-woman business and offers items not found in every nursery, in addition to some common houseplants that are her favorites. Generally, her list includes flowering and foliage plants, succulents, begonias, hanging plants, ferns, bromeliads, and daylilies.

White Flower Farm, Litchfield, Connecticut 06759. (203) 567-9415. A subscription to White Flower Farm's Gardening Publications Service includes spring and fall editions of *The Garden Book* and three editions of *Notes*; the cost is $4.00 (a $4.00 credit is given for use on an order of $15.00 or more). Open daily 9:00 a.m. to 5:00 p.m. from April 1 to October 31. Closed on Saturday and Sunday from November through March. Guided tours are available for $1.00 per person ($50.00 minimum). An entrance fee of 50 cents is charged from May 20 to September 1. Mainly a perennial nursery carrying a wide range of plants, trees, and shrubs with some unusual houseplants such as spathiphyllum, clivia, *Jasminum polyanthum*, and gloxinias.

Wileywood Nursery, Box 2628, Lynnwood, Washington 98036. (206) 775-9768. Plant list with descriptions. Nursery located at 17414 Bothell Way Southeast, Bothell. Open daily 9:00 a.m. to 4:00 p.m. Visitors welcome. Extensive offering of hanging and bush-type fuchsia varieties. Instructions on potting the rooted cuttings are included. Also available are some rhododendrons, unusual plants, and shrubs.

Wilson Brothers Floral Company, Roachdale, Indiana 46172. (317) 596-3455. Color-illustrated catalog. Greenhouse is on US 231, 5 miles west of Roachdale. Open daily 8:30 a.m. to 5:00 p.m. Visitors welcome. Since 1918 this company has specialized in unusual houseplants, geraniums, African violets, and begonias. Plants for terrariums and hanging baskets are offered also. Catalog includes general culture notes for indoor and outdoor planting of geraniums.

World Gardens, 845 Pacific Avenue, Department R, Willows, California 95988. (916) 934-4701. Catalog. Specializing in unusual seeds and tropical plants, World Gardens offers exotic plants from around the world: carob, blue ginger, black pagoda, bird of paradise, Hawaiian air plant, chain of love, devil's tongue, night jessamine, peacock flower, to name a few.

The evolution of indoor gardening

Man's desire to raise plants in containers, rather than simply leaving them to grow in the wild, can be traced back to the empires of the Sumerians and Egyptians, 3500 years ago. One thousand years later, the Chinese began using plants decoratively. Seneca, Virgil, and Horace, writing 2000 years ago, described the Roman custom of cultivating exotic fruits and plants. Plants housed in stone containers were placed in courtyards and open-air rooms solely for decoration.

During the early Middle Ages, most Westerners took a more austere view of things. Plants were less ornamental and more practical. Most were cultivated in monastery courtyards and used basically for food and healing. After 1291, however, the Crusaders returned from the Near East with such exotic plants as jasmine, carnations, and roses. (By contrast, the Spanish, influenced by the Arabs, had long been fascinated by terrariums and indoor gardens with pools. It was their vision of Paradise on earth.)

It is said that Western Civilization really began with the Renaissance, and this is certainly true of the art of gardening. Explorers consciously began to bring exotic plants back from the far corners of the globe. By the sixteenth and seventeenth centuries, the Germans, French, and English were all planting decorative gardens, and some were using pots of flowers on windowsills much as we do today. By the end of the seventeenth century, Louis XIV had had a glass-windowed building (a forerunner of today's greenhouse) constructed for him at Versailles. It housed and kept alive over 1500 plants and trees. In the eighteenth and nineteenth centuries, over 5000 plants from Australia, the two Americas, Africa, and India were introduced to professional botanists and gardeners, who cared for them and found newer, more thorough methods of classifying them.

Today, an indoor plant, tree, or even garden is considered a necessity by most designers, architects, and homeowners. Dwellings are being built not only to accommodate plants but specifically to make them feel "at home" indoors. The outside and inside are merging as R. Buckminster Fuller would have us believe—and civilization seems to be all the better for it.

When your plants arrive in the mail

Open the package at once and check your order: Have you received all the plants you requested? Were substitutions made without your permission? Are any of the plants seriously damaged? If any of these problems exist, write the supplier promptly. Some will replace plants if you notify them soon enough.

Unwrap the plants carefully. Most plants will be in a pot wrapped in newspaper or corrugated paper. Some will then be wrapped in a plastic sleeve.

Inspect the plants carefully for pests or diseases. State law mandates that plants to be shipped must be inspected at the source, but accidents will happen. If you find evidence of disease or infestation, discard the plant or return it to the supplier for replacement. Even if the plant appears healthy, keep it in isolation for at least a week.

Place the plant on a tray or flat and water it thoroughly if the soil appears very dry. If not, just mist it for the next few days. Place the plant in a warm, humid, shady location. Over a week's time, gradually move it to a brighter light. Exposing it to too much light too soon will probably harm it, since it has been in complete darkness for two to five days during shipping.

Bringing plants into the country

"Know Before You Go" is the title of a Customs Service brochure summarizing the rules regarding the importation of foodstuff and plants into the country. Its title indicates the best policy to follow if you're thinking of bringing plants back from your vacation abroad. Ask before you leave. The USDA has rather stringent requirements concerning the importation of plants, and with good reason. Pests or diseases not naturally present in the country have been introduced, with devastating results, through the seemingly innocent medium of foreign plants. To avoid disappointments, the USDA suggests you follow this procedure:

Write to the U.S. Department of Agriculture
Animal & Plant Health Service
Plant Protection & Quarantine Programs
209 River Street
Hoboken, New Jersey 07030

Request a plant import license number. Tell them where you'll be going, and your probable port of entry.

In two to three weeks you'll receive a questionnaire. Note whether you'll be bringing in seeds or plants, and specify that they are for your own use, and not for sale or commercial distribution. Several weeks after you return the questionnaire, you'll receive (1) a form stamped with your license number; (2) mailing labels with your license number; (3) a summary of USDA regulations on bringing plants or seeds into the country.

You can bring the plants you purchase back with you, or mail them back. If you mail them, they must be sent to one of the USDA plant inspection stations. Whether you mail them or carry them with you, when you're ready to return home you'll have to remove each plant from its container, carefully wash away all traces of soil, and pack the plants in a slightly moist neutral medium, such as vermiculite, perlite, or sterlized peat moss.

The USDA has issued a booklet explaining everything you need to know about bringing plants into the country. "Travelers Tips On Bringing Food, Plant, And Animal Products Into the United States," USDA Program Aid #1083, is available for 30¢ from the Superintendent of Documents Government Printing Office. Your county agent, or local USDA office, may also have copies on hand.

Reprinted from *The Plant Buyer's Handbook*, by Richard E. Nicholls, Running Press, 38 S. 19th St., Philadelphia, Pennsylvania 19103, 1976, paperback, 142 pages, $3.95.

Societies

American Camellia Society, Box 212, Fort Valley, Georgia 31030. The $10.00 annual membership fee entitles members to *The Camellia Journal* and a copy of *The American Camellia Yearbook*. A camellia garden in Fort Valley is open to the public.

American Fuchsia Society, Hall of Flowers, Golden Gate Park, San Francisco, California 94122. Members receive a monthly magazine giving details of fuchsia culture. Dues are $5.00 per year.

American Hibiscus Society, Route 1, Box 491F, Fort Myers, Florida 33905. The society maintains a seed bank; various pamphlets, a quarterly magazine, books, and nomenclature lists are available to members. Dues are $5.00 per year.

Epiphyllum Society of America, Membership Secretary, Box 1395, Monrovia, California 91016. Membership includes a subscription to the bimonthly bulletin which contains information on growing the orchid cacti. Dues are $3.00 per year.

The Houseplant Club, 7 Greenbriar Drive, Savannah, Georgia 31406. The club publishes a bimonthly bulletin and lesson on cultivating a particular houseplant. Members have access to a seed and plant exchange and help with plant problems. Dues are $4.50 per year.

National Fuchsia Society, 260 Bennett Avenue, Long Beach, California 90803. Membership includes a subscription to a monthly magazine on fuchsia cultivation. Dues are $6.00 per year.

Palm Society, 1320 South Venetian Way, Miami, Florida 33139. Through the society, members can learn how to care for palms, and are able to order seeds through a seed bank for a nominal fee. Dues are $12.50 per year.

Care of newly-acquired plants

Even the healthiest of plants may droop and lose some leaves a few days after you get it home. This is known as trauma, or shock, and is due primarily to the plant's attempt to adjust from the moist, warm, bright environment the grower has provided to the dryer, cooler, darker one that exists in most homes. To help a newly-acquired plant through this transitional stage, follow these steps:

1. Buy most of your plants in the spring or the fall, when the weather is mildest. Both extreme heat and extreme cold can injure plants.

2. When you get the plant home, water it thoroughly several times. This flushes away excess fertilizer which could harm the plant when its growth slows in its new home.

3. Put new plants in a warm, airy location that receives bright, diffused light. Keep near a humidifier, if you have one, or mist plants frequently. In cases of severe droop, you can form an emergency greenhouse by encasing a plant in a clear plastic bag for a day.

4. Isolate the new plant from your collection until you are sure it has no diseases or pests that could spread to other plants.

Humidity

Humidity, or moisture in the air, is necessary for your health and for houseplants to thrive. Only a few succulent species will endure very low humidity without suffering. The relative humidity around the most popular foliage and flowering plants should be between 40 and 50 percent. Some tropicals must have even higher humidity to reach optimum beauty, and these are the species most often restricted to greenhouse and terrarium gardening.

What it does

Adequate moisture in the air permits plants to grow normally, without undue stress. You can measure humidity with a small hygrometer, available from garden stores (approximately $10.00). When humidity drops too low, plants must protect their lives by guarding water. They do this by losing leaves, slowing growth, and failing to open flowers. The situation becomes critical when low humidity is accompanied by high temperatures or very strong light. Warm air holds more moisture so relative humidity drops; strong light overheats the cells, causing more water loss through stomata.

Emergency treatments for plants suffering from low humidity include enclosing the whole plant in a clear plastic bag, misting foliage, and making cuttings from the last remaining healthy growths on a plant soon to perish. You can avoid having houseplants suffer from low humidity by providing extra moisture in the air where plants are growing. Airborne evaporated water and soil moisture must be in balance. More water on the soil will not make up for drastically low humidity.

How to do it

Arrange waterproof trays, several inches deep, under the plant pots. Fill the trays with water; then set pots on wire or wooden grids above the water. Plastic grates sold for fluorescent light fixtures are also suitable for suspending containers above water.

An alternative is to fill trays with gravel, perlite, or pebbles, then pour in water to keep the tray filling moist. Water will evaporate up and around the foliage, thus creating a microclimate of humid air. Roots may escape into the tray, but this is not harmful to the plants; it only makes moving them around somewhat difficult.

United we grow

Grow plants in groups. By keeping plants together, the moisture lost naturally through the leaf pores and soil surface will contribute to the well-being of each individual in the group, rather than be immediately lost into the air. Misting foliage with room temperature water in the mornings also helps raise humidity while cleaning the leaves.

In rooms where these methods fail to keep humidity above 40 percent, grow succulents or install a humidifier to furnish a constant supply of evaporated water. Small, portable humidifiers are inexpensive but require con-

How to increase humidity

Peat moss: Place a potted plant in a waterproof container and surround it with moist peat moss. Add water when necessary to replenish lost moisture.

Grouping: Grow plants in groups so the moisture they lose through their leaves and soil benefits the whole group before it is dispersed through the air.

Trays: Fill waterproof trays with pebbles (perlite, gravel, a brick, overturned clay saucer, or plastic grate may also be used). Then pour in water, and refill as it evaporates. Never allow

the water level to reach the bottom of the pot, or plants will become waterlogged and develop root rot.

Misting: Spray plants with a fine mist of warm water to increase humidity and freshen the foliage. Mist frequently, since this method raises humidity only briefly.

stant filling. Larger units may attach to the water line but are often suitable only in large sunrooms, greenhouses and dry basements.

Capture humidity

Humidity can be captured and held around plant groups by hanging clear plastic material over and around the collection. This is easy to do in tiered light gardens and bay windows, or within living areas. Many delightful miniature houseplants do best in terrariums. By letting in light while preserving humidity, the clear-glass or plastic containers provide a perfect home for miniature sinningias, ferns, begonias, and other tropical treasures.

The ultimate in terrariums is the modern plant case with built-in lights, heating, and ventilating controls. These freestanding cabinets with sliding-glass doors are an expensive but attractive way to grow smaller tropicals in rooms with less than ideal light and humidity.

Charles Marden Fitch

Books

The Apartment Gardener, by Florence and Stanley Dworkin, Signet Books, The New American Library, 1301 Ave. of the Americas, New York, New York 10019, 1974, paperback, 400 pages, $1.50. Pages 80 to 86 have helpful hints on how to provide humidity for plants in an apartment.

The Complete Book of Houseplants, by Charles Marden Fitch, Hawthorn Books, 260 Madison Ave., New York, New York 10016, 1972, hardbound, 308 pages, $10.95. This book includes instructions for providing humidity around houseplants. Well illustrated.

The Complete Book of Terrariums, by Charles Marden Fitch, Hawthorn Books, 260 Madison Ave., New York, New York 10016, 1974, hardbound, 150 pages, $8.95. Hundreds of miniature plants including begonias, sinningias, ferns, and other tropical houseplants are described—along with directions for creating humid terrarium landscapes. Color and black-and-white photographs.

HumidiPlant and **HumidiGrow** are two indoor humidifier units that maintain high relative humidity in plant areas. Both models are electrically operated and completely automatic. HumidiPlant dispenses 1 gallon of water mist in 10 hours, and HumidiGrow dispenses 1½ gallons in up to 15 hours. Both shut off automatically and both have 2-year warranties. Available at many gardening supply stores.

For information write:
Kaz
614 West 49th Street
New York, NY 10019

Cordless electric sprayer is a battery-powered, hand-held tank with a 39-inch flexible hose and 20-inch spraying wand. The molded plastic unit is lightweight and perfect for increasing humidity or spraying fertilizer or pesticides.

For catalog and buying information, write:
Disston
601 Grand Street
Pittsburgh, PA 15219

Supplies & equipment

Plastic trays protect windowsills from water marks. They can hold pots up to 4 inches in diameter. The trays, measuring 22 x 3¼ x ¾ inches, come in clear, smoke, or evergreen. Also available is a *Wide Sill-Saver* which measures 22 x 5 3/16 x 1 3/32 inches and an *Extenda-Sill* designed for narrow sills.

For information write:
Opus
437 Boylston Street
Boston, MA 02116

Humidi-care plant trays are made of water-proof plastic. Ridged floor construction eliminates the need for saucers, gravel, or pebbles. The trays come in four convenient sizes; suitable for windowsills, tables, and shelves, and for grouping plants.

For buying and mail-order information, write:
Diffusa-Lite Company
Box 38
Lenni, PA 19052

Hankscraft plant moisturizer holds 1 gallon of water and will vaporize approximately 11 ounces per hour. Produces up to 12 hours of cool vapor with one filling. The air filter lifts out for easy cleaning.

For information write:
Gerber Products Company
445 State Street
Fremont, MI 49412

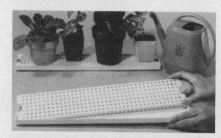

Sani-tray provides humidity for your plants and at the same time acts as a drainer. Fits a windowsill; rubber feet protect furniture. 18 x 3 1/2 x 5/8 inches. White.

For mail-order catalog send 10 cents to:
Dorothy Biddle Service
DBS Building, Dept. TC
Hawthorne, NY 10532

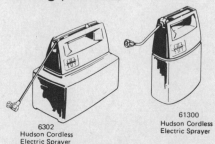

61300
Hudson Cordless
Electric Sprayer

6302
Hudson Cordless
Electric Sprayer

Cordless electric sprayers are useful for misting or pesticide spraying. Compact, lightweight, and easy to use; there is no cord or hose to bother with. Special nozzle adjusts to to any cone spray pattern. Polyethylene housing; permanent battery recharges overnight. Available in three sizes. Sold at garden centers. No mail order.

Free catalog may be obtained by writing:
H.D. Hudson Manufacturing Company
500 North Michigan Avenue
Chicago, IL 60611

Hybrids

Our most outstanding houseplants are often hybrids created for adaptability and floriferousness. A hybrid is formed when two different plants are crossbred to produce offspring which combine characteristics of each parent. The sexual union results in seedlings having actual genes from each parent. With most types of indoor plants, a careful selection is made from the resulting seedlings (each individual will be slightly different) to obtain those clones that best meet the hybridizer's goals.

Once selected, the individual seedlings are increased by asexual propagation (cuttings, divisions, tissue culture) so that the propagations will be identical with the chosen clone. Seedlings from the original cross which do not show desirable characteristics are destroyed. Plant hybridizers make hundreds of crosses and have to grow thousands of seedlings just to find a few that are improvements over existing types.

Making your own

You can make your own hybrids easily. With careful selection of parents, your chances of creating attractive offspring are very good. Of course, parents always love their "children" better than anyone else, so your favorites may not have commercial value, but they will be exciting additions to your personal collection.

Many of my hybrids in various tropical plant genera are better under my conditions than commercially available selections because I have bred them to suit a personal taste and the immediate environment.

Here's how

Start your hybridizing project with indoor plants you already grow well. Suitable are amaryllis, begonias, columneas, sinningias (gloxinias and miniature sinningias), and African violets. Quickest to bloom will be begonias and various gesneriads, all of which show flowers within a year if grown well. Amaryllis require 3 years to bloom.

Your task as a hybridizer is to study the potential parents and choose two individuals that have very desirable characteristics. For example, I recently crossed a dwarf white-flowering sinningia with a taller lavender-striped clone that has dark foliage. Some of the offspring are compact pink-flowered types with striped blooms and bronze-toned foliage.

To cross the parents you must first emasculate the female (pod) parent to prevent self-pollination. Do this before the pollen is ripe, usually just as the bloom opens. Use long-handled scissors or delicate tweezers to take off the anthers.

Now collect pollen from the male parent. The pollen must be ripe before being placed on the female so it may be necessary to collect the anthers a day or so before you want to make the cross. Let the anthers dry on a clean piece of paper. Pick up dry pollen with a damp finger or No. 1 brush. Large anthers can be carried to the female parent with tweezers.

Dust pollen over the stigma of the pod parent. In amaryllis, begonias, gloxinias, and single African violets, the reproductive parts are well exposed. With miniature sinningias and double blooms, you may have to cut away the petals to reach the male and female organs. In begonias, male and female flowers are separate; female flowers have a three-sided ovary, and male flowers have distinct clusters of anthers.

Let the seed mature

Once a cross has been made, the pollen grains send microscopic tubes down through the stigma into the ovary where sperm are released to fertilize the egg of each ovule. If parents are compatible, seed will form. Columnea and gloxinia fruit mature in four to five months, miniature sinningias and amaryllis ripen in four to six weeks. Harvest the seed then, and plant.

Charles Marden Fitch

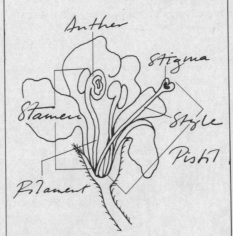

Anatomy of an african violet

A working knowledge of the structure of a flower is necessary before you can hybridize by hand-pollination. The African violet flower is bisexual; that is, it contains both male and female organs.

The male organ is called a stamen and consists of a yellow, saclike anther and filament.

The female organ, the pistil, is longer and more prominent than the stamen. It grows at an angle away from the male organ, perhaps to discourage self-fertilization in nature. The pistil has a sticky, disklike swelling at its tip (stigma) which retains the grains of pollen produced by the anther.

The five green sepals at the base of the flower form a protective covering, first for the developing bud, and then for the seed pod.

African violet hybrids

Here's an example of how easy hybridization can be. Those who work with African violets have one or more of these goals: deeper purer color in new combinations, new flower shapes, smaller plants that flower profusely, and longer-lasting flowers on strong stems.

To begin, choose two varieties of African violets. Designate one a female and one a male plant.

1. Prevent self-pollination of the female plant by removing the anthers with long-handled scissors or tweezers. Do the same with the male plant, but reserve the pollen by letting the anthers dry on a clean piece of paper.

2. Pick up the dry pollen on a damp fingertip, fingernail, or paintbrush. Dust the pollen over the sticky stigma of the female plant.

When the seed pods shrivel and turn brown, (6-9 months), harvest the seed and plant it.

Cultivar name registrars for plants related to indoor gardening

Various organizations, societies, and institutions act as plant registration authorities. These registrars assist the developer of a new plant in properly selecting and publishing a cultivar name. If you are interested in developing a cultivated variety of a plant, either a hybrid or natural variant, contact the registration authorities for details.

Aloe
South African Aloe Breeders Association, A. Koeleman, Chairman, P.O. Box 16393, Pretoria North, South Africa.

Amaryllidaceae (including nerine and excluding narcissus and hemerocallis)
American Plant Life Society, Dr. Hamilton P. Traub, Editor, 5804 Camino de la Costa, La Jolla, California 92037.

Begonia
American Begonia Society, Mr. Rudolf Ziesenhenne, Nomenclature Director, 1130 North Milpas St., Santa Barbara, California 93103.

Bougainvillea
Division of Vegetable Crops and Floriculture, Attn: Dr. B. Choudhury, Head, Indian Agricultural Research Institute, New Delhi 12, India.

Camellia
International Camellia Society, Mr. Charles Puddle, Bodnant Gardens, Tal-Y-Cafn, Colwyn Bay, Denbingshire, North Wales, United Kingdom.

Cyclamen
Laboratorium voor Tuinbouwplantenteelt, Landbouwhogeschool, Postbus 30, Wageningen, The Netherlands.

Fuchsia
American Fuchsia Society, Hall of Flowers, Golden Gate Park, San Francisco, California 94122.

Gerbera
Aukland Carnation and Gerbera Society, Mr. T. R. Cunningham, 38 Gordon Rd., Mt. Albert, Aukland 3, New Zealand.

Gesneria (excluding saintpaulia)
American Gloxinia and Gesneriad Society, Inc., Mr. Paul Arnold, Registrar, 26 Hotchkiss St. S., Binghamton, New York 13903.

Hebe
Nomenclature Committee, Botanic Gardens, Rolleston Ave., Christchurch 1, New Zealand.

Hedera
American Ivy Society, Henri K. E. Schaepman, Registrar, National Center for American Horticulture, Mt. Vernon, Virginia 22121.

Lantana
Arnold Arboretum, Jamaica Plain, Massachusetts 02130.

Leptospermum
Nomenclature Committee, Botanic Gardens, Rolleston Avenue, Christchurch 1, New Zealand.

Lily
Royal Horticultural Society, Vincent Square, London, SW1P 2PE, England.

Orchid
Royal Horticultural Society, Vincent Square, London, SW1P 2PE, England.

Pelargonium
Australian Geranium Society, NSW Div., Mrs. H. Llewellyn, Convenor, Nomenclature Committee, 'Nyndee' Torkina Ave., St. Ives, NSW, Australia.

Rose
American Rose Society, Attn.: Harold S. Goldstein, Registrar, 4048 Roselea Place, Columbus, Ohio 43214.

Saintpaulia
African Violet Society of America, Attn: Mrs. Fred Tretter, Registrar, 4988 Schollmeyer Ave., St. Louis, Missouri 63109.

Tulip
Royal General Bulbgrowers' Society, Mr. H. A. G. de la Mar, Gen. Secretary, Parklaan, Hillegam, The Netherlands.

Information compiled by Freek Vrugtman, Curator of Collections, Royal Botanical Gardens, Box 399, Station A, Hamilton 20, Ontario, Canada.

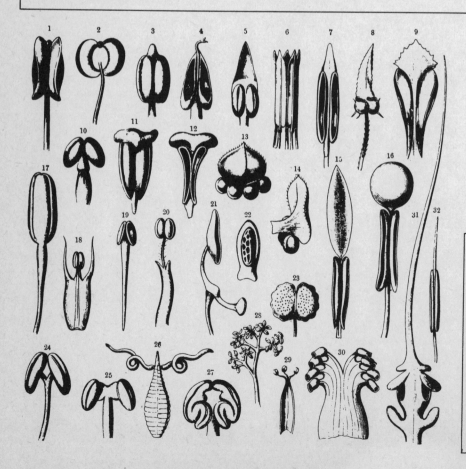

Books

Breeding Plants for Home and Garden, Handbook of the Brooklyn Botanic Gardens, 1000 Washington Ave., Brooklyn, New York 11225, 1974, paperback, 77 pages, $1.75. Illustrated articles include several on breeding indoor plants.

Helen Van Pelt Wilson's African Violet Book, by Helen Van Pelt Wilson, Hawthorn Books, 260 Madison Ave., New York, New York 10016, 1970, paperback, 238 pages, $3.95. Chapter 8, "How to Hybridize," provides detailed instructions for breeding African violets, including illustrations showing precise steps in pollination.

Hydroponics

Hydroponics is a centuries-old but still little-known method of gardening. This highly efficient, intensified growing technique is so effective it is even planned for use by American astronauts in future space shuttle programs.

In hydroponics, an inert soil substitute — like gravel — is used and a balanced nutrient solution is fed to plants daily, allowing them to grow bigger and faster in smaller spaces than they ever could in an ordinary garden.

For example, hydroponically grown tomatoes ripen in 8–10 weeks and produce four to five times as much fruit as similar plants grown in the same amount of space in the soil. Cucumbers ripen in 5 days and bibb lettuce is ready in 40 days, seedling to harvest.

Hydroponic gardening conserves water and fertilizer, which are re-used — over and over. Insect and disease problems are minimized since sterile, nonorganic growing mediums are used in place of soil and plants are usually grown indoors or in a screened greenhouse.

It has been our experience that the convenience and efficiency of hydroponic gardening makes it an ideal way to raise family crops. We have been able to produce all the vegetables and flowers and many of the fruits we want any season of the year. We have found that home gardening doesn't have to require a great amount of time, effort, or space. Even a very small place is big enough for a hydroponic garden!

Reprinted from Discovering Hydroponic Gardening, by Alexandra and John Dickerman, Woodbridge Press Publishing Co., Santa Barbara, California 93111, 1975, paperback, 144 pages, $2.95.

Advantages

'Why bother with chemicals, tanks and such things, when all you have to do is to put seed in the ground, water it and leave the rest to Nature?'

There are several answers to this question:

 (1) no need to fertilise (build up the fertility of the soil);
 (2) no cultivation;
 (3) no crop rotation;
 (4) virtually no weeds;
 (5) a tendency towards uniform results;
 (6) cleanliness;
 (7) larger yields;
 (8) less labour;
 (9) better control;
 (10) ease of starting off new plants;
 (11) a means of upgrading poor plants;

Reprinted from Hydroponics, Growing Plants without Soil, by Dudley Harris, David and Charles Co., North Pomfret, Vermont 05053, 1975, hardbound, 218 pages, $14.95.

Books

Advanced Hydroponics, by James Douglas, Drake Publishers, 801 Second Ave., New York, New York 10017, 1975, hardbound, $8.95.

Beginner's Guide to Hydroponics, by James Douglas, Drake Publishers, 801 Second Ave., New York, New York 10017, 1972, hardbound, $6.95, paperback, $3.95.

Discovering Hydroponic Gardening, by Alexandra and John Dickerman, Woodbridge Press Publishing Co., P.O. Box 6189, Santa Barbara, California 93111, 1975, paperback, 144 pages, $2.95. Multifaceted book on gardening without soil. This book delves into the different methods of hydroponics and explains what plants to grow, where to grow them and how to keep them healthy. Also included are sections on indoor growing of fresh vegetables, mushrooms, and flowers hydroponically. Drawings and photographs.

Gardens Without Soil — House Plants, Vegetables and Flowers, by Jack Kramer, Charles Scribner's Sons, 597 Fifth Ave., New York, New York 10017, 1976, 128 pages, $8.95. This book defines hydroponics and assists the beginner in choosing the proper method. Also includes information about light, temperature, and air circulation. Tips on insect and disease control with specific instructions on growing houseplants, vegetables, and flowers.

Home Hydroponics: How To Do It, by Lem Jones, Beardsley Publishing Co., 5523 N. Homestead Lane, Paradise Valley, Arizona

85253, 1975, hardbound, $10.00, paperback, $5.95. Includes step-by-step instructions with numerous drawings and photographs; plus detailed greenhouse building plans and a list of suppliers.

Hydroponic Gardening: The Magic of Hydroponics for the Home Gardener, by Raymond Bridwell, Woodbridge Press Publishing Co., P.O. Box 6189, Santa Barbara, California 93111, 1972, hardbound, $6.95, paperback, $3.95.

Hydroponics: Growing Without Soil, by Dudley Harris, David and Charles Co., P.O. Box 57, North Pomfret, Vermont 05053, 1975, hardbound, 218 pages, $14.95. Simple to complex units are described with illustrated steps. In-depth technical information, plus tables and diagrams for large-scale hydroponic growing.

The Indoor Water Gardeners How-to Handbook, by Peter Loewer, Popular Library Books, 600 Third Ave., New York, New York 10019, 1973, paperback, $1.25; Walker and Co., 720 Fifth Ave., New York, New York 10019, 1973, hardbound, $5.95. For those who wish to raise plants without the bother of obtaining the proper soil or worrying about light and temperature conditions. This book explores and details the keys to indoor water gardening, with sections on starting your water garden. Includes what types of plants to grow and how to grow them. With illustrations.

Hydroponic watering systems

Plants grown hydroponically must be supplied with a nutrient solution. This solution can be supplied to trays growing large quantities of plants, such as vegetables and flowers, in several ways.

Manual watering

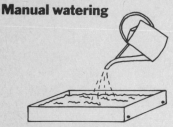

Method I

Sprinkle the nutrient solution with a watering can. Let the excess run out through drainage holes, and collect it in a bucket for reuse.

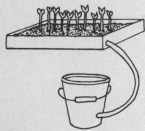

Method II

Connect a bucket to the tray with plastic tubing. Fill the bucket with nutrient solution and the tray with planting medium and the plants. Every day, raise the bucket above the tray, supporting it on a shelf or chair. When all the solution has run into the tray, lower the bucket below the tray, allowing the solution to return to the bucket for reuse.

Automatic pump system

Put the nutrient solution into an airtight container. Use a simple aquarium pump to force the solution into the planting medium. Turn the pump off to allow the solution to return to the airtight container. To make the system fully automatic, incorporate an electric timer and set it to turn on the pump for about two hours every day.

Wick watering

Put the nutrient solution in the bottom tray and the planting medium and the plants in the top tray. Place wicks made of synthetic fabric in the solution and pass the ends through holes drilled in the top tray, embedding them in the planting medium. The solution will constantly be drawn up into the tray.

Simple hydroponics

In this system the planting medium, which may be pebbles, gravel, pearl chips, or coarse sand, serves to give the plant physical support only. Nourishment is supplied

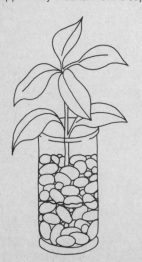

by a water-soluble fertilizer, dissolved one-quarter strength in water.

Start with a waterproof glass, plastic, or ceramic container. Do not use metal, which will be corroded by the fertilizer. Most people find transparent containers, such as glass cannisters, apothecary jars, tall drinking glasses, and photograph display cubes, the prettiest.

Wash the container and the planting medium with soap and water.

Place a handful of the medium in the container. Add a few tablespoons of charcoal to keep the water pure.

Use plants that have been grown in pots, or cuttings that you have rooted in water. Wash off any potting soil clinging to the roots, and trim off any rotted or damaged roots. Place the plants in the gravel; add more gravel up to the original soil line.

Mix the fertilizer solution separately. Then pour it into the container until half the planting medium is immersed. Replenish the water as necessary. About once a month pour out the old solution and replace it completely.

Supplies & equipment

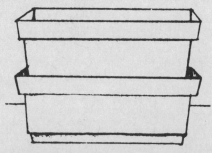

Hydroponic gardening equipment is available in complete one- or two-tray systems. The components of each system—trays, nutrient tank, and hardware—are also offered separately.

For information write:
Tiffany Industries
Greenhouse Products Division
145 Weldon Parkway
Maryland Heights, MO 63043

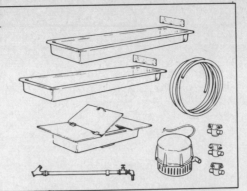

Gardening Without A Garden, a hydroponics instruction book by Dr. E. Saub, includes drawings and illustrations for the do-it-yourself enthusiast, with a special section on the "wick system method."

To obtain the book send $3.00 to:
Dr. Saub
555 North Colgate Street
Anaheim, CA 92801.

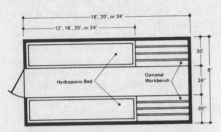

Hydroponic supplies, equipment, and books as well as a completely hydroponic greenhouse, are offered by Water Works.

For brochures and mail-order information, write:
Water Works Gardenhouses
Box 905
El Cerrito, CA 94530

Hydroponic garden tubs for home use, either indoors or out, are available in kit form from Pacific AquaCulture. The unit, in various sizes, includes a ready-to-assemble redwood box, vinyl liner, pump, and timer. Also available are nutrient mix, pH test kit, jiffy starter kit, literature, and instructions.

For brochure, literature, and information write:
Pacific AquaCulture
3A Gate 5 Road
Sausalito, CA 94965.

A manually-operated beginner's hydroponic kit includes a six-month supply of nutrients, growing tray, growing medium, feeding line, fittings, and instructions.

For information write:
Texas Greenhouse Company
2717 St. Louis Avenue
Fort Worth, TX 76110

Indoor garden, a hydroponic kit for growing vegetables, herbs, and flowers, includes a metal rack, two steel growth trays in baked green enamel, two cool-white fluorescent lamps with 48-inch fixture. Overall dimensions: 58 x 48 x 24 inches. Use with a soilless mixture and plant food. Attractive deluxe kit includes 3-shelf, walnut-finish particleboard plant display stand.

For information and brochure write:
Home Grow Products
Tube Craft
1311 West 80th Street
Cleveland, OH 44101.

Three hydroponic growing kits, containing everything you need for hydroponic gardening, are available from Environmental Dynamics. All include growing medium, nutrient mix, tomato and flower seeds, pH tester, and instructions. The Hydroponic Starter Kit, geared toward beginners, includes a wick-watering planter. The Gravity Hydroponic System is a manually-operated nutrient recycling system. The Hydroponic Growing System is a complete 12-lesson course with step-by-step illustrations, growing experiments, a performance log, charcoal, and planters. The pH water-tester kit and hydroponic nutrient kit are available separately. A large selection of books on hydroponic gardening is also offered.

For information write:
Environmental Dynamics
Box 996
Sunnymead, CA 92388

Insect pests

Where do they come from, those little buggers that chew and suck the life out of houseplants? You won't like the answer. It's you, the well-intentioned gardener, who usually brings them home on newcomers from the plant shop or the garden, on your hands and tools, and in unsterilized potting materials. It's not all your fault, though. They may arrive as eggs so small that you'd need a microscope to see them.

Minor infestations of most critters respond to handpicking with a cotton swab soaked in isopropyl alcohol or hydrogen peroxide. Another old stand-by for thwarting foliage pests is dipping or spraying with a solution of two teaspoons mild detergent in one gallon of warm water. This will not kill the bugs, only loosen them so that they can be washed away. Therefore, it is important to cover the soil with plastic to prevent bugs from washing down into it. After thoroughly saturating the foliage, let it dry. Then rinse the plant with clear, warm water.

Either of these methods must be followed by another application every two or three days. If you don't seem to be getting anywhere after a week or ten days, you'll be faced with a decision: throw the plant out or turn to insecticides.

Contact insecticides destroy pests with piercing-sucking mouthparts. Stomach insecticides are used to control insects with chewing mouthparts. Insecticides used as contact poisons will also work as stomach poisons.

Insecticides may be used in a variety of ways. They may be dissolved in water and used as a spray, dip, or soil drench. When spraying and dipping, ½ teaspoon of mild detergent added per gallon of solution will improve wetting power and cut down residue.

Systemic insecticides are applied to the soil or foliage and absorbed by plant tissues and circulated in the plant juices, poisoning the pest's food supply. Another way to control pests is with fumigants. To do this, enclose the plant in a plastic bag with a no-pest strip for several days.

Some of the names you might see when buying pesticides are pyrethrum, rotenone, nicotine sulfate, carbaryl, diazinon, malathion, and dimethoate. Pyrethrum and rotenone are made from plant derivatives and are the least dangerous of insecticides to use around the home. Nicotine sulfate is another relatively safe insecticide. The trade name of carbaryl is Sevin; it is used for chewing insects. Diazinon controls many soil and foliage pests. Malathion is useful for a broad range of pests. Dimethoate is used under various trade names as a systemic.

For stubborn infestations, chemical treatments may have to be repeated every few days. No matter which insecticide treatment you choose, always read the label thoroughly. Make sure that it will kill the bug you have identified without killing the plant that has it. Follow instructions to the letter and heed all warnings.

Isolation and proper plant hygiene are the keys to pest-free indoor gardening. But infested plants should be put in quarantine immediately—so should new plants or plants you bring in from the garden. Sanitation is important, too. Keep foliage clean, pick off dead or dying plant parts, and remove dead material when it falls into the pot. Use only sterilized potting medium and hygienically clean containers.

Gayle Fankhauser

Books

First Aid for House Plants, by Shirley Ross, McGraw-Hill Book Co., 1221 Avenue of the Americas, New York, New York 10020, 1976, paperback, 216 pages, $5.95. Pest diagnosis and treatment chart is unusually thorough, and stands alone without much further explanation. What's especially good about this book is its plant-by-plant discussion of the most common pests and ailments.

The Gardener's Bug Book, by Cynthia Wescott, Doubleday and Co., 245 Park Ave., New York, New York 10017, 1946, hardbound, 689 pages, $12.95. The definitive handbook of plant pests and their control. The depth of treatment in this text will overwhelm many houseplant people, but for those who have large, valuable plant collections in home, garden, or greenhouse, Wescott's book is a must.

Houseplant Rx, by George and Katy Abraham, A. B. Morse Co., Countryside Books, Barrington, Illinois 60010, 1976, paperback, 48 pages, $1.50. Lists and describes 21 common insect pests, how they do their damage and how to eradicate them. Includes discussions of chemical controls, but emphasizes non-chemical ones. Extensive diagnostic chart for plant ailments and color photos of afflicted plants.

The Indoor Gardener's First Aid Book, by Jack Kramer, Simon and Schuster, 630 Fifth Ave., New York, New York 10020, 1975, hardbound, 128 pages, $6.95. Some pest discussions and illustrations could be more informative, but otherwise a helpful book. One section is devoted to ailments and pests usually found on specific plants. Charts and lists provide quick reference.

The Plant Doctor, by Richard Nicholls, Running Press, 38 S. 19th St., Philadelphia, Pennsylvania 19103, 1975, paperback, 108 pages, $3.95. A comprehensive book on doctoring plants. Chapters on good routine care are brief but get quickly to the point. Diagnostic chart is cross-referenced to full explanations in text. Discusses most common pests and explains how to choose and use insecticides.

Rx For Ailing House Plants, by Charles M. Evans and Roberta Lee Pliner, Random House, 201 E. 50th St., New York, New York 10022, 1974, paperback, 106 pages, $3.95. Discusses cultural and parasitic diseases as well as insect pests. Includes diagnostic charts and helpful explanations of chemical and non-chemical controls and pest prevention.

Aphid   Mealybug   Scale   Spider mite   Thrip   Whitefly

Insect control chart

Description	Detection	Treatment
Aphids These pear-shaped sucking insects, often called plant lice, are 1/16 to 1/8 inch long and may be almost any color. Adults may have wings or waxy-looking fuzz. Clear, sticky honeydew is secreted, which attracts ants, black sooty molds. Some species live in soil and attack roots. Often provoked by damp conditions.	Look for aphids on undersides of leaves, especially at tender growth tips. May have to knock out plant to examine soil for root-feeding aphids. Plant distress signals: waning plant vigor, stunted growth, puckering leaves, deformed buds.	Handpick small infestations. Soap and water technique also recommended, especially for removal of honeydew and molds. More serious infestations may be treated with contact, systemic, or fumigant type insecticides. Drench soil with contact poison if root aphids are suspected.
Mealybugs Sucking insect with soft, oval body, white, waxy-looking fuzz. Usually quite visible, up to 3/16 inch long. May feed on foliage or roots. Clear, sticky honeydew secreted, which attracts ants and black sooty molds.	Look for mealybugs and sacks of eggs at leaf and stem axils, on undersides of leaves, especially along veins. Suspect underground mealybugs if you notice stunted growth, sudden wilting between waterings, defoliation.	Above ground, handpick with alcohol and then, if infestation is heavy, treat with contact, systemic, or fumigant. Drench soil with contact or systemic poison if root-feeding mealybugs are present.
Scales Small, sucking insects that develop hard, shell-like covering and remain stationary. Shape may be oval, hemispherical, or like an oyster shell. They vary in size from 1/16 to 1/4 inch long. Colors range from white to brown, grey, and black. A honeydew substance is secreted, attracting sooty molds and ants. Soft scales do not develop a shell and retain their larval legs and, hence, are mobile.	Look for scales on stems, branches, and the midribs and veins of leaves. Plant distress signals: yellow spots on leaves, yellowed leaves dropping off, stunted growth, wilt. The shells have a waxy texture and are easily scraped off with a fingernail.	Handpick or wash with soap and water for small infestations. Use malathion as a dip or spray for more severe attacks, spraying every 3 to 4 weeks. Don't confuse fern spores with scale. Spores are found on leaflets and scale is usually on the midrib of the frond. Never spray ferns with malathion; use nicotine sulfate instead.
Spider mites Tiny oval bugs (really spiders) may be almost any color but usually reddish brown, green, or yellow. Since they average 1/50 inch long you may need a magnifying glass to see them. Mites pierce plant tissue and suck juices. Will proliferate in hot, dry environments.	Look for fine mealy-textured webs on undersides of leaves or laced between plant parts. If you see specks and can't tell if they are mites, tap suspicious plant parts over piece of white paper. If specks fall and scamper across paper, they are mites. Plant distress signals: mottled-looking leaves with bronze or gray cast; new growth is dwarfed, deformed, turns brown and dry.	Handpicking or soap and water might work, but bugs and eggs are so small that chances are you'd never get all of them. Broad-spectrum contact and systemic poison will have some effect on mite populations. However, special contact formulas called miticides are the best choice. Some brand names include Dimite, Kelthane, Tedion.
Thrips Minute winged insects, about as wide as a fine needle. Those that fly or jump when plant is touched are adults and can be tan, brown, black. Less-active young may be white, yellow, orange. Thrips do their damage by scraping and sucking on foliage.	Look for the insects themselves and also for tiny black blobs of excrement they leave as they feed. Plant distress signals: silvery streaks, papery scars on foliage; tips of new leaves curl under; flower buds drop or are deformed when they open.	Mild cases can be treated with sprays or dips in soap and water. Use contact, systemic, or fumigant for more severe infestations. When using systemics, spray with soap and water first to force off flying adults before they attack other plants.
Whiteflies Most obvious whiteflies are the white, mothlike adults, about 1/16 inch long. Yellow, crawling larvae and tan scales fringed with white, waxy filaments are visible immature stages of this pest. All stages suck plant sap; scale stage secretes clear, sticky honeydew.	Usually hide on undersides of leaves. Adults flutter away like a cloud of snowflakes when the plant is disturbed. Sooty mold may develop on honeydew secreted by scale forms. Plant distress signals: leaves turn pale, thin, develop stippled look.	Soap and water may thin out the population but will have little effect on scales that will soon become adults. Sprays and dips containing malathion, a contact poison, or dimethoate, a systemic poison, will offer more positive control. Fumigants are also recommended because they contain these mobile pests. Soil-applied systemics are effective but must be used with a soapy water or clear water spray to remove the adults before they fly to new headquarters in your plant collection.

Supplies & equipment

Black leaf 40, a nicotine-sulphate solution, is a biodegradable insecticide effective on aphids, spider mites, thrips, and similar sucking insects. It is non-caustic and does not injure foliage or leave unsightly residue. The company also carries a wide range of other insecticides, fungicides, fertilizers, potting soils, and other gardening aids.

For mail-order information write:
**Black Leaf Products Company
667 North State Street
Elgin, IL 60120**

Science Products Company manufactures a wide range of pesticides, including a houseplant spray and a red spider spray. Their products are nationally distributed and are available at most garden-supply centers. No mail order.

Red arrow insect spray contains pyrethum and rotenone. For the indoor gardener, it is useful in combatting mealybug and whitefly. Available east of the Mississippi only in garden centers and florist shops. No mail order

For buying information write:
**B.G. Pratt Division
Gabriel Chemicals, Ltd.
204 21st Avenue
Paterson, NJ 07509**

Insecticides in minicontainers designed for the indoor plant grower are available from Bonide Specific and general purpose formulations are available for spraying and soil treatment. They are sold in the East and Midwest in garden centers and hardware stores.

For buying information write:
**Bonide Chemical Company
2 Wurz Avenue (off Commercial Drive)
Yorkville, NY 13495**

Ladybugs control harmful aphids and other insects. Quantities available range from 1 pint up to 1 gallon.

For mail-order information write:
**Fountain Sierra Bug Company
Box 114
Rough and Ready, CA 95975**

Beneficial insects for pest control can be obtained from Bio-Control Company, which will ship ladybugs and Chinese praying mantises. Included are instructions on when to use and how to store the insects. For house gardens, small quantities are available: ladybugs packed in ½-pint containers, Chinese praying mantis eggs in cases of 200.

For literature and mail-order information, write:
**Bio-Control Company
10180 Ladybird Drive
Auburn, CA 95603**

Mite-e-funge controls mites and fungus on a wide variety of plants. Squeeze duster applicator eliminates leaf burn and allows easy application. Does not harm beneficial insects. Contains 98 percent sulfur.

Botanic controls a broad spectrum of plant pests, including aphids, thrips, and whiteflies. May be used as a dust or diluted with water as a spray. Contains pyrethrins, rotenone, and ryania.

Also offered are ladybug eggs and praying mantis eggs, which can be hatched in the garden or greenhouse to ward off insects organically.

For brochures and mail-order information, write:
**Organic Control
Box 25382
Los Angeles, CA 90025**

Indoor plant insect spray controls certain insects on African violets and many other houseplants. Contains pyrethrins and rotenone. Available nationally in retail outlets that handle indoor-plant products.

For additional information write:
**Chevron Chemical Company
Box 3744
San Francisco, CA 94119**

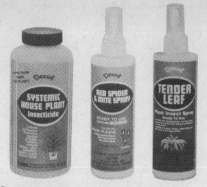

Systematic insecticide kills insects from inside the plant. Sprinkled in the soil, it is absorbed by the root system. Sucking insects are killed for up to six weeks. Will not harm tender foliage. No lingering odor.

Red spider and mite spray contains Kelthane and comes in a non-aerosol, pump container. It can be used directly on hardy plants and also sprayed on windowsills and doors to keep out insect pests.

Tender leaf plant insect spray, for use on delicate plants, is an emulsion containing nicotine and light petroleum hydrocarbon. It comes in a non-aerosol, pump container. Kills a wide range of insect pests.

Dexol products are sold through distributors, but Dexol welcomes requests for catalogs and buying information. Write:
**Dexol Industries
1450 West 228th Street
Torrance, CA 90501**

Houseplant insecticide is a highly perfected formula of pyrethrum, rotenone, and malathion. Highly effective for all-around plant protection indoors. Available nationwide in nurseries, garden centers, and retail stores.

For mail-order information write:
**Plantabbs Corporation
Timonium, MD 21093**

All-purpose i-bomb aerosol insect spray controls many plant pests and is safe for plants.

African violet aerosol insect spray is specially formulated for use on African violets as well as other plants. It will not leave stains or harm blooms.

For free brochures and mail-order information, write:
**Plant Marvel Laboratories
624 West 119th Street
Chicago, IL 60628**

Joy of gardening

How important is it to our emotional well-being to have daily contact with nature? To experience the peace and solitude of a garden, or feel the relaxation of a walk through the park? These intangibles cannot be analyzed by a computer, but if, as has been said, the maturity of a community can be measured by the quality of its gardens, our growing concern for plants and nature is a very healthy sign.

If you live in an urban environment, as I do, your alienation from the earth is real, and it really increases the higher up you live in an apartment house. We might even say that the need for living plants increases with the magnitude of the floor number, and this applies to offices as well.

Along with the trend to high-rise living I see a swing to the natural: in foods, furniture, fashion, even in behavior. We want to be more honest with ourselves so that we can deal more realistically with life. Drugs and alcohol may be used as brief escapes from reality, but no one should want to depend on them. Traditional psychotherapy is sought by some, others seek the answer in transcendental meditation and other forms of consciousness raising.

To whatever discipline the word "therapy" is applied, we tend to think or hope, that it will work magic in our lives. I maintain that there are no instant cures to life's ups and downs, but rather "supportive holds" that help us put daily difficulties and annoyances into a proper perspective. An involvement with plants can be such a supportive hold.

If you live and work with plants around you, there is always something that needs to be done for them and that will simultaneously help you get through everyday anxieties. As you wait for an important telephone call or recover from a difficult personal or professional confrontation, picking off dead leaves and flowers, watering a plant, or cleaning its leaves with a damp tissue can reduce anxiety far better than chain smoking, a stiff drink, or a tranquilizer.

The more I recognize the symptoms of stress in my life, the more I realize that plants suffer stresses too. Concerning myself with relieving theirs helps me to forget, and thus relax, the tightness in my own body as I nurture my plants.

Putting this into practice in one's own life doesn't require a whole roomful of plants. It takes only a few to give a range of plant stresses sufficient to relieve your own. Even a single plant may suffer a whole range of stresses in a relatively short time; the need for more or less water, more or less fertilizer, more or less light, a smaller or larger pot, a different growing medium, protection from hot and dry or cold drafts of air, and for protection from insect invasions. The greater your attention to these needs, the greater will be your sense of gratification when your plants thrive.

The more involved you become with your plants, the more you will identify with them. They have cyclical needs just as we do. When the leaves of a prayer plant or axalis fold up at night, the plant is resting. After a period of leaf growth and flowering, bulbs like amaryllis and gloxinia go into dormancy for weeks or months. If plants take a rest every night, and require an annual vacation, it seems obvious to me that I need a similar regimen if I am to be healthy and productive.

Stress, anxiety, tension: they are all a part of living and have always been. It's just that today we are living faster and longer, and we are trying to accomplish more in business as well as personal relationships. Although the obvious answer to your problems and mine may be to take a vacation, to work less, or to live in a less urbanized society, none of these options may be ours. Plants are a natural alternative available to all.

They can help us get through a tough day, a lonely night, or a long period of anxiety. When you're on top of the world, having plants can make life even sweeter, and when you come down, they'll be a support to you.

Plant therapy requires no prescription. It can be refilled as often as you feel the need. Addiction to gardening, indoors or outdoors, one plant or a thousand, is a desirable state.

Excerpted and reprinted by permission from *Plants As Therapy* by Elvin McDonald, Praeger Publishers, 200 Park Ave., New York, New York 10017, 1976, 194 pages, hardback, $7.95.

Horticultural therapy

The concept of people benefiting from being around and working with plants is being used in various institutional situations around the country. Mental health clinics, retirement homes, prisons, and rehabilitation centers have all found that a gardening program is of great value to the patients and students.

As an increasing number of people became interested in using horticulture as a therapeutic and rehabilitative tool, a national organization was formed, The National Council for Therapy and Rehabilitation through Horticulture. The Council coordinates professional, educational, therapeutic, and rehabilitation programs and organizations throughout the country. Services provided include a newsletter, a resource library, meetings, seminars, a manpower exchange bank, job placement service, and consultation services.

If you're interested in finding out what horticultural therapy programs are available in your area or in learning about the educational programs and training available to those interested in becoming horticultural therapists, contact: National Council for Therapy and Rehabilitation through Horticulture, Mount Vernon, Virginia 22121.

Libraries

In its own quiet way, this just might be the most important and valuable section in this book. For in it lies a storehouse of knowledge, perhaps an entire education—and it's yours for the asking. All of the horticultural libraries listed here are open to the public for reading, study, and research. Some specialize in a specific area such as woodland plants. But most contain more information, on an endless variety of subjects, than any one book possibly could (even this one). Libraries not only contain books, but also pamphlets, photographs, maps, catalogs, periodicals, and beautiful examples of botanical art and illustration. They are also one of the nicest places to meet and exchange ideas with interesting people who, just like you, are involved with plants.

California
**California State
Polytechnic University at Pomona**
3801 West Temple Avenue
Pomona, California 91768
Open to the public; primarily reference, but some book lending; specializing in areas of agriculture, ornamental horticulture, and landscape design.

**County of Los Angeles
Department of
Arboreta and Botanic Gardens**
301 North Baldwin Avenue
Arcadia, California 91006
Open to the public for reference only; specializing in woody plants of Southern Africa and non-woody exotics as well as house and garden plants.

Colorado
Helen Fowler Library
Denver Botanic Gardens
909 York Street
Denver, Colorado 80206
Open to the public 9 to 5 Mon. thru Sat., 12 to 5 Sun. Circulation limited to members of the Gardens; participates in interlibrary loan. Botanical and horticultural books; particular strength in orchids, houseplants, landscape architecture and design, vegetable gardening, and plant ecology. Also 180 periodicals and many state and federal pamphlets.

Illinois
Chicago Horticultural Society Botanical Garden Library
P.O. Box 400
Glencoe, Illinois 60022
Open to the general public for lending and reference; areas of specialization include general horticulture, gardening, and landscape architecture.

Sterling Morton Library
The Morton Arboretum
Lisle, Illinois 60532
Open to the general public for reference and borrowing; collection concerned with all aspects of temperate-zone woody plants and with botany and horticulture generally.

Kentucky
Agricultural Library
University of Kentucky
Lexington, Kentucky 40506
Open to the public 8 to 11 Mon. thru Thurs., 8 to 5 Fri., 2 to 5 Sat., 2 to 10 Sun. Participates in interlibrary loan; books cover all phases of plants; section on floriculture also maintained.

Massachusetts
Morrill Biological Sciences Library
University of Massachusetts/Amherst
Amherst, Massachusetts 01002
Open to the public; lending privileges extended when university borrower's card is obtained; areas of specialization include ecology and botany.

Massachusetts Horticultural Society Library
300 Massachusetts Avenue
Boston, Massachusetts 02115
Open to the public 9 to 4:30 weekdays; borrowing books limited to Society members; collection strong in all horticultural and related fields; contains one of the world's largest collections of nursery catalogs.

Worcester County Horticultural Society Library
30 Elm Street
Worcester, Massachusetts 06108
Open to the public Mon. thru Fri. 9 to 4. Very little circulation of materials takes place; wide range of periodicals, pamphlets, books—old and new—in all areas of horticulture; also houses the country's largest pomology collection.

Minnesota
Andersen Horticultural Library
University of Minnesota
Landscape Arboretum
3675 Arboretum Drive
Chaska, Minnesota 55318
Open to the general public; no circulation of materials; it is a reference reading library that specializes in horticulture, landscape architecture, and natural history.

Missouri
Missouri Botanical Garden Library
2345 Tower Grove Avenue
St. Louis, Missouri 63110
Founded in 1859, this is the nation's oldest independent botanical library; a collection of some 300,000 items is maintained, including bound books and periodicals, manuscript items, photographs, maps, botanical art and illustration, and unbound pamphlets. Primarily for research; anyone with a serious interest in botany and horticulture may use the library, preferably by writing or calling in advance. Open 9 to 5 Mon. thru Fri.

New Hampshire
Biological Sciences Library
Kendall Hall
University of New Hampshire
Durham, New Hampshire 03824
Open to the general public; New Hampshire residents have borrowing privileges; may participate in interlibrary loan. Contains substantial collection of horticultural material.

New York
Herbarium Library
County of Monroe Department of Parks
375 Westfall Road
Rochester, New York 14620
Open to the public; does not have lending privileges. Strictly reference dealing with botany and horticulture.

New York Botanical Gardens Library
Bronx, New York 10458
Open to the public as a research and reference center, circulation to members of the Garden. Open Mon. thru Sat. 11 to 4 from Sept. thru June and from 11 to 4 Mon. thru Fri. for July and August.

Ohio
Kingwood Center Library
900 Park Avenue West
Mansfield, Ohio 44906
Nonprofit educational institution operated as a public library; open 8 to 5 Tues. thru Sat. Specializing in horticultural information.

Ohio Agricultural Research and Development Center Library
U.S. 250 and Ohio 83 South
Wooster, Ohio 44691
Open to the public; borrowing privileges extended exclusively to staff and graduate students of the Center. Specializing in sciences related to agriculture.

Eleanor Squire Library
The Garden Center of Greater Cleveland
11030 East Boulevard
Cleveland, Ohio 44106
Open to the public; circulation is limited to members of the Center; strong subject areas include flower arranging and general gardening; a 50,000 card index of illustrations of flowering plants is also maintained.

Oregon

Kerr Library
Oregon State University
Corvallis, Oregon 97331
Open to the general public, with circulation to the faculty, students, and staff of the university as well as residents of the area; specializes in most areas of horticulture.

Pennsylvania

Hunt Botanical Library
Carnegie-Mellon University
Pittsburgh, Pennsylvania 15213
Open to the public 9 to 5 Mon. thru Fri. It's not a circulating library but participates in resource sharing activities in the Pittsburgh area; major strength in works published between 1550 and 1850, particularly those on systematic botany, herbs, early agriculture and gardening; a collection of botanical art is maintained.

Morris Arboretum Library
9414 Meadowbrook Avenue
Philadelphia, Pennsylvania 19118
Open to the public, but is not a lending library; botany and horticulture are thoroughly represented with an emphasis on plant geography; a collection of teacher's resource materials has also been started.

The Pennsylvania Horticultural Society Library
325 Walnut Street
Philadelphia, Pennsylvania 19106
Open to the public 9 to 5 Mon. thru Fri.; borrowing privileges limited to members of the Society. Particular specialization in ornamental horticulture; also an extensive collection of nineteenth-century landscape and gardening books and journals.

Temple University Library
Ambler Campus
Ambler, Pennsylvania 19002
Open to the general public, circulation limited to the faculty, students, and staff of the university; participates in interlibrary loan service; collections in landscape design and horticulture; horticulture pamphlets and recent seed and nursery catalogs also maintained.

Tennessee

Cheekwood Library
The Tennessee Botanical Gardens and Fine Arts Center
Cheekwood
Nashville, Tennessee 37205
Open to the public Tues. thru Sat. 9 to 5, Sun. 1 to 5; lending privileges open to members of the Gardens; participates in interlibrary loan policy. Extensive collection covering all aspects of horticulture.

Virginia

H.B. Tukey Memorial Library
The American Horticultural Society
Mount Vernon, Virginia 22121
Not open to the public; maintained for use by the members of the Society, some lending privileges extended to local residents; popular literature and horticulture texts are available for reference.

Washington

University of Washington Arboretum Library
Seattle, Washington 98195
A branch of the University of Washington library system, open to the public 8 to 5 Mon. thru Fri.; it is not a circulating library; books available on areas of horticulture and floriculture, pests and diseases.

Washington, D.C.

National Arboretum Library
U.S. National Arboretum
24th & R Streets, N.E.
Washington, D.C. 20002
Open to the public 8 to 4:30 Mon. thru Thurs.; material may be used on site, no loans; extensive collection of horticultural and botanical books and periodicals, with emphasis on woody plants.

Smithsonian Institution Libraries
Washington, D.C. 20060
Open to the public, but appointment preferred; lending privileges extended only to staff; participates in interlibrary loan; strong areas are: taxonomic botany, plant anatomy, and morphology. Some popular and horticultural material maintained.

Ontario, Canada

The Civic Gardens Centre Library
Edwards Gardens
777 Lawrence Avenue East
Ontario, Canada
Open to the general public 9:30 to 4 Mon., Tues., Thurs., and Fri., 9:30 to 9 Wed., 10 to 4 Sat.; borrowing privileges restricted to members of the Centre; collection is devoted to all aspects of horticulture; two shops are also maintained, one specializing in horticultural books, the other carrying materials for flower arranging and drying.

Royal Botanical Gardens Library
Box 399
Hamilton, Ontario, Canada
Open to the public weekdays 9 to 5; lending privileges extended to staff members of the Gardens only; collections emphasize botany, ornamental horticulture and floriculture, flower arranging and landscape architecture.

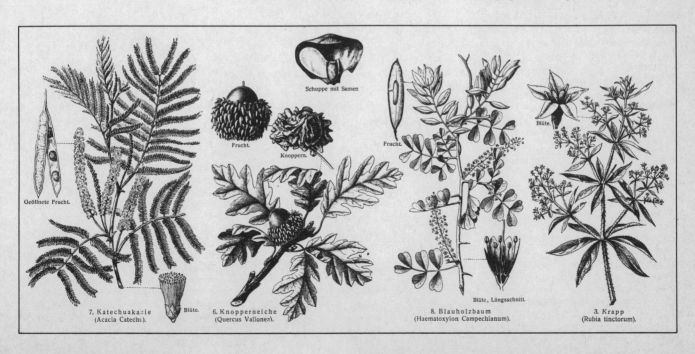

Geöffnete Frucht.

Schuppe mit Samen

Frucht.

Knoppern.

Frucht.

Blüte.

Blüte, Längsschnitt.

Blüte.

7. Katechuakazie (Acacia Catechu).   6. Knopperneiche (Quercus Vallonea).   8. Blauholzbaum (Haematoxylon Campechianum).   3. Krapp (Rubia tinctorum).

Light

Your houseplants must have light to live. While some plants can exist on very little light, most need a fair amount, and some won't survive, much less thrive, without quite bright light. It's important to understand the light needs of a plant you want to grow or else your investment of money, time, and love may be lost.

In general, plain green foliage plants require less light than varicolored-leaf and flowering plants, but there are many exceptions. Ask when you buy a plant, or consult houseplant reference books to find out the light needs of a particular variety. While to most plants only the general degree of brightness is important, in some cases the directness or diffused nature of the light is also a necessary consideration. To a relatively few plants, the day length is a crucial factor.

Observe the places where you might put the plant to see what light is available throughout the day. Are the spots in intense sun much of the day, or do they have sun only in the morning, or no direct sun at all? Match as closely as possible the light needs of the plants to the brightnesses of the available locations.

After placing a plant in your chosen spot, keep a close watch on it for several weeks. If there is too little light (perhaps the most frequent situation), you will see symptoms such as tall, weak-looking new growth, all the leaves turned in one direction toward the brightest light, general paleness, leaf drop, and cessation of flowering. The more extreme the symptoms, the greater the need for more light. Don't wait very long to move the plant to a brighter location or provide supplementary light.

On the other hand, if the problem is too much or overly intense sunlight, you'll see leaves curling up or becoming bleached, or becoming sunburned with brownish, burned-looking spots. Move the plant at once or shade it, if you can see that it's getting burned, before the damage is too great.

If the plant stays healthy but does not grow or flower much over a period of months, or leaves lose their variegation but the plant remains healthy looking, then it's probably receiving enough light to maintain itself but not enough to thrive. Whether or not you should give it more light depends on what you want—a plant of the present size or one that will grow rapidly and bloom.

The happiest situation, of course, is when the plant you've chosen happens to thrive in the location where you most want the plant for decorative purposes. But there are tricks you can use to modify a situation to make it at least tolerable, if not perfect, for the plant. White and light-colored hard surfaces, such as walls or furniture, can reflect light back onto a plant, helping it in a low-light situation. Mirrors can do the same thing, and reading-lamp light striking a plant in the evening hours helps. More elaborate would be the installation of special plant lights.

To reduce and diffuse light, try a translucent window shade or lacy curtains.

Wendy Schrock Dreyzin

Rotating plants
If your plants lean toward the light source, rotate them every few days to keep the growth pattern even.

Books

The Facts of Light about Indoor Gardening, Ortho Books, Chevron Chemical Co., Ortho Division, 200 Bush St., San Francisco, California 94104, 1975, paperback, 97 pages, $3.98. This is a very thorough book on all aspects of light and your plants. It explains how your plants use light, which plants to grow in which lighting situation, how to measure your available light, how to increase light, and many related topics.

Houseplants for Five Exposures, by George Taloumis, Abelard-Schuman Limited, 257 Park Ave. South, New York, New York 10010, 1973, hardbound, $7.95; New American Library, 1301 Avenue of the Americas, New York, New York 10019, 1975, paperback, $1.50. This book describes plants to grow in windows that face north, south, east, and west, and plants for the fifth, or "decorative exposure," which includes areas eight to ten feet or more away from windows, where a plant adds to the decor. Also a general houseplant care section.

House Plants to Grow If You Have No Sun, by Elvin McDonald, Popular Library, 600 Third Ave., New York, New York 10016, 1975, paperback, 191 pages, $1.50. The bulk of the book is a plant encyclopedia giving preferred light level, light tolerance range, and other cultural information about each plant. The emphasis is on plants that tolerate low light levels. Many unusual plants are included.

Measuring light

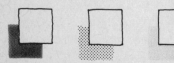

To determine the intensity of light, use this simple cast-shadow method. Use any hard-edged object such as a piece of paper or cardboard.
Bright: An object casts a distinct shadow.
Moderate: An object casts a pale fuzzy-edged shadow.
Low: An object casts almost no shadow at all.

Use a photographic light meter to measure light levels for your plants
Using a light meter (the one in your camera will work) is the most accurate way to assess the amount of light available for your plants. To measure, first set the ASA index to 200; next, set the shutter speed to 1/30 of a second. Now place a sheet of white paper where the top third of the plant's foliage would be. Turn the paper so it faces the light source. Focus the meter on the paper; be careful to avoid shading it or blocking the sun. Read and record the f-stop. An f-stop reading of 5.6 to 8 means the light is low; 8 to 11 indicates medium light and 11 to 16 is good light.

Magazines

Where to turn for the most up-to-date information on plants? Magazines, of course. The plant periodicals listed here are published either quarterly, bimonthly, monthly, or semimonthly, which means they are able to keep you posted on the latest developments in plants, products, and procedures. Some include decorating tips, craft how-to's, and personality profiles; all are written in a down-to-earth style.

Magazines

American Horticulturist. A bimonthly magazine with much of its space devoted to indoor gardening. Subject matter covers the entire breadth of horticulture, with emphasis on the latest developments and the newest trends. Excellent photography and illustrations complement the helpful articles. The yearly subscription rate is $15.00, which includes membership in the American Horticultural Society. For subscription information, write *American Horticulturist*, The American Horticultural Society, Mt. Vernon, Virginia 22121.

The Avant Gardener. Published twice a month in a newsletter format. Contains interesting and helpful articles on the latest developments and trends in plants, products, cultural methods, and more. Devotes between one-third and one-half of its content to indoor gardening. The subscription rate is $10.00 per year. For a subscription, write *The Avant Gardener*, P.O. Box 489, New York, New York 10028.

Flower and Garden. Published monthly, devoting up to one-half of its content to indoor gardening. Intended for both the beginner and the moderately involved home gardener. Emphasis is on practical topics and procedures presented in easy-to-understand, nontechnical language. Newsstand cost is 50 cents a copy while subscription rates are $5.00 per year. Publishing and subscription service address is *Flower and Garden Magazine*, 4251 Pennsylvania, Kansas City, Missouri 64111.

Greenleaves. A quarterly publication available at newsstands only. Almost all of its content is devoted to indoor gardening and is designed to appeal to "plant people." Some topics explored include plant care, propagation, decorating, consumer reports, product reviews, and more. Available at newsstands for $1.50 per copy. The publishing office address is Popular Publications, 420 Lexington Ave., New York, New York 10017.

Horticulture. A monthly publication devoting a substantial amount of content to indoor gardening. Diverse in its editorial approach. *Horticulture* covers areas ranging from down-to-earth how-to articles to photographic essays and human interest profiles. The newsstand price is $1.25 a copy with subscription rates at $9.00 per year. For subscriptions, write *Horticulture* Subscription Service, 125 Garden St., Marion, Ohio 43302. The publishing address is 300 Massachusetts Ave., Boston, Massachusetts 02115.

Houseplants and Porch Gardens. A bimonthly (as of September 1977, a monthly) publication dealing mainly with indoor gardening. Contains features on plant care and propagation along with easily understood how-to's concerning different facets of gardening. Written in a down-to-earth, nontechnical manner. Regular column on plant problems. Each issue contains approximately 48 pages of color photographs. Available at newsstands and plant shops for $1.25 an issue. Subscription rates are $6.00 for 6 issues, $12 for 12 issues. For subscriptions, write to *Houseplants and Porch Gardens*, Box 2461, Boulder, Colorado 80302.

Plants Alive. A monthly publication devoted almost entirely to indoor gardening. Special features include a monthly greenhouse calendar, instructing the reader on what should be done in the greenhouse each month, along with advice on container gardening and an emphasis on how-to articles. Available at newsstands at $1.25 an issue, subscription rates are $9.60 per year. For subscriptions write *Plants Alive*, 1255 Portland Place, Boulder, Colorado 80302. Editorial offices are located at 5509 1st Ave. South, Seattle, Washington 98108.

Popular Gardening Indoors. A bimonthly devoted entirely to indoor gardening, featuring professional and amateur gardeners and their plants. Covers such areas as plant culture and care, decorating with plants, mail-order sources of unusual plants, plant cooking recipes as well as features on crafts and construction. Available at newsstands for $1.25 an issue with a yearly subscription rate of $7.50. For subscriptions, write *Popular Gardening Indoors*, 1200 Garden St., Marion, Ohio 43302. Publishing offices are located at 383 Madison Ave., New York, New York 10017, and the editorial office is at 249 E. 57th St., New York, New York 10022.

Miniature roses

New hybrid mini roses are available in an extraordinary range of flower types and color combinations. Best of all, these tiny shrubs will bloom when only 6 to 8 inches tall. Mini roses in my basement light garden provide flowers all year long, but these perfect little blooms are most appreciated inside when cold weather has put the outdoor garden to sleep.

Light

Strong direct sun for at least 5 hours per day will grow sturdy bushes with maximum flower production. If morning sun comes through the window and lights the bushes directly until at least mid-day, mini roses will do well even in mid-winter. However, sunlight is often rare during northern winters and not all of us have sunny windows or a sun porch. Fortunately, broad spectrum fluorescent light is equal to sun for growing mini roses.

The mini roses I grow under fluorescent lights in the dark basement outbloom roses dependent on sun through west to south windows. A fixture with 3 or 4 fluorescent lamps will provide strong enough light for perfect roses. Use Wide Spectrum Gro-Lux, Agro-Lites, or Vita-Lites, since they are designed for plants with high light requirements. Keep the lamps close to the foliage, 4 to 6 inches away, and leave them on for 12 to 14 hours per 24 hour period. A longer time, to 18 hours, will make bushes grow faster, but normal flowering is adequate with the 12 to 14 hour day under the broad spectrum lamps.

Temperature

Sturdy growth occurs with nights 8 to 10 degrees colder than daytime highs. Since mini roses are hardy, they will accept very cool temperatures, but for maximum indoor growth and increased flowering, keep nights in the 60 to 65 degree F. range. Daytime temperatures as high as 80 degrees are satisfactory so long as the relative humidity remains above 50 percent. Wash foliage off under a stream of warm running water every few weeks to keep it clean and to discourage spider mites.

Containers

Pot mini roses in 4- to 6-inch plastic pots with a bottom layer of gravel and hardwood charcoal chunks for sharp drainage. Other containers are suitable if they have adequate drainage. Mini roses like to remain evenly moist, but they won't thrive if the roots sit in water or soggy soil.

Soil mixtures

The modern soilless peatlike mixes such as Jiffy, Vita-Bark, and Pro formulas are perfect for potted roses. Terra-Lite Rose Bush Planting Soil is a recently introduced mix that works well for mini roses indoors. Modern "soils" based on peat moss, perlite, and vermiculite provide few nutrients so fertilizer must be added as plants grow. Use slow-release products, supplemented occasionally with fish emulsion or seaweed fertilizer. My indoor roses are fed Ortho 5-10-5 timed release fertilizer, Osmocote, or MagAmp, which release nutrients at every watering for several months.

Selections

To start your collection, try these hybrids which do especially well as pot plants:

White: Popcorn, Starglo (sometimes blushed yellow in the center), White Madonna.

Light Pink: Baby Betsy McCall, Pearl Dawn, Stacey Sue.

Dark Pink: Bonny, Judy Fischer, Mimi.

Red: Beauty Secret, My Valentine.

Yellow: Littlest Angel, Rise 'n' Shine.

Blends: Green Ice (opens white, turns pink, matures green), Magic Carrousel (white with dark pink petal edges), Rosmarin (white and shades of pink), Sassy Lassy (red, yellow, pink), Tiny Warrior (rose, pink, silver-white).

Charles Marden Fitch

Charles Marden Fitch, a horticultural writer and photographer, has grown plants for more than twenty years. He has taught advanced classes at the New York Botanical Garden, and has also lectured on international travel, horticulture, and natural science.

More suggestions

Suggestions from Harm and Chip Saville of Nor'East Miniature Roses:

We have found that some varieties of miniature roses make splendid hanging basket subjects. We have used, with excellent results:

Red Cascade	Spring Song
Sugar Elf	Pink Mandy
Green Ice	Frosty

We suggest extra heavy fertilizing and extra humus in the potting mix. Some miniatures grow much smaller than others. Below, we have tried to group those that will appeal to people who prefer the smallest ones.

Baby Cheryl	Red Imp
Baby Ophelia	Rosmarin
Bo-Peep	Rouletti
Cinderella	Stacey Sue
Granate	Sunnyside
Kara	Sweet Fairy
Midget	Tea Party
Pearl Dawn	Yellow Bantam

Charles Marden Fitch

Plant sources

Armstrong Nurseries, Box 4060, Ontario, California 91761. (714) 986-5114. Color-illustrated catalog. Miniature tree roses.

Roses by Fred Edmunds, 6235 Southwest Kahle Road, Wilsonville, Oregon 97070. (503) 638-4671. Color-illustrated catalog. Open Monday through Saturday 8:00 a.m. to 4:30 p.m. (Closed Saturday April to November.) Large selection of outdoor roses and some miniatures suitable for indoor culture. Miniatures available most of the year.

Herbs 'N Honey Nursery, Route 2, Box 205, Monmouth, Oregon 97361. (503) 623-4033. List. Open Monday through Friday 8:00 a.m. to 4:00 p.m. Visitors are welcome but should call ahead to make appointment. Miniature roses, also herbs.

McDaniel's Miniature Roses, 7523 Zemco Street, Lemon Grove, California 92045. (714) 469-4669. List with descriptions. Open 9:00 a.m. to 5:00 p.m. Monday through Saturday. Over 250 varieties of miniature roses, including bush tree, climbers, and hanging-basket types. Roses listed by color. Growing instruction sheet sent with every order.

Mini-Roses, Box 4255, Station A, Dallas, Texas 75208. (214) 946-3487. Catalog issued twice a year. Descriptive list includes newest varieties plus many other choice ones. Also, climbing miniatures. Instructions for growing in hanging baskets. Instant rose food available.

Miniature Plant Kingdom, 4125 Harrison Grade Road, Sebastopol, California 95472. Catalog. Open 9:00 a.m. to 3:00 p.m. daily. Specialists in miniature roses; miniature climbers available.

Moore Miniature Roses, Sequoia Nursery, 2519 East Noble Avenue, Visalia, California 93277. (209) 732-0190. Color-illustrated brochures. Open Monday through Saturday 9:00 a.m. to 5:00 p.m. Varied selection of miniature roses listed with descriptions according to flower shade and common name. Small tree roses and hanging-basket varieties, plus unusual miniature moss roses.

Nor'East Miniature Roses, 58 Hammond Street, Rowley, Massachusetts 01969. (617) 948-2408. Color-illustrated catalog issued twice a year. Open daily to visitors, 9:00 a.m. to 5:00 p.m. More than 100 different varieties of miniature roses grown in the firm's green-houses, approximately 250,000 plants in all. Collections of 5, 10, 25, and 50 plants available. Also, special potting mix specifically for miniature roses. Many helpful suggestions. Growing instructions sent with every order.

Small World Miniature Roses, Box 562, Rogue River, Oregon 97537. (503) 582-1998. Catalog. Open daily during daylight hours at 6383 East Evans Creek Road, Rogue River. Visitors welcome. Over 200 different varieties of miniature roses are offered, with about 15 new ones added each year.

Star Roses, The Conard-Pyle Company, West Grove, Pennsylvania 19390. (215) 869-2426. Color-illustrated catalog mailed fall and spring. Retail garden center. Visitors welcome to drive through rose fields, also the Living Catalog and The Robert Pyle Memorial Rose Garden. The nursery has been in business since 1897. Large selections of hybrid teas, grandifloras, floribundas, climbers, shrubs, and miniatures. Introducers of the first miniature roses in the United States. Excellent, concise "Rose Fact Sheet" with information on color, bud-shape, bloom-size, fragrance, growth habit, and uses. Catalog includes color photographs with essay-type descriptions of many spectacular roses. Nursery also carries other ornamental plants, including azaleas, junipers, blue hollies, chrysanthemums, delphiniums, and other perennials.

Stocking Rose Nursery, 785 Capitol Avenue, San Jose, California 95133. (408) 258-3606. Color-illustrated catalog. Open daily 8:00 a.m. to 5:00 p.m.; closed Thursdays and holidays; Sunday 10:00 a.m. to 5:00 p.m. Varied selection of roses from hybrid teas, grandifloras, and floribundas to climbing roses. Catalog includes planting instructions and care. Miniature tree roses available.

Tillotson's Roses of Yesterday and Today, Brown's Valley Road, Watsonville, California 95076. (408) 724-3537. Illustrated catalog $1.00. Open Monday through Friday. Display garden is in full bloom from May 20 through June 10. Old, rare, and unusual roses, and a few selected newer varieties. Their specialty is "roses of history," including tender species and a few miniatures.

Melvin E. Wyant, Rose Specialist, Johnny Cake Ridge, Mentor, Ohio 44060. (216) 942-2511. Color-illustrated catalog mailed twice yearly. Display garden open to visitors. Specializing in roses, including miniatures, and related garden supplies. Plant descriptions and growing information.

Charles Marden Fitch

Charles Marden Fitch

Books

Books on growing miniature roses are relatively scarce. Most commercial growers supply a complimentary how-to leaflet with every order. In-depth information will be found in two recently published books:

The Complete Book of Houseplants Under Lights, by Charles Marden Fitch, Hawthorn Books, 260 Madison Ave., New York, New York 10016, 1975, hardbound, 275 pages, $9.95. This volume presents details on growing mini roses under lights; also shows many light garden designs.

The Complete Book of Miniature Roses, by Charles Marden Fitch, Hawthorn Books, 260 Madison Ave., New York, New York 10016, 1977, hardbound, 300 pages, $12.50. An encyclopedic covering of miniature rose culture, history, breeding, new hybrids, and sources. Sections on indoor and outdoor culture, propagation, grooming, showing, and so forth.

The case of the missing miniature

The pigmy rose, a forerunner of today's miniatures, was thought at one time to be lost forever to cultivation. However, in 1918, a specimen was found in Switzerland, growing on the windowsill of a small cottage.

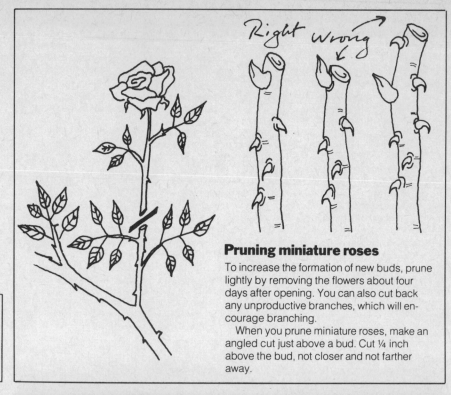

Pruning miniature roses

To increase the formation of new buds, prune lightly by removing the flowers about four days after opening. You can also cut back any unproductive branches, which will encourage branching.

When you prune miniature roses, make an angled cut just above a bud. Cut ¼ inch above the bud, not closer and not farther away.

Charles Marden Fitch

Societies

American Rose Society, Harold S. Goldstein, Box 30,000, Shreveport, Louisiana 71130. Membership dues are $15.50 per year and members receive the monthly magazine, *The American Rose.*

Charles Marden Fitch

Miniatures

Miniature sinningias

Oxalis hedysaroides rubra

Fittonia verschaffeltii 'Minima'

Replicas of their bigger brothers and perfect in every detail, fascinating miniature plants enable the gardener to have any type of garden he wants, regardless of where he lives and what type of space he has at his disposal.

Almost every plant family has tiny members, and searching them out is part of the fun. In each case, the requirements of the plant are similar to the larger varieties in the family.

To begin with, determine what the plant requires in terms of light, temperature, water, humidity, and feeding. If you plan to group plants in a landscape, use a dish deep enough to hold at least four inches of soil, and make sure the plants are compatible in terms of their cultural requirements.

A miniature landscaped garden is easier and less expensive than it sounds, mainly because the plants are so small. For example, if you have always avoided growing plants because a room is dark and special lighting equipment is expensive, remember that a simple light unit will probably supply adequate light for your miniaturized garden. Likewise, if you've always shied away from a tropical garden because of the high humidity required, simply enclose your miniature tropical plants in a lucite container or terrarium. If the sculptured formal garden has always been out of your reach for reasons of space, try landscaping one in a large dish.

And so it goes. With miniatures, all the gardens you thought you could never have are yours for the asking. Look closely at them. You'll find they'll provide you with worlds within worlds — all within your own four walls.

Ruth Katzenberger

Books

Little Plants For Small Places, by Elvin McDonald, Popular Library Books, 600 Third Ave., New York, New York 10016, 1974, paperback, 205 pages, $1.50. All about miniature gardening. How to grow and maintain over 800 varieties of miniature plants and trees, indoors or out. Special features include how to raise miniature African violets, orchids, begonias, and roses; helpful charts; and a list of specialty suppliers and greenhouses.

Miniature Plants Indoors and Out, by Jack Kramer, Charles Scribner's Sons, 597 Fifth Ave., New York, New York 10017, 1971, hardbound, 114 pages, $5.95. Beautifully presented with many black-and-white photographs, line drawings, and easy-to-read type. Suggestions for use in the garden and in the home.

Oxalis martiana 'Aureo-reticulata'

Planting a dish garden

The most important factor in planting a dish garden is the choice of plants. They all should have similar growth requirements: light, water, humidity, temperature, and potting mix. You can use almost any shape dish for your grouping, as long as it is deep enough to hold four inches of soil.

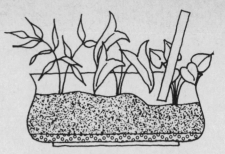

1. Place a layer of drainage material, such as pebbles or gravel, in the container (place a clay shard over the drainage hole first, if the container has one).

On top of this, add a shallow layer of the appropriate potting mix.

2. Remove the plants from their pots. Arrange and rearrange them in the container until you have created a landscape that you like. Do not crowd the plants—they must have enough room to grow.

3. Press the plants gently into place, and then fill in the spaces between them with more potting mix. Use a stick or spoon to tamp down gently.

If you like, add rocks, twigs, or a ground cover such as moss to the landscape.

To maintain the garden, water with a sprinkling can to avoid dislodging the roots. Pinch and prune the plants regularly to keep them from growing too large for the container.

Some miniatures to try

Gesneriads
Alloplectus nummularia, Gesneria cuneifolia, Codonanthe carnosa, Phinaea multiflora, Koellikeria erinoides, plus the miniature African violets and miniature sinningias (such as Snowflake, Bright Eyes, Krishna, Dollbaby, and Wood Nymph).

Ferns
Adiantum bellum and *hispidulum, Asplenium trichomanes, Camptosorus rhizophyllus, Cheilanthes lanosa, Doryopteris pedata, Polystichum tsus-simense,* and *Nephrolepis exaltata* 'Fluffy Duffy.'

Begonias
Red Planet, Miyo Berger, *prismatocarpa,* Midget Maze, It, Persian Brocade, *bowerae nigramarga,* Spaulding, Zaida, Baby Rainbow, Bantam Gem, Red Berry, and Shorty.

Orchids
Aerangis rhodasticha; Neofinetia falcata; Kingiella philippinensis; Oncidium pusillum, cheirophorum, longipes, and *triquetrum;*

Odontoglossum rossii; Epiphronitis veitchii; and *Pleurothallis chrysantha.*

Geraniums
Salmon Comet, Snow White, Pigmy, Robin Hood, Ruffles, Dopey, Fairy Tales, Frills, Sugar Baby, and Pompeii.

Peperomias
Peperomia rubella, velutina, orba, and *glabella* 'Variegata.'

English ivy
Glacier, Triloba, Jubilee, Minima, Walthamensis, and Needlepoint.

Bromeliads
Tillandsia ionantha, Cryptanthus species, and *Billbergia morelii.*

Cactus and succulents
Haworthia limifolia and *pilifera, Gymnocalycium bruchii, Hatiora salicornioides, Sedum lineare* 'Variegatum,' *Crassula teres, Opuntia microdasys,* and *Mammillaria baumii.*

Basket plants
Chlorophytum bichetii, Cymbalaria muralis,

Helzine soleirolii, Hoya minima, Ficus pumila, Saxifraga stolonifera 'Tricolor,' and *Episcia dianthiflora.*

Some others
Sansevieria 'Hahnii,' *Pilea depressa, Cyclamen neopolitanum, Fittonia verschaffeltii* 'Minima,' *Oxalis hedysaroides rubra, Allophyton mexicanum,* and *Selaginella kraussiana.*

Plant sources

Miniatures are available from many of the plant sources listed in *African Violets, Begonias, Bromeliads, Bulbs, Cactus and Succulents, Carnivorous Plants, Ferns, Geraniums, Gesneriads, Houseplants, Miniature Roses,* and *Orchids.*

Faucaria tigrina

Begonia bowerae nigramarga

Allophyton mexicanum

Moving plants

The good china and precious knick-knacks were once the main concerns on moving day. Now, it's the plants. But just as with breakables, a little forethought goes a long way toward preventing plant casualties.

A short crosstown move is sometimes most dangerous for plants because planning for them is often neglected. Plants placed carelessly in an auto may fall over with soil spilling, pots cracking, and branches breaking. Or heat and sun may cook them or cold temperatures or drafts give them a nasty chill. Don't let any of these calamities happen to your plants.

There's no one correct way to move plants — just a number of common sense tricks that do the job. To prevent spilling soil, you might water and drain each plant before moving, and then cover the soil with foil or wet paper. A plastic bag over or wound around each small plant and pot, tied together at the end, both saves mess if the soil should spill and protects the plant against drying drafts. Place pots in divided liquor shipping cartons, or use crumpled newspaper to hold pots upright and separate in undivided boxes.

Hanging baskets and very large plants pose special problems. While holding stems up, roll baskets in butcher paper or newspaper, florist-style. Large plants may be difficult to wrap, though you can usually cover the pot and soil with a plastic bag, tying it around the main stem.

Choose a closed car over an open pickup truck for moving plants, and warm the car in advance if it's a cold day. Place plants on the floor rather than the seat, and if a large plant must be placed on its side, then be sure it's stabilized so it won't roll around. A sheet laid lightly over plants is ample protection against hot sun for a short drive.

A long-distance move is of course more complex. Some states require Department of Agriculture certificates for your plants, certifying that they are free of certain pests, before you'll be allowed to bring them across the state border. Contact your local USDA office (look in U.S. Government listings in the phone book) or call a county extension agent for informa-

How to pack your plants

1. Cover the top of the pots with aluminum foil to keep the soil from spilling out.

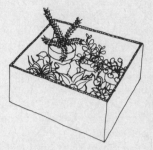

2. Group small plants in a box or container, using wads of newspaper to keep them from tipping over.

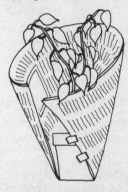

3. To conserve moisture or protect from cold during long hauls, encase the plants in plastic bags. During warm weather you may have to loosen the plastic occasionally to keep the plants from becoming too hot. In hot weather use newspaper for wrapping plants.

4. To transport trailing plants safely, make a newspaper cone to hold the vines up out of the way. Ask a friend to hold up the stems while you make the cone, fasten with tape or staples.

tion on this. Getting plants certified is usually a simple and inexpensive process.

If you're moving by auto, you may have to entrust your very large plants to the moving company, but try to keep your little ones with you. Since space will undoubtedly be a problem, take only your hard-to-replace favorites, and give away or sell all others.

Again, you must protect against heat, cold, spilling, breaking, and excessively dry air. You must also pack in such a way that plants can be easily unpacked for watering, and they cannot go for more than a couple of days without some light, though bright sun should also be avoided. Remember to park in a sheltered spot when you stop to eat, to avoid heat build-up in the summer, and to take plants into your motel room at night (especially important during winter months).

If you're moving by plane, the plants may be able to travel on the same plane if you make a cargo de-

partment reservation when you buy your own ticket. Ask about box size limitations, and prune plants, if needed, to fit. Cut small air holes and write "This side up" and "Live plants" all over the cartons; then insulate well with newspaper. Just before flight time, place the watered and drained plants in the boxes, stuffing empty spaces with crumpled newspaper; then jiggle and tip to be sure the plant won't move much if the airline cargo handlers toss the box around.

No matter how you make your move, unpack plants first when you arrive at your new home. Give them moderate light at first, depending on how long they've been in transit, and gradually over several days move them into brighter spots.

If a plant pouts at first, be patient. Just as with people, moving can be a shock to the plant's system, and it may take a little time for the plant to become accustomed to its new home.

Wendy Schrock Dreyzin

Mushrooms

In the world of edibles, the mushroom has long been king, both for its delicate flavor and the royal price it commands. These facts considered, it's good news for gardener and gourmet alike that the mighty mushroom can now be grown at home. The secret is in the new mushroom kits on the market. Costing about $5.00, a kit will provide you with a six-week crop of mushrooms; all ready for you to pick at their peak of perfection.

There are various kits on the market, available through mail-order sources and large gardening supply houses. When selecting one, remember that kits without needlessly elaborate packaging are generally the best, and that clear, detailed instructions are an absolute necessity.

Exacting conditions

In addition to what it will do for your table, growing mushrooms is a fascinating gardening experience. The culture is unlike that of almost any other plant, and the conditions that must be maintained are rigorous enough to offer a stimulating challenge to any gardener.

Temperature (between 50 and 65 degrees F. is ideal) and light levels (little or no light) must be carefully maintained. So must the moisture and humidity levels specified on the package. All of this means frequent monitoring, of course, and it isn't unusual for the gardener to develop a feeling of kinship with his little patch of soil.

The real thrill, however, comes about fourteen days after you've begun. That's when the first hint of the coming harvest appears: a layer of white fuzz on the surface of the soil. A few days later, tiny mushrooms appear. Approximately a week after that, the caps begin to flatten—the

sign that you can harvest your first crop. That's the bumper crop. It continues for a week and is soon followed by a second one. Smaller crops will appear for the next four weeks.

At least it was fun

The total yield, despite the long harvest period, is not all that large. In fact, you're almost guaranteed to gain more experience than mushrooms from this garden. True aficionados of the mushroom, however, may want to proceed to the more expensive packs sold by large commercial growers. Depending on how you handle them, these can yield between 10 and 20 pounds of produce.

Either way, the homegrown mushroom is a passport to some very tasty gardening. And who's to say that the fruit of your labor can be measured only by the weight of its yield?

Jill Munves

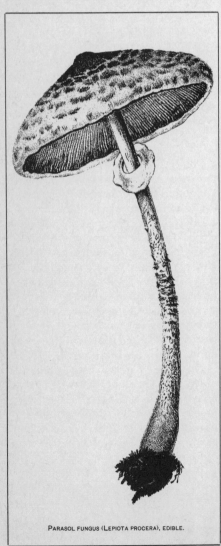

PARASOL FUNGUS (*LEPIOTA PROCERA*), EDIBLE.

Plant sources

Alberta Nurseries and Seeds, Bowden, Alberta, TOM OKO, Canada. Color-illustrated catalog. Pretested mushroom spawn is offered in a sterilized media; will keep for an indefinite period of time. Available by the quart.

American Science Center, 5700 Northwest Highway, Chicago, Illinois 60646. Catalog 50 cents. Mushroom-growing kit includes processed spawn preplanted in compost and easy-to-follow instructions. Two sizes available.

W. Atlee Burpee, Warminster, Pennsylvania 18974; Clinton, Iowa 52732; or Riverside, California 92502. Color-illustrated catalog. Pure culture process mushroom spawn, sold in packets.

Edmund Scientific Company, 1006 Edscorp Building, Barrington, New Jersey 08007. Catalog 50 cents. Mushroom-growing kit includes processed spawn preplanted in compost and easy-to-follow instructions. Two sizes available.

Ferndale Gardens, Faribault, Minnesota 55021. Color-illustrated catalog. Preplanted mushroom kit includes spawn, soil, and instructions.

Henry Field Seed and Nursery Company, Shenandoah, Iowa 51602. Color-illustrated catalog. Pure culture mushroom spawn is offered; full instructions included.

Lakeland Nurseries, 340 Poplar Street, Hanover, Pennsylvania 17331. Color-illustrated catalog $1.00. Mushroom kit includes growing tray, special soil, mushroom spawn, and instruction booklet.

Mellinger's, North Lima, Ohio 44452. Catalog. Pure culture mushroom spawn is available in two quantities; cultural instructions included. Also offered are kits which include bedding, casing, instructions, and spawn of one of four

mushroom species: the wood ear (*Auricularia polytricha*), oyster (*Pleurotus ostreatus*), enokitake (*Flammulina velutipes*), or common mushroom (*Agaricus bisporus*).

Nichols Garden Nursery, 1190 North Pacific Highway, Albany, Oregon 97321. Catalog. Pure culture process mushroom spawn is available in packets.

R. H. Shumway Seedsman, 628 Cedar Street, Rockford, Illinois 61101. Full-color catalog. Mushroom spawn in crumbled form; sold in quart, 3-quart, and 5-quart quantities.

Spring Hill Nurseries, 110 Elm Street, Tipp City, Ohio 45371. Color-illustrated catalog. Mushroom-growing kit includes spawn, soil, directions, and recipes.

Stokes Seeds, Box 548, Main Post Office, Buffalo, New York 14280. Catalog. Lambert's mushroom spawn in two forms, fine mold cultures and larger, shredded flakes. Free pamphlet on indoor mushroom culture with order.

Office plants

As our business environment increasingly leans toward the sleek, easily used architectural materials of cement, glass, and steel, we create very functional, very open interiors. The price for such efficiency is starkness, sterility, and a lack of warmth. Enter the professional space planner, interior designer. Schooled and experienced in working with open as well as more traditional office designs, they make the expensive space work.

Function and efficiency is their first concern. But in creating the total environment, the aesthetics and more subtle finishing ingredients are equally called for. What more effectively than healthy, thriving plants can soften the dominant, angular lines of current architecture or more subtly direct traffic, diffuse sound or visually screen?

In using plants most creatively in the office environment, space planners are more and more consulting with and using the services of a new professional—the interior landscape designer. The effective use of plants

in the business environment is a relatively new development. Many offices at one time or another have tried using plants—usually with expensively disappointing results brought about by selecting the wrong plants for the conditions existing, inadequate or improper lighting, and improper care. The interior landscape specialist works daily with introducing plants into offices.

The space planner knows where plants are wanted, what functions they are to perform. The interior landscaper then selects varieties, suggests necessary lighting in order to save expensive wiring and lighting changes later (to give most important design input the interior landscaper should become involved in the design program during the earliest planning stages), and then offers important maintenance program alternatives.

The most ideal program for an office occurs when the interior landscape designer not only provides the plants but maintains them under a full replacement guarantee, assuring that

the plants will continually perform their original design function.

How does a company or space planner go about selecting an interior landscape specialist? Since they represent such a young industry, there are few established guidelines. But the following should be helpful: 1) Ask for examples of previous projects and check carefully with the companies. 2) Select several of these and personally review them. Important note—they should have been under maintenance for at least six months, preferably a year or longer. Nearly any interior planting can look good at the time of installation. It's six months and longer that truly professional maintenance makes itself evident. 3) Does the interior landscape firm use plants which have been conditioned for office use by gradually acclimating them to the interior environment, from the ideal conditions of Florida or California as well as local greenhouses? Ask to review their conditioning area. Acclimated plants are slightly more expensive but because of long-term hardiness are well worth the investment.

4) Finally, does the firm belong to the national Interior Landscape Association, recently established to recognize the professionals of interior landscaping, establish standards for the industry, and ultimately provide more effective interior planting for the business community?

For more details on ILA, contact the Society of American Florists and Ornamental Horticulturists, 901 North Washington St., Alexandria, Virginia 22314.

In essence then, the safest, most effective way to incorporate plants into your office, as it currently exists or as you have plans for it, is to go the expert—the professional interior landscape designer.

Donald Gammon

Donald Gammon is president of The Greenery, a firm specializing in interior landscapes, located in Cambridge, Massachusetts.

Books
The Office Gardener, by Jacqueline Heriteau, Hawthorn Books, 260 Madison Ave., New York, New York 10016, 1977, hardbound, $9.95, paperback, $5.95.

Orchids

Orchids form the largest plant family, comprising more than 30,000 species found in all areas of the world except the perpetually frozen polar regions or arid, desert wastes. These adaptable plants inhabit the seacoasts of North and South America, reach to the snow boundaries of the Andes Mountains, and are as common as roses in the cities and small towns of Asia, where natives still backpack huge quantities of orchids from the jungle hills to sell for pennies in the great, open-air flower markets.

The history of the orchid is a romantic one, filled with legend and thus rife with many misconceptions. Many people today feel that orchids may be too expensive. This undeserved reputation originated during the mid-to-late nineteenth century, where orchids were primarily grown on the estates of the English and European aristocracy. Since most plants came directly from the jungle, after long, expensive, collecting trips, prices were naturally high for the few specimens which survived the harsh, sea journeys and the improper understanding of their culture.

Today, after decades of experimentation with orchid seed germination and both greenhouse and indoor culture, orchids can be grown by anyone with a thumb only remotely green — and at a price accessible to every budget. Their cultural requirements, while as varied as one might expect in such a large and diverse family, have been carefully documented in the books listed at the conclusion of this article. It is essential, however, that the beginning indoor orchid grower clearly understands the basic environment he must offer his first orchids.

Light

The two major concerns of orchid culture are light and temperature. Most orchids, both species and hybrids, have been placed in one of three light categories. High-light orchids, such as vanda, dendrobium, and cymbidium, require nearly full sunlight and are thus unsuitable for most indoor culture. Medium-light orchids, by far the majority, require a minimum of 1500 footcandles of light to flower successfully. Well-lighted windows, solariums, or high-intensity fluorescent light units may prove adequate for such genera as cattleya, oncidium, brassia, miltinia, and epidendrum. Low-light orchids, the most suitable for home culture, may be easily grown on any windowsill or in any fluorescent light unit offering a minimum of 1000 footcandles of light. The most popular low-light orchids are paphiopedilum and phalaenopsis. Orchids from one light zone may often adapt to the zone nearest to them.

Cattleya

165

Temperature

Orchids are also divided into three temperature ranges. Beginning growers should remember that species orchids, those found in nature, are more rigid in their temperature demands than the man-made hybrid orchids. Hybridizing experiments have begun to break the temperature barriers which have thwarted growers for many years. Basically, warm-temperature orchids such as vanda and phalaenopsis require 70- to 75-degree F. day and 65- to 70-degree F. night temperatures. Intermediate-temperature orchids, such as cattleya, oncidium, epidendrum, and a host of less well-known genera, require 65- to 70-degree F. day and 55- to 65-degree F. night temperatures. Cool-temperature orchids, such as cymbidium, odontoglossum, and some paphiopedilum, flourish at day temperatures around 55 to 60 degrees F. with a night temperature at 50 degrees F. One basic requirement is a minimum 10-degree differential between day and night temperatures.

Orchids are adaptable plants, as mentioned earlier, and many plants may adjust to a wide range of temperatures. Experimentation, reading, and experience are the only real teachers.

Orchid culture is one of the most vigorous of all plant hobbies. More than 350 orchid societies exist in upwards of 40 countries, most operating under the guidance of the international organization, the American Orchid Society, based at the Botanical Museum of Harvard University in Cambridge, Massachusetts. Since the days of orchids as the "hobby of kings," interest in these exotic but easily cultured plants has grown to tremendous proportions. The orchid industry in the United States alone is a multimillion dollar business, and many firms can offer fine, healthy plants at reasonable prices through the mails to interested people.

And as a final note—while orchids are among the loveliest of all flowers, so are orchid people among the friendliest of all people. Anyone interested in growing his or her first orchid will be sure to find a helping hand and a word of advice and encouragement from any of the thousands of orchid growers in the United States today.

Richard Peterson

Richard Peterson grows a wide range of orchids under fluorescent lights in his home, office, and greenhouse. In 1971, he was made associate editor of the American Orchid Society Bulletin. *In 1973 he became the bulletin's editor.*

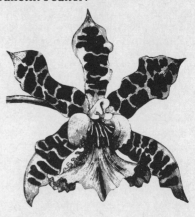

Phalaenopsis

Orchids are divided into two basic growth types: monopodial and sympodial. Monopodial orchids have a central stem which grows continuously from the tip. Inflorescences are produced from the stem between the leaves, usually alternately from side to side. Phalaenopsis are an example of this. Sympodial orchids, such as cattleyas and paphiopedilums, possess a rhizome which sends out a shoot. This develops into a stem and leaves and eventually, produces flowers. In due time, from the base of this growth, a new shoot develops, and so on in a continuous cycle. The buds are often, though not always, protected by a sheath.

Reprinted from *Handbook on Orchid Culture*, American Orchid Society, Botanical Museum of Harvard University, Cambridge, Massachusetts 02138, 1974, paperback, 80 pages, $2.00 postpaid.

Books

Handbook on Orchid Culture, by the American Orchid Society, Botanical Museum of Harvard University, Cambridge, Massachusetts 02138, 1974, 80 pages, $2.00. A color-illustrated "how-to" journal which includes detailed information on the culture of most common and widely available orchids plus specific instructions on fluorescent light, windowsill, and greenhouse culture.

A History of the Orchid, by Merle Reinikka, University of Miami Press, Coral Gables, Florida, 1972, 316 pages, $15.00. Readable biographical sketches of the people and events involved in the cultivation of orchids from the early nineteenth century to the present.

Home Orchid Growing, by Rebecca Tyson Northern, Van Nostrand Reinhold Co., 450 W. 33rd St., New York, New York 10001, 1970, 347 pages, $22.50. This book relates each step in the process of growing orchids, both in the greenhouse and indoors under artificial light. All phases of growing are handled, from pollination and seed stages to caring for the mature plant. Over 500 species of orchids are discussed; 100 color illustrations.

Orchids As House Plants, by Rebecca Tyson Northern, Dover Publications, 180 Varick St., New York, New York 10014, 1976, 142 pages, $2.50. Aimed at those who wish to grow orchids in the home, including living rooms, sun porches, and basements. The book explains the basic needs of orchids and where to grow them in the house, both by natural and artificial light. It includes the description and care of orchids that do well as houseplants. Contains 63 illustrations.

You Can Grow Orchids, by Mary Noble, published by the author at 3003 Riverside Ave., Jacksonville, Florida 32205, 1975, 136 pages, $4.95. Good introductory guide.

Societies

American Orchid Society, Gordon Dillon, Botanical Museum of Harvard University, Cambridge, Massachusetts 02138. The Society was founded in 1932 to spread interest in orchids. Membership is open to anyone. The fee is $15.00 per year and entitles the member to the Society's monthly magazine, various special pamphlets, and to attend monthly meetings of local chapters.

There are 350 affiliated chapters in over 40 countries, and every three years the World Orchid Conference is held, during which tours associated with the Conference are offered. In the United States, there are shows yearly and meetings twice yearly.

Cymbidium Society of America, 469 West Norman Avenue, Arcadia, California 91006. The Society was started in 1950. Membership is open to anyone interested in its activities, which include attending and entering competitions, as well as learning how to judge such competitions. The high point of the calendar is the annual orchid show, held in Southern California. Membership costs $10.00 per year, which includes a subscription to the Society's bimonthly magazine.

Repotting orchids

Repot orchids once every two years, in the early spring. Use a clay or plastic pot, and either a highly organic terrestrial orchid mix, or osmunda fiber, or shredded tree bark mixed with sphagnum moss, depending on the particular orchid you have.

To prepare the plant for repotting, remove the support stakes, if any, and knock the plant out of its old pot. Trim away any dead leaves or roots, and carefully remove and discard as much of the old growing medium from the roots as possible. Check the plant thoroughly for scale or other insects.

To prepare the new pot, place a large clay shard over the drainage hole, followed by about one inch of smaller shards to ensure good drainage. Then half fill the pot with the potting mix.

Single-stemmed (monopedial) orchids

This type of orchid has a single, upright stem and is planted much as you would any other houseplant. Place the orchid in the center of the prepared pot with the top of the root crown ½ inch below the rim of the pot. Pour in potting mix, packing it in tightly.

Multiple-stemmed (sympodial) orchids

1. Orchids with multiple stems grow horizontally, with their stems tied to a support stake. First divide the plant, leaving at least three pseudobulbs on each division. You can also cut back the roots to 2 inches if they are very long and tangled. Both the front and back division can be potted in separated containers giving you two plants.

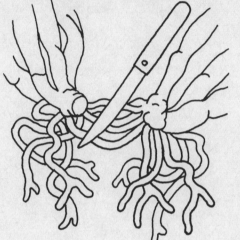

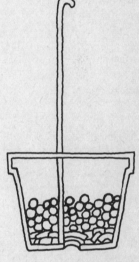

2. Insert the wire stake in the prepared pot, slightly off center.

3. Hold the division in the new pot with the oldest end against the side. The rhizome should be ½ inch below the rim of the pot. Pour in potting mix, working it in between the roots and pressing down tightly. Tap the pot on the table to help the mix settle into place. Continue adding mix, pressing it down and tapping the pot as you work. When finished, the potting mix will be ½ inch below the rim of the pot, with the rhizome lying in a trench on top (do not cover the rhizome).

4. Support each existing vertical stem by tying it to the wire stake.

5. As the orchid grows and sends up new stems, tie them to the stake.

Plant sources

Alberts and Merkel Brothers, 2210 South Federal Highway, Boynton Beach, Florida 33435. (305) 732-2071. Orchid catalog 75 cents, tropical foliage catalog 75 cents; both $1.35. Open Monday through Saturday 8:00 a.m. to 4:30 p.m. In business since 1890, these horticulturists now specialize in a varied selection of cattleya hybrids, phalaenopsis, paphiopedilums, dendrobiums, and numerous vandas. Catalog gives brief description and flowering times. Orchid mini-bottles and hybrid seedlings; suggested book list and orchid supplies. Also tropical foliage plants.

The Beall Company, Box 467, Vashon Island, Washington 98070. (206) 463-9151. Catalog. Greenhouses are located at 91st Avenue Southwest and Southwest 186th Street. Open Monday through Saturday 8:00 a.m. to 4:00 p.m. Visitors welcome. The eighty greenhouses on Vashon Island are used to raise a wide selection of orchids, especially cattleyas, cymbidiums, miltonias, vandas, paphiopedilums, and miscellaneous species and hybrids. Catalogs are issued about every six weeks with descriptions of different genera of orchids in each. In business for 70 years.

Black River Orchids, Box 110, 77th Street, South Haven, Michigan 49090. (616) 637-5085. Catalog. Open Monday through Saturday 9:00 a.m. to 4:00 p.m. Tours by appointment (50 cents per person). Varied selection of orchid plants for growing and cut flowers —extensive listing of species. Many unusual orchids plus separate hybrid listing and African orchid collection listing. Orchid supplies and books available.

Coastal Gardens, 137 Tropical Lane, Corpus Christi, Texas 78408. (512) 882-9896. Catalog. Open Monday through Friday 9:30 a.m. to 3:30 p.m. Appointments preferred. Specialists in orchid hybrids and seedling production. Catalog includes descriptions of seedlings. Mature plants are listed.

Edelweiss Gardens, 54 Robbinsville-Allentown Road, Box 66R, Robbinsville, New Jersey 08691. (609) 259-2831. Plant list 35 cents. Open daily until 4:00 p.m. Selection of orchids for growing in the home includes jewel orchids, brassavolas, dendrobiums, epidendrums, and paphiopedilums.

Finck Floral Company, 9849 Kimker Lane, St. Louis, Missouri 63127. (314) 843-4376. Price lists with descriptions. Visits by appointment only. Small selection of phalaenopsis, miniature oncidiums, cattleyas, and miltonias. Also bromeliads, carnivorous plants, and ferns.

Fort Caroline Orchids, 13142 Fort Caroline Road, Jacksonville, Florida 32225. Catalog. Open Wednesday through Sunday 11:00 a.m. to 5:00 p.m. Appointment appreciated. Extremely large number of genera, both as hybrids and species. Description of flower, blooming season, and cultural information.

Fox Orchids, 6615 West Markham Street, Little Rock, Arkansas 72205. (501) 663-4246. Catalog 50 cents. Visitors welcome. Numerous cattleya hybrids listed by color plus species listings of many other genera. Many paphiopedilums; also some bromeliads, tropical water plants, and houseplants. Very wide range of specialized supplies. Extensive book list.

Paphiopedilums

Arthur Freed Orchids, 5731 South Bonsall Drive, Malibu, California 90265. (213) 457-9771. Catalog issued twice yearly. Open Monday through Saturday 10:00 a.m. to 4:00 p.m. Visitors welcome. This company breeds and grows orchids which can be grown in the house and do not require special greenhouse care. Wide selection of phalaenopsis (white, pink, peppermint striped) and unique choice of intergeneric seedlings and plants. Also doritaenopsis, ascocenda, paphiopedilum, dendrobium, and many hybrids. Bare-root and in-pot shipments of both seedlings and mature flowering plants. Catalog gives general culture notes.

Great Lake Orchids, Box 1114, Monroe, Michigan 48161. (313) 242-5995. Catalog. Collection of orchids including cattleya hybrids, paphiopedilums, and phalaenopsis hybrids for beginners. Plants shipped with fertilizer and culture instructions.

Herb Hager Orchids, 30th and Capitola Road, Box 544, Santa Cruz, California 95061. (408) 475-2425. Brochure. Selection of phalaenopsis orchids; also some renanthopsis and doritaenopsis.

Orchids by Hausermann, Box 363, Elmhurst, Illinois 60216. (312) 543-6855. Illustrated catalog $1.00. Nursery at 2 North 134 Addison Road, Villa Park, Illinois. Open Monday through Saturday 7:00 a.m. to 4:30 p.m. Varied selection of orchids, particularly cattleya, dendrobium, paphiopedilum, phalaenopsis, and botanicals. Large choice of meristemmed cattleyas and cymbidiums in a range of colors, all propagated at the nursery. The catalog includes many beautiful color photos. A special section on suitable varieties for home growing, orchid growing supplies, recommended publications, and growing information.

Spencer M. Howard, Orchid Imports, 11802 Huston Street, North Hollywood, California 91607. (213) 762-8275. Plant list. Open by appointment only. Specializing in orchids from Southeast Asia, Brazil, Central America, Mexico, and Columbia for over 25 years. Varied collection of different species. New choices in each quarterly listing.

Lager and Hurrell, 426 Morris Avenue, Summit, New Jersey 07901. (201) 273-1792. List. Greenhouses open Monday through Saturday 9:00 a.m. to 4:00 p.m. Small selection of blooming-size bare-root plants, including brassavola, cattleya and allied genera, plus cymbidium, dendrobium, epidendrum, maxillaria, phalaenopsis, and others. Basic orchid supplies and some publications.

Ann Mann's Orchids, Route 3, Box 202, Orlando, Florida 32811. (305) 876-2625. Price list 25 cents. Open by appointment only. Large selection of hybrids and species of cattleyas, some vandas, and miscellaneous genera. Many plants, orchids, and other exotics, collected on biannual trips to the Caribbean and Central America. Orchid/exotic plant collecting trips also arranged and directed for amateur collectors. Cultural handbook on orchids available for $2.50.

Rod McLellan Company, 1450 El Camino Real, South San Francisco, California 94080. (415) 871-5655. Illustrated catalog and brochures. Greenhouses may be visited at above address or at 2352 San Juan Road, Watsonville, California 95076. (408) 728-1797; 422-1143. Open daily 9:00 a.m. to 5:00 p.m. Free guided nursery tours 10:30 a.m. and 1:30 p.m. daily at South San Francisco facilities; Saturday and Sunday only at Watsonville greenhouses. Over 70 acres of greenhouses are devoted to orchids and houseplants, making this nursery "the world's largest orchid hybridizer." Supersoil orchid-planting mixes and a full range of growing supplies are available.

Penn Valley Orchids, 239 Old Gulph Road, Wynnewood, Pennsylvania 19096. (215) 642-9822. Color-illustrated catalog $1.00. Open by appointment only. Specialize in paphiopedilum orchids; offer an incredibly large selection. Also extensive choice of cattleya alliance and some unregistered crosses. Some seedlings.

Santa Barbara Orchid Estate, 1250 Orchid Drive, Santa Barbara, California 93111. (805) 967-1284. Catalogs. Open Monday through Saturday 8:00 a.m. to 4:30 p.m.; Sunday 11:00 a.m. to 4:30 p.m. Large selection of exhibition type indoor and outdoor orchids, featuring cymbidiums, paphiopedilums, masdevallias, lycastes, and *Dendrobium nobile* hybrids. Flasks of seedlings. Separate brochure for different orchids—very large choice of cymbidiums. Useful orchid blooming calendar. Good selection of orchids for cool growing conditions.

Alvim Seidel, Orquideario Catarinense, Box 1, Rua (Street) Roberto Seidel, 1981, 89280, Corupa, Santa Catarina, Brazil. Illustrated catalog $2.00. Very extensive listing of orchid species and varieties. Company is experienced in exporting plants. Bromeliads, *Marantaceae*, and tropical plant seeds also available.

Shaffer's Tropical Gardens, 1220 41st Avenue, Capitola, California 95010. (408) 475-3100. Color catalog $1.00 (refundable with order). Open Monday through Saturday 9:00 a.m. to 5:00 p.m.; Sunday 11:00 a.m. to 5:00 p.m. Specialized breeders of phalaenopsis orchids, plus some cymbidiums, paphiopedilums, ascocendas, and related species. Fertilizers, insecticides, and other orchid supplies and books available. Houseplants available only at the nursery.

Fred A. Stewart Orchids, Box 307, 1212 East Las Tunas Drive, San Gabriel, California 91778. (213) 283-4590; 287-8974. Color-illustrated catalog $1.00. Open Monday through Saturday 8:00 a.m. to 5:00 p.m.; Sunday noon to 5:00 p.m. Visitors welcome. Extensive collection of orchids concentrating on five major types: cattleyas, cymbidiums, paphiopedilums, phalaenopsis, and ascocendas. Owning 60,000 square feet of greenhouse space, this company is a pioneer hybridizer of cattleya, cymbidium, and paphiopedilum orchids. Large, detailed color photographs included in the regular catalog; also special 16-page cymbidium catalog. Culture sheets for cattleya, cymbidium, paphiopedilum, phalaenopsis, and other botanicals. Orchid supplies are available.

More information available
Countless books on botanical, taxonomic, scientific, and cultural aspects of orchids, suitable for advanced growers, are available, and the American Orchid Society would be pleased to send interested readers whatever information is available.

Cattleya

Ascocenda

Organic gardening

House or greenhouse plants thrive only in conditions similar to those of their natural environment. The organic gardener provides the appropriate levels of sun or fluorescent light, humidity, water, and temperature, but departs from his nonorganic counterpart through the use of organic soils, fertilizers, and insecticides.

Soil mixes

Four types of organic soil mixtures will satisfy the needs of any indoor plant. The basic ingredients are garden loam for some nutrients and a soil mixture "skeleton"; compost or leaf mold for soil structure improvement, increased water retention, slowly released plant nutrients, trace elements, and anchorage for roots; and coarse, sharp (builder's) sand for improved aeration and drainage. The majority of houseplants will require an all-purpose soil: 2 parts garden loam, 1 part compost or leaf mold, and 1 part sharp sand. Some plants, such as the gesneriads, require a more humusy soil: 1 part garden loam, 2 parts compost or leaf mold, and 1 part sharp sand. Cacti and succulents will do well with 1 part compost or leaf mold and 1 part sharp sand. Ephiphytes, such as orchids and holiday cacti, require 1¼ part compost or leaf mold and 1 part sharp sand. A more alkaline soil can be provided with 1 tablespoon of ground limestone per 2 quarts of soil, a more acid soil with a monthly application of ½ teaspoon of vinegar per quart of water.

Fertilizers

Organic fertilizers are released slowly and will not burn root hairs. A balanced program of fertilization can be provided with a mixture. The components are: seaweed concentrate with nitrogen, phosphorus, potassium, and many trace elements present (such as Maxicrop); fish emulsion, a deodorized concentrate with nitrogen, phosphorus, and potash; Sturdy, an organic concentrate with phosphorus and potash (Charles Bateman Ltd., Box 25, Thornhill, Ontario, L3T 3N1, Canada). Dissolve the seaweed concentrate in 1 gallon of water (keep out of sun) to make a stock solution. Mix together ½ teaspoon of stock solution, 1½ teaspoons of fish emulsion, and ¼ teaspoon of Sturdy. Dilute the mixture to 1 quart with water. This soluble organic fertilizer can be used as a watering solution or foliar spray.

Insect control

Mild insect infestations can be controlled with a soapy water spray (1 tablespoon flaked Ivory or Octagon per gallon room-temperature water) left on plants for two hours prior to rinsing with room-temperature water. A botanical insecticide, pyrethrum-rotenone (such as Red Arrow Insect Spray), will subdue severe attacks by red spider or other mites, aphids, thrips, or white fly. Mealybugs or scale can be smothered with an insecticide of natural oils in a hemlock base (Cedoflora, Cedo Products Corp., 903 Allen Road, North Syracuse, New York 13212). To avoid plant damage it is always wise to test a leaf before spraying the whole plant.

Raymond P. Poincelot

Raymond Poincelot is trained in plant biochemistry and does research in plant biology at the Connecticut Agricultural Experimental Station, focusing on the effects of chemicals on the environment.

Let it rot

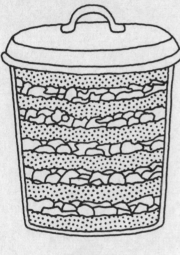

Composting in a small garbage can allows you to utilize good kitchen waste you'd generally just throw away: onion skins, orange peels, spoiled foods, and more. In addition, if it is made right you can have all the compost you need for apartment farming without muss, fuss, or smell. Here are the steps:

1. Obtain two or three 5- to 10-gallon plastic cans with lids. I find mine by asking a painting contractor for his old 5-gallon paint cans. You can also buy small garbage cans from a hardware, discount, or similar store.

2. Buy a sack of sand from your local hardware store, and place a 2-inch layer of sand on the bottom of the garbage can or plastic pail.

3. Add a 2- to 3-inch layer of garbage. On top of this place a 1-inch layer of sand. After this, layer the garbage and sand until you reach the top. Keep the lid on top.

4. When the first can is full, start on the next. Good compost takes two to three months.

Reprinted from *The Apartment Farmer*, by Duane Newcomb, J.P. Tarcher, Inc., 9110 Sunset Blvd., Los Angeles, California 90069, 1976, paperback, 154 pages, $4.95.

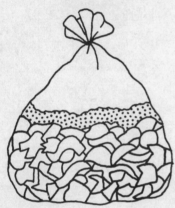

To make compost in a plastic bag, pour in waste materials and add a layer of nitrogenous material such as bone meal or manure. Close the bag tightly. Do not open the bag until the material has decomposed (about three months).

Organic Control, Inc.   Ladybug

Books

The Basic Book of Organic Gardening, edited by Robert Rodale, Rodale Press, 33 E. Minor St., Emmaus, Pennsylvania 18049, 1971, paperback, 362 pages, $1.50. Written for those with just a small plot, suburban garden, or even a small farm. This book discusses the value and cultivation of specific vegetables and fruits. Included are instructions on how to plant, what to plant, and what to do with the finished product. Also included is a complete list of where to order organic products by mail throughout the country, as well as an explanation as to why organic foods are necessary.

Compost – A Cosmic View with Practical Suggestions, by Carolyn Goldsmith, Harper and Row Publishers, 10 E. 53rd St., New York, New York 10022, 1973, paperback, $1.95. An entertaining, sometimes poetic, look at compost. This book tells how to make compost, why we use it, and gives practical and interesting suggestions on how to use it.

Gardening Indoors with House Plants, by Raymond P. Poincelot, Rodale Press, 33 E. Minor St., Emmaus, Pennsylvania 18049, 1974, hardbound, 266 pages, $8.95. All aspects of house plants and their culture are covered comprehensively, with thoroughness and precision, but in a lively interesting style. Hundreds of questions encountered by beginners and experienced hobbyists are answered. Fluorescent-light requirements and specifics on temperature, soil, humidity, light, and watering needs of over 200 ornamental houseplants are provided. Also included are instructions for growing vegetables, fruits, herbs, and forcing spring bulbs indoors. There is much more, including 100 photographs, numerous illustrations, and it is the only book written on house plants for the organic gardener.

Organic Gardening Under Glass, by George and Katy Abraham, Rodale Press, 33 E. Minor St., Emmaus, Pennsylvania 18049, 1975, hardbound, 308 pages, $8.95. This book gives extensive coverage of most plants grown under glass. As such, it is a useful reference for new greenhouse gardeners or experienced hobbyists. Greenhouses, soils, controlled environments, insects, diseases, and plant propagation are a few of the other subjects covered. Includes illustrations and photographs and is recommended for the greenhouse owner who wishes to use organic methods.

Homemade pest controls

All-purpose sprays

With the following two recipes, you can make pesticides that will control common houseplant pests such as aphids, thrips, whiteflies, and red spider mites. Both work on the principle that insect pests don't like to be saturated with garlic, onion, horseradish, pepper, and soapsuds any more than you do.

Recipe #1

Crush, or mash in a blender:
green onion tops
horseradish
hot red peppers
spearmint leaves

Add:
1 quart soapy water
1/4 cup detergent

To use:
Combine 1 part solution with 8 parts water.

Recipe #2

Chop fine:
one small onion

Add:
1 teaspoon cayenne pepper
1 cup water

To use:
Let steep for 1 hour, then strain into sprayer.

Multipurpose controls

Nicotine: Soak several cigar or cigarette butts in a gallon of water overnight. Pour the solution into the soil to kill fungus gnats, springtails, and centipedes. Never use tobacco sprays on members of the tobacco family, such as tomatoes, browallias, ornamental peppers, night jessamine, and brunfelsia.

Soapsuds: To kill soft-bodied pests such as aphids, make a mild soap-and-water solution. Dip plants into the solution. Let them dry, then rinse well with plain water. To rid plants of fungus gnats, sprinkle 1/2 cup of a laundry-soap solution on top of the soil. To remove scale, scrub the affected areas with a toothbrush dipped in a soap or detergent solution; rinse well. For whiteflies, dissolve 1 teaspoon household detergent in 1 gallon of water; spray undersides of leaves. Repeat three times at five-day intervals.

No-pest strips: Although these strips emit chemical fumes, they can be confined within a very limited area. Enclose the infected plant, together with a no-pest strip, in a plastic bag. In a few days, the fumes given off by the strip will kill scale and mealy bugs.

Controls for specific pests

Aphids: Soak the tobacco from two or three cigarette butts in a quart of water; add a little soap. Dip plants in the solution or use as a spray. Let plants dry; then rinse with plain water.

Red spider mites: Mix 1/4 cup buttermilk, 2 cups flour, and 2 1/2 gallons water. Spray or sprinkle on infested leaves.

Whiteflies: Paint a card yellow; let dry and coat with a sticky substance, such as Tack Trap (available from Animal Repellents, Griffin, Georgia 30223). Place the card near the infested plant. The flies, attracted by the yellow color, will go to the card and stick to it.

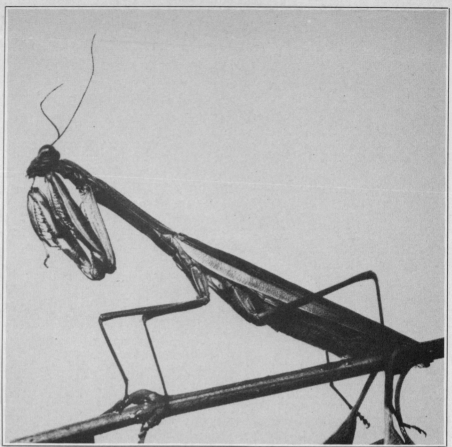

Organic Control, Inc. *Praying mantis*

Magazine for organic living

Organic Gardening and Farming. A monthly publication concerning itself with all aspects of organic gardening and living. Includes periodic pieces on greenhouses and indoor planting, such as greenhouse construction, growing vegetables in the greenhouse, raising and using herbs, and advice on growing houseplants. Subscription rates are $6.85 for 1 year and $12.25 for 2 years. For further information and subscriptions, write *Organic Gardening and Farming,* 33 E. Minor St., Emmaus, Pennsylvania 18049.

Removing garden stains

Stains on your hands are easily removed, plus your hands are softened by using the following method: First, wash your hands in cold water; follow by rubbing with a mixture of 1 teaspoon sugar, 1 teaspoon lemon juice, and 1 teaspoon vegetable or olive oil.

Learn more about seaweed

Seaweed has been used for many years as medicine, in human nutrition, as fertilizer, and as feed for livestock. Today, more and more people are researching and studying its benefits. An interesting book is available which recounts seaweed's history plus how to use it for growing plants. *Seaweed in Horticulture and Agriculture,* by W.A. Stephenson, 1968, paperback, 240 pages, is available by sending $5.50 to Maxicrop, U.S.A., Box 964, Arlington Heights, Illinois 60006.

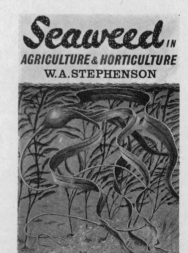

Photographing plants

Photographs of your indoor plants make original decorations, unusual holiday greeting cards, form a record of each houseplant, and provide visual illustration in programs and articles for plant societies. You can learn to take clear, correctly exposed and artistically pleasing photographs in color with a few hours of reading and practice with several rolls of film.

Equipment

Most indoor plants present a total area of interest less than 12 inches square. This means that your camera must be able to focus close. In addition, you should be able to view directly through the lens to precisely judge composition, depth of field, and spatial relationships. You can do all this with a single-lens reflex camera. Viewfinder cameras, especially the inexpensive types such as Instamatics, do a fine job with landscapes and big shrubs, but they are not the best cameras for close-up photography.

Single-lens reflex cameras are made by many different manufacturers. Most suitable are 35mm or 120 roll film cameras that provide 20 or 36 pictures per roll of film. Some of the best known are Canon, Hasselblad, Leicaflex, Nikon, and Minolta. Prices range from a low of about $150.00 for a camera with normal lens to over $1,000.00 for versatile professional level equipment. Close focusing is done by adding screw-in close-up lenses to the normal lens, by placing extension tubes between the lens and camera body, or by using a special close-focusing macro lens.

Modern single-lens reflex cameras have built-in, behind-the-lens meters which measure available light. Some offer an automatic mode, but I suggest using the camera in manual so you have full control of exposure. This gives best results with variations in background brightness and subjects which are white or very dark.

Two controls, the shutter speed and the f/stop (lens opening), determine exposure. Film sensitivity to light (film speed), expressed in an ASA number, determines how much exposure is required. For example, the best color slide film for true colors and fine grain is Kodachrome with an ASA of 25 or 64 – a relatively slow or insensitive film. The faster slide films are rated at ASA 160 to 500, much more sensitive to light, but with less perfect rendition of color, more grain showing in enlargements. In between are negative color films which have an ASA of 80 to 400. These yield negatives from which prints are usually made at the time of processing.

If you want slides, select a film type ending in *chrome* (Kodachrome or Ektachrome). If you want mainly prints, select Kodacolor or Fujicolor. Slides can later be made from negatives, and prints may also be made from slides if required later. My favorite is Kodachrome 25, exposed with electronic flash for indoor plant photos.

Lights

The easiest light source to use is the sun or photoflood lamps because your camera meter can read the intensity directly. Put your camera on a sturdy tripod to permit slow exposures. The smaller the camera f/stop (lens opening), the greater the depth of field (depth of acceptable sharpness). However, small f/stops require long exposures, hence the need for a tripod. Be sure the film you use is matched to your light source. The instructions packed with the film will guide you.

With electronic flash you can use small f/stops at faster speeds, usually 60th on 35mm cameras, but the actual exposure is much faster since it is determined by the flash, usually 500th to well over 1,000th of a second.

Backgrounds

Put your plant subject about 2 feet or more in front of a background of black velvet or clean blue paper unless you want the background to show. (Most backgrounds where the plants actually grow indoors only detract from the main subject.) Carefully compose the picture. You may want to diffuse direct sun through frosted plastic or fiberglass to avoid harsh shadows, or photograph by reflected light. A greenhouse with white shaded glass or fiberglass roof provides ideal soft light. Take your meter reading off a Kodak Neutral Test Card, available at good camera stores. Use white cardboard or aluminum foil as reflectors to fill in shadows.

For flash exposures, use guide numbers provided by the equipment manufacturer. Shoot a test roll and then make notes for precise results in the future. (Professionals use flash meters which cost $70.00 to over $300.00 each.) Automatic flash units can't be trusted with dark or light colored flowers until you learn to compensate for the flash behavior.

Shoot and have your roll processed within several weeks. Don't have a Christmas cactus on the same roll as summer blooming roses because colors change when films get old. When your roll is complete, send it to the best lab available, such as a regional Kodak lab. Cheaper "bargain" labs often ruin film by processing your important film in old chemicals and by careless handling.

Charles Marden Fitch

Books

Photographing Nature, Life Library of Photography, 1971, hardbound, 234 pages, $9.95. This advanced book is well illustrated and has several sections with useful information on photographing indoor plants.

Tips for Taking Flower Pictures, Kodak publication AC-39 and **Close-Up Pictures with Kodak Instamatic Cameras,** Kodak publication AB-20, give details on using simple cameras for close-ups. Kodak says: "You can obtain a copy of these pamphlets from your photo dealer or request them from Eastman Kodak Co., Photo Information Department 841, 343 State St., Rochester, New York 14650. For prompt delivery of these pamphlets, please send a self-addressed, business-size envelope with the pamphlet title and number written on the package. We will pay postage."

The Here's How Book of Photography, Eastman Kodak Co., Rochester, New York, 14650, 1971, 394 pages, $9.95. Good chapter on creative close-ups of garden flowers.

Pinching, pruning and shaping

Most house plants, if allowed to develop without restraint under natural conditions would become full-sized trees, shrubs or vines or rangy herbaceous plants. Only a very few are naturally small or compact. The challenge of pot gardening is to keep the naturally large ones at manageable size and in pleasing proportions. The basic technique for accomplishing this is pruning.

Horticultural basis of pruning

A young tree must elevate its foliage above the surrounding underbrush and into the light in order to survive. Accordingly, for the first year or so it is apt to consist of a single, leafy stem growing straight up. Many single-stemmed woody house plants are really tropical trees in this juvenile stage.

As the growing tip of the young tree extends upwards, additional leaves and ultimately branches appear at intervals along the new growth, and the older leaves lower down on the stem die and fall off. This is inevitable. Proper culture may prolong the life of a leaf, but sooner or later every fiddle-leaved fig and every rubber tree will lose its lower foliage and look leggy. At this point, pruning will induce the plant to branch earlier and oftener than it would in its natural development, thus restoring its attractiveness.

The explanation for this is the presence of lateral buds along the stem—so-called axillary buds in the niches (known as axils) where the leaf stalks join the stem, and adventitious buds scattered in between. Each of these lateral buds is capable of developing into a branch. But its development is inhibited by a hormone-like substance produced by the terminal bud at the end of the growing shoot. When the terminal bud is removed by pruning, the lateral buds, both axial and, to a lesser extent, adventitious, begin to grow, and new leaves develop along their growing shoots.

Techniques of pruning woody plants

When the terminal bud is pruned, a new growth will usually begin in one or two axillary buds immediately below the cut. This means that the cut should be made just above the height where you want the branch to appear and at a place where there is a bud to develop into a new leader—i.e., at the base of a leaf if the leaf is still attached, otherwise at a node, the swelling that marks the place where a leaf previously grew. Cuts made at axils or nodes will heal readily without dying back. An internodal cut dies back to the next node, forming an unsightly stub.

Once the branches have begun to grow, they, in turn, can be induced to develop lateral branches by pruning. Removal of the end bud of a branch has the same effect on it that removal of the terminal bud has on the stem. And the same is true of the multiple shoots of woody shrubs. Repeated pruning will produce numerous branches and twigs from which the gardener can retain those that are pleasing to the eye, cutting away and discarding the others.

Pinching

The foregoing explanation shows that the horticultural effect of pruning comes from the removal of the terminal buds. The same result can be obtained simply by pinching off the terminal buds from time to time. Pinching is particularly effective on fast-growing plants during the spring and summer, when the pinched bud is rapidly replaced.

Shaping herbaceous plants

Begonias, philodendron, geraniums, African violets, and other herbaceous plants are just as amenable to shaping by pruning and pinching as trees and shrubs. Frequent pinching during the growing season keeps them compact and encourages the multiplication of side branches. Occasional severe pruning, usually in late winter or early spring, will result in a renewal of the entire plant. When a tropical perennial is grown in the house, protected from the vicissitudes of the weather and devouring animals, there is nothing but the gardener's clippers to remove the old growth and make way for the new.

Reprinted by permission from *Garden In Your House*, by Ernesta Drinker Ballard, Harper and Row, 10 East 53rd St., New York, New York 10022, 1971, hardbound, $8.95.

Pinching back

Pinching back, which should only be done when a plant is actively growing, is simple to do. It encourages a plant to branch out, which results in a fuller, bushier shape. Some plants, such as wandering jews and coleus, will become unpleasantly leggy if not pinched regularly. Flowering plants will produce more blooms if pinched back.

To pinch back a plant, remove the growing tip of the main or side stems by cutting with a scissor or actually pinching it off with thumb and index finger. This causes the lateral (side) buds to develop.

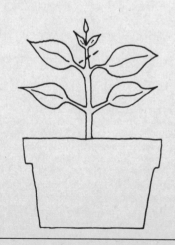
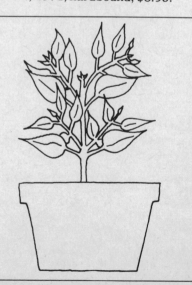

Easy topiary

You can add interest to your plant collection by training a variety of plants to grow into almost any shape. One approach involves using frames and supports that you buy or make yourself. These supports range from the simple fan-shaped trellis to circles, spheres, candelabras, and even hearts. If you decide to make one yourself, use stiff, rust-proof wire or bamboo. Solder the cross pieces together, or bind them with thinner rust-proof wire or synthetic cord.

To make sure the support is well-anchored and to avoid injuring the roots, insert the support in the pot before potting the plant. As the plant grows, it will climb and cling to the support (some may need coaxing and tying).

The best plants to use are climbers and trailers such as grape ivy, Swedish ivy, English ivy, wandering jew, philodendron, wax plant, bougainvillea, fuschia, creeping fig, and velvet plant.

Fancy plants

The second approach to indoor topiary is growing plants in wire mesh forms that actually take the place of the usual pot. These, too, may be bought ready-made or you can construct them from chicken wire. This method allows for even greater design possibilities. You can have a menagerie of green living animals, a fleet of airplanes, or even your name.

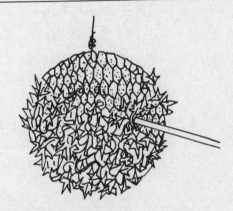

2. Then, using plenty of patience and a thin stick, stuff the form with moist sphagnum moss by forcing small pieces through the spaces in the wire. If you want to disguise the wire, cover it with a layer of damp, uncut moss, securing the moss lengths with rust-proof wire. Next, pry open a hole in the moss with the stick and insert the roots of a plant. Use young ferns for simple forms; rooted ivy cuttings work for all shapes.

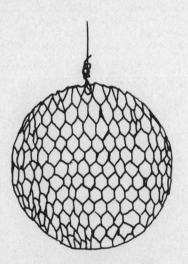

1. First buy or construct the shape you want. Use wire snips for cutting, your hands for forming and shaping, and pieces of rust-proof wire for securing. Add a length of wire at top for hanging.

3. If you use ivy, don't attempt to cover the entire shape at this time. As the cuttings grow, pin down the new shoots with lengths of rust-proof wire bent into a hairpin shape.

4. Mist your topiary daily. Water it by immersing it in a sink or bucket of water for at least five minutes; let drain and return it to its hanging place. Feed the plant every two or three weeks by adding fertilizer to the water.

Controlling growth by root pruning

A plant, especially a woody one, will keep growing forever if you put it in a larger pot each time you repot it. To keep such a plant from growing too large for its location, prune back the roots and stems whenever it needs repotting and then repot it in the same pot with fresh soil.

1. Remove the plant from its pot and pick out or wash out some of the old soil clinging to the roots.

2. Prune the root ball around the sides and along the bottom. Use a sharp knife to trim away ½ to 1 inch of roots, depending upon the size of the plant.

3. Repot the plant (see *Repotting*). Then prune the stems proportionately to the pruning the roots received to maintain a good balance. Water the plant thoroughly.

Books

The Complete Handbook of Pruning, edited by Roger Grounds, Macmillan Co., 866 Third Ave., New York, New York 10022, 1973, hardbound, 155 pages, $12.95. A well-illustrated book dealing with the essential questions of how, why, and when to prune. Also included are instructions for the pruning of over 250 species.

Plant Pruning in Pictures, by Montague Free, Doubleday and Co., 245 Park Ave., New York, New York 10017, 1961, 286 pages, $7.95. This book contains useful advice and techniques for pruning trees, shrubs, houseplants, vegetables, and fruits. Also instructions for producing specialized results by pruning, such as espalier and pollarding. Includes advice on insect and disease control. 320 photographs and 74 line drawings.

Pruning Handbook, Sunset Books, Lane Publishing Co., Menlo Park, California 94025, 1972, 96 pages, $2.45. This book deals with the various procedures of pruning and pruning tools. Also includes a 74 page section of different plants and a 10-page glossary.

Trained and Sculptured Plants, Handbook of the Brooklyn Botanic Garden, 1000 Washington Ave., Brooklyn, New York 11225, order No. 36, $1.75 postpaid. Well-illustrated guide book on specialized training and pruning.

Supplies & equipment

Spiral trellis makes topiary easy. The trellis is made of epoxy-coated heavy-gauge steel. Available in black, white, or green.

For information write:
Berkshire Products
219 Ninth Street
San Francisco, CA 94103

Three-dimensional frames for topiary are constructed of welded steel and will not sag or collapse even when full growth is attained. When the bodies are filled with dampened sphagnum or sheet moss and rooted cuttings or small plants are inserted, fast, uniform coverage is achieved.

For mail-order catalog, send 50 cents to:
Floral Art
Box 1985
Springfield, MA 01101

Topiary frames add a new dimension to your gardening experience. Sturdy metal frames in a variety of shapes make it easy to create your own menagerie. Included with every frame are instructions, plus suggestions of plants.

For brochure and mail-order information, write:
Topiary
41 Bering Street
Tampa, FL 33606

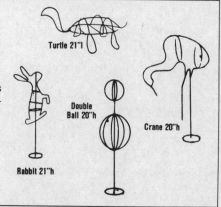

Turtle 21"l

Double Ball 20"h

Crane 20"h

Rabbit 21"h

Tulip trellises constructed of Vermont ash are durable yet handsome. Instructions are included for assembly and finishing. The 2-, 3-, or 6-foot heights will complement any climbing plant.

For brochure and mail-order information, write:
Plant Furniture
Box 94
Waitsfield, VT 05673

Plant processes

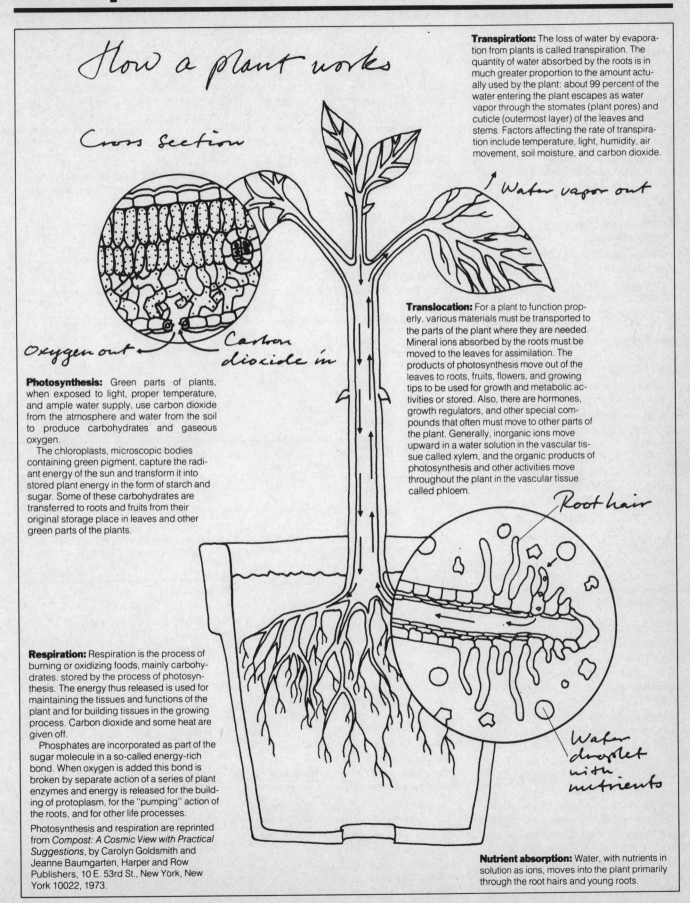

How a plant works

Cross section

Oxygen out

Carbon dioxide in

Water vapor out

Root hair

Water droplet with nutrients

Transpiration: The loss of water by evaporation from plants is called transpiration. The quantity of water absorbed by the roots is in much greater proportion to the amount actually used by the plant: about 99 percent of the water entering the plant escapes as water vapor through the stomates (plant pores) and cuticle (outermost layer) of the leaves and stems. Factors affecting the rate of transpiration include temperature, light, humidity, air movement, soil moisture, and carbon dioxide.

Translocation: For a plant to function properly, various materials must be transported to the parts of the plant where they are needed. Mineral ions absorbed by the roots must be moved to the leaves for assimilation. The products of photosynthesis move out of the leaves to roots, fruits, flowers, and growing tips to be used for growth and metabolic activities or stored. Also, there are hormones, growth regulators, and other special compounds that often must move to other parts of the plant. Generally, inorganic ions move upward in a water solution in the vascular tissue called xylem, and the organic products of photosynthesis and other activities move throughout the plant in the vascular tissue called phloem.

Photosynthesis: Green parts of plants, when exposed to light, proper temperature, and ample water supply, use carbon dioxide from the atmosphere and water from the soil to produce carbohydrates and gaseous oxygen.

The chloroplasts, microscopic bodies containing green pigment, capture the radiant energy of the sun and transform it into stored plant energy in the form of starch and sugar. Some of these carbohydrates are transferred to roots and fruits from their original storage place in leaves and other green parts of the plants.

Respiration: Respiration is the process of burning or oxidizing foods, mainly carbohydrates, stored by the process of photosynthesis. The energy thus released is used for maintaining the tissues and functions of the plant and for building tissues in the growing process. Carbon dioxide and some heat are given off.

Phosphates are incorporated as part of the sugar molecule in a so-called energy-rich bond. When oxygen is added this bond is broken by separate action of a series of plant enzymes and energy is released for the building of protoplasm, for the "pumping" action of the roots, and for other life processes.

Photosynthesis and respiration are reprinted from *Compost: A Cosmic View with Practical Suggestions*, by Carolyn Goldsmith and Jeanne Baumgarten, Harper and Row Publishers, 10 E. 53rd St., New York, New York 10022, 1973.

Nutrient absorption: Water, with nutrients in solution as ions, moves into the plant primarily through the root hairs and young roots.

Plant societies

The evolution of horticultural societies in this country is a minicapsule of American history, for the two developments easily go hand in hand.

As early colonies were established and pioneers began moving farther west, they were essentially an agrarian society concerned with developing the land, acquiring and propagating plants and seeds, and producing healthy crops; all crucial to individual survival as well as to the community's economic progress.

Means of exchanging information

Initially, communication about new ideas came through advertisements and mail-order catalogs. And the first organizations which formed in the early days were aimed at improving this dissemination of knowledge of developments in crops, foods, trees, medicinal herbs, and so forth. Essentially, the early societies provided the first trading posts for these ideas.

Emphasis on practicality dominated, and there was only sporadic mention of flowers and the more exotic and subtropical plants, though interest here picked up with new developments in heating hothouses and the increasing popularity of flowering plants.

Knowledge of agriculture, horticulture, and botany were often a measure of a man's stature and wealth. Horticultural records are dotted with names of preeminent statesmen like Benjamin Franklin and Thomas Jefferson.

European heritage

Since much of the early American society was heavily influenced by European culture and customs, it was natural such influences would be felt in horticulture. And, since many of the early horticulturists had trained in Europe and were well acquainted with the Royal Horticultural Society of London and the Jardin des Plantes in Paris, it was only a matter of time until groups sprang up here.

One of the first groups to take a specific interest in the area of horticulture was the American Philosophical Society in Philadelphia, organized in 1769 by Benjamin Franklin, who served as its first president. Although not devoted to horticulture, Franklin set the precedent at the outset for the society's keen interest in new information about plants, herbs, and trees.

The group's founding was followed by the work of numerous scientific academies, universities, museums and technical groups which published their own papers touching on various aspects of horticulture. And it was these groups which continued to provide much of the recorded knowledge in this area until well into the nineteenth century when the first, and still preeminent, horticultural societies were founded.

One of the early horticultural magazines noted the growth of societies in the nineteenth century by reporting that some fifty groups came into existence in the second part of the century as opposed to only one being formed before 1820.

While there is a note of a society being formed in New York in 1818, it languished and was virtually extinct within 15 years. In contrast, New York's group today is a very active one, with varied activities.

Societies today

Credit for being the oldest continuing society is given to the Pennsylvania Horticultural Society, which, though founded on November 20, 1827, was not officially incorporated until 1831.

Off to a quick start, the group soon sponsored the first of its renowned flower shows (one noted achievement through the years being the introduction of the poinsettia plant). Today, this active group serves the entire Delaware Valley area, and publishes a magazine for its members called *The Green Scene*.

The reputation of the Massachusetts Horticultural Society, founded March 17, 1829, is also well established through its library and many ongoing activities. Currently, the Boston-based group is the only regional society to publish a monthly magazine, *Horticulture*, which is aimed at a national audience.

While there are a number of other active local and regional societies in existence today, such as those in California, many of the stronger groups have tended to be in the East.

The only national society, the American Horticultural Society, was started in 1923 by noted horticulturist Benjamin Y. Morrison, also the first editor of the *American Horticulturist Magazine*, still published for the group's 30,000 plus members. The society is located at River Farm, once owned by George Washington and not far from his own home at Mt. Vernon, Virginia.

Officials at A.H.S. say that their organization today is no longer one geared to horticultural academicians.

"We're a lot less technical now," says one executive there.

In retrospect, there is a pattern of a gradual progression away from the scholarly and technical approaches of those early societies as they move to a more generalized gardening approach.

Ernesta Ballard, president of the Philadelphia Horticultural Society, agrees that there is a "proliferation" of organizations today. But she divides them into three groups: the social clubs with restrictive memberships, the plant societies where interests are very specialized, and the general horticultural societies.

As an A.H.S. official says of horticultural groups today: "We're trying to give out as much worthwhile and practical information and be as responsive as we can to the needs of many people from the person with a window box to the big gardener."

Penny Girard

Societies

American Horticultural Society
Mount Vernon, Virginia 22121

The American Horticultural Society was founded in 1924 and today has 30,000 members. It represents horticultural institutions, arboretums, and other plant institutions.

The purpose of the Society is to promote and encourage national interest, research, and education in horticulture and all its branches.

Membership is open to anyone interested in the Society's purposes. The dues, $15.00 per year, include subscriptions to the bimonthly magazine and the Society's award-winning newsletter. Other benefits include a free seed exchange program each spring, discounts on gardening publications, tours to spots of interest, and awards as incentives for work done in horticulture.

American Society for Horticultural Science

National Center for American Horticulture
Mount Vernon, Virginia 22121

Founded in 1903, the Society mostly serves professionals. Its objectives are to promote and encourage horticultural research and education within the United States and around the world.

Membership is open to anyone actively interested in furthering the Society's objectives. The dues start at $40.00 per year and vary according to membership category. This includes a subscription to *HortScience*, a bimonthly publication, and *Journal of American Horticulture*, published in alternate months.

Annual meetings, workshops, and elections are held to further increase the usefulness of the society.

California Horticultural Society

California Academy of Sciences
Garden Gate Park
San Francisco, California 94118

The California Horticultural Society was founded in 1932 by area gardeners who wanted to organize a society to deal with a wide range of horticultural interests. The Society is dedicated to advancing knowledge and appreciation of ornamental horticulture in California. It offers a means for members to share information and develop their skills as gardeners. The Society also promotes the introduction of lesser known plants for garden use and gives recognition to achievements in horticulture. It is geared to serve all plant enthusiasts, be they beginners or experienced professionals.

Benefits of membership in the Society include field trips to horticulturally interesting places, access to the Society's library and seed exchange program, and attending the annual society dinner. Members also receive a quarterly publication, *Pacific Horticulture*, which contains articles concerning horticulture; *The Bulletin*, which reports the Society's activities; and a biannual *Membership Roster*.

Membership is open to anyone wishing to join; the fee is $12.50 per year ($5.00 for students.)

Florida State Horticultural Society

P.O. Box 552
Lake Alfred, Florida 33850

The Florida Horticultural Society, founded in 1888, is one of the oldest organizations of its kind. It serves as an open forum where growers, processors, research workers, and many others can discuss and resolve problems of mutual concern. An organization for the advancement of Florida horticulture, the FHS compiles information and keeps members abreast of important advances in Florida horticulture. The Society's activities provide members with many practical new horticultural methods, money-saving procedures, and common-sense answers to current problems. Membership is open to anyone interested; the annual fee is $10.00 ($5.00 for students).

The Horticultural Society of New York

128 West 58 Street
New York, New York 10019

The Society was chartered in 1902 as a nonprofit organization devoted to education. Its purpose is to collect and disseminate information on all topics related to the culture and care of all plants and to stimulate knowledge and love of horticulture. Among the many privileges enjoyed by members are reduced rates on all Society programs, which include courses, lectures, flower shows and special events, horticultural tours, a circulating library, and joint programs with other botanical gardens. Members receive a monthly *Bulletin* that contains articles of horticultural interest and a *Newsletter* that keeps members abreast of Society activities. Membership is open to those who have an interest in the purposes of the Society; the annual fee is $15.00.

Kansas State Horticultural Society

Waters Hall
Kansas State University
Manhattan, Kansas 66502

Following the Civil War, many people in Kansas were interested in various phases of horticulture and felt the need of a state organization. And so, in 1867, the Kansas Horticultural Society was started. The Society's purpose is to serve the people of Kansas in promoting horticulture.

In 1963 plans were laid for ten horticultural organizations to group together. These range from a garden club association to a vegetable growers' group to a Christmas tree association. Each organization conducts its own organizational business, with the Horticultural Society acting as the voice of all. Since each organization has its own newsletter, ten different newsletters are prepared and then compiled and published by the Society. One may join one or more of these organizations with fees ranging from $3.00 to $25.00. Fees are used to maintain annual meetings and field days and to bring in outside speakers.

Massachusetts Horticultural Society

300 Massachusetts Avenue
Boston, Massachusetts 02115

The Massachusetts Horticultural Society has something for everyone—from the beginning gardener to the professional. In fact, one of its stated goals is to "offer personal assistance with whatever kind of gardening, landscaping, or conservation you're interested in." In line with this, the Society offers a wide range of classes, workshops, symposia, and excursions throughout the year (all available to members at reduced rates), and also maintains a service—The Horticultural Hotline—which offers members expert horticultural advice over the phone.

Members receive monthly copies of *Horticulture*, America's oldest gardening magazine, and of *Nasturtium*, the Society's newsletter. Other benefits include invitations to attend private showings and to visit privately owned gardens, access to the Society's famous library (which offers a mail-lending service), and discounts on garden books. The annual membership fee is $15.00.

Michigan State Horticultural Society

Jerome Hall, Jr.
Room 302, Horticulture Building
Michigan State University
East Lansing, Michigan 48824

The Michigan State Horticultural Society was founded in 1870. It was known as the Michigan Pomological Society until 1880, when it changed to its current name.

The Society seeks to encourage people to have a greater love for choice fruit products; to awaken more interest in Michigan's horticultural possibilities, and to offer growers practical suggestions along modern cultural and marketing methods.

Membership in the Society is open to any interested individuals. The annual fee is $5.00. The Society holds an annual convention and five regional meetings each year, at which an annual compilation of papers is presented as well as other selected papers.

The Pennsylvania Horticultural Society

325 Walnut Street
Philadelphia, Pennsylvania 19106

The Pennsylvania Horticultural Society, founded in 1827, is the oldest horticultural society in the United States. Its purpose is to disseminate horticultural information and promote the pursuit of the science. Currently, it has over 5,500 members.

Benefits of membership include receiving telephone assistance with indoor-plant problems, access to extensive horticultural files and the largest horticultural library in the area (books can be received by mail), free tickets to various flower shows, and a free plant each year. One can also participate in PHS trips abroad, take part in how-to workshops, and visit spots of horticultural interest. All members also receive a monthly newsletter, a 32-page bimonthly magazine—*The Green Scene*—and the annual yearbook. Membership is open to anyone interested; the fee is $15.00 per year ($7.50 for students). The Philadelphia Flower and Garden Show takes place in March.

Worcester County Horticultural Society

30 Elm Street
Worcester, Massachusetts 01608

The Worcester County Horticultural Society is an educational institution, organized to advance the knowledge and science of horticulture and related subjects. Founded in 1842, the Society has over 1,100 members. It is housed in one of the most beautiful horticultural halls in the country, where it maintains an extensive library. (The library is open to the public from 8:30 to 4 on weekdays.)

The Society sponsors exhibitions of fruits, flowers, vegetables, and gardens throughout the year. It also offers a series of lectures and educational classes on horticultural subjects and tours of gardens of interest and importance.

Membership in the Society costs $10.00 per year ($5.00 for students), and entitles one to various benefits, such as free admission to the Spring Flower Show and participation in special events at reduced rates. All members also receive the Society's bimonthly newsletter, which includes a calendar of horticultural events and activities.

Poisonous plants

If you enjoy plants, but have little children or pets around, take a few minutes to make a quick check on whether or not any of your plants may be poisonous. Surprised? Well, don't be. Some plants, and parts of others, actually do contain some damaging poisons. Although statistics are somewhat sketchy on the number and the seriousness of plant-caused poisonings, they are not to be scoffed at. The growing interest in plants, as well as the large assortment of plants available, increases the chances of such accidents occurring.

Defining poisonous

To consider a plant poisonous, it must cause severe disturbances or death when ingested. The poison may affect the digestive system, the liver or kidneys, or the nervous system. Saying that a person has been poisoned can mean anything from a stomachache to convulsions to death.

An ounce of prevention

Although the majority of plants won't pose any problems, some of the more dangerous ones are found in many homes and gardens. This should not cause undue alarm: the fact that there are poisonous plants doesn't mean that you should avoid having any of them around your home. Some have lovely foliage, flowers, and fruits. But it may mean just a little extra effort to keep them away from little fingers and mouths. A word of caution beforehand can save a lot of worries later.

Most poisonings from plants occur to children under the age of five—the same age when parents have to teach children to watch out for other dangerous things, such as cars and stoves.

Be aware of these

Looks can be deceiving. Take, for example, the common philodendron, recommended as one of the easiest plants to grow, especially for novices. The entire plant is poisonous, as is the delicate lily-of-the-valley. Another is the dieffenbachia, more commonly called the dumbcane, named because chewing its stalks or leaves can temporarily numb one's tongue.

Christmas is a time to watch because of some of the unusual and colorful plants for sale then. The bright red berries of the Jerusalem, or Christmas, cherry, which resemble small cherry tomatoes, are poisonous, as are the leaves and flowers of the azalea plant. And even the popular mistletoe can be dangerous if any of the berries go beyond the lips.

Plan ahead

Make a list of the plants you have (know the scientific names) which are dangerous, and keep it with the number of your doctor or nearest Poison Control Center. That way you or your babysitter will know the specifics. If poisoning does occur, don't induce vomiting unless the doctor tells you to. Find out from the child what he ate, how much, and how long ago.

The key to the whole issue of poisonous plants is understanding and education. Be aware of the dangers, but don't overreact and panic. Children should be brought up to enjoy plants, not fear them.

Penny Girard

Books

Deadly Harvest, by John M. Kingsbury, Holt, Rinehart, and Winston, 383 Madison Ave., New York, New York 10017, 1965, hardbound, $4.95, paperback, $1.95.

Human Poisoning from Native and Cultivated Plants, by James W. Hardin and Jay M. Arena, Duke University Press, 6697 College Station, Durham, North Carolina 27708, 1973, hardbound, $6.75.

Some poisonous plants

Name	Poisonous part
Anemone species (windflower)	all parts
Anthurium species (tailflower)	all parts
Buxus sempervirens (boxwood)	leaves
Caladium species (caladium)	all parts
Colchicum autumnale (autumn crocus)	bulb
Daphne species (daphne)	berries
Dieffenbachia species (dumbcane)	all parts
Hyacinthus orientalis (hyacinth)	bulb
Lycopersicon esculentum (tomato)	foliage
Narcissus species (daffodil)	bulb
Nerium oleander (oleander)	all parts
Philodendron species (philodendron)	all parts
Rhododendron species (azalea)	leaves, flowers
Solanum tuberosum (potato)	leaves, buds and green skin on tuber

Pots

I'm all for clay pots: some of my best friends are in them. That's not to discount plastic pots, because they've proved their worth too; they're easier to clean and sterilize (which every pot should experience, incidentally, to remove any spores or bugs left by former tenants). Plastic pots hold water longer, if you have to go away without arranging with a plant sitter. And they are cheaper, too.

But there's something about the organic warmth of a clay pot which strikes a tender note in old planter-uppers. The classic pot is porous; it breathes and it lets out moisture so the roots more quickly absorb the oxygen they need, while the moistened clay sides of the pot cool the soil. The shape allows easy removal of the plant for checking or repotting. Even the drainage hole, protected with its crocking, performs just like the plant doctor ordered. In fact, the pot shape is as near perfect in form and function as the diaper is for the baby.

Plant purists grimly cling to the proposition that a plant in a clay pot should have no distractions. They may be quite right. However, as you may have guessed when you thumb through this book, my ideas of plant parenthood stray from the straight and narrow windowsill row of pots. I believe that the addition of a sculptural container or form, whether serious or lighthearted, ceramic or wood or basket, gives any plant a dimension it can't have otherwise. For example, the two containers on the cover are old friends, but every time a new plant is put in either one of them, I experience a whole new pleasure. An Episcia cascading over a face becomes poetic; a Beaucarnea is a wild explosion of hair on the little tree trunk. It's simply a matter of lifting out one four-inch pot and inserting another to change moods.

This book is written on the premise that everything changes (even diapers have changed!) and some of these changes include using plants in fresh visual ways to give them more importance. Toss around the idea of being innovative when you clothe a new plant. Changing a baby can turn over a new leaf for Plant Parenthood.

Q. *I have been given some old clay pots from a friend's greenhouse. They have thick crusts of a kind of white mold. Is there any way to remove that?*

A. This white crust is not mold but an accumulation of fertilizer salts over the years. Soak the empty pots in a wash tray in a solution of a cup of household bleach to two gallons of water for at least eight hours. Scrub with a stiff brush, rinse and neutralize the pots by soaking for another eight hours in a solution of one cup of vinegar and two gallons of water. Wash with soap and water and dry. Any stubborn spots can be removed with a wire brush.

Q. *Why do my pots leave bleached circles on the floor? I put saucers under the pots.*

A. This is not usually leakage but rather condensation. Air space under the saucer will eliminate the problem. Three equal slices from a wine cork, about a quarter inch thick, will lift almost any saucer size and plant weight.

Q. *Clay saucers are so expensive. I wondered if there is something else I can use under my pots.*

A. Inexpensive painted metal trays (plain dark colors), old glass pie plates. You can also apply Rustoleum metal spray paint to flexible aluminum cake and pie tins which are sold in packages in supermarkets.

Q. *What can I do? My clay pots are too wide for my windowsill.*

A. Get a one-inch piece of shelving six inches wide and the length of your sill. One wood screw at each end will hold it in place (and if you're renting, you can remove the board and fill the screw holes before you leave). Cover the board with contact paper, or make a mosaic tile top if you have the urge. If there's radiator under the window, attach a wider board to deflect the rising heat.

Reprinted by permission from *Plant Parenthood*, by Maggie Baylis, 101 Productions, 834 Mission St., San Francisco, California 94103, 1975, paperback, 192 pages, $4.95.

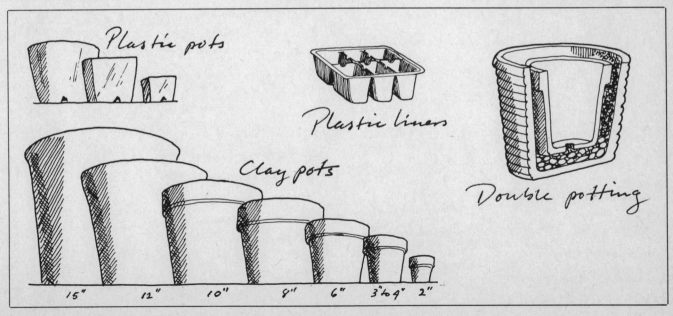

Plastic pots

Plastic liners

Clay pots

Double potting

15"   12"   10"   8"   6"   3" to 4"   2"

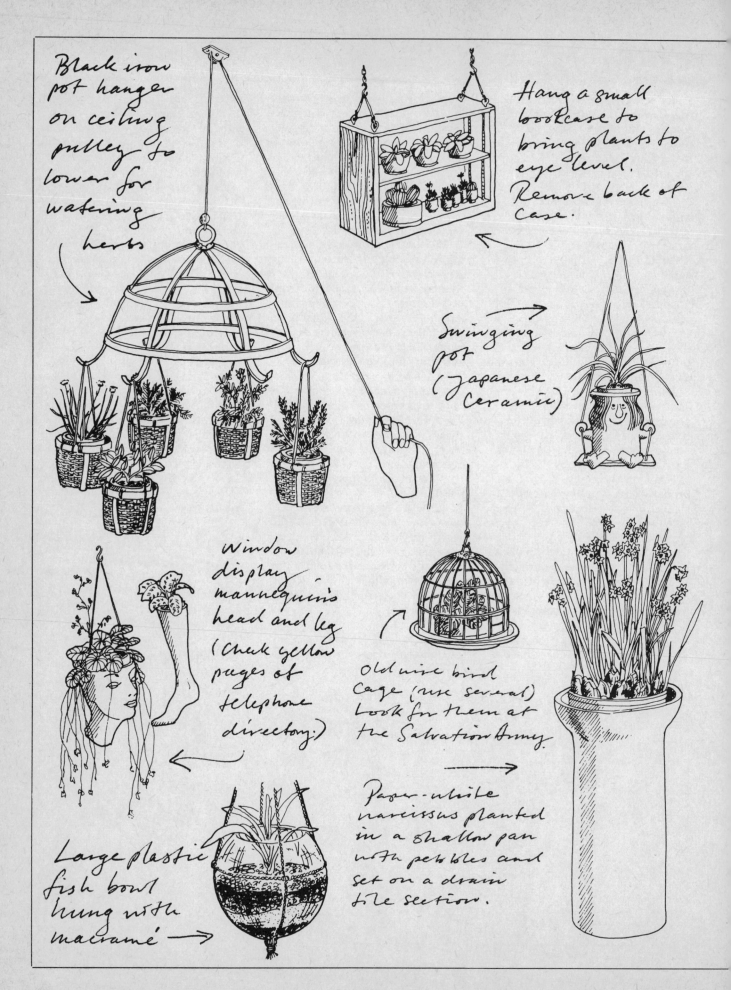

Black iron pot hanger on ceiling pulley to lower for watering herbs

Hang a small bookcase to bring plants to eye level. Remove back of case.

Swinging pot (Japanese ceramic)

Window display mannequin's head and leg (check yellow pages of telephone directory)

Old wire bird cage (use several) look for them at the Salvation Army.

Paper-white narcissus planted in a shallow pan with pebbles and set on a drain tile section.

Large plastic fish bowl hung with macramé →

Wood tub →

Drill drainage holes.

Build a plywood tray with 3/8" by 1 3/8" edges; line with fiberglass like a boat to waterproof.

Rest a nursery container on bricks to raise it in an oversize jar or basket until it is ready to be permanently potted.

Half barrel

if inside is not treated, apply cuprinol wood preservative as directed.

Soil level 1 1/2" below top

use a large pebble tray or get a pan to catch drain.

1" x 1" strips glued together →

3/8" x 1 3/8" molding to make a 12" sq. trivet →

Child's project: Clay slab box and cones →

Two play-dough bowls set one upside-down on the other for a craft project. (Recipe: 4 parts flower, 1 part salt, 1 1/2 parts water. Mix dry ingredients, add water & knead. Mold figure; bake at 300°-325° one hour or until done. Spray or brush on clear plastic finish.

Mexican clay fish pot with succulents

Line a basket with newspapers & a resin sealer to waterproof.

Supplies & equipment

Round and square pots and hanging planters are available in assorted colors, sizes and materials; magnum-size plants are available in several colors and two styles, modern and standard. A granitelike planter measures 24 inches across and weighs only 14 pounds.

For more information and free mail-order catalog (specify retail), write:
Golden Earth Enterprises
512 Lambert Road
Brea, CA 92621

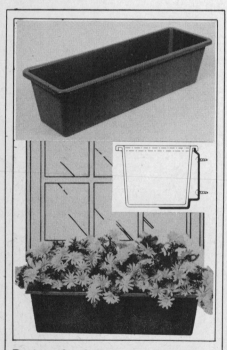

Rectangular planters for windows, walls or railings are made of fiberglass, and come in sizes ranging from 18 x 7 x 5 inches to 36 x 8 x 6 inches. Colors are white, green, black, avocado, lemon, or orange. Zinc-plated steel wall brackets are also available separately, providing support on walls or posts. They are sold at garden centers, hardware, and department stores. No mail orders.

For catalog write:
Molded Fiber Glass Tray Company
East Erie Street
Linesville, PA 16424

Planters in the round are available as 10-inch diameter pots in five heights and as 15-inch diameter pots in two heights. They are water-tight for direct planting, or can be used upside down as a display pedestal. Finished in chrome mylar, natural cork, or split bamboo.

For mail-order information write:
Wall Designs Ltd.
199 East Post Road
White Plains, NY 10601

Planters that look like weathered wood and carved clay are available in many shapes and designs for various uses. They are manufactured by Rubbermaid and are sold nationally at retail stores. No mail order.

For catalogs and buying information, write:
Rubbermaid
1147 Akron Road
Wooster, OH 44691

Breath of life pots are made of munkresite, a unique semipermeable substance. Air circulates through the plants' soil and roots; water evaporates through the pot walls, yet will not seep through the bottom to stain furniture. Made by hand, they are individually designed in a variety of sizes, colors, and shapes.

For further information write:
Breath of Life Planters
1287 66th Street
Emeryville, CA 94608

Tile-a-plants are handsome, square planters and pedestals decorated with a selection of polished metal, cork, or wood tiles. All of the planters are available in a variety of sizes. The planters are sold in various retail outlets.

For free catalog and mail-order information, write:
Metalco Industries
258 Hendricks Road
Mineola, NY 11501

177 176

Decorator planter cubes are part of the extensive lines of ready-to-assemble furniture offered by JS Permaneer. Plant directly into them, put pots in, or slip on the top piece and use them as display stands. The water-resistant cubes range from 12 to 36 inches in height and are finished in pecan vinyl veneer.

The cubes are sold in retail stores across the nation.

For free catalog sheets and buying information, write:
JS Permaneer
201 Progress Parkway
St. Louis, MO 63043

Contemporary design planters are ideal for large plants and trees. Sizes range from 14 to 48 inches. The sleek, modern design is complemented by the decorator colors available. Durable, maintenance-free construction.

For free brochure write:
Syntropics
Box 2587
Sarasota, FL 33578

185

Featherock is an unusual landscape stone. Heavy and robust in appearance, it is extremely light in weight: one-fifth the weight of ordinary stone. Color varies from silver gray to charcoal and is very easy to shape, cut, and drill. Available nationally at selected stores, building supply yards, and garden centers.

For brochure and address of nearest supplier, write:
Featherock
2890 Empire Avenue
Box 6190
Burbank, CA 91510

Versatile clear plastic containers for use as terrariums and decorative planters in several colors and shapes. The firm also features several series of distinctive planters that are made of burned copper, brass, chrome, and natural cork cubes. These items are available at department stores, nurseries, garden centers, and gift shops. No mail order.

For brochures write:
Visual Design Manufacturing Company
Box 36441
Houston, TX 77036

Natural, red clay planters and pots are available in many varied shapes and sizes. Also included are glazed, clay pots in bright colors. Stock sizes range from 3½ through 10 inches. Each pot is handcrafted and is gently packed by size in convenient inner boxes and protective master cartons.

For mail-order information write:
CDP Corporation
Box 587
Richardson, TX 75080

Gardens-in-a-can are tin cans 4¾ inches tall and 4 inches in diameter, packed with soil and seeds. Just open and follow directions. The cans are attractively labeled with a different design for each of the herbs and flowers offered. The cans are available principally in the South and West in boutiques, beauty salons, and garden centers.

For mail-order information write:
Garden-In-A-Can
11046 McCormick Street
North Hollywood, CA 19601

Potting soil

Why is soil important?

If you want your plants to stay healthy and flourish for a long time, a good soil mix at planting time is essential. Soil holds the plant upright and provides air, water, and nourishment to the root system. It should be porous enough to allow proper drainage and air and water penetration.

Ingredients of soil mixes

The following are important components in soil mixes. Whether you buy packaged soil or make your own (several recipes follow), it is helpful to know what each ingredient does. All are readily available; all are relatively inexpensive.

Compost is the residue of partially decomposed animal or vegetable matter and adds humus, the organic portion of the soil.

Sand makes soils more porous. Coarse builder's sand is used, since beach sand is too fine and salty to be useful.

Loam is good garden soil that contains a proper balance of humus, sand, and clay.

Perlite is a white, lightweight material made from volcanic rock. It contains no nutrients, but aids in drainage and aeration.

Vermiculite is a lightweight material made by expanding mica. It absorbs and holds water and dissolved nutrients, and increases drainage and aeration.

Sphagnum moss (peat moss) has a large water-holding capacity and increases acidity.

Hydrogel, a recently developed synthetic, absorbs and holds more than 20 times its weight in water. The water is released to the plant roots as needed, helping to prevent both over-watering and drying out.

Tree bark is used in soil mixes for growing orchids, bromeliads, and other epiphytes.

Composted manure is rich in humus and nutrients and is an excellent addition to soil mixes.

Packaged soil mixes

Packaged all-purpose potting soils, as well as mixtures for specific types of plants, are readily available. They are convenient and generally quite good. Some are "soilless" mixes, based on the Cornell Foliage Plant Mix and the Cornell Epiphytic Mix, which are combinations of organic and inorganic materials plus nutrients. They are generally lightweight and easy to handle.

Mixing your own

If you require a large amount of potting soil and prefer to mix your own, the following general formulas will serve as a guide. Many call for sterilized soil or loam. You can buy this or sterilize your own. To do so, spread *moist* soil in shallow pans. Bake for 30 minutes at 185°F. There may be some odor, but it will soon disappear.

Soil mixes

All-purpose potting mix
1 part sterilized soil
1 part sand or perlite
1 part sphagnum moss
1 part composted manure

Tropical plant mix
1 part sterilized soil
2 parts sphagnum moss
1 part sand or perlite

Cacti and succulents
1 part sterilized soil
1 part sphagnum moss
1 part sand
1 part gravel or perlite

Terrarium mix
2 parts composted manure or leaf mold
2 parts sphagnum moss
2 parts peat humus
1 part sand
1 part perlite

Soilless mixes

Cornell foliage plant mix
½ bushel sphagnum peat moss
¼ bushel vermiculite, No. 2
¼ bushel perlite (medium-fine grade)
8 tablespoons ground dolomitic limestone
2 tablespoons superphosphate (20% powdered)
3 tablespoons 10-10-10 fertilizer
1 tablespoon iron sulfate
1 tablespoon potassium nitrate
3 tablespoons granular wetting agent (e.g. Aqua-Gro, etc.)

Cornell epiphytic mix
⅓ bushel fir bark fine grind (⅛ to ¼ inch)
⅓ bushel sphagnum peat moss
⅓ bushel perlite (medium-fine grade)
8 tablespoons ground dolomitic limestone
6 tablespoons superphosphate (20% powdered)
3 tablespoons 10-10-10 fertilizer
1 tablespoon iron sulfate
1 tablespoon potassium nitrate
3 tablespoons granular wetting agent

David A. Pottinger

About peat moss

Peat is an organic material formed in cool, wet places such as swamps and bogs. About 40 percent of the peat produced in the United States comes from Michigan. It is used as a mulch and soil conditioner.

The two most commonly available varieties are *peat humus* (sometimes called Michigan peat) and *sphagum moss* (also called peat moss). Peat humus is dark brown or black, thoroughly decayed hypnum peat moss, and has some value as a soil conditioner. Sphagnum moss is a light-brown, very effective soil conditioner that holds a lot of water and acidifies the soil. However, it is usually sold completely dry and, when dry, is quite difficult to wet. It is advisable to thoroughly moisten sphagnum moss before mixing it with soil, and hot or warm water will penetrate the material much faster than cold water.

The importance of pH

Simplified, pH is a scale for measuring the relative acidity or alkalinity of soil, based upon the concentration of hydrogen ions. It is a logarithmic scale numbered from 1 to 14, with a pH of 7.0 being neutral, above 7.0 alkaline, and below 7.0 acid.

Various plants have been classified according to their pH requirements, and it is necessary to provide a plant with its proper soil needs to get the best results. Acid-loving plants like a soil with a 4.5 to 5.5 pH, but most other plants do best in soils that have a 5.5 to 7.2 pH.

Inexpensive soil-test kits are available to determine a particular soil's pH. These are handy, easy to use, and come with charts listing ideal pH levels of individual plants.

Adding lime will raise a soil's pH (alkalize), and adding sulphur, aluminum sulphate, or sphagnum moss will lower a soil's pH (acidify).

Supplies & equipment

Power plant is a pure organic potting soil formulated from earthworm castings and other organic nutrients. It is steam sterilized and ready for use. It will not burn plants and is perfectly balanced.

Red hybrid earthworms are used primarily for soil conditioning. Plant growers may also obtain breeder stock and raise their own earthworms. The rich humus the worms produce is a most beneficial natural fertilizer.

For literature and mail-order information, write:
Clear Creek Farms
5300 Clark Road
Paradise, CA 95969

Sifter selects finest garden soil by eliminating rocks, clods, leaves, and debris. Constructed of redwood and galvanized steel, it is lightweight and easy to use. Coarse and fine texture screens are included.

For catalog and mail-order information, write:
Gardening Goodies
Box 5081-T
Beverly Hills, CA 90210

Red hybrid worms are domesticated earthworms that have been selectively bred to be exceedingly active in breeding and feeding. These characteristics make them more beneficial to plant growth than any other type of worm. They condition and aerate the soil; in addition, their castings add nutrients.

For brochure and mail-order information, write:
Longmire's Worm Farm
Ettersburg Star Route
Garberville, CA 95440

Fertilmix potting soil is intended for use in planters, hanging baskets, and terrariums. It may also be used for starting seeds, rooting cuttings, and transplanting. Also available are soil builders such as vermiculite, peat moss, perlite, and hydrated lime. No mail order, but products can be purchased in major chain stores, hardware stores, and garden centers.

Potting materials for orchids and tropical plants are available in a complete range. Included are: seven grades of tree fern; six grades of redwood bark; four grades of Douglas fir bark; tree fern and redwood bark mixes; mixed brown and black osmunda fiber; live, long-fibered sphagnum moss; natural sheet moss; perlite; vermiculite; and terrestrial and seedling mix.

For mail-order information write:
Tropical Plant Products
1715 Silver Star Road
Box 7754
Orlando, FL 32804

The polyloam portable garden is a solid block of "synthetic" soil that can be used to grow plants without worrying about seeds or insects.

For mail-order information write:
Challenge Pacific
10633 Shadow Wood Drive
Houston, TX 77043

Milled sphagnum moss, produced from long-fibered, crude sphagnum moss and marketed under the name Nodampoff, is ideal for starting seeds. Various potting soils are also available, including a general mix and one especially made for African violets.

For more information and catalog, send 50 cents to:

Mosser Lee Company
Millston, WI 54643

Terra-lite soils, long a standard in the nursery business, have been adapted and tailored to the specific needs of home gardeners and houseplant enthusiasts. These potting soils are lightweight and premixed for convenience and ease of handling. They come in eight different formulations, and all are rich in horticultural vermiculite and Canadian sphagnum peat moss. Special mixtures are made for African violets, tomatoes and vegetables, seed starting, cacti and succulents, terrariums, and rosebushes. In addition, two all-purpose potting mixes and two soil conditioners (vermiculite and perlite) are available.

For more information and a booklet, *The Secrets in the Soil*, write:

W.R. Grace and Company
62 Wittemore Avenue
Cambridge, MA 02140

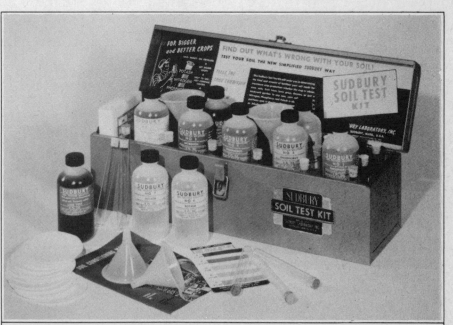

Soil-testing kits range from the elaborate and expensive Custom Portable Soil Lab, designed for professionals by Sudbury, to the more modest Home Gardener Kit, which will make approximately 70 tests for nitrogen, phosphorous, potash, and acidity levels.

Economy-size refill solutions are available for all kits.

Sold nationally in garden, hardware, and department stores. For information write:
Sudbury Laboratory, Inc.
Sudbury, MA 01776

Problems

Problem	Cause	Cure
Bruising Tips of leaves, leaf edges turn brown and die back.	Plant is being brushed against.	Cut away damaged sections of foliage, being careful to keep as much of leaf and stem intact as possible. Place plant in a location where people and pets cannot get at it.
Drainage Water remains on surface of soil after watering. Wilting, slow growth, leaves turn yellow, older leaves drop off rapidly. General deterioration of plant.	Compacted soil caused by improper soil or insufficient drainage material over drainage holes. Compressed soil does not allow oxygen to get to the roots, drying process happens too quickly.	Remove all damaged foliage. Repot plant, using proper soil for plant and providing proper amount of drainage material at bottom of pot.
Soil is constantly wet. Plant shows signs of overwatering.	Overwatering. If you have not been overwatering plant, waterlogged soil probably caused by improper drainage.	See "Watering."
Fertilizer Leaves pale bleached in color, or has yellow spots on leaves, yellowing of leaf beginning at edges and spreading over whole leaf. Older leaves drop off. Stems weak and limp. No flowering.	Too little fertilizing.	Fertilize more frequently, and especially during the growing season of the plant. Remove damaged foliage.
Yellowing of foliage at edges and over leaf. Yellow spots, crisp brown spots, scorched edges on leaves. Wilting. No flowers. Root damage.	Too much fertilizing. (Also see "Salt Damage.")	Flood soil with water and allow to drain twice. Remove fertilizer salts if accumulated on pot with warm water and a stiff brush. Remove damaged foliage. Fertilize less often or use about half as much fertilizer as you have been using.
Dark, undersized leaves, and stunted growth.	Phosphorous deficiency. (Also see "Underwatering.")	Use superphosphate to correct this.
Plant yellowish green in color. Undersides of leaves often turn purple.	Nitrogen deficiency	Use a fertilizer high in nitrogen every other feeding.
Humidity Leaf tips brown, margins of leaves yellow, no new growth or stunted growth, wilting, shriveling, buds drop off.	Too little humidity.	Place pot on bed of moist pebbles. Don't allow bottom of pot to touch water. Spray-mist leaves daily. In winter, use a humidifier.
Promotes molds and mildews, decay and rot characteristic of overwatering, soft discolored growth.	Too much humidity. Succulents and cacti are especially vulnerable.	Lower humidity, mist plant less often and ventilate plant's growing area well (avoid drafts). Move succulents away from humidity-loving plants.
Light Pale, discolored leaves, yellow foliage, tips of leaves and margins turn brown and die. No new growth, or if new growth it shrivels and dies. Older plants lose leaves from bottom up; young plants elongated, misshapen, underdeveloped leaves, inadequate branching, especially succulents and cacti. In winter, growth is soft and discolored. Variegated leaves turn solid green, yellow, drop off. Poor or no blooms.	Too little light.	Plant needs brighter exposure. If growing under artificial light, move closer to tubes, closer to center area of tubes, or the wattage must be increased, and lights remain on longer.
Scorch marks, spots on leaves that turn grayish. Plant looks bleached out. Plant might go limp, shrivel up and die if no sun is needed. Growth might be small.	Too much light.	Shield plant from light with curtain or other plants, or move it away from light source. If using artificial light, move plant farther away from center of tubes, or use lower wattage.

Problem	Cause	Cure
pH, acid and alkaline soil Discolored leaves, yellowing of leaf margins, yellow top leaves, retarded growth, no root-development.	Too alkaline soil (iron or magnesium deficiency). Plants that prefer a more acid soil (pH 5–6.5) are: shrimp plant, camellia, century plant, gardenia, citrus, palm, asparagus fern, podocarpus.	Acid fertilizers help lower the pH for acid-loving plants. Add peat and sphagnum to soil (they are acid substances but will also absorb excess acid and alkaline elements). Soil testers are available, but read the directions carefully in order to test accurately.
Pollution Brown crisp spots, yellow spots, bleached leaves, dropping leaves, soft growth, wilting, drying of foliage from base upward.	Polluted, stagnant air.	Increase ventilation around growing area. In damp weather, keep plants on dry side. Avoid excess moisture on leaves. Remove damaged foliage.
Salt damage White salts on soil, pot side, rim. Brown crisp spots on leaves, scorched leaf edges. New growth dwarfed, thick.	Too much fertilizer.	Flood the plant with water until water pours out of drainage holes. Scrape off accumulated salts from pot's rim and sides with stiff brush and warm water. Give plant more light. Fertilize less frequently or use half the amount you have been using.
Temperature Soft, discolored foliage, curled leaves, brown edges. Soft, discolored foliage. Lower leaves turn yellow with brown spots, edges of leaves dry and curl under. Foliage dies from base upward, older leaves drop off. Flowers have short life. Plants leggy, elongated, especially succulents. Yellowing leaves fall suddenly, glossy translucent tissue.	Too cool temperatures. Drafts will cause stems to rot from top down. Too warm temperatures. Sudden changes in temperature.	If plant has been severely damaged by temperature, remove from pot and check roots. If brown and soft they are rotted. Discard plant. If roots white and healthy, prune roots back to keep them in balance with the surviving top growth. Repot plant, remove damaged top growth. Keep plant away from drafts, air conditioners, radiators.
Watering Rotting, wilting, bleaching of foliage. Mass yellowing of leaves and they drop off. Leaves curl, tips turn brown, die back. Weak new growth. Flowers blight. Soil always wet. Plant stems weak, limp, wilted. Leaves curled under, lower leaves yellow with brown spots and fall off. Brown crisp spots, scorched edges on leaves and flowers. Short flowering period, flower buds drop. Dark, undersized leaves, older leaves drop off. New growth dies, and soon whole plant dies. If plant is allowed to wilt more than a few times, it might die. Cactus and succulent leaves turn yellow and shrivel.	Overwatering. These symptoms also can indicate fungus diseases, but overwatering often precedes such diseases. When overwatering reaches advanced stages, diseases occur. Improper watering or underwatering.	Remove plant from pot to check the root and also check the soil and the drainage holes to make sure they are not clogged, and check to see there is enough drainage material in the bottom of the pot. If roots white and healthy, repot plant and stir up surface soil to aerate it, or repot plant in a warm, well-ventilated area until new growth appears. Resume proper care. If roots soft, brown, and mushy, discard plant. Thoroughly soak plant at each watering. Water over entire soil surface, slowly, until excess water drains out of drainage holes. Don't let plant sit in water for more than an hour. Let plant dry out enough to meet its proper requirements between waterings. Remove damaged foliage. Cover plant with plastic bag to speed recovery. Most plants will pick up soon after watering.

Reprinted by permission from *First Aid for House Plants,* by Shirley Ross, McGraw-Hill Book Co., 1221 Avenue of the Americas, New York, New York 10020, 1976, paperback, 216 pages, $5.95.

Propagation

Propagating plants, growing new plants from already existing ones, is becoming more and more popular with indoor gardeners. The reasons for this are many. For one, it is the least expensive way of creating an extensive plant collection. For another, it is the most reliable: a plant started at home generally has a better chance of survival than does a full-grown plant that is abruptly shifted from the ideal environment of the nursery to the more rigorous environment of the home. Not least of all, it is exciting to see a leaf, a stem, or a cutting take root and flourish.

Sexual and asexual reproduction

Along with the new interest in propagating plants at home has come a new interest in *why* it works — and how.

There are two major forms of plant reproduction, sexual and asexual. In the former, the female egg cell is fertilized by the male pollen. The resulting seed bears an embryo that will grow into a plant when the right conditions for its growth are met. Asexual, or vegetative propagation, is based on a piece of a plant being able to send out roots from the cut surface.

Not surprisingly, it is asexual reproduction that has stirred the most interest in plant propagation. Outside of the realms of science fiction, only plants are capable of cloning — reproducing an exact replica of themselves from a portion as small as a leaf or stem taken from the parent plant. (Under laboratory conditions, even a single cell can be used.) For the indoor gardener, this form of propagation is also interesting because it is much quicker than growing plants from seed.

Five common methods

The following section deals with propagating plants by five such vegetative methods. Using stem or leaf cuttings is the most common. In this process, a stem or leaf is cut from the parent plant, allowed to develop roots, and then planted in its own pot. Air-layering involves cutting part of the way through a stem on a plant and allowing roots to develop *before* cutting the new plant away from the parent. Divisions and offsets are more familiar methods of plant propagation. Offsetting is used with plants such as spider plants that produce miniature replicas of themselves. Division involves unpotting a plant, dividing it into separate plants and repotting each of them. Plants that can be divided form multiple crowns at the soil level and have no central upright stem.

Guidelines

Each of these methods is suited to various plants, and the one you choose depends on the plants. Whichever methods you use, the following rules of thumb will prove helpful.

Always start from healthy plants. Although it is possible to propagate plants indoors the year round, your chances of success are better if you start either in early spring or late summer, just as new growth is starting. Never propagate when plants are in, or nearing, the dormant stage.

In addition, use a good medium for propagating. Basically, a good medium fulfills three requirements: it is able to hold moisture, yet provides good drainage and aeration. All three are essential to successful propagation. Without moisture, roots cannot develop, but without drainage and good aeration, the roots are likely to rot. The following materials are all good choices:

- Sterilized soil, sand, and peat moss (covered with a layer of sand).
- Finely ground sphagnum moss.
- Builder's-grade sand.
- Horticultural-grade vermiculite.
- Various combinations of the above.

Jill Munves

Runners, offsets, stolons, suckers, and viviparous propagation

1. Runners, offsets, and stolons are all similar in that a plantlet usually grows on an aboveground stem. These tiny plants can be cut off from the parent plant and potted or rooted in small pots while still attached to the parent.

2. Suckers are new plants that start from a root or underground stem. Break or cut off these plants, trying to keep some roots attached, and plant in the appropriate soil mix.

3. Viviparous propagation means that tiny plants form on the mature leaves of the parent. Place the leaf bearing the new plantlets on the propagating medium and keep moist until roots form.

How to multiply your plants

Reprinted from *House-plants*, Better Homes and Gardens, Meredith Corporation, 1716 Locust, Des Moines, Iowa 50336, 1971.

Leaf cutting	Root division	Stem cutting	Air-layering	Runners or offsets
African violet	Aspidistra	Christmas cactus	Croton	African violets
Gloxinia	Airplane plant	Coleus	Dieffenbachia	Airplane plant
Kalanchoe*	Boston fern	Crown of thorns	Dracaena	Apostle plant
Peperomia	Chinese evergreen	Dracaena	Fatshedera	Asparagus fern
Philodendron*	Devil's ivy	English ivy	Fiddle-leaf fig	Boston fern
Rex begonia	Echeveria	Grape-ivy	Jade plant	Bromeliads (some species)
Sansevieria	English ivy	Impatiens	Rubber plant	Orchids (some species)
Scindapsus*	Maranta	Nephthytis	-or any plant that	Pick-a-back plant
Sedum species	Pandanus	Peperomia	you can start	Strawberry saxifrage
*Cutting must include	Peperomia	Rubber plant	by means of a	-or any plant you can start
a leaf bud and leaf.	Sansevieria	Velvet plant	stem cutting.	by division

Leaf cuttings

1. Cut a mature, vigorous leaf off the plant using a sharp knife.

2. Insert the leaf at an angle into a moist propagating medium such as vermiculite, sand, or perlite. Maintain high humidity by enclosing the leaf in a plastic bag or covering it with a plastic tent. In a few weeks, roots and then small leaves will appear.

3. Instead of a sterile propagating medium, some plants, such as the African violet, can be rooted in plain water. Either place the leaf in about two inches of water in a tall glass (this adds humidity), or suspend it in a shorter glass by cutting a cardboard or aluminum foil collar.

Stem cuttings

2. Put the cutting into a container of water or moist rooting medium. More uniform rooting is attained if a rooting powder and bottom heat are used.

1. Using a sharp knife or razor blade, cut off a 3- to 6-inch tip of a plant stem. The cutting, or slip, must have at least three nodes, and the cut should be made just below one. Remove the flower buds, flowers, and lower leaves.

3. Maintain high humidity by using one of the propagating units available, or by placing the rooting container in a clear plastic bag. Don't let the plastic touch the leaves. Transplant cuttings when a good root system has developed.

Division

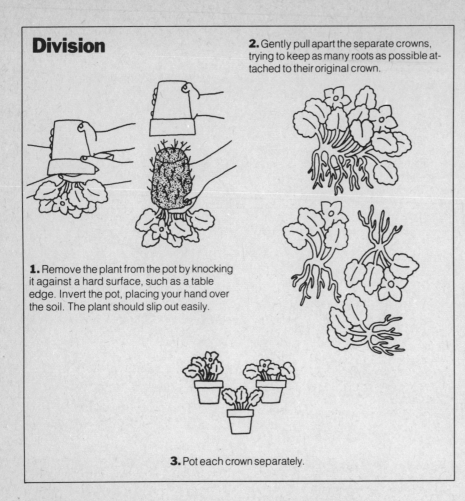

2. Gently pull apart the separate crowns, trying to keep as many roots as possible attached to their original crown.

1. Remove the plant from the pot by knocking it against a hard surface, such as a table edge. Invert the pot, placing your hand over the soil. The plant should slip out easily.

3. Pot each crown separately.

Air layering

1. Using a sharp knife, cut three-quarters of the way through the stem at a 45-degree angle, just below a node and at the height you want the new plant to be. Sprinkle the cut with rooting powder; to keep the cut from healing shut, insert a toothpick.

2. Wrap wet sphagnum moss around the cut, followed by a piece of plastic. Tie at the bottom and top with string or wire twists. Check periodically to be sure that the moss is still moist. If not, add more water with a kitchen baster.

3. When the roots become 2 or 3 inches long, cut the stem all the way through, just below the roots. Leave the tender new roots wrapped in moss and handle carefully when potting.

Books

New Plants from Old, by Charles M. Evans, Random House, 201 E. 50th St., New York, New York 10022, 1976, 118 pages, hardbound, $8.95, paperback, $4.95.

Plant Propagation: Principles and Practices, by Hudson T. Hartmann and Dale E. Kester, Prentice-Hall, Englewood Cliffs, New Jersey, 1975, hardbound, 702 pages, $17.25. A complete text written by two University of California professors. Deals with every facet of plant propagation. Included are chapters on plant nomenclature, soil mixtures for propagation, and different techniques used in propagation. There are also sections on grafting and budding and tissue culture.

Plants from Plants — The Secrets of Propagating More Than 60 Different Kinds of Houseplants for Next to Nothing, by Suzanne Crayson, J. B. Lippincott Co., E. Washington Square, Philadelphia, Pennsylvania 19105, 1976, paperback, 120 pages, $5.95. The art of creating new plants from already existing ones. Included is advice on equipment, preparing your supplies, and different methods of propagation with instructions on caring for your propagated plant. In addition, there is an 88-page section on the propagation of specific plants, listed alphabetically from African violet to wandering jew. With over 60 illustrations.

Propagating House Plants, by Arno and Irene Nehrling, Hearthside Press, 445 Northern Blvd., Great Neck, New York 11021, 1971, hardbound, $7.95; Bantam Books, 666 Fifth Ave., New York, New York 10019, 1976, paperback, $1.95. Detailed step-by-step guide on propagating indoor plants with advice on keeping your propagated plants healthy and growing. Indispensable.

Supplies & equipment

Astral dome mini greenhouse is 100 percent clear Plexiglas. The two-piece unit is 15 inches long and comes complete with a heating device and specially formulated soil that is suitable for plantings, seed propagation, rootings, and cuttings.

For free brochures and buying information, write:

**Cal-Mil Plastic Products
6100 Lowder Lane
Carlsbad, CA 92008**

Plant propagator lets you root cuttings and grow plants from seed in a controlled environment. A uniform 70- to 75-degree-F. temperature is thermostatically controlled. Humidity, soil warmth, and oxygen can also be controlled. It comes complete with see-through dome, twelve 2-inch plastic pots, vinyl edging for direct planting, and an instruction booklet. One-year warranty.

For information write:

**Kaz
614 West 49th Street
New York, NY 10019**

Offshoot and **sprout** are hanging containers designed to hold plant cuttings or flowers. Made of clear plastic, they are approximately 3 inches in diameter and come with 4 feet of monofilament for hanging.

For information write:

**Opus
437 Boylston Street
Boston, MA 02116**

Electric seed starter comes complete with planting box, a 12-foot electric heating cable, plastic cover sheet, and supports. It provides a constant 70-degree F. growing temperature, accelerating seed germination and helping to produce healthy plants. The unit weighs 1½ pounds and provides 3 square feet of growing space. Available nationwide, mainly through seed catalogs.

Electric soil cable can be "planted" in a window box. With its preset, automatic soil thermostat, it will maintain a uniform temperature of 70 degrees F. Both are available nationwide in chain and other retail stores.

For mail-order information write:

**Plantabbs Corporation
Timonium, MD 21093**

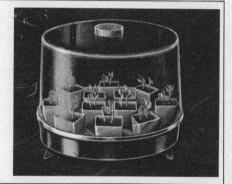

The electric green house is a miniature greenhouse that maintains an even temperature of 75 degrees F., and can be used for incubating seedlings and cuttings. The plastic unit measures 17 by 12½ inches and is vented to control condensation.

For information write:

**Berkshire Products
219 Ninth Street
San Francisco, CA 94103**

Airlayer grow-kit contains everything you need to perform this centuries-old method of plant propagation. Directions are included. The kit can also be used for rooting cuttings, as described on the instruction sheet.

For information and catalog, send 50 cents to:

**Mosser Lee Company
Millston, WI 54643**

Hormex rooting powder is available in six formulas of increasing strengths. These ensure successful rooting of all types of plants, from the easy-to-propagate to the extremely-difficult-to-propagate. The powders are sold in nurseries, garden centers, flower shops, and department stores.

For information write:

**Brooker Chemical Corporation
Box 9335
North Hollywood, CA 91609**

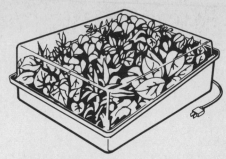

The greenery is a miniature greenhouse, measuring 25 x 15 x 12 inches. Made of high-impact plastic, it is ideal for rooting cuttings and starting seeds. The Greenery has a removable roof and sides for easy-to-use accessibility; adjustable roof vents for climate control; and a reservoir tray for watering. Available in retail outlets.

For catalog, prices, and direct ordering, write:
Mr. Chain
1805 Larchwood Street
Troy MI 48084

Heated seed starter kits come complete with special seed-starting soil. Heating elements are embedded in their plastic trays.

Heated sash bed consists of a plastic tray and a clear plastic hood, with an electric heating cable and automatic thermostat molded into its base.

Soil warming cable with hermetically sealed, automatic thermostat comes in lengths from 12 to 60 feet.

Soil warming mat utilizes the same cable and thermostat, bonded to nylon mesh.

All products sold nationally at garden centers, hardware, chain, and department stores. No mail order. For free catalog write:
Easy Heat Lawn and Garden Products
U.S. 20 East
New Carlisle, IN 46552

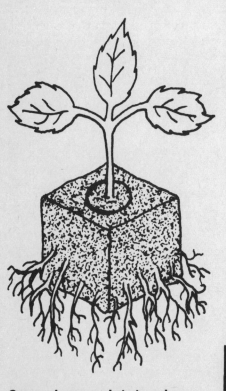

Seed-starter cubes, seaweed-based, and called Sea-Gro, contain natural seaweed nutrients. Trace elements and vitamins are completely organic, non-toxic, and improve germination.

Free catalog is available. Also booklets: *The Good Earth Can Do You Dirt* (25 cents) and *The Organic Supplement* (50 cents). For information write:
Sudbury Laboratory
572 Dutton Road
Sudbury, MA 01776

Super solo-gro seed-starter cubes are made of a special combination of peat, arcil-lite, and seaweed, a formulation especially suited to germination and seedling growth. The soil structure provides good drainage and allows oxygen to reach the roots for healthier plants and better root systems.

For mail-order information write:
Hy-Trous Corporation
3 Green Street
Woburn, MA 01801

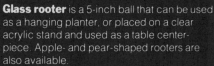

Glass rooter is a 5-inch ball that can be used as a hanging planter, or placed on a clear acrylic stand and used as a table center-piece. Apple- and pear-shaped rooters are also available.

For catalog send 25 cents to:
Vermont Crafts Market
West Hill, Box 17
Putney, VT 05346

Bo-kay seed flats are suitable for green-house and indoor use. Made of fiberglass, they resist mildew, mold, plant-feeding chem-icals, and humidity. Sizes range from 21½ x 11 x 2½ inches to 24½ x 21⅛ x 2 11/16 inches. The slotted bottom allows moisture and drainage control during seed germi-nation and plant growth. Available at garden centers, hardware and department stores, nurseries, and chains. No mail order.

For free catalog write:
Molded Fiber Glass Tray Company
East Erie Street
Linesville, PA 16424

Repotting

The first rule of repotting is: do it only if really necessary. Slight under-potting rarely harms a plant, but over-potting often contributes to root rot. A small root system is simply unable to absorb all the moisture held by a large quantity of soil.

When roots start growing out of drainage holes or appear suddenly on the soil surface, or if the plant appears to be slowly rising out of its pot, it's time to take a look at root space. Other symptoms of a need for a larger pot may be soil that seems to dry out un-usually fast, a feeling of hardness when the soil is touched, or general debility that is not easily explained by any other cause.

To find out for sure, place your fin-gers around the main stem of the plant, and turn the plant and pot up-side down. If the plant starts to fall out, it is probably not too tightly potted. If it resists falling out, rap the pot rim on a counter edge and tug slightly at the upside-down plant until the soil ball comes loose. Only if the soil ball is covered with roots, and they appear to be wrapping round and round, is it time to consider a larger pot. The preferred season to repot is when the plant is in rapid growth. Young plants may need repotting each spring or even twice during the spring-summer season.

Plants that have reached adult size, on the other hand, don't crowd their pots with roots nearly so quickly. Their preference most springs may be for the old topsoil to be scraped off with a spoon and replaced by fresh. Only very infrequently will they need a few outer roots pruned (be sure to prune the plant's foliage proportion-ately) followed by placement in a fresh bed of soil in the same size pot as before.

When repotting is definitely called for, start by choosing a new pot 1 to 2 inches larger in diameter than the present pot. Gather potting soil, drain-age material (broken pot pieces or gravel), and plastic screen (available at hardware stores) if desired for covering drain holes.

The object is to transfer the plant with as little shock to its system as pos-sible. Prepare the new pot by soaking it (if clay) in warm water, covering the drain hole with screen or a broken pot piece, and adding a thin layer of drain-age material covered by a thin layer of moist soil mix.

Remove the plant from the old pot, and with fingers gently pull off and discard easily detachable old soil mix and drainage material. If roots are very tangled, loosen a bit with fingers or pointed stick, but try not to break them.

Place the plant in the new con-tainer and fill in with soil so that the plant is at the same height in the new pot as it was in the old. Tamp soil light-ly with fingers, water thoroughly with lukewarm water (some people like to add very weak fertilizer or transplant-ing solution), and drain.

Set the plant in a warm, indirectly lighted spot for a week or 10 days; then move to its regular position. Either mist frequently at first, or cover with a plastic bag until roots have established themselves and foliage feels firm.

Wendy Schrock Dreyzin

Removing a plant from its pot

1. Water the plant slightly an hour before you plan to remove it from the pot. Using one hand to support the plant and the soil surface, and the other to hold the pot, invert the plant and its pot. Knock the rim of the pot sharply on the edge of a bench or table to release the plant.

2. Pull the pot up and away. The soil and roots will slide out intact. (If they do not, care-fully run a clean knife between the pot and the soil.) Roots that have filled the pot and are visible outside the soil are a sign that the plant has outgrown its pot and should be replanted in a larger one. If the roots are not yet visible, use the same size pot for repotting.

Repotting

Make sure the pot you use is clean. If you are reusing an old pot, scrub it to remove any soil or deposits. An unglazed clay pot, old or new, should be soaked overnight in water to pre-vent it from absorbing the moisture in the pot-ting soil, causing it to dry out too quickly.

1. Place a piece of broken clay pot over the drainage hole. If the pot is 6 inches or larger in diameter, add a 1-inch layer of drainage material such as pebbles, gravel, or more pieces of broken pot. Pour in a layer of moist potting mixture.

2. Remove the plant from its old pot and gently work loose and discard as much of the old soil as possible. Center the plant on the layer of soil. In pots up to 5 inches in diame-ter, the root ball should be ½ inch below the rim of the pot. In larger pots, leave 1 inch. Fill in the sides with more potting soil until it reaches the top of the root ball. Tamp the soil down gently to secure the plant. This will also remove air pockets which would cause the water to drain through too quickly, bypassing the roots. Water the plant thoroughly; then set it in a shady place for a few days before mov-ing it to its permanent location.

Seed starting

The world of horticulture is full of miracles. Perhaps the most wondrous event lies dormant, often in a particle no larger than a speck of dust. For every seed, no matter how large or small, is a potential plant.

Everything's provided for

A plant seed is the result of the union of male and female cells; when a plant is propagated from seed, it is a form of sexual reproduction. All seeds are basically the same in spite of the tremendous variety in their shapes, textures, and sizes. Every seed—be it a dustlike begonia seed, a grain of rice, or a coconut—contains an embryo plant and the food to nourish it enclosed in a protective shell.

Conditions to meet

If germination is to occur, causing the tiny plant to burst out of its shell, certain conditions must be met. There must be enough moisture to soften the protective coating and cause the seed to swell, but not so much that it rots. The temperature must be at the correct level to bring the seed out of dormancy—neither so high nor so low that it gets damaged. And the seed cannot be buried so deeply that the new plant dies before it reaches the soil surface and the light it needs. Seed germinating is a tricky business, but not so tricky as it is in nature, where many more seeds die than grow into adult plants.

If you are a beginner, don't try to start seeds from your own plants, except as an experiment. Seeds often have to go through a certain period of dormancy or need special treatment before they will germinate. In most cases, you should buy seeds from a reputable nursery or other source to increase the likelihood of good results.

Supplies needed

Containers: Small seed flats, miniature greenhouses, clay, plastic, or peat pots, cottage cheese or margarine cartons, or aluminum foil loaf pans (at least 1½ inches deep) can be used. All should be provided with holes for drainage and to permit bottom watering. Self-watering pots can also be used.

Seedling mediums: Seed-starting mediums must be relatively sterile to prevent damping-off, a fungus disease that attacks young seedlings causing them to rot at soil level. Satisfactory mediums include: vermiculite; milled sphagnum moss; Jiffy Mix, or other starter mixes offered in garden supply stores or in catalogs; equal parts vermiculite, milled sphagnum moss, and perlite; equal parts vermiculite and perlite; or sterilized potting mixes lightened with perlite.

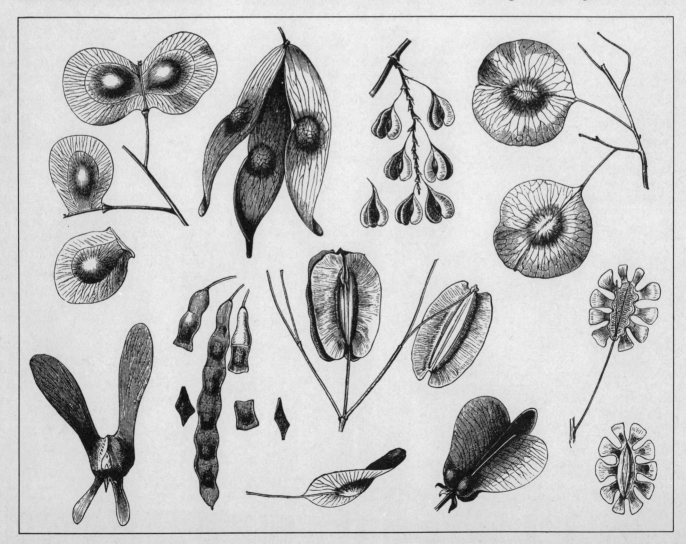

Procedure

Sowing seed: Fill container to within ½ inch of top. Do not pack tightly. Water from bottom for several hours or overnight to be sure medium is thoroughly moistened, and let drain. Label a plant stick with the name, date, and source of the seed for future reference, and insert the stick in the container.

For ease in sowing, open the packet of seed over a piece of creased white paper and let the seeds spill out. Sow thinly and evenly. Never cover fine seed with mix, but press it lightly into the medium. Barely cover seed the size of a pin head. Cover larger seed only so it cannot be seen. When seed is sown, water again from bottom or mist top. Drain and place the container in a plastic bag or cover with a tent of plastic, propping it up with plant sticks so it does not rest on the medium. If possible, temperature should be maintained at 65 to 70 degrees F. Bottom warmth can be provided by use of an inexpensive heating cable. Put in bright light but never in direct sun.

Under flourescent lights, seeds germinate well when containers are placed 6 to 10 inches from the tubes. Check daily to be sure the medium is adequately moist, for moisture is the most important factor for germination.

After germination

When the seedlings are visible, remove the plastic bag and provide strong light. Some indoor plants thrive in full sun while others need diffused light. It is important to learn the needs of individual species so they can be given the proper light and temperature for good growth. The first leaves to appear are the seedling leaves which are not typical of those of the mature plant. After a week or ten days, apply a diluted solution of a water-soluble fertilizer and continue weekly until the seedlings are large enough to be handled, usually from ¼ to ½ inch high depending upon variety. At this point lift the seedlings carefully, permitting as much of the medium to cling to roots as possible. Transplant to individual 1- or 2-inch pots, small flats or other containers, spacing them 2 inches apart each way and using a rich potting mix as a medium. When leaves touch each other, move to individual pots of sufficient size to fit the root systems. When a pot has become filled with roots, transplant to the next size pot.

Elda Haring has been gardening for thirty years, running the gamut from herbs, perennials, and annuals to vegetables, shrubs, and trees.

Flowers into seeds

Seed formation is an essential step in the survival cycle of most plants, and this process begins in the flower.

All flowers are based on one general plan. Many have succeeded in hiding their similarities by evolutionary changes, but the basic parts are there, if we look closely enough. The following illustration shows the floral organs of a typical flower:

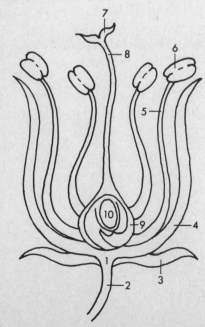

The *receptacle* (1) is attached to the plant stem by a special stalk known as the *pedicel* (2). The receptacle holds the *sepals* (3), which are collectively called the *calyx*. Occasionally sepals are brightly colored, as in tulips and lilies, but usually they are green. Sepals form a protective layer over the *petals* (4), which are usually brightly colored to form the initial attraction for insects, and are collectively called the *corolla*. Inside the corolla there are the *stamens* or male floral organs. The stamens consist of the *filament* (5) and the *anther* (6). The anther is the site of pollen formation. The female floral organ is called the *pistil* and is composed of the *stigma* (7), which receives the pollen and is held by the *style* (8), which in turn is attached to the *ovary* (9), where the *ovules* (10) or seeds develop.

Reprinted from *Seeds and Cuttings* by H. Peter Loewer, Walker and Co., 720 Fifth Ave., New York, New York 10019, 1975, hardbound, 96 pages, $6.95.

How to start seeds

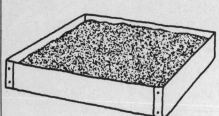
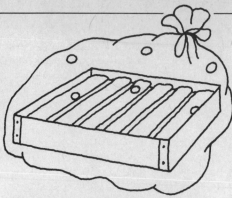
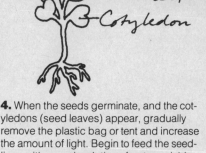

1. Fill a container such as a seed box or flat with a sterile germinating medium. Moisten the medium from the bottom.

2. Create shallow troughs in the medium and drop in the seeds. Most seeds will be easier to control if you empty the packet onto a creased sheet of clean paper. Then tap them out, one by one or a few at a time, depending on the size. Sprinkle large seeds with just enough medium to cover them. Tiny seeds shouldn't be covered at all, merely pressed gently into the damp medium. Label the seeds for future reference.

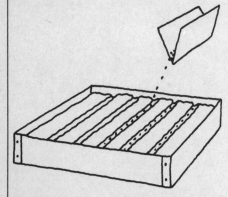

3. After sowing, water the germinating medium again, from the bottom or by misting it lightly. Be careful not to wash away any seeds. To maintain the high humidity the seeds need, cover the container with a clear plastic bag or tent. Poke a few holes in the plastic for ventilation. Place it in indirect light and keep the temperature at about 65 to 70 degrees F. (You may need a heating cable to accomplish this.) Check the moisture frequently: at least once a day.

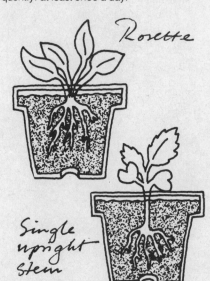

Rosette

Single upright Stem

4. When the seeds germinate, and the cotyledons (seed leaves) appear, gradually remove the plastic bag or tent and increase the amount of light. Begin to feed the seedlings with a weak solution of water-soluble fertilizer, unless you choose a growing medium which has nutrients of its own. Soon the next set of leaves, the true leaves, will appear. At this point seedlings will measure ¼ to ½ inch high, and can be transplanted.

5. Move the seedlings to individual pots, using a rich potting mix as the medium. When transplanting, avoid injuring tiny root systems. One way to avoid injury is to slice the germinating medium into cubes as you would a cake. Lift the entire cube, leaving the tiny root ball intact.

6. When transplanting, some seedlings should be planted at the same depth at which they grew in the germinating medium. This type of seedling is characterized by a rosettelike form, with all the leaves originating at the soil level. The other type has a growing point at the tip of a single upright stem. It can be planted deeper than originally, as long as the leaves are above the surface.

Books

The Complete Book of Growing Plants from Seed, by Elda Haring, Hawthorn Books, 260 Madison Ave., New York, New York 10016, 1971, 240 pages, hardcover, $8.95, paperback, $5.95. Tips for growing from the author's own notebook record of personal experiences. Includes a chapter devoted to growing houseplants from seed.

The Complete Book of Houseplants, by Charles Marden Fitch, Hawthorn Books, 260 Madison Ave., New York, New York 10016, 1972, hardbound, 308 pages, $9.95. Well-written and easily understood, the book contains a section on growing houseplants from seed.

How To Grow House Plants From Seed, by Elvin McDonald, Mason Charter, 641 Lexington Ave., New York, New York 10022, 1976, hardbound, 189 pages, $8.95. Liberally illustrated, this book gives clear and concise instructions for growing indoor plants from seed, plus information on special requirements of 200 indoor plants.

Time-Life Encyclopedia of Gardening: Flowering House Plants, by James Underwood Crockett, Time-Life Books, 777 Duke St., Alexandria, Virginia 22314, 1971, hardbound, 158 pages, $6.95. Many beautiful watercolors illustrate this book in which plants from seed are a feature.

Water, Light and Love, by Dee and Gene Milstein, Applewood Seed Co., 833 Parfet St., Lakewood, Colorado 80215, 1976, paperback, 96 pages, $3.95. This book discusses containers, planting media, germination requirements and care of seedlings. Emphasis on wildflowers, tropical plants, and culinary herbs. Special germination chart for 200 plants.

Wyman's Gardening Encyclopedia, by Donald Wyman, Macmillan Co., 866 Third Ave., New York, New York 10022, 1971, 1222 pages, $18.95. A section on growing plants from seed is included in this encyclopedia.

Supplies & equipment

The supplies and equipment described in Propagation are also ideal for starting plants from seeds indoors.

Sprouts

If you need a little prompting to start sprouting seeds in your kitchen cabinet, try chewing on these findings.

For the calorie-conscious, sprouts are an ideal addition to a menu because they are so low in calories. One cup of wheat sprouts has only eight calories, while one cup of alfalfa sprouts or sprouted mung beans has sixteen calories, and one cup of soybean sprouts has sixty-five calories.

For vitamin fans, sprouts should become an important staple in the diet because they contain all the vitamins and many of the minerals that the body needs. For example, one-half cup of 3-day-old soybean sprouts was found to contain as much Vitamin C as six glasses of orange juice.

Sprouts are easily digested because the sprouted grains and legumes contain all eight essential amino acids that make up complete protein. Sprouts are also a healthy kind of quick-energy food because the germinated seeds have a high level of simple sugars. This nutritional bounty is not only nourishing, but it is also inexpensive; sprouts cost about seven cents per pound.

Simple to do, and also good for you; give sprouting a try.

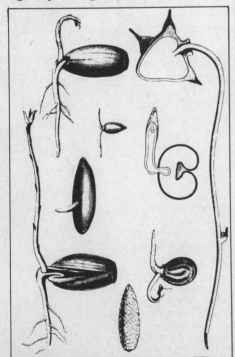

Warning
Use only seeds specifically designed for sprouting; seeds for sowing, if treated chemically, should not be used.

Sprouting methods

Jar
Almost any seed or bean (almonds, chia seeds, flax, and oats are the exceptions) can be sprouted in a jar. Choose a jar with a wide mouth and use a piece of cheesecloth secured with a rubber band for the cover. Lay the jar on its side between rinsings, with one end elevated to drain away excess water. To protect from light, cover a clear glass jar with a cloth or a paper bag, or store in a cabinet.

Commercial sprouter
To sprout several types of seeds and beans conveniently at one time, you might consider investing in a set of stackable containers. Specially made for sprouting, they are made of clear plastic, have individual compartments for each seed, and a system that eliminates daily rinsings. This type and other commercial sprouters are available at health food stores, and come with instructions.

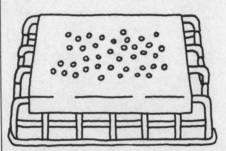

Paper towel
Seeds that require open air are best sprouted using this method; these are almonds, chia, flax, and oats. Alfalfa, buckwheat, corn, and cress can also be sprouted this way. Place a towel over an inverted wire basket or cooling rack. Arrange the layer of seeds on the towel and place another over it. In this method, the seeds are not actually rinsed, merely dampened with a spray bottle.

Flowerpot
An unglazed clay flowerpot makes a good sprouting container when coupled with two clay saucers. Alfalfa seeds are the most popular seeds to sprout in clay pots, but barley, lentils, millet, peas, soybeans, and sunflower seeds also respond well. Plug up the drainage hole with a wad of nylon netting; remove it for rinsing and draining. Tilt the pot in the bottom saucer to help excess water drain away, and cover the top with the second saucer. Do not use a glazed pot, unless you are sure the glaze contains no lead.

Seed and bean sprouting

There are basically four methods used in seed sprouting. All but one call for equipment found in most homes. The jar method is probably the most popular and is used as an example in describing the general procedure. Start with ¼ cup of seeds or beans.

General procedure: Jar method
1. Pick over the seeds or beans and remove the cracked or discolored ones; they will not sprout. Place the seeds in a jar or one of the other sprouting containers suggested. Cover the seeds with water and place the cover over the jar. Place it in a warm, dark place for 12 hours; seeds will absorb water, soften, and double in bulk.

2. Drain off the soaking liquid, which may be reserved for cooking dishes such as soups and stews. Replace the cover on the jar and make sure the seeds are only one or two layers thick and that there is plenty of room for air to circulate. Place the jar in a warm, dark place.

3. Rinse the seeds one to five times a day, depending upon the type of seed (see chart). With each rinsing, swish the water around thoroughly, then drain. Continue rinsing for three to seven days (see chart). When they are ready for harvesting, drain well. You can expose them to sunlight for several hours to further increase their nutritive value. Store sprouts in airtight containers in the refrigerator for up to one week.

Eating and cooking with sprouts

The easiest way to serve sprouts is just as they are– they make a great substitute for potato chips and other junk foods. But the cooking possibilities are almost endless, since sprouts can be used in all these dishes:

Salads: Add chopped or whole raw sprouts to green salads, potato salad, egg or tuna fish salad, tomato salad.

Desserts: Add chopped or whole raw sprouts to applesauce, fruit cups, or yogurt. A pretty, healthful dessert might consist of layers of fresh fruit slices, yogurt, and sunflower seed sprouts, topped with coconut.

Bread: Add chopped or whole raw sprouts to bread, muffin, waffle or pancake batter before baking.

Soups: A garnish of raw sprouts freshens canned soups. Add whole raw sprouts to homemade soup near the end of the cooking time.

Main dishes: Substitute raw whole sprouts for lettuce on sandwiches. Use sprouts in egg dishes such as omelets and egg foo yung. To make vegetable burgers, combine 2 cups each cooked, mashed soybean sprouts and lentil sprouts with 2 eggs, 3 slices whole wheat bread (cubed), and chopped onion, parsley, or mushrooms. Add milk to moisten (about ¼ cup), and flavor with soy sauce and herbs. Mold into patties, coat with flour, and fry until crisp.

Plant sources

Burgess Seed and Plant Company, 67 East Battle Creek Street, Galesburg, Michigan 49053. Color-illustrated catalog. Alfalfa, barley, buckwheat, mung bean, rye, wheat, lentil, pinto bean, and red kidney bean seeds are offered for sprouting. Also available is a collection of seeds for sprouting, five different seed sprouting kits, and a sprouter's cookbook.

W. Atlee Burpee, Warminster, Pennsylvania 18974; Clinton, Iowa 52732; or Riverside, California 92502. Color-illustrated catalog. Mung beans, soybeans, and garden cress seeds for sprouting are offered; also, a seed sprouter.

Henry Field Seed and Nursery Company Shenandoah, Iowa 51602. Color-illustrated catalog. Mung beans.

Johnny's Selected Seeds, Albion, Maine 04910. Catalog 50 cents (credited to first order). Organically grown adzuki and mung bean seeds.

Lakeland Nurseries, Hanover, Pennsylvania 17331. Color-illustrated catalog. Seed-sprouting kit includes three dishwasher-safe, screen tops in colorful styrene (fine, medium, and coarse sizes) and packets of alfalfa, mung bean, and wheat seeds. Refill seed packets are also available. Instructions included.

The Natural Development Company, Box 215, Bainbridge, Pennsylvania 17502. Illustrated catalog. Corn, wheat, alfalfa, mung beans, buckwheat, and large and small soybean seeds are offered for sprouting. Also, Swiss-designed seed sprouter.

Sprouting Chart

Seed or Bean	Yield (from ¼ cup dry seeds)	Sprouting time and length of root at harvest	Number of daily rinsings
Adzuki	1 c.	4 days; ¾ inch	2
Alfalfa	½ c.	3 days; 1 inch	2
Almond	½ c.	4 days; ¼ inch	3
Barley	½ c.	3 days; ½ inch	3
Buckwheat	½ c.	3 days; ½ inch	1
Chia	1 c.	3 days; ½ inch	5
Corn	1¼ c.	6 days; ½ inch	3
Cress	3 c.	3 days; 1½ inches	2
Flax	3 c.	3 days; 1½ inches	2
Lentil	½ c.	3 days; 1 inch	3
Millet	½ c.	3 days; ¼ inch	3
Mung	1 c.	3 days; 2 inches	4
Oat	½ c.	4 days; same size as seed	1
Pea	½ c.	3 days; same size as seed	3
Radish	3 c.	3 days; ¾ inch	3
Rye	½ c.	3 days; same size as seed	3
Sesame	½ c.	3 days; same size as seed	5
Soybean	¾ c.	4 days; 2 inches	5
Sunflower	½ c.	7 days; smaller than seed	2
Wheat	1 c.	3 days; ½ inch	2

Supplies & equipment

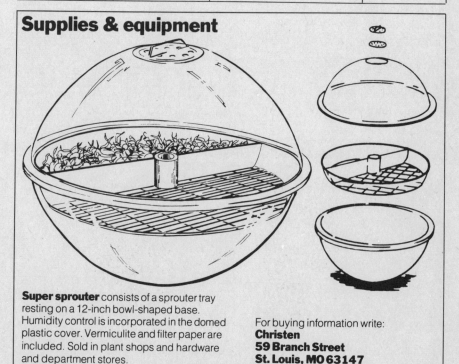

Super sprouter consists of a sprouter tray resting on a 12-inch bowl-shaped base. Humidity control is incorporated in the domed plastic cover. Vermiculite and filter paper are included. Sold in plant shops and hardware and department stores.

For buying information write:
Christen
59 Branch Street
St. Louis, MO 63147

Nichols Garden Nursery, 1190 North Pacific Highway, Albany, Oregon 97321. Catalog. Organically grown seeds for sprouting: alfalfa, red clover, peppergrass, black radish, mung bean, and lentil. The company offers a sprouting kit that includes three meshes of screens. Also available is *Sprouts To Grow And Eat* by Esther Munroe, a paperback book that tells all about sprouts and how to use them.

Geo. W. Park Seed Company, Greenwood, South Carolina 29647. Color-illustrated catalog. Mung beans.

Thompson and Morgan, Box 24, 401 Kennedy Boulevard, Somerdale, New Jersey 08083. Color-illustrated catalog. Lentil, alfalfa, alphatoco, adzuki, fenugreek, triticale, mung bean, and soybean seeds are offered for sprouting. Also available is a mixture of seeds for sprouting, the book *Sprouts To Grow And Eat*, and a seed sprouter.

Talking to plants

In the past few years something's been afoot, or rather amouth, in the plant-and-people world. Not only have people begun talking about their plants, they've also started talking to them. What's more, they're singing to them, reading to them, and buying record albums for them.

Not since Dr. Spock told us how to take care of our children have so many of us sought the advice of experts. Plant lovers are running out to buy manuals that teach them how to behave with their begonia, relate to their rhododendron, and communicate with their coleus.

Communicate. That's been the key word these past few years, and plant life has been caught right smack in the middle.

Actually, plant communication isn't that new. It began with Darwin, who played his bassoon for his *Mimosa pudica.* He complained that it didn't seem to make any difference. But then, in 1950, an Indian scientist discovered that the protoplasm of plants was affected by a tuning fork, and that movement was accelerated by a violin and a raga, a South Indian song of devotion.

It seems that it's not the music itself, but the vibrations the music makes. The same is true with talk. Or is it?

"Look, don't discuss scientific evidence with me," said one plant procurer recently. "I've got all the evidence I need in my living room." She eagerly led the skeptical guest into a plant-filled room. "Look at this dracaena," she said proudly, pointing to a lush specimen. "Every morning, I read it Ann Landers. At night, I sing it lullabies. Or maybe *Top 40* tunes. And let me tell you something—this plant is growing like the police are after it."

"Well," sighs an official at the New York Botanical Gardens—where scientific experimentation is the rule—"I think that people are running around looking for spiritual things. It's all possible, I suppose, but it's not probable."

One plant consultant in New York, William T. Wheeler, is much more positive about the possibilities. "My plants like music and they like being talked to. Energy is the key to it all. Plants have energy and they pick up energy from things like talk and music, even thoughts. When I'm away from my plants, I think about them, and they can feel my thoughts."

There is one plant doctor in Manhattan who has conducted his own experiments with plants and music and has come up with all sorts of conclusions (more plants prefer Joan Baez to The Who, for example). In fact, at least three long-playing record albums of plant music have been released.

But what is the answer? Is all the talk *just* talk?

"Look," says one skeptic. "It's all a gimmick. But if a person's going to talk to his plants, then he's going to pay attention to his plants and notice that they need water or light or whatever."

And so, the answer is that there is no answer. But look at it this way: if we think we can make plants grow and thrive by talking to them and singing to them and kissing them and giving them love, just think what we can do for each other.

Rick Mitz

Rick Mitz is a writer who types to his plants. They like it best when he writes about popular music, television, sociological phenomena and...plant life.

Supplies & equipment

Plant Serenade is a record album designed to encourage your plants with "a collection of tonal experiences." Produced by an acoustics expert who researched the use of music in stimulating plant growth, the album is available through Sunset House Catalog and Spencer Gifts Catalog.

To order the album directly, send $5.95 plus $.90 postage to:
**Jerem Productions
185 Maryland Avenue
Staten Island, NY 10305**

Environments, a recorded series of natural sounds, will help your plants grow better. Recommended titles include *Gentle Rain in a Pine Forest* and *Dawn Dusk at New Hope.* They are available in selected record shops.

For mail-order information write:
**Syntonic Research
175 Fifth Avenue
New York, NY 10010**

Galvanic skin response monitor with precise solid-state sensitivity can be used to research plant response to light, touch, heat, smoke, and sound. Powered by long-life batteries. Ninety-day warranty and full instructions.

For catalog send 50 cents to:
**Edmund Scientific Company
101 East Glouster Pike
Barrington, NJ 08007**
or
**American Science Center
5700 Northwest Highway
Chicago, IL 60646**

PlanTalker lets you listen to your plants. It is a simple, solid-state, electronic instrument that converts the minute electrical responses of plants into audible sounds. Available only from manufacturer.

For free information write:
**E.X.I.T.
Department PT
Box 201
Dracut, MA 01826**

Temperature

Temperature is almost as important for houseplants as the light requirements. Fortunately for indoor gardeners, most common houseplants thrive at normal household temperatures: up to 75 degrees F. during the day and 65 degrees F. at night. The most important single thing to remember in providing plants with the proper temperature is that, regardless of their temperature classification, all plants must have a drop in nighttime temperature. A 10-degree decrease is optimal, but even a few degrees will do. In most cases, the temperature drop that automatically occurs in all homes at night is sufficient.

There are one or two other factors that should be pointed out. Plants cannot tolerate drafts and they will die if subjected to direct heat. In most cases, solving these problems is easy. If you have plants on a draughty windowsill, add weatherstripping, storm windows, or simply tack sheet plastic over the window.

If you want to have plants on or near a radiator, put them on a thick shelf of wood or asbestos. This will adequately reduce the heat that reaches them.

A final word on temperature and the plant: If you have longed for certain plants with exacting requirements, but have avoided getting them because you thought you could not provide the proper temperature, get a portable thermometer and take a close look at temperatures in different parts of the room. Check the window first. You'll probably find that it is as much as 10 degrees cooler than the general temperature of the room. Check near the radiator, and you note a rise in temperature. With a bit of experimentation (and taking the proper precautions if you put plants near windows or radiators), you'll probably find that you can add an armload of exotic plants to your less demanding houseplants. In a word, the secret to success is less in the selection than in the placement.

Jill Munves

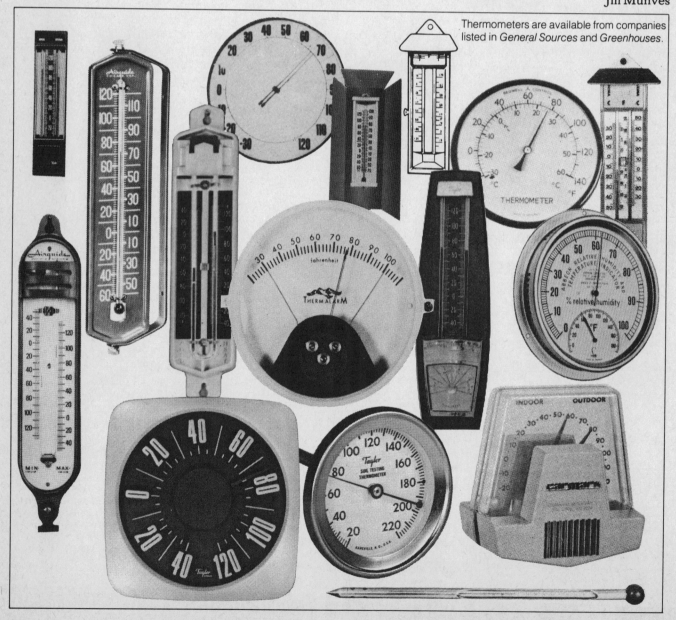

Thermometers are available from companies listed in *General Sources* and *Greenhouses*.

Terrariums

Enclosed miniature gardens, or terrariums, have had their ups and downs throughout history. Their early ancestor was the Wardian case. Dr. Nathaniel B. Ward (1791-1868) designed the case to be used by plant collectors of the period who were off to obscure corners of the world discovering plants. Dr. Ward's case ensured that at least a portion of the plants would survive the arduous journey back to Europe.

Terrariums again had a meteoric rise in popularity in recent years. Unfortunately, the meteor burned out rather quickly because of misconceptions about terrariums. Billed as the greatest thing to happen to indoor gardening since plants, people were told terrariums needed no care. All life out of its natural habitat needs at least some care and attention.

Ideal environment

By their very nature, terrariums create an ideal growing environment. The warmth and humidity provided is like a shot in the arm to plants, with the noticeable effect being the plant's rapid growth. Sometimes within weeks a terrarium will become completely overgrown. Commercially prepared terrariums are often guilty of this because fast growing, inexpensive plants are most commonly used. The logical alternative is to choose plants that are either very slow growing or are naturally small. Even then, regular pruning will be necessary to maintain the desired scale of this miniaturized world.

Pests and problems

Not only are terrarium conditions ideal for plants, but also for insect and disease pests. To ensure against this, thoroughly wash the container and rinse with a disinfectant such as Clorox, before planting; also keep terrarium tools clean. Another must is to use sterilized planting mixes. Finally, inspect all plant material prior to planting for evidence of insects and diseases. It's a good policy to treat plants with a pest control before planting. If problems show up in a completed terrarium, control measures will again have to be used. Contrary to popular belief, a terrarium is not a completely closed system. Ventilation is vital to help keep diseases in check and plants healthy. A loose-fitting lid or one that is regularly removed is essential.

Containers for terrariums can be any shape and size, as long as there is enough space for the plant's roots, plus drainage material. The most important requirement is transparency; there must be no color tint to the glass (no matter how much you'd like to use those wine jugs). But with the wealth of containers available there should be no trouble meeting the criteria. From beautifully designed leaded-glass forms to coffee tables to old fish bowls, the choices are limitless.

Plan your terrarium

Some people buy the plants first and then plan the terrarium, and others plan before selecting the plants. Whichever, be sure to plan before you plant. Terrariums may be as simple as a single, jewellike, miniature African violet or as elaborate as an entire landscape. In creating miniature landscapes, avoid crowding the plantings; create open areas, low spots, and terraced hills. Use rocks, driftwood, sand, shells, and other natural materials for special effects.

The aim in a terrarium is to establish a rain cycle; water evaporating and then precipitating. Tiny droplets of water on the side of the terrarium are natural. Water the terrarium when these droplets no longer appear and the surface of the soil shows evidence of drying. Add water in small amounts until it begins to appear in the drainage layer. Any excess water condensation on the glass should be wiped off; then remove the top for several hours.

Terrariums need bright light, but never direct sun; the heat buildup and sunburn will destroy the plants. The ideal temperature range for tropical terrariums is 65 to 75 degrees F.

Books

The Complete Book of Terrariums, by Charles Marden Fitch, Hawthorn Books, 260 Madison Ave., New York, New York 10016, 1974, hardbound, 150 pages, $8.95. Handsomely illustrated and well written by an experienced horticulturist.

Fun With Terrarium Gardening, by Virginia and George A. Elbert, Crown Publishers, One Park Ave., New York, New York 10017, 1973, paperback, $3.95. Covers the various aspects of terrarium gardening with special emphasis on using glass gardens for home decor.

Gardens in Glass Containers, by Robert C. Baur, Hearthside Press, 445 Northern Blvd., Great Neck, New York 11021, 1970, hardbound, 191 pages, $6.95. From apothecary jars to brandy snifters, fish bowls, and intricate landscapes in jugs and bottles, this book tells how to make and care for terrarium gardens easily and economically. Chapters on aquatic bottle plantings and dried arrangements under glass reflect the diversified facets of this fascinating form of indoor gardening.

Terrariums, Handbook of the Brooklyn Botanic Garden, 1000 Washington Ave., Brooklyn, New York 11225, order No. 78, $1.50 postpaid. Includes bottle and water gardens; suggests plants to choose and how to use them effectively.

The World of Terrariums, by Charles L. Wilson, Jonathan David Publishers, 68-22 Eliot Ave., Middle Village, New York 11379, 1975, hardbound, 143 pages, $14.95. Besides telling how to make and maintain terrariums, this book gives explicit information on the functional basics of gardening in glass containers — miniature worlds with self-contained climates that manufacture oxygen and moisture in a continuous cycle. Sixty-two black and white photographs, 18 color plates, 15 drawings.

Societies

The Terrarium Association, Robert C. Baur, 57 Wolfpit Ave., Norwalk, Connecticut 06851. The Terrarium Association was founded in 1974 by Robert C. Baur. It is a national organization with members in seven foreign countries.

Membership costs $7.00 per year, which includes information cards on the different kinds of terrariums and four copies of *Terrarium Topics,* a four-page newsletter written for both beginning and advanced terrarium gardeners. The Terrarium Association also provides information on where to buy terrarium plants and bottle-planting tools, how to conduct a terrarium workshop, and how to judge flower-show entries.

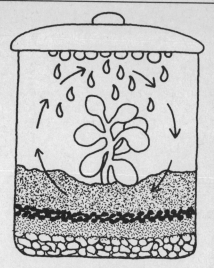

How a terrarium works

A properly assembled terrarium is an almost totally self-sufficient microclimate. Plants absorb the moisture you add to the soil through their roots and lose it through their leaves. The water condenses on the glass container, runs down the sides, and re-enters the soil to begin the rain cycle all over again. During the day, the plants absorb carbon dioxide in the air and give off oxygen in return. At night they take in the oxygen they have released during the day and give off carbon dioxide to be utilized the next day.

Basic planting techniques

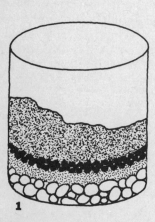

1

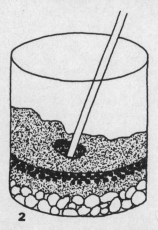

2

3

4

Whether your terrarium is a simple jelly jar with a single plant or an elaborately landscaped aquarium tank, the planting procedure is the same.

1. Start with a clean container. Pour in 1 to 2 inches of coarse sand, gravel, or small pebbles for drainage (the depth depends on the size of the container). Then add a layer of peat moss, sphagnum moss, or dead leaves. This acts as a separating layer which keeps the soil from sifting down into the drainage material. Next comes a layer of charcoal chips to sweeten the soil and keep the terrarium from smelling sour. Finally, pour in the potting soil. It should be light and loose, and slightly moist. There are special packaged terrarium potting soils available. The depth of this layer depends upon the length of the plant's roots. At this time, you can form the major hills and valleys, if any.

2. Prepare the plants for planting. You can use small rooted cuttings, or young slow-growing or miniature potted plants. Knock potted plants carefully out of their pots and remove as much of the soil from the roots as possible. With a stick or other suitable instrument, make a depression in the soil large enough for the root ball of the first plant.

3. Insert the plant and fill in the hole with soil; tamp down. Repeat the procedure for each plant, being careful not to disturb the roots of previously planted plants.

4. When all the plants are in, you can add a ground cover, like moss, if you wish, along with rocks, sticks, and other objects to complete the illusion of a miniature landscape.

Make sure the soil is damp enough and put the lid on. The terrarium should not require any additional watering for some time. Keep it in a fairly cool location that receives only indirect light. When droplets cease to appear on the sides of the container, water again lightly.

Sand layering

To brighten the base of your terrarium, add layers of colored sand before planting. Novices are advised to stay with simple layers and contours, and then progress to more realistic landscapes.

To sand layer, you will need the following supplies: fine-textured, colorfast, dyed sand (available at plant and terrarium stores and some variety stores); a spoon with the sides bent up with pliers to control the flow of sand; a knitting needle or dowel with a point; and a lazy susan (optional).

If you like, you can make a full-size sketch of your final design. Remember that the layers of sand will add height to the planting, so plan the design, the height of the container, and the plants accordingly. Make sure your container is clean and thoroughly dry; moisture upsets the flow of sand. If you have one, put the container on the lazy susan and turn it as you work to reach all sides easily.

1. Pour in drainage material, charcoal, peat moss, and potting soil as usual, but confine them to a mound in the center of the container. This core will keep the sand from slipping back into the center.

2. To make a simple design of horizontal stripes or contours, or to form the foreground of a realistic landscape, pour or spoon three to five layers of sand into the container. Pour one layer at a time, turning the container around to reach all sides. To make each layer level, give the container several brisk twists from side to side. For irregular, contoured layers, just pour each layer of sand, making some mounds higher than others.

Add more potting soil to the center as necessary, keeping it higher than the sand. When the design is complete, pour a final layer of potting soil over it, making it a part of the design.

Set the plants in the potting soil as usual, and water the terrarium sparingly.

Sandscapes
As your skill increases, try forming realistic landscapes of mountains, grass, and birds. First pour a simple, contoured base to represent the foreground.

Grass
Pour in a layer of green sand; then pour a layer of a contrasting color on top. Insert the knitting needle or pointed dowel, sliding it along the inside of the container. Poke it through the top layer and into the green layer, creating a valley into which the top sand will flow. The jagged pattern that results from repeating the process around the container resembles tufts of grass.

Mountains
To form a single mountain, pour a spoonful of sand against the side of the container. To form a mountain chain, continue pouring mountains all around the container, allowing some sand to flow down and join the mountains at their bases.

Birds in flight
Pour a layer of sky up to the height at which you want the bird to be. Pour a tiny, thin mound of bird-colored sand on top.

Poke the knitting needle or pointed dowel into the center of the mound, forming the head and wings.

Pour another layer of sky over it to hold the bird in place.

Plants for terrariums

Acorus gramineus variegatus (miniature sweet flag)
Adiantum species (maidenhair fern)
Ajuga reptans (bugle weed)
Anoectochilus sikkimensis and *roxburghii* (jewel orchids)
Asplenium platyneuron (ebony spleenwort)
Asplenum nidus (bird's nest fern)
Begonia miniatures
Boea hygroscopica (Oriental streptocarpus)
Caladium humboldtii (miniature caladium)
Calathea micans (miniature maranta)
Carex foliosissima albo-mediana (miniature variegated sedge)
Chameadorea elegans (parlor palm)
Cheilanthus gracillima (lace lip fern)
Chimaphila maculata (pipsissewa)
Cryptanthus 'It' (earth star)
Cuphea hyssopifolia (false heather)
Cyperus alternifolius gracilus (umbrella plant)
Diastema quinquevulnerum
Episcia dianthiflora (lace-flower vine)
Euonymus fortunei radicans gracilis (dwarf winter creeper)
Ficus pumila minima (miniature climbing fig)
Ficus radicans (rooting fig)
Fittonia 'Minima', *F. vershaffeltii* (nerve plant)
Fragaria virginiana (wild strawberry)
Gesneria cuneifolia (firecracker)
Gloxinia sylvatica
Goodyera repens and *pubescens* (rattlesnake plantain)
Hedera helix 'Jubilee,' 'Needlepoint,' and 'Pixie' (miniature English ivies)
Helxine soleirolii (baby's tears)
Koellikeria erinoides (dwarf bellflower)
Ludsia discolor (jewel orchid)
Malpighia coccigera (miniature holly)
Maranta leuconeura (prayer plant)
Mikania ternata (purple haze vine)
Mitchella repens (partridgeberry)
Myrsine nummularia
Myrtus communis microphylla (dwarf myrtle)
Nautilocalyx bullatus and *picturatus*
Oxalis hedysaroides rubra (firefern)
Oxalis martiana 'Aureo-reticulata' (gold-net sour clover)
Pearcea hypocyrtiflora
Pellaea rotundifolia (buttonfern)
Pellionia daveauna (trailing watermelon begonia)
Peperomia species
Petrocosmea parryorum (hidden violet)
Phinaea multiflora
Pilea depressa (miniature peperomia)
Pilea microphylla (artillery plant)
Polyscias fruticosa (Ming aralia)
Polystichum tsus-simense (tsus-sima fern)
Pteris species (brake fern)
Punica granatum nana (dwarf pomegranate)
Saintpaulia miniatures (African violet)
Saxifraga stolonifera (strawberry geranium)
Sedum lineare 'Variegatum' (carpet sedum)
Selaginella species (club moss)
Serissa foetida variegata (yellow-rim serissa)
Sinningia pusilla (miniature gloxinia)
Sinningia miniature hybrids
Smithiantha hybrids (temple bells)
Streptocarpus cynandrus and *rimicola* (miniature cape primroses)
Syagrus weddelliana (terrarium palm)
Viola species (wood violets)

Supplies & equipment

Terrariums and accessories include trapezoids, cubes, and spheres in clear plastic and attractive glass-and-ceramic mushroom and ball shapes. A three-gallon bottle has all necessary accessories including stand, soil, tools, and fill tube. Available in hardware, department, and garden stores, as well as mass-merchandising chains.

For buying information write:
**Christen
59 Branch Street
St. Louis, MO 63147**

Terrariums in several decorative shapes and sizes come equipped with astral domes and humidity controls. Transparent acrylic is used to maximize light transmission. The terrariums are washable and lightweight.

For brochures and mail-order information, write:
**Cal-Mil Plastic Products
6100 Lowder Lane
Carlsbad, CA 92008**

Sand painting kits are easy plant-enhancers and contain everything needed except the plants. Three styles are available. All kits include five bags of colored sand, special potting soil, decorative pebbles, instruction book, and container. Available at department stores, nurseries, garden centers, and gift shops.

For brochures write:
**Visual Design
6335 Skyline Drive
Houston, TX 77027**

Handblown crystal terrariums are available in an assortment of shapes and sizes. Available shapes include a bubble ball, brandy snifter, three-gallon bottle, and bell bottle (which is also suitable for a lamp base).

For brochure and buying information, write:
**Riekes-Crisa
Box 1271, Downtown Station
Omaha, NE 68101**

Pirate's chest terrarium is handmade in Mexico of glass and brass. The top is hinged at the rear for easy access. 4½ inches high by 5 inches wide by 4 inches deep.
For more information and ordering details, write:
Artisans International
St. Peters, PA 19470.

Bubble tables make perfect terrariums. The three-leg black wrought iron base is 16 inches high and holds a 24-inch Plexiglas bubble. Top it with one-quarter-inch polished plate glass or a second bubble. Either way it makes an unusual, but highly functional piece of plant-growing furniture.

For brochure and mail-order information, write:
Dilworth Manufacturing Company
Box 158
Honey Brook, PA 19344

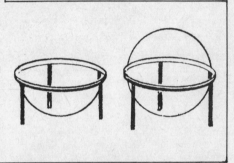

Leaded-glass terrariums made with stained glass, mean instant beauty in indoor gardens. Created with plants in mind, two styles are available: an eight-sided oval and a cathedral shape. Terrariums can be accented with shades of amber or blues and greens.

Send 25 cents for catalog to:
Vermont Crafts Market
West Hill, Box 17
Putney, VT 05346

Leaded-, stained-glass terrariums are custom made to your order in any of a dozen color combinations. All are hand-crafted in the Tiffany copper foil technique and may be ordered in antique copper or antique patina. There are both sitting and hanging styles. The hanging terrariums are supplied with 3 feet of chain and ceiling hooks.

For catalog write:
Creative Stained Glass, Ltd.
10 West Downer Place
Aurora, IL 60506

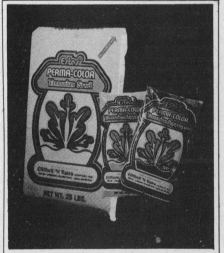

Colored mineral aggregates and sand can be used for making unusual terrariums and sand paintings. A variety of colors and package sizes are available.

For color brochure and buying information, write:
Clifford W. Estes Company
Box 105
Lyndhurst, NJ 07071

Trees

For that special place, for that corner that needs dramatic accents, or for severe interior architecture that needs softening, tree plants (sometimes called decorator or specimen plants) are the answer. And do not overlook the fact that trees can cover a multitude of sins; for example, an ugly wall or cracked plaster. Finally, the lush, green, alive feeling of a plant is always desirable indoors.

Once there were only a handful of large treelike plants for the home: *Dracaena marginata* and a few palms. Now there is an array of plants to choose from, for two reasons. Because of the sophisticated heating and cooling systems available, more and more large plants can be grown indoors. And the new houseplants that fall into the category of outdoor or field trees — for example, grevillea and bamboo — perform just as well, if not better, indoors as outdoors.

The choice for the indoor gardener is vast. There is little reason not to have the lush effect of a large tropical palm in the living room or a leafy hibiscus in the kitchen. But deciding just what plant to select, where to put it, and how to grow it may puzzle you.

What does the room need?

Because so many plants are available and some are quite expensive, consider just what conditions you can provide for the plant and where the plant will go. Each indoor tree — like an outdoor one — has a character and feeling, and you must match the tree to the place in the home. Each tree requires certain conditions in order to grow.

First, determine where the plant will go. Then consider other factors. What are the conditions in the area? Should the tree be tall or bushy? What kind of container does the tree need?

Reprinted from *Indoor Trees*, by Jack Kramer, Hawthorn Books, 260 Madison Ave., New York, New York 10016, 1975, hardbound, 164 pages, $9.95.

Trees for the living room

The palms
Caryota mitis (fishtail palm): Feathery fronds with tips like fishtails.
Chamaedorea species (parlor or bamboo palms): Soft fronds and bamboolike stems.
Chrysalidocarpus lutescens (areca palm): Airy palm fronds, fast grower.
Howeia forsteriana (kentia palm): Use as single stem or group; feathery fronds.
Phoenix roebelenii (pigmy date palm): Elegant palm with a single, stout stem.
Rhapis excelsa (lady palm): Fanlike fronds.
Rhapis humilis (rattan palm): Tall and bamboolike.

The palm look-alikes
Beaucarnea recurvata (ponytail plant): Swollen base topped with a tuft of narrow leaves.
Cordyline varieties (ti plant): Large, lush, green or variegated leaves.
Dracaena deremensis 'Warneckei' (striped dracaena): Narrow, green and white striped leaves.
Dracaena fragrans massangeana (cornstalk plant): Broad, green and yellow leaves.
Musa nana (dwarf banana): Large, broad, lush leaves.
Pandanus veitchii (variegated screw pine): Green and white swordlike leaves; fountain shape.

Repotting large plants and trees

When a plant's roots grow out of the drainage holes and appear on the soil surface, it's time to transfer it to a larger pot. Larger plants, planted in large pots, are heavy and awkward. They require special handling.

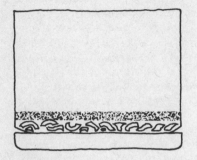

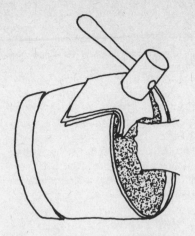

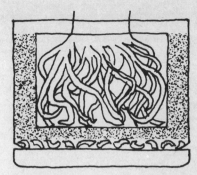

Procedure

1. Choose a new pot that is 2 inches wider and deeper than the old one. Prepare it by placing a layer of drainage material, such as clay shards from broken pots, in the bottom. Then add about 2 inches of potting mixture.

2. Water the plant to make it easier to remove from the pot. Carefully tip the pot onto its side. Then gently tap the rim with a mallet or hammer, protecting the pot with several thicknesses of newspaper or cloth. Turn the pot a bit and tap it again. This will release the soil ball from the pot.

3. Remove some of the old depleted soil from the roots and trim away any that are overly long. Set the plant in its new pot, making sure the old soil level falls about an inch below the pot's rim. (Add more soil to the bottom layer, if necessary.) Add more potting mixture around the sides, tamping it down slightly. Water the plant thoroughly, and set it in a shady place for a few days before you move it to its permanent location.

The araliads

Brassaia actinophylla (schefflera): Glossy, green, compound leaves.
Cussonia spicata (spiked cabbage tree): Long stems with giant snowflakelike leaves.
Dizygotheca elegantissima (false aralia): Airy effect; small fingerlike leaves.
Fatsia japonica (Japanese aralia): Large, deeply lobed leaves.
Pseudopanax lessonii (false panax): Leathery leaves on upright plants.
Schefflera arboricola (Hawaiian elf schefflera): Smaller leaves than the brassaia.
Tetrapanax papyriferus (rice-paper plant): Large, hand-shaped leaves.
Tupidanthus calyptratus (mallet flower): A brassaia look-alike; more adaptable and more expensive.

Some others

Abutilon x hybridum (flowering maple): Maple-like leaves and bell flowers.
Araucaria heterophylla (Norfolk Island pine): Needled evergreen with soft, drooping branches.
Bambusa multiplex (hedge bamboo): Densely clumping, tall canes.
Citrus species (orange, lemon, grapefruit): Glossy leaves and fragrant flowers.
Coccoloba uvifera (sea grape): Leathery, round leaves on an open-growing shrub.
Codiaeum variegatum pictum (croton): Large shrub with brightly variegated leaves.
Coffea arabica (coffee): Thin trunk and branches, with shiny leaves.
Dieffenbachia picta (dumbcane): Tall grower, large variegated leaves.
Ficus benjamina (weeping fig): Small, pendulous, deep green leaves.
Ficus elastica (rubber plant): Classic plant with large, thick leaves.
Ficus lyrata (fiddleleaf fig): Large plant with very large leaves.
Ficus retusa nitida (Indian laurel fig): Small leaves on large tree.
Grevillea robusta (silk oak): Skinny trunk and feathery leaves.
Jacaranda acutifolia (mimosa-leaved ebony): Lanky growth, feathery leaves; raise as a seedling.
Ligustrum lucidum 'Texanum' (waxleaf privet): Small leaves, stiff, open growth.
Mahonia lomariifolia (Chinese holly grape): Tall and dramatic; compound leaves with angular effect.
Nandina domestica (heavenly bamboo): Delicate, graceful plant, small leaves.
Persea americana (avocado): Lanky growth, large leaves.
Podocarpus macrophyllus 'Maki' (Japanese yew): Columnar form with narrow leaves.
Sparmannia africana (African linden): Big hairy leaves on bushy plant.

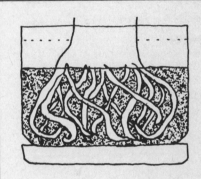

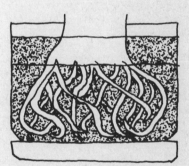

Top dressing

Some plants— trees especially— eventually grow too large to repot easily. To freshen the soil without removing the plant from its pot, scoop out the top 2 or 3 inches, and replace it with new potting soil.

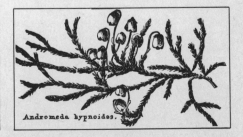

Andromeda hypnoides.

Vacations

Mini greenhouses

This method conserves water present in the soil. Water your plants thoroughly just before you leave and place them in a cool location, away from direct light. Cover them, as a group or individually, with a sheet of clear plastic to form a tent. Poke a few air holes in the tent and make sure the plastic does not come into direct contact with the foliage.

For a deluxe greenhouse, line your bathtub with bricks or stacks of newspaper. Moisten the bricks or newspaper with water, and then place the plants on top. Cover them with a sheet of clear plastic, and your plant will stay moist longer than in a mini-greenhouse.

Wick watering

This method actually allows you to water your plants while you're away. First, water the plants thoroughly and, except for hairy-leaved plants, mist the foliage. Arrange the plants around a large container of water which has been placed on a higher level than the plants. Form a wick for each plant from cotton wicking or from clothesline (wash out the sizing). You can wrap the middle portion of each wick with aluminum foil to reduce evaporation. Put one end of the wick in the water and the other in the soil of each pot.

Note: To make sure the system is working and to gauge the amount of water needed for the duration of your vacation, set it up a week or two before you plan to leave.)

There are two kinds of vacations of concern to an indoor gardener: your own trips away from home, and your plants' summer vacations. "Plants' vacations?" you may ask incredulously. Yes, some people do give their plants a vacation from their usual decorative positions. Let's consider this first.

Plant vacations

The term plant vacation doesn't mean sending them to a swank resort; it merely means setting them outdoors for the summer. While this is not essential if you lack the space or inclination, it does seem to give most plants a healthy boost. Sunshine, fresh moist air, and other natural factors encourage vigorous growth, so the extra effort involved gives you sturdier, larger, prettier plants.

Choose a cloudy day, if possible, after the weather has become warm and settled to move plants outdoors. Set them in a shady spot. While low-light plants may stay in this location all summer, you should gradually over several days move sun-lovers into brighter positions. Keep a sharp watch, however, for signs of sunburn that would call for a move back into deeper shade.

While most people simply set potted plants out onto a deck or patio, there are two possible disadvantages: they may need very frequent watering and a strong gust of wind may blow them over. For these reasons, some gardeners prefer to bury the pots up to the rims in flowerbeds. The disadvantages to this are that soil pests are encouraged to move in, and roots may grow out of drainage holes into surrounding soil unless holes are covered by screen material. If a sheltered patio spot is available, it would seem preferable.

Wherever the plants are, regular attention to watering and feeding is needed if the benefits of moving outdoors are to be gained. When it's hot and dry, even twice-a-day watering may be necessary.

When night temperatures in fall start dropping below 60 degrees F., it's time to start bringing plants back in. Each plant should be inspected for pests and treated or discarded if infested. Healthy plants can be gradually moved from sun to shade to indoors, more beautiful as a result of their outdoor holiday.

People vacations

Your own vacations away from home are no problem when houseplants are outdoors. You simply arrange for whoever is watering your outdoor garden to water the vacationing potted plants at the same time.

If your plants are indoors, you'll want to make special arrangements depending on the length of your trip. For a trip of two weeks or less, they can do without watering if you take these precautions: water all plants very well (and drain them) just before leaving, set them in a cool, indirectly lighted spot, and either cover a group with a large plastic-bag tent or cover plants and pots individually with plastic bags. Poke some small air holes in the plastic. While your plants may not love this treatment, it will keep them alive until you return.

If you travel frequently, consider investing in self-watering pots. Though expensive, they will make travel preparation easier for you and will prevent the setback to plants that frequent use of the plastic tent method might cause.

For the really long trips, hiring an experienced plant sitter is the only good solution.

Wendy Schrock Dreyzin

Vegetables

Roll over dieffenbachia, move over sansevieria, make way for a garden of vegetable delights. Fresh beets, salad greens, onions, carrots, tomatoes, cucumbers, and more can be at your fingertips when you have your own indoor vegetable garden. You need no experience, and no gardening tools other than kitchen utensils, to be able to harvest all year long. Of course, you won't be able to grow enough to keep a family of ten constantly in salad greens, but you will be able to experience a part of nature that has, up to quite recently, been denied apartment dwellers. And you need not limit your indoor vegetable patch to the ordinary; you can grow specialty and hard-to-find items that will satisfy any gourmet palate.

Light and space

A window makes a perfect vegetable garden. Most windows will accommodate at least three shelves (or two shelves and a row of hanging baskets). This adds up to space for at least twenty pots. Southern windows, which receive direct sun for a good part of the day, are best for fruit-producing vegetables such as tomatoes, beans, cucumbers, and eggplants. An eastern exposure provides low-intensity morning sun and indirect light during the rest of the day. This is the place to raise root and leafy vegetables, such as carrots, radishes, beets, and salad greens. West windows are good for almost any vegetable, since they receive light for most of the day. A northern exposure does not provide enough light for most vegetables; it must be supplemented with artificial light. If you want to invest in artificial-light fixtures, vegetables can be grown anywhere in your home. Unused corners, tabletops, bookcases, shelves, and closets can be pressed into service with the addition of fluorescent or special plant lights. Those that will grow best under artificial light are generally the leafy and root vegetables: spinach, radishes, carrots, beets, lettuce, Chinese cabbage, celery, endive, green onions, and watercress. Some fruit-bearing types may also do well, especially tomatoes and cucumbers. Others can be started under artificial light and then moved to a bright window to mature.

Window greenhouses

Another investment you might consider is a window greenhouse. This is an excellent way to expand the space in which you can grow your crop (see *Window Greenhouses*).

Containers

Let your imagination run free when choosing containers for your vegetables. You can use anything from plain terra-cotta, plastic, or styrofoam pots to coffee cans and plastic bags, or even more decorative items such as antique stoves, wheelbarrows, wagons, tubs, kettles, cookie jars, wicker baskets, and trunks. Just be sure there is adequate drainage. If there are no natural drainage holes in the container, drill or poke a few in the sides, close to the bottom, and in the bottom. You should also add a layer of drainage material such as pebbles or gravel.

Potting soil

The growing medium for indoor vegetables must be light in weight (since containers are large), porous, and have good drainage. It should also be sterile to cut down on the likelihood of insects and diseases attacking the plants. You can purchase special potting soil for container vegetable gardening, or mix you own from equal parts of coarse sand, peat moss, and commercial potting soil.

Planting

Buy seeds from reputable nurseries, and ask for varieties specially developed for indoor or container gardening. These will be called midget, miniature, dwarf or double dwarf, and they take up a minimum of room.

You can germinate the seeds in the containers in which they will be grown, in seed flats, or in tiny, biodegradable pots. Always plant more seeds than necessary (see *Seed Starting*). When they sprout, thin out seedlings, leaving the healthiest plants.

Watering and fertilizing

Vegetables require a lot of water. You may need to water some plants every day, especially the fruit-producing types growing in bright, warm windows. This frequent watering tends to wash away the nutrients in the soil, which must be replenished with fertilizer. Either add a timed-release vegetable food to the soil before planting, or use a water soluble fertilizer with a high phosphorous content. Leafy vegetables need a fertilizer high in nitrogen.

Nancy Bruning

Seed starting
Vegetable seeds can be germinated in a number of ways. The delicate seedlings require no transplanting, and so suffer no shock, if started in biodegradable pots or cubes. Plant two or three seeds per pot or cube. When they are old enough for you to determine the strongest, thin out to one plant and plant the seedling, peat pot and all, in the container you've chosen for it.

Plant sources
Seeds of vegetable varieties for growing indoors are available from many of the companies listed in *General Sources*.

Thinning
Always sow more seeds than you will need. Some seeds will not germinate at all, and some will send up smaller, weaker sprouts than others. When the seedlings have their second set of true leaves, thin out the surplus at the soil line using small scissors.

Books

Making Vegetables Grow, by Thalassa Cruso, Alfred A. Knopf, 201 E. 50th St., New York, New York 10022, 1975, hardbound, 229 pages, $8.95. Detailed book on helping people grow their own vegetables. It covers choosing a garden site, what soil is and what soil to use, the size of the garden, when and where to plant, fertilizing care, and harvesting. Included are in-depth looks at 42 different vegetables.

A Manual of Home Vegetable Gardening, by Francis C. Coulter, Dover Publications, 180 Varick St., New York, New York 10014, 1973, paperback, $6.95. An A-B-C guide for growing vegetables for backyard gardeners. The book deals with the most common vegetables and is written mainly for one who's never gardened.

The New Vegetable and Fruit Garden Book, by R. Milton Carleton, Henry Regnery Co., 180 N. Michigan Ave., Chicago, Illinois 60601, 1976, paperback, 387 pages, $5.95. A complete look at vegetable and fruit gardening for both the veteran and the beginner, including tips on new fertilizers, soil needs, tools, climate, insect and disease control. Also covers growing herbs to spice up vegetables, grapes for making wine, and fruits for desserts.

The Vegetable, Fruit and Nut Book— Secrets of the Seed by Barbara Friedlander, Grosset and Dunlap, 51 Madison Ave., New York, New York 10010, 1974, 287 pages, hardbound, $9.95, paperback, $4.95. Well-written guide to growing, buying, preparing, eating, and enjoying vegetables, fruits, and nuts. Arranged alphabetically—complete with plant-care charts, consumer and storage information. Contains illustrations, some myths, and a little poetry. Good reading.

The New York Times Book of Vegetable Gardening, by Joan Lee Faust, Quadrangle, The New York Times Book Co., 3 Park Ave., New York, New York 10016, 1975, hardbound, 282 pages, $9.95. A direct and practical approach to gardening, including many organic gardening practices left out of other books; basics which take you from seed sowing to growing and harvesting; information on cold frames, greenhouses, mulching, and weeding.

Raise Vegetables Without a Garden, by George Abraham and Katy Abraham, A.B. Morse Co., Countryside Books, 200 James St., Barrington, Illinois 60010, 1975, Illus., paperback, 88 pages, $2.95. Basically for the urban dweller who has no space for a garden, this book tells how to raise vegetables almost anywhere— i.e. containers, jars—and enjoy the same benefits a garden yields. It covers container selection, soil mix, varieties of vegetables, herbs and fruits, and freezing, canning, and preserving the harvest.

All About Vegetables, edited by Walter L. Doty, Ortho Books, Chevron Chemical Co., Ortho Div., 200 Bush St., San Francisco, California 94104, 1973, paperback, 112 pages, $3.98. This book gives a comprehensive analysis of growing vegetables, from choosing the soil to serving them on the family table. Included are planting tables, recipes, and in-depth looks at individual vegetables and herbs.

The Apartment Farmer—the hassle-free way to grow vegetables indoors, on balconies, patios, roofs and in small yards, by Duane Newcomb, J. P. Tarcher, 9110 Sunset Blvd., Los Angeles, California 90069, 1976, paperback, 154 pages, $4.95. Written for the city dweller, this book discusses the aspects of raising your own vegetable garden. Included is advice on soil, watering, and planting; tips on what vegetables will grow in the apartment environment; what equipment will be needed. There is even a chapter on growing your own gourmet vegetables, herbs, and sprouts.

Burrage on Vegetables, revised edition, by Albert C. Burrage, edited by Susan A. Hollander and Timothy Hollander, Houghton Mifflin Co., 2 Park St., Boston, Massachusetts 02107, 1975, hardbound, 224 pages, $8.95. Presents a time-tested garden plan for high yields. Includes recipes designed to make the most of garden-fresh flavor and to keep it through preserving and freezing. A step-by-step guide from planting to serving.

The Food Lovers Garden, by Angelo M. Pellegrini, Madrona Publishers, 113 Madrona Pl., East Seattle, Washington 98112, 1975, 253 pages, hardbound, $7.95, paperback, $3.95. Aimed at the city dweller and suburbanite, this book shows how to grow vegetables and herbs no matter how small your plot of land. Includes how, what, and when to plant; how to care for and harvest what you grow; and recipes for putting the end product to its best use.

The Green Thumb Book of Fruits and Vegetables, by George Abraham, Prentice-Hall, Englewood Cliffs, New Jersey 07632, 1970, hardbound, $7.95. This book gives good practical ideas for starting a vegetable garden. It includes basic information on planning and maintaining the garden, and growing an assortment of vegetables.

Quantities of vegetables to grow in 4-inch and 8-inch pots

	No. of plants in 4-inch pots	No. of plants in 8-inch pots
Looseleaf lettuce	1	2
Mustard greens	1	3
Spinach	1	2
Beets	2-4	8-20
Carrots	2-4	12-24
Green onions	4-8	16-30
Garlic	2-4	4-16
Turnips	2-4	2-16
Radishes	4-8	16-30

Reprinted from *The Apartment Farmer*, by Duane Newcomb, J. P. Tarcher, 9110 Sunset Blvd., Los Angeles, California, 1976, paperback, 154 pages, $4.95.

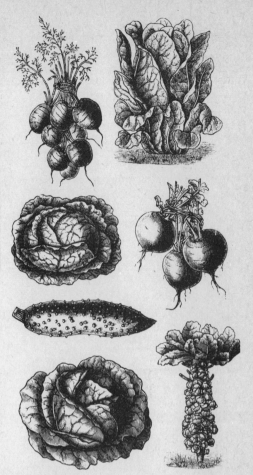

Bread-and-butter pickles

One of the pleasures of home gardening is the taste of fresh-picked vegetables all year round. You might, however, like to try your hand at pickling for a change of taste.

To make about three quarts of pickles:

    2 quarts cucumbers
    4 or more onions
    ¼ cup salt
    3 cups cider vinegar
    2½ cups sugar
    1 tablespoon mustard seed
    1 teaspoon celery seed
    ½ stick of cinnamon
    ¼ teaspoon ground cloves

Wash cucumbers and peel the onions. Cut them into very thin slices and place in a bowl. Sprinkle them with the salt and refrigerate for twelve hours or overnight.

Drain the vegetables; rinse well in cold water and drain again. Make a syrup by combining the vinegar, sugar, and spices in a saucepan. Bring to a boil; add the vegetables and bring just to a boil again.

Place the pickles in sterilized glass jars and seal them. Process in a boiling water bath for twenty minutes (consult your cookbook for detailed instructions on boiling).

Containers for indoor vegetable gardening

If you use a wooden container, such as a wooden box or wine barrel, coat the inside with asphalt paint to prevent the wood from rotting. Line wicker baskets with plastic. To prevent root rot, make sure all containers have drainage holes or a layer of drainage material (pebbles, gravel) at the bottom.

Water

If there is one phase of plant culture that is the gardener's nemesis, watering is it. Too much water will readily kill a plant, as will too little, for both conditions invariably destroy the plant's roots and, hence, its ability to maintain itself. It is no wonder then that neophyte gardeners invariably ask how often they should water their plants. Unfortunately, there is no precise answer. Not only do different plants have different water requirements, but even the same plant will need more or less frequent waterings depending on a host of other factors: the type and size of the pot, the humidity level, the type of soil used, the amount of drainage, and the light and temperature levels.

How the above factors influence watering schedules is given in a general way in the accompanying list, but the only way to know for sure when a plant needs to be watered is to observe it. Except for plants that need to be kept constantly moist, a general rule of thumb is that when the soil is beginning to dry out (the soil one inch below the surface is barely moist to the touch and the topsoil is dry), the plant needs to be watered. With a few weeks of observation, you'll have a good sense of how often your plants need watering. But remember that the schedule may change if other factors in the environment are altered.

Happily, none of the vagueness of the "how often" question beclouds the "how much" question. Whenever a plant needs watering, it must be watered thoroughly—until water drains out of the holes at the bottom of the pot. If you are using a planter without drainage holes, proceed slowly, adding a little bit of water at a time and stopping when the soil can absorb no more. Be especially careful not to overwater these plants, for there is no way to drain away the excess water without removing a lot of topsoil. If you are using a conventional pot, be sure to empty the excess water from the saucer underneath it after about thirty minutes. Allowing a plant to sit in water is just as destructive to its root system as overwatering it.

In essence, then, the mystique of watering isn't really so mysterious. It all boils down to observing your plants and using adequate water when watering is needed. Most plant lovers will find that there is one small secret for complete success. Plants cannot tolerate cold tap water. Let it sit overnight in an uncovered jar.

Jill Munves

How to water plants

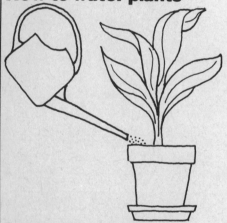
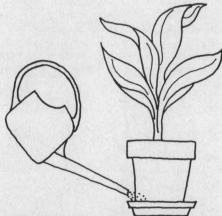

Top watering: To water plants from the top neatly and effectively, use a long-spouted watering can. Water the plant until water runs out the drainage hole. Let it stand 30 minutes, then empty excess water to prevent root rot.

Bottom watering: Fill the pot's saucer with water. When the water has been drawn up to the top of the soil through the pot's drainage hole, empty the saucer to prevent root rot.

Immersion: Immerse the pot in a large water-filled container, such as a pail or sink. When the plant is thoroughly soaked (bubbles stop rising), remove it and let it drain awhile.

Factors affecting frequency of watering

Containers: Plants in small containers and containers made of clay tend to need more frequent waterings than plants in large or plastic containers.

Soil: Plants in heavy, water-retentive soil (large proportion of peat moss) will retain water for longer periods of time than will those in a light, aerated soil (large proportion of coarse sand and perlite).

Temperature: the higher the temperature, the more water a plant will need.

Humidity: Dry air increases the frequency of needed waterings; moist air decreases it.

Light: The more light a plant is exposed to, the more water it is likely to need.

Drainage: A plant in a pot with poor drainage will need less frequent watering than one in a pot with good drainage.

Growth periods: A plant that is rapidly growing needs more water than one that is resting or in a state of dormancy.

Moisture meters

When to water is perhaps the most perplexing question that faces a plant owner. You realize that improper watering will cause a sure decline of the plant, but it's awfully hard to tell if your frequency of watering is correct.

A moisture meter can be part of your answer. While not totally reliable (the salt content of your soil can affect the meter reading), these electronic instruments are much better than guesswork at determining the wetness of the soil at various levels below the surface. You'll find a moisture meter most useful if you have big plants in large or deep pots of soil.

There are several different kinds and brands of moisture meters available. Most require small batteries, while some operate merely by chemical interaction with the moist soil. The flow of the very weak electric current thus generated (which you can't feel) is what the meter actually monitors. If no current flows, a "dry" reading is given by the meter; if current flows, a relatively "wet" reading is given, depending on the strength of the current.

One brand of moisture meter gives you a reading by means of red lights. If no lights glow when the prong is inserted into the soil, the soil is dry. One light glowing means the soil is damp, two lights that it's wet. Another brand of meter makes clicking sounds, slow clicks meaning relatively dry soil, and fast clicks that it's relatively wet. Other brands have dials or scales with needles that tell you the degree of dampness.

Moisture-light meters are a more recent development. With these, you not only know whether or not to water, but also whether or not the plant needs more light. Of course, the light meter only measures the present light; you'll have to consult a chart of plant light needs to determine whether your spot is bright enough for the particular variety you're growing.

Supplies & equipment

Water genie is a 12-inch-long cotton wick. One end is a special compressed tip, which is inserted into the flowerpot. The other end sits in a reservoir of water. Through natural capillary action, it delivers the precise amount of water needed by the plant. Depending on the size of your water container, the wick will keep plants watered properly for days or weeks without a refill. Available through retail outlets.

For mail-order information write:
Mardon Gardens
637 Quaker Road
East Aurora, NY 14052

Plant watering tools and fittings for greenhouse, indoor, and outdoor use are produced by The Dramm Company. The line includes water breaker nozzles, hose handles of varying lengths (up to 48 inches), dribble tubes and rings, special nozzles adapted to specific water pressure, multi-irrigators, and automatic watering controls. Available in garden centers, hardware, chain, and department stores. No mail order.

For information write:
The Dramm Company
Box 528
Manitowoc, WI 54220

Aqua-kane is a meter designed to measure soil moisture at root level. When the 12-inch probe is inserted to the desired depth, the meter will instantly register from dry to saturated. No batteries or maintenance required. Available at dealers in the U.S. and Canada.

For catalog and mail-order information, write:
RCF Developments
2509 Browncroft Boulevard
Rochester, NY 14625

Moist-o-meter is a moisture meter made of tough plastic and heavy brass for lifetime use. Available with 6-inch or 18-inch probes. Battery and watering information included. One year warranty. Available in garden and flower shops throughout the country.

For mail-order information write:
Karl's Enterprises
9306 Idyl Place
Lakeside, CA 92040

Environment plant-care meters promote luxuriant plant growth by eliminating over- or under-watering; too little or too much light. Sturdy construction utilizes no wires, batteries, or recharging. Large, easy-to-read dials for immediate visibility. Two models available: the Model RO-1 measures moisture only; the Model RO-2 measures both moisture and light levels.

For information write:
Environment Corporation
401 North Velasco
Houston, TX 77003

Garden angel is a portable moisture meter with a "winking" light that indicates over-watering, soil dryness, or a need for fertilizer. The battery-operated unit is marketed by Turf Service Laboratories and is sold, primarily in the western United States, in plant stores, garden centers, and hardware stores.

For brochures and mail-order information, write:
Turf Service Laboratory
11762 Western Avenue
Stanton, CA 90680

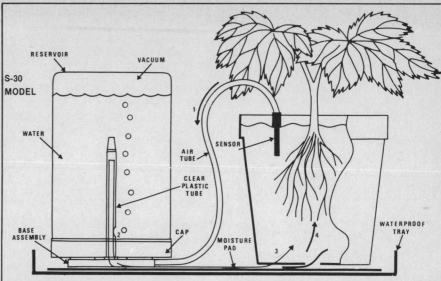

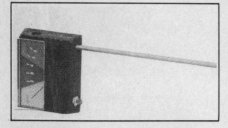

Help-a-plant is a metering device that indicates moisture levels in plant soils on a numerical dial. A deluxe model is offered which measures light as well as moisture level. A chart showing the moisture and light needs of 250 plants accompanies each unit.

For mail-order information write:
Sid Kleiner Enterprises
4121 Gail Boulevard
Naples, FL 33940

Plantenders are automatic watering systems. Each has a water reservoir operated by a unique moisture sensor that gauges the soil's water content.

Planter plantenders consist of double-walled pots, with wood-grained vinyl covering. Plants can be directly potted in these.

The hotai figurine is also a plantender made of heavy vinyl plastic; it can be used in window boxes, on trays, or with larger plants. The figurine is 10 inches high and holds 65 ounces of water. There is a smaller, plain version, holding 38 ounces of water.

The poletender is an effective and inexpensive way to water plants. It is especially effective with large foliage plants.

Black plastic plantender trays are available in three sizes, all furnished with a felt-type pad and nylon wicking. The trays can be used alone or with the figurine or plain water reservoir.

The biggest plantender (15 inches in diameter) is designed for large potted plants. The 2½-gallon reservoir saves valuable watering time. The unit can be placed in the bottom of a large 16- to 18-inch decorator pot.

To obtain brochure and mail-order information, write:
Plantamation
Millstone
Seaman, OH 45679

Houseplant water indicator monitors soil moisture level. The monitor is a 1-inch, wafer-like disc which is pink but turns blue when plant needs watering. One disc is effective for a year or longer. The monitors are available three to a package.

For mail-order information write:
3M Company, Plant Care Systems
Box 33600
St. Paul, MN 55133

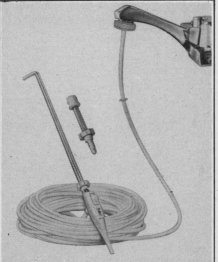

Indoor watering hose is 50 feet long and can be attached to any standard faucet. Plants can be watered with the 8-inch nozzle, which has an on-off switch. Interchangeable mist attachment, faucet adapters, and washers are included. Available generally at all types of retail outlets.

For buying information write:
Northern Electric Company
5224 North Kedzie Avenue
Chicago, IL 60625

Mister-spritzer is a 50-foot indoor watering hose and mister that provides a 100-foot watering diameter from kitchen or bathroom faucets. No tools are required. Comes complete with both kitchen and bathroom faucet adapters. The product is available nationwide through chain and hardware stores. No mail-orders.

For further information write:
Cleveland Cotton Products
Box 6895
Cleveland, OH 44101

Hydro-pot, a new type of care-free gardening container, is a pot-within-a-pot. The outer pot contains a 3-to-5-week water and food supply. The plant nested inside the inner pot draws food and water at its own rate. Available in garden centers, greenhouses, and at Sears stores.

For mail-order information write:
**Agricultural Institute of Research and Development Corporation
Box 16374
Houston, TX 77022**

Self-watering plant survival kits are available in four different models. Each kit provides special nutrients, woven glass umbilical cords, a water reservoir container, and redwood platforms.

For catalog and mail-order information, send 50 cents to:
**Alprax Enterprises, Ltd.
Rotterdam Industrial Park, Building #4
Box 2636
Schenectady, NY 12309**

The spritzer is a 24-ounce, trigger-powered sprayer for watering plants.

For mail-order information write:
**New Humor Company
Box 29033
Dallas, TX 75229**

Aquatil is a granular powder able to absorb more than 20 times its weight in water. Mixed into a plant's soil, it slowly releases water to the plant as needed. Helps prevent over- and under-watering, and increases the length of time plants can go without watering.

For 25-cent sample or mail-order information, write:
**Medpro
275 Highway 18
East Brunswick, NJ 08816**

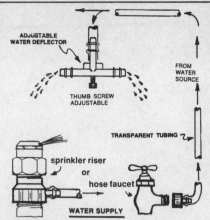

Thirst Quencher Systems specializes in indoor plant watering systems. The Thirst Quencher Hanging Basket Watering System provides simultaneous, individually controlled watering for hanging plants. Can be used with or without the system timer, which makes watering automatic. The Mini-Reel comes with 60 feet of white tubing on a reel, attaches to standard faucets, and has a no-drip wand and spray tip for misting. Model RF has a cartridge fertilizer adapter. Micro-Reel is a smaller edition of the Mini-Reel. Available at plant shops, home improvement centers, chains, and nurseries.

For free brochures and mail-order information, write:
**Thirst Quencher Systems
2440 Ridge Park Lane
Orange, CA 92667**

Aqua bellows is an expandable bottle that holds up to two quarts of water. Its long curved spout lets you water hard-to-reach plants with a minimum of bending and stretching. Another plus: it won't drip. In blue plastic.

For free brochure and mail-order information, write:
**The Magrath Company
Box 148
McCook, NB 69001**

Viterra hydrogel granules act like tiny sponges, absorbing and holding more than 20 times their weight in water. They help prevent over-watering and also keep soil from drying out. Water is released only as needed. Available in two forms: a package you can mix in with your own potting soil or as part of Burpee's Special Potting Mixture, which also includes peatmoss, perlite, vermiculite, and slow-release fertilizers.

For mail-order catalog write the Burpee headquarters nearest you:
**W. Atlee Burpee
Warminster, PA 18974**
or
Clinton, IA 52732
or
Riverside, CA 92502

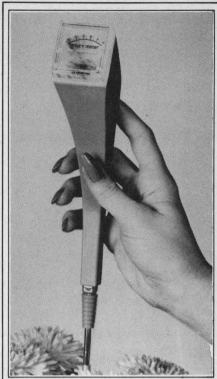

Mist'r meter is a device that measures moisture at the plant roots. The Mist'R Sun measures moisture and light. Available nationally at hardware stores, chain, and department stores.

For mail-order information write:
**Korex Industries
51 El Pueblo Drive
Scotts Valley, CA 95066**

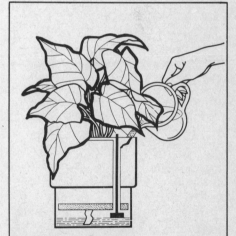

Self-watering planters prevent over- and under-watering. The units contain an internal water reservoir that is filled through a concealed funnel. The planters are sturdy and well designed, and they come in white, black, chocolate, and terracotta colors. Larger units are built with casters. Available in gift and flower shops and in department stores.

For a free catalog and mail-order information, write:
**American ESA Corporation
Box 477
Sturbridge, MA 01566**

water reservoir   air reservoir

Grosfillex is a line of self-watering indoor planters imported from France by London Garden Associates. A water reservoir in the bottom feeds water to topsoil as needed through a wick. Watering funnel (concealed inside pot) has built-in water level indicator. Planters are available in square, round, and rectangular shapes and in three colors. Larger units are equipped with castors.

For catalog and mail-order information, write:
London Garden Associates, Ltd.
Box 333
Ridgefield, CT 06877

Sav-a-plant I is a meter for testing soil moisture at root level, giving a precise numerical reading. Save-A-Plant II combines moisture and light metering. Exposing the interchangeable filters that come with the meter, you can measure not only the light intensity, but whether or not your plants are getting the right type of light. Instruction book included with each unit. Available in department and hardware stores or nurseries.

For mail-order information write:
A.M.I. Medical Electronics
116 East 27th Street
New York, NY 10016

Inplant spa is a miniature device that automatically waters plants. For use, the ceramic core base is inserted into the soil and a flexible tube is immersed in a nearby water reservoir. Available at garden centers, supermarkets, and hardware stores nationally.

For free brochure and mail-order information, write:
Edison Packaging Corporation
U.S. Highway No. 1
Edison NJ 08817

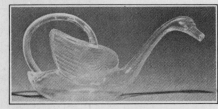

The swan, a leakproof watering can with a one-quart capacity makes watering more fun. Water pours from its mouth like a fountain.

For mail-order information write:
Souhan Design
Box 36384
Dallas, TX 75235

Mark four moisture meter is a compact unit that gives an instant moisture reading. It has an easy-to-read dial, comes complete with a watering guide for over 200 plant varieties, and is fully guaranteed. Available at chain and hardware stores nationwide. No mail-order.

For more information write:
Cleveland Cotton Products
Box 6895
Cleveland, OH 44101

Water mist'er indoor watering hose and mister snaps onto any faucet. A 50-foot vinyl hose, faucet adapters, watering wand, and misting attachment are included. Push-button operation provides variable water intensity, from trickle to full flow. Five-year guarantee.

For mail-order information, write:
Plantrac Corporation
38 West Mall
Plainview, NY 11803

Window greenhouses

In recent years window greenhouses have proven to be a popular and inexpensive means of gardening indoors. These mini-greenhouses are ideal for growing herbs, flowers, and also for starting seeds in late winter and early spring for outdoor planting.

Actually, the window greenhouse is nothing more than a miniature conservatory attached to the outside sill and framing of any suitable window. They are simple to make or inexpensive to buy. Many are sold in garden centers or you can order them direct from a greenhouse supply company. Any window can be rigged for one of these handy mini-greenhouses. They come in all sizes. You can buy or make one that fits your window exactly, or have it extend as much as 18 inches beyond each side of the window frame for extra space.

Location is important. If you plan to use your window greenhouse all year long, choose a southeast exposure. In mild regions, heat from the house may be sufficient to keep the window greenhouse warm. In cold regions, a small heating unit that fits right into the window extension may be necessary. You can also provide bottom heat by burying a heating cable in the trays that support your pots or flats. These heating cables, sold mainly to help seed germination, can be bought through most seed mail-order houses or in garden supply centers.

When south-facing windows get hot on sunny days, you can open the ventilator that provides fresh, cooler air. Or you can install an automatic vent opener, equipped with a thermostat.

In summer, a south-facing window greenhouse will need some kind of shading. Inexpensive matchstick bamboo screening works fine, or you can paint the outside panes with a commercial shading compound. If trees are nearby, you may not need additional shading.

North-facing window greenhouses may be harder to keep warm in winter than south-facing ones, but they can be used for most cool- and shade-loving plants in spring, summer, and fall. If you live in sunny southern regions, you'll find a north-facing window greenhouse excellent any time.

We recommend making galvanized trays 1 inch deep to fit the shelves in your window greenhouse. Fill these trays with crushed stone or pea gravel and keep them wet to maintain humidity levels.

One avid gardener harvested between 20 and 40 pounds of tomatoes each winter from her homemade window greenhouse. For these kinds of harvests, your window should have a southern exposure, and be able to hold a night temperature of 60 degrees F. all through the winter. Heating cables at the bottom are needed as tomatoes like a warm soil.

One of the easiest ways to acquire a window greenhouse is to use your basement window. Most window wells are a waste of space. They are about 2 feet deep and 3½ feet wide. A light bulb can be used as a source of heat. The top of the window well must be covered at night and on cold days, using a piece of heavy plate glass or plexiglass. Seedlings develop into sturdy plants just like those grown in a regular greenhouse. For added warmth, you can open the basement window to the well, allowing heat to circulate into the mini-greenhouse. Some people use a covered-over cellar door for a "free" greenhouse. When it's cold you can leave the basement door open or use auxiliary heat of some sort.

George and Katy Abraham

Books

Gardening Under Glass: An Illustrated Guide to Living with a Greenhouse, by Jerome A. Eaton, Macmillan Co., 866 Third Ave., New York, New York 10022, 1973, hardbound, $8.95. Covers all aspects of greenhouse gardening including choosing a site and building a greenhouse. Simple explanations on day-to-day maintenance of plants.

Organic Gardening Under Glass, by George and Katy Abraham, Rodale Press, Emmaus, Pennsylvania 18049, 1975, hardbound, 308 pages, $8.95. Useful for both organic and non-organic gardeners; covers fruits, vegetables, and ornamentals in the greenhouse.

Greenhouse Gardening For Fun, by Claire Blake, William Morrow and Co., 105 Madison Ave., New York, New York 10016, 1967, paperback, $2.95. A practical guide with all the shortcuts to give the beginning greenhouse hobbyist more joy than work.

Sources

Greenhouse windows by Guaranteed Products are available in sizes ranging from 30 by 30 inches to 60 by 60 inches. Side vents let you adjust air flow and temperature. All units are designed and constructed to stand up to heavy environmental demands.

For further information and free catalog (specify retail), write:
Golden Earth Enterprises
512 Lambert Road
Brea, CA 92621

One-piece window greenhouse units made of Plexiglas are easily installed in standard 2-foot 8-inch-wide windows. For larger windows, an extender kit is available. The units are simply designed and require little maintenance. They come complete with wire shelves and an installation kit. There is a money-back guarantee.

For brochure and mail-order information, write:
Window Greenhouses
Box 26273
Richmond, VA 23260

Window bubble is made of clear, rigid, heavy-duty Plexiglas and can turn a cellar window well into a greenhouse. Available in various styles and shapes designed to cover both rectangular and semicircular wells. Certain models have redwood extensions or wood sides. Models can be ordered according to your individual specifications. For price and availability information, send a photo or drawing showing dimensions.

For brochure and mail-order information, write:
Dilworth Manufacturing Company
Box 158
Honey Brook, PA 19344

Aluminum-frame window greenhouse is available, completely assembled, from Texas Greenhouse. It has single-thickness glass panels, adjustable metal shelves, and a vertical sliding vent on each side. The easy-to-install greenhouse comes in 11 sizes ranging from 50 to 65 inches wide, 41 to 56 inches high, and 12 to 16 inches deep.

For information write:
Texas Greenhouse Company
2717 St. Louis Avenue
Fort Worth, TX 76110

Window greenhouse, distributed by Reliable Greenhouses, comes completely assembled for easy installation. It can fit over or replace an ordinary window. Available in either single-thickness or insulated glass. The frame is aluminum, available with a bronze or white finish. Complete with aluminum humidity pan and wire insect screens, it also includes galvanized steel-rod shelves. The side vents provide proper air circulation; fixed top prevents leakage and vibration. May be obtained in standard sizes, ranging from 50 inches wide, 41 inches high, and 12 inches deep to 65 inches wide, 56 inches high, and 16 inches deep.

For brochure and mail-order information, write:
Reliable Greenhouses
Box G
Route 53
Norwell, MA 02061

Janco window greenhouse is an aluminum-and-glass unit which can easily be installed in minutes. All parts slip together, so no tools are needed for assembly. It comes complete with an insect screen, humidity pan, vinyl-coated plant shelves, and operation and assembly instructions, and features an adjustable roof vent. The greenhouse is available in a variety of sizes, and several optional accessories are offered at additional cost.

For brochures and mail-order information, write:
J. A. Nearing Company
10788 Tucker Street
Beltsville, MD 20705

Sun-glo window box is a greenhouse unit that features an unusual double-wall construction. A tinted outer wall, made of acrylic, and a special inner wall serve to diffuse light and provide good light levels in the greenhouse. The frame and hardware are made of aluminum. The units are available in several sizes: 55 or 61 inches long, 54 or 72 inches high, and 60, 90, or 120 inches wide (all measurements are approximate). All units are constructed to stand up to heavy environmental demands, and all are shipped disassembled. An instruction booklet and installation tools are included. Units are available in nurseries and garden centers on the West Coast.

For additional information write:
Sunglo Greenhouses
3714 South Hudson Street
Seattle, WA 98118

Glass-and-aluminum window greenhouses that can be assembled in a few minutes (without tools) are manufactured by Lord and Burnham. The standard 16-inch deep greenhouses are from 33 to 48 inches wide and 52 to 72 inches high. Custom sizes (up to 60 inches wide) are also available. Features are: an adjustable roof sash, an insect screen, open-work shelving, and a removable bottom pan for pebbles and gravel. Installation and operating instructions are included. A small heater and a fluorescent light fixture are available at additional cost.

For brochures and mail-order information, write:
Lord and Burnham
Dept. HC
Irvington, NY 10533

Directory of sources